To Chris
From the very beginning. What a good man you've become. I love you!

Acknowledgments

SO MANY HARD-WORKING PEOPLE worked on this book, I hardly know where to begin. Many people worked behind the scenes, each as valuable as the next. First, I'd like to thank Megan Belanger for believing in me enough to let me write this book. To Kezia Endsley, whose great patience and wonderful grammatical skills kept me going through the process. To Lisa Bucki, who used her incredible knowledge of Microsoft Office to keep me on track. To Jill Flores, for exercising all her patience and layout talents in making this a beautiful book. To the proofreader and indexer rolled into one, Kelly Talbot, who made the book even better. Finally, to Heather Talbot, Stacy Hiquet, and all the others working madly behind the scenes to get this book to market. To all of you, thank you from the bottom of my heart.

And finally, a huge note of appreciation goes to my husband of almost 42 years. Vern, thank you for your patience and understanding of the *many* late-night hours, for fending for yourself or both of us at supper time, and for keeping me encouraged and supplied with Diet Coke and working chocolate. I love you.

PICTURE YOURSELF
Learning
Microsoft® Office® 2010

Diane Koers

COURSE TECHNOLOGY
CENGAGE Learning™

Picture Yourself Learning Microsoft®
Office® 2010
Diane Koers

**Publisher and General Manager,
Course Technology PTR:** Stacy L. Hiquet

Associate Director of Marketing: Sarah Panella

Manager of Editorial Services: Heather Talbot

Marketing Manager: Jordan Castellani

Acquisitions Editor: Megan Belanger

Project Editor: Kezia Endsley

Technical Reviewer: Lisa A. Bucki

Interior Layout: Jill Flores

Cover Designer: Mike Tanamachi

Indexer: Kelly Talbot Editorial Services

Proofreader: Kelly Talbot Editorial Services

For product information and technology assistance, contact us at
Cengage Learning Customer & Sales Support, 1-800-354-9706

For permission to use material from this text or product, submit all requests online at **cengage.com/permissions**

Further permissions questions can be emailed to
permissionrequest@cengage.com

Microsoft, Windows, Word, and the Word launch icon are either registered trademarks or trademarks of Microsoft Corporation in the United States and/or other countries.

All other trademarks are the property of their respective owners.

All images © Cengage Learning unless otherwise noted.

Library of Congress Control Number: 2008940750
ISBN-13: 978-1-59863-890-5
ISBN-10: 1-59863-890-4

Course Technology, a part of Cengage Learning
20 Channel Center Street
Boston, MA 02210
USA

Cengage Learning is a leading provider of customized learning solutions with office locations around the globe, including Singapore, the United Kingdom, Australia, Mexico, Brazil, and Japan. Locate your local office at: **international.cengage.com/region**

Cengage Learning products are represented in Canada by Nelson Education, Ltd.

For your lifelong learning solutions, visit **courseptr.com**
Visit our corporate website at **cengage.com**

Printed in the United States of America
1 2 3 4 5 6 7 12 11 10

About the Author

DIANE KOERS owns and operates All Business Service, a software training and consulting business formed in 1988 that services the central Indiana area. Her areas of expertise have long been in the word-processing, spreadsheet, and graphics areas of computing as well as providing training and support for Peachtree Accounting Software.

Diane's authoring experience includes over 40 books on topics such as PC Security, Microsoft Windows, Microsoft Office, Microsoft Works, WordPerfect, PaintShop Photo Pro, Photoshop Elements, Lotus SmartSuite, Quicken, Microsoft Money, and Peachtree Accounting, many of which have been translated into other languages such as French, Dutch, Bulgarian, Spanish, and Greek. She has also developed and written numerous training manuals for her clients.

Diane and her husband enjoy spending their free time camping, fishing, traveling, and playing with their four grandsons and Sunshine, their cute little Yorkshire Terrier.

Table of Contents

Introduction

WELCOME TO THE WORLD of Microsoft Office 2010! This new *Picture Yourself Learning* guide from Cengage Learning will help you master the many and varied features of one of Microsoft's most popular products—Microsoft Office 2010. Microsoft Office is a powerful and popular suite of programs that will support many aspects of your everyday work style. For example, information is provided to help you write a letter, create a spreadsheet, produce a professional-looking presentation, and manage your schedule and electronic mail. In addition, you'll learn how to create your own professional-appearing newsletters and other publications as well as create your own Web page, using Microsoft Publisher.

Each of the individual programs interact with the other programs in the suite. For example, you might need to prepare a business report in Word that contains graphs and charts based on data you enter in an Excel spreadsheet. Perhaps later, after you have delivered your report (possibly using Outlook's e-mail), you might need to prepare and schedule a PowerPoint presentation.

Through this book you learn how to create Office documents; however, what you create is totally up to you! Your imagination is the only limit to what you can do with them after that. This book cannot begin to teach you everything you can do with Microsoft Office, nor will it give you all the ways to accomplish a task. What I have tried to do is give you a fast, fun, and easy way to get started with this exciting suite of programs.

Book Structure

This book is divided into 25 chapters, which fall into seven parts. In Part I, I show you how to use basic Office commands; things that are common among most Office applications. Although it's not the most exciting part of the book, it's certainly the most practical. Look out then! Things start to be lots of fun! In Parts II, III, IV, V, VI, and VII you learn the basics of six popular Office applications: Word, Excel, PowerPoint, Access, Outlook, and Publisher.

Who Should Read This Book?

I make a couple of assumptions about the readers in this book. One, I assume you have worked with your computer enough to handle the mouse and be familiar with some terms such as save, open, and close. Secondly, most importantly, and most obviously, since you're reading this right now, I assume that you want to know more. Okay, I am going to try and fill you with knowledge.

Whether you are computer challenged or have used Microsoft products before, you will be able to quickly tap into the user-friendly integrated design and feature-rich environment of Microsoft Office 2010.

Cengage Learning's *Picture Yourself* guides use a visual approach with illustrations of what you will see on your screen, linked with instructions for the next mouse movements or keyboard operations to complete your task. Computer terms and phrases are clearly explained in non-technical language, and expert tips and shortcuts help you produce professional-quality documents.

This book can be used as a learning tool or as a task reference. The easy-to-follow, highly graphical nature of this book makes it the perfect learning tool. No prerequisites are required from you, the reader, except that you know how to turn your computer on and how to use your mouse.

In addition, anyone using a software application always needs an occasional reminder about the steps required to perform a particular task. By using the *Picture Yourself Learning Microsoft Office 2010* guide, any level of user can look up task instructions quickly without having to plow through pages of descriptions.

Added Advice to Make You a Pro

You will notice that this book uses a lot of steps and keeps explanations to a reasonable amount to help you learn faster. Included in the book are a few elements that provide some additional comments to help you master the program, without encumbering your progress through the steps:

▶ Tips offer shortcuts when performing an action, or a hint about a feature that might make your work in Office quicker and easier.

▶ Notes give you a bit of background or additional information about a feature, or advice about how to use the feature in your day-to-day activities.

Read and enjoy this *Picture Yourself Learning* book. It certainly is the fastest and easiest way to learn Microsoft Office 2010. If you have any comments about this book, please feel free to contact me at diane@thepeachtreelady.com.

–Diane

Part I
Getting Started

You are about to embark on a journey into the world of Microsoft Office 2007. Office is a collection of multiple products and, depending on the flavor you purchase, you probably have Word, Excel, PowerPoint, Outlook, and possibly Publisher. Each application has its own purpose. You typically use Word for letters, Excel for math calculations, PowerPoint for presentations, Outlook for appointments and e-mail, Access for data management, and Publisher for newsletters. Each program is unique, yet all the programs have common features. The chapters in this section take you through some of the common functions used within all the different programs.

Discovering Office Common
Features

PICTURE YOURSELF SITTING DOWN at your new computer, ready to begin using it. You've already mastered the game of Mahjong Titans, so now you're going to explore Microsoft Office. Microsoft Office isn't really a single program; rather, it's a collection of several applications. Some of the Microsoft Office 2010 applications include:

- ▶ **Word**, which you use to write letters, faxes, and other such documents.

- ▶ **Excel**, which you use to view and manage numbers and data.

- ▶ **PowerPoint**, which you use to create presentations and slide shows.

- ▶ **Access**, which you use for managing similar types of data.

- ▶ **Outlook**, which serves as an e-mail program as well as a personal information manager.

- ▶ **Publisher**, which you use to create publications, newsletters, brochures, and Web pages.

Applications May Vary

The specific applications included with your version of Office vary with the different Microsoft Office 2010 packages.

In most Windows programs, you see menus and toolbars from which you select your options. In Office, Microsoft's interface provides you with the right tools at the right time. Instead of the traditional look, Office applications provide tabs with icon and button-laden Ribbons containing your favorite features. Galleries and themes are also relatively new additions, helping you maintain consistency and style in your documents' appearance.

Opening Office Programs

CHOOSE START> All Programs>Microsoft Office, which displays a list of Office applications. Click the application you want to open. If you select Word, Excel, or PowerPoint, a blank document, workbook, or presentation appears on your screen ready for you to begin entering your data. You'll start working with Word in Chapter 2, Excel in Chapter 8, and PowerPoint in Chapter 14. Figure 1-1 illustrates the opening screens for Word, Excel, and PowerPoint.

Desktop Shortcuts

To place an Office application icon on your Windows desktop, right-click the application name from the Start>All Programs>Microsoft Office menu and choose Send To>Desktop (create shortcut).

If you open Access (Chapter 18) or Publisher (see Chapter 25), a list of templates appears and the first time you open Outlook (Chapter 21), a startup wizard appears prompting you to configure Outlook and set up your e-mail accounts.

Whenever you finish working with a specific application, you exit the program to release the program from your computer's memory. Click the File tab and choose Exit or click the Close button in the upper-right corner of the application window. You may be prompted to save your file. Click Yes or No if prompted to save your file.

Figure 1-1
Ready to begin working in your Office application.

Closing the File Only

Optionally, click the File tab and choose Close. The current file closes, but the current program remains open.

Working with Office Elements

Designed to adjust to the way you work, instead of the traditional Windows menu bar and standard toolbars, the Office applications use a Ribbon. Take a look at Figure 1-2, and let's take a stroll through an Excel window and review some of the Office elements.

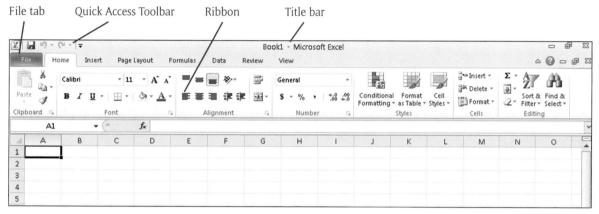

File tab   Quick Access Toolbar   Ribbon   Title bar

Figure 1-2
The Office Ribbon is designed to provide the right tool at the right time.

▶ **Title bar:** Across the top you see a title bar that shows the program title and the document title. If you are working with a document created in an earlier version of Office, you may see the words Compatibility Mode displayed. You'll learn about Compatibility Mode later in this chapter.

▶ **File tab:** The first tab on the Ribbon, the File tab is where you see the Backstage view and access many common file functions such as Open, Save, and Print. It's also where you'll exit the application when you are finished.

▶ **Quick Access Toolbar:** The Office Quick Access Toolbar, which is the only toolbar, provides fast and easy access to basic file functions. Hover your cursor over any of the three icons next to the File tab. By default, the Office Quick Access Toolbar (QAT) functions include Save, Undo, and Redo. You can click the arrow next to the QAT and customize it to better meet your needs.

▶ **Ribbon:** If you hover your cursor over the Ribbon area containing tabs, which are task-orientated screens, a description of the feature appears in an Enhanced ScreenTip. The tabs are also broken down into subsections called groups, which break the tasks into smaller areas. Figure 1-3 shows the Excel Insert tab, which includes the Tables, Illustrations, Charts, Links, and Text groups. As you click a different tab, the Ribbon changes to reflect options pertaining to the selected tab.

Customize the Ribbon

Beginning with Office 2010, you can now customize the Ribbon. See "Customizing Applications" later in this chapter.

Tabs   Groups

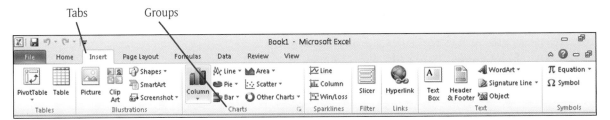

Figure 1-3
Related items appear in groups.

▶ **Dialog Box Launcher:** Many options include an icon at the bottom right edge of the group option. Office calls this the Dialog Box Launcher, and clicking it opens a related dialog box. Figure 1-4 shows the Dialog Box Launcher with the Page Setup dialog box.

Close a Dialog Box

Click the Cancel button to close a dialog box without making any changes.

▶ **Galleries:** Some Ribbon buttons display a down arrow, which means there are more choices available. In Figure 1-5, you see an arrow on the Excel Format as Table button. Click the arrow to display a gallery of table styles. (Click the arrow again to close the gallery.)

Dialog Box Launcher

Figure 1-4
See additional options through a traditional dialog box.

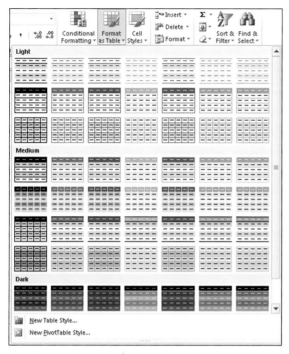

Figure 1-5
Click the arrow to expand the gallery.

Figure 1-6
Display helpful information on the status bar.

▶ **Status bar:** Along the bottom of the Office application window you see a status bar that tells you if your keyboard's Num Lock or Caps Lock is on, along with a variety of other options. You can customize what displays in the status bar by right-clicking anywhere on the status bar. The application displays a list of options in the Customize Status Bar menu similar to the one seen in Figure 1-6. Click any option without a checkmark next to it to activate the feature, or click any option with a checkmark to deactivate the feature.

Selecting Commands with the Keyboard

Sometimes you don't want to take your hands off the keyboard to make a choice from the Ribbon. Fortunately, Office provides easy ways to select commands using the keyboard instead of the mouse. Follow these steps to make a keyboard command selection:

▶ If appropriate for the command you intend to use, place the insertion point in the proper word, paragraph, or cell.

▶ Press Alt on the keyboard. Shortcut letters and numbers appear on the Ribbon. The letters control Ribbon commands, and the numbers control Quick Access Toolbar commands. See Figure 1-7.

Figure 1-7
Make command selections using the keyboard.

► Press a letter to select a tab on the Ribbon; for this example, press P. The application displays the appropriate tab and letters for each command on that tab.

► Press a letter or letters to select a command. The application displays options for the command you selected.

► Press a letter or use the arrow keys on the keyboard to select an option. If you use the arrow keys, press the Enter key after making a selection. The application performs the command you selected, applying the option you chose.

Step Backwards

Press the Escape key to revert the keyboard controls back one step.

Change Focus

Press F6 to change the focus of the program, switching between the document, the status bar, and the Ribbon.

Exploring the Backstage View

NEW TO OFFICE 2010 is the Backstage view, which appears under the File tab. It contains many file-related choices such as Save, Open, and Print. But, the Backstage view is more than just a menu. It's a full information center.

Take a look at Figure 1-8. With a document open, in this example an Excel file called Capital Budget, you see three columns of information. The first col-

umn is where you see the file commands and represents actions you can select. The second column currently displays tasks relative to, in this case, the file Capital Budget. As you make selections from the first column, the choices in the second column change. The third column contains information about the current document including the author, the file creation and modification dates, file size, and other document properties.

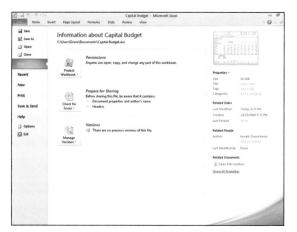

Figure 1-8
Backstage view.

Now click the Print option from the first column. As you see in Figure 1-9, the second column changes and now displays options related to Printing. If you click the Recent button, you see a list of documents you recently worked with. You can click any document to open it. See "Opening an Existing File" file later in this chapter.

Click the File tab to close the Backstage view and return to your open file.

File tab

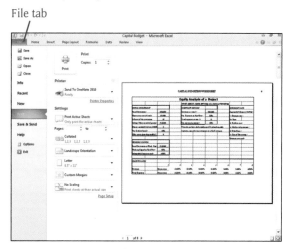

Figure 1-9
Viewing the Print options.

Don't Click the X

Don't click the Close box (X) in Backstage view. Doing so closes the entire application.

Working with Files

WHENEVER YOU WORK with an Office application, the application is creating a file. In Word, you create a document file; in Excel, a workbook file; in PowerPoint, a presentation file; in Access, a database file, and in Publisher, a publication file. You can create the file and just throw it away when you're finished or you can save it on a disk drive for future reference.

Saving a File

The first time you save your file, the application prompts you for a name and a folder in which to save it. Click the File tab and choose Save or click the Save button on the Quick Access Toolbar. The Save As dialog box appears, as shown in Figure 1-10.

Navigation Pane   Save in folder

File name   File type

Figure 1-10
Saving a file for future reference.

From the Save As dialog box, you enter the following information:

▶ **Location:** By default, Office applications save your files in your Documents folder. If you want to save your file in a different folder, use the Navigation Pane to navigate to the folder or disk drive where you want to save the file.

▶ **Name:** In the File Name text box, type a descriptive name for the file. File names can contain any characters except an asterisk, slash, backslash, or question mark.

▶ **Type:** Each application has a specific file type it uses as a default. Word 2010 and Word 2007 documents use a .docx file type while Excel workbooks use the .xlsx file type. Most of the time you'll want to use the default file type, but if not, click the Save As Type down arrow and select a different file type. If someone who doesn't have Office 2010 or Office 2007 will be opening your file, you might consider saving your file in a format that more closely matches their version, such as Word 97–2003. Older Word versions use a .doc file extension, and older Excel workbooks use the .xls file extension.

Click the Save button. Office saves the file in the location and with the name you specified. After assigning the file a name and a location, each time you click the Save button, the saved file is updated with any changes.

Depending on the file type you chose, Office may prompt you for additional information. In Figure 1-11, for example, you see a dialog box warning you of your workbook features used in Excel 2010 that aren't available when saving a file in an Excel XP or 2003 format.

Figure 1-11

Some Office 2010 features are not available in earlier Office versions.

Save Often

Don't wait until a project is finished to save it. A good rule of thumb is to save your work at least every 10 minutes.

Perhaps you want to make some changes to your file but you're not sure if you will like the changes. Or, maybe you wrote a proposal to a company and you need a similar one for a different company. One way to work around the changes is to save the file with a different name or in a different location. Office then keeps the old version with the original name or location and keeps the modified file with a different name or in a different location.

File Naming Rule

No two files can have the exact same name in the exact same folder. You can place them in different folders, save them as different file types, or vary the name by at least one character.

To save a revised file without overwriting the original, click the File tab and choose Save As, which displays the Save As dialog box. From the Save As dialog box you can enter a new file name, select a different folder, or choose a different file type.

Creating a New File

As mentioned earlier in this chapter, when you open most of the Office applications, a blank document appears. You can also generate a new document at any time by clicking the File tab and choosing New. The application then displays the new Backstage view prompting you for more information. Figure 1-12 illustrates the window that appears when you choose Office>New in PowerPoint. You click the template you want to use and then click the Create button. By default, Office names each new file by the next numerical increment, such as Presentation2 or Workbook3.

Create button

File type arrow

Figure 1-12
Create any number of new files.

Figure 1-13
Open a previously saved file.

---

2. If needed, select the appropriate folder from the Navigation Pane.

3. Select the file you want to open.

Keyboard Shortcut

Optionally, press Ctrl+N to create a new file without opening the dialog box.

Opening an Existing File

When you've worked on and saved a file previously, you can reopen it to review or modify the file.

1. Click the File tab and choose Open. An Open dialog box similar to the one shown in Figure 1-13 appears.

Another Keyboard Shortcut

Optionally, press Ctrl+O to display the Open dialog box.

Display Other File Formats

Click the file type arrow to display files saved in other formats.

---

4. Click the Open button. The document appears, ready for you to edit.

Compatibility Mode

If the file you open was created in a previous version of Office, the words Compatibility Mode appear on the title bar, next to the document name (see Figure 1-14).

Compatibility Mode indicator

Figure 1-14
Some Office 2010 functions are not available when working in Compatibility Mode.

Converting a Prior Version File to Office 2010

If you originally created a file in a prior than 2007 version of Microsoft Office, you may find you want to convert it to an Office 2010 file so you can take advantage of the great new features provided by Office 2010. The steps are similar but not quite exactly the same in all Office programs. Begin by opening a file created in the earlier Office version. The application title bar indicates the document is in Compatibility Mode.

▶ **Word:** Click the File tab and from the Backstage view Info screen, choose Convert. (See Figure 1-15.) Word displays a message indicating you are about to convert the current document. Click OK. Word replaces the older version of the document, using the same name you used for the older version of the document. If the older version was a Word 97-2003 or earlier document, Word 2010 changes the extension to .docx.

▶ **Excel:** Click the File tab and from the Backstage view Info screen, choose Convert. Excel displays a message indicating you are about to convert the current workbook.

Click OK and another conversion message appears. Click Yes and Excel saves the file in the new format. Excel replaces the older version of the workbook, using the same name you used for the older version of the document. If the older version was an Excel 97-2003 or earlier document, Excel 2010 changes the extension to .xlsx.

▶ **PowerPoint:** Click the File tab and from the Backstage view Info screen, click Convert. The Save As dialog box appears. Click Save. PowerPoint saves a copy of the presentation with a .pptx extension. The original presentation remains with a .ppt extension.

▶ **Access:** Click the File tab and choose Save & Publish. Then click Save Database As and choose Access Database. Access saves a copy of the database with an .accdb extension. The original database remains with an .mdb extension.

No Conversion Needed

No conversion is needed for Publisher and Outlook files.

Convert button

Figure 1-15
Converting an older Word file.

Renaming a File

When you first save your file, you're prompted to name it. But perhaps you didn't give it a name intuitive enough to know what the file represents. If you use the File tab>Save As command and save your file with a different name, you have both the original file and the new file. If you just want to rename the existing file, you can use the Open or Save As dialog boxes. Follow these steps:

1. With the Office application open, but not the file you want to rename, click the File tab and choose Open. The Open dialog box appears.

Use the Save As Dialog Box

Optionally, click the File tab, choose Save As and proceed using the Save As dialog box.

---

2. Locate and click once on the file you want to rename. Do not double-click the file as double-clicking the file will open it.

3. Choose Organize>Rename (see Figure 1-16). The original file name becomes highlighted.

Organize menu

Figure 1-16
Choose a new file name.

4. Type the new file name and press Enter when you are finished typing. Excel renames the file.

5. Click the Cancel button, or press the Escape key, to close the Open (or Save As) dialog box.

Deleting a File

Similar to renaming files, you can also use the Open or Save As dialog boxes to delete unwanted files. With the application open, click the File tab and choose Open or Save As. Either the Open or Save As dialog box appears. Locate the file you want to delete and choose Organize>Delete. A confirmation dialog box appears like the one you see in Figure 1-17. Choose Yes to delete the file, and then click the Cancel button (or press the Escape key) to close the dialog box.

Figure 1-17
Delete unwanted files.

Previewing with Live Preview

MOST OFFICE 2010 applications include a feature called Live Preview where you can see how formatting choices look in your document before you actually apply them to the document. By pointing to formatting options such as fonts or styles, you can see the effect on your document. If you want a different look, you simply move your cursor to a different option to view its effect.

Additionally, you can use Live Preview to view tables, charts, shapes, and graphics. However, Live Preview works only with Word, Excel, PowerPoint, and Outlook applications; it doesn't work completely in Publisher or at all in Access.

Take a look at Figure 1-18 where you see the effect of selecting a different font immediately display on the Word document heading. If you decide you like the effect, just click on the font to actually apply it to the text.

In Figure 1-19, choosing a different theme for a PowerPoint presentation allows you to see its effect on the current slide. If you don't want the new effect, just move your cursor to a different effect, or move the cursor off the Ribbon to make no changes.

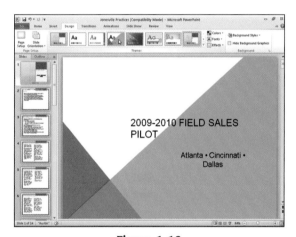

Figure 1-19
View style changes before actually applying a change.

Figure 1-18
Preview how font changes affect your document.

Customizing Applications

ACH OFFICE APPLICATION comes with predefined settings, but you can tailor many settings to better meet your needs. You can set a default file location, change the default font, and many other choices. So, what does the *default* mean? Default settings are what the program assumes you want, unless you specify otherwise. Think of them as the standard settings.

To customize your application, click the File tab and choose Options. A dialog box displaying options for the current program appears. Figure 1-20 shows you the settings for Word.

Figure 1-20
Word options.

From the Options dialog box, you choose from one of the categories on the left side, which then displays the related options on the right side of the box. For example, if you click the Save category, you see options such as a default file format and a default file location. (See Figure 1-21.)

After you change any options, click the OK button to save your changes.

Figure 1-21
Word's Save options.

Modifying the Quick Access Toolbar

Earlier in this chapter you discovered the Office Quick Access Toolbar, which is the only toolbar available in Office applications. By using the Quick Access Toolbar you are only a single mouse click away from saving your file or using the Undo or Redo functions. That's great, but wouldn't it be nice to have other frequently used functions also a single mouse click away?

You can easily add (or remove) buttons to the Quick Access Toolbar. Microsoft provides several ways to add or remove buttons, but the most straightforward method is through the Options dialog box. The following steps show you how to accomplish this task:

1. Click the File tab and choose Options, which displays the Options dialog box.

2. Click Quick Access Toolbar. Options for customizing the Quick Access Toolbar appear.

3. Click the down arrow next to Choose Commands From and choose All Commands. All the commands appear in the list on the left side.

4. Choose the command you want to add to the Quick Access Toolbar and click the Add button. See Figure 1-22 where I've added the Open and the Quick Print buttons.

Choose commands from arrow   Add button

Figure 1-22
Adding icons to the Quick Access Toolbar.

5. On the right column, click any command and click the Up or Down arrow to change the icon arrangement.

Restore the Default Settings

Click the Reset button and choose Reset Only Quick Access Toolbar to reset the QAT to the default toolbar.

6. Click OK when you are finished.

Individual Application Toolbars

Although each Office application has a Quick Access Toolbar, with the same three default tools, customizing the Toolbar in one application does not change it in the others.

Customizing the Ribbon

New to Office 2010 is the ability to create a customized Ribbon tab. You'll find this very helpful when you are working on a specific project and you find yourself using the same tools over and over again and the tools you use are on different Ribbon tabs. Save yourself mouse clicks, wrist strain, and most importantly time, by creating a customized Ribbon tab. Just follow these steps:

1. Click the File tab and choose Options, and then, click Customize Ribbon.

2. From the right side column, click the New Tab button. A New Tab (custom) section appears with New Group under it.

3. With the New Group selected, from the left column, click the tool you want to add and click the Add button. The tool appears under the new group.

Choose Different Categories

If you don't see the tool you want, click the Choose Commands From arrow and select a different category.

4. Add groups by clicking the New Group button. See Figure 1-23 where you see I've added four groups to the New Tab. The first group contains the New, Open, and E-mail buttons.

Rearrange Buttons

Rename the new custom tab or group by clicking the new tab or group and choosing Rename.

Figure 1-23
Creating a customized Ribbon tab.

5. Click the up or down arrows to reorder the buttons, group, or even the new tab.

6. To remove a newly added tool, group, or tab, click on it and choose Remove.

7. Click OK when you are finished. Take a look at Figure 1-24 where you see I renamed the tab to My Projects.

Figure 1-24
The newly created customized Ribbon tab.

Part II
Word

There are a number of essential things we need. Air and water certainly fit the bill, and many of us consider chocolate and true love right at the top. If you are using a computer, a good word processing program is essential—and you have it. Microsoft Word is the most popular word processing program in the world. Its abundance of features and ease of use make it unmatched. Whether you're making a grocery list or writing the great American novel, Word is the program for you. The chapters in this section explains the fundamentals of working with Word. Even if you have worked with other word processing programs, I am sure you will find Word's ease of use enriching.

Getting Started with

Word

PICTURE YOURSELF AS A SMALL CHILD looking through a glass door. The world looks huge when viewed through the perspective of a toddler, but generally children aren't afraid to explore the world around them. That's how they learn. In this chapter, you begin exploring and learning of the world of Microsoft Word.

Microsoft Word is a powerful word processing program that takes your documents far beyond what you can produce with a typewriter. Whether you want to write a simple letter to a friend, produce a newsletter for a professional organization, or even write a complicated, multiple-page report containing graphics and tables with numerical data, you can create it in Word.

If this is your first opportunity to use Microsoft Word, you may be a little overwhelmed by all the buttons and items on the screen. Just remember that although Word is a powerful program, it's also very easy to use, which is why most businesses have adopted it as a company standard. Don't worry. You'll be creating your first document after just a couple of mouse clicks.

Exploring the Word Window

A S MENTIONED IN CHAPTER 1, many items you see when you open the Word window are common to several other Office applications such as the Ribbon, tabs, groups, and status bar. The following list illustrates a few elements specific to Word (see Figure 2-1).

Ruler   Insertion point   View controls

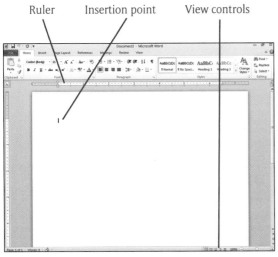

Figure 2-1
Word screen elements.

▶ **Mouse pointer:** The shape of the mouse pointer will change as you move it to different areas on the screen.

▶ **Ruler:** Use the rulers to measure the document settings within the page margins. (See Chapter 4, "Managing Word Pages," for information on setting margins.)

Show Rulers

By default, Word does not display the rulers. Show the rulers by choosing View>Show>Ruler.

▶ **Document screen:** The white area of the screen is where your typed text appears.

▶ **Insertion point:** The blinking vertical line in the document screen indicates where text will appear when you begin typing.

▶ **View controls:** Buttons on the status bar show you your document from various perspectives. (See Chapter 4 for more about changing views.)

Moving Around the Screen

A S YOU TYPE A FEW LINES of text, you'll notice that you don't need to press the Enter key at the end of each line. The program automatically moves down (or wraps) to the next line for you. Word calls this feature word wrap. You need only to press the Enter key to start a new paragraph.

To make changes to your document, you'll need to move the insertion point. Take a look at several methods Word provides for moving around the screen.

Using Click and Type

You can position the insertion point anywhere on the document using the Click and Type feature. Double-click your mouse pointer where you want to type. Word determines and sets any necessary paragraph formatting based on where you double-click.

Click and Type Restriction

The Click and Type feature works only if you are using Print Layout or the Web Layout view.

Before double-clicking the mouse, pay close attention to the appearance of the mouse pointer. If there are lines to the right of the I-beam pointer, the text you type will flow to the right of the insertion point. If the lines are to the left, the text will flow to the left of the insertion point, and if the lines are below the I-beam, the text will be centered at the insertion point (see Figure 2-2).

Click and Type insertion point

Figure 2-2
Using Click and Type.

Different than a typewriter where you have to use the carriage return at the end of every line, in a Word document, you don't use the Enter key (which is the equivalent of the carriage return), until you reach the end of a paragraph. When you reach the end of a line, you just keep typing because Word knows where the margins are. You'll learn about setting margins in Chapter 4.

You can see the margins, too: the dotted rectangle on the page shows you where they are. Just keep typing and Word will wrap the text within the margins.

Using the Scroll Bars

The Word document screen includes two scroll bars; a vertical scroll bar and a horizontal scroll bar; however, depending on the current view and the document zoom amount, you may not see the horizontal scroll bar. Figure 2-3 illustrates a document with both scroll bars visible.

Horizontal scroll bar   Vertical scroll bar   Scroll box

Figure 2-3
Word document scroll bars.

Click the arrow at either end of the scroll bar to move the document up or down in the window, or click the arrow at either end of the horizontal scroll bar to move the document left or right. Displaying text by using the scroll bars does not move the insertion point. You still need to click the mouse wherever you want to locate the insertion point.

Drag Scroll Box

Optionally, drag the scroll box up or down to quickly move through a document.

Using the Keyboard

As you've seen, you can work on any part of the document that appears on your screen simply by clicking the mouse pointer where you want to work. You can also move around in a Word document by pressing the Up, Down, Right, or Left arrow keys on the keyboard. Each press of the key moves the insertion point one character or one line at a time.

There are also a number of shortcut keys designed to speed up the process of moving around in a Word document. Table 2-1 illustrates these shortcut keys.

Table 2-1 Word's Movement Shortcut Keys

To Move	Do This
A word at a time	Press Ctrl+Right arrow or Ctrl+Left arrow
A paragraph at a time	Press Ctrl+Up arrow or Ctrl+Down arrow
A full screen up at a time	Press PageUp
A full screen down at a time	Press PageDown
To the beginning of a line	Press Home
To the end of a line	Press End
To the top of the document	Press Ctrl+Home
To the bottom of the document	Press Ctrl+End
To a specified page number	Press Ctrl+G, enter the page number, and then press Enter

Using the Go To Command

If you have a lengthy document, use the Go To command to jump to a specific location in the document. Follow these steps:

1. Choose Home>Editing and click the Find button drop-down arrow.

2. Choose Go To. The Find and Replace dialog box appears with the Go To tab in front (see Figure 2-4).

Go To Alternatives

Two optional methods for displaying the Go To option are to press the F5 key or press Ctrl+G.

Figure 2-4
Quickly locate specific pages in your document.

3. Type the page number you'd like to display and then click Next or press the Enter key. Word displays the specified page with the insertion point located at the beginning of the specified page.

Editing Text

UNLESS YOU'RE A PERFECT TYPIST, you'll probably make a few mistakes in your document. Or maybe you'll change your mind about some of the text in the document. In a word-processing document such as Word, corrections and changes are easy to make, and in some instances typing errors are even automatically corrected for you. In Word, if you make a mistake, or change your mind, you just go back and change the text.

Adding New Text

Suppose you are typing a letter to someone and forgot to add a thought you wanted in an early paragraph. When you want to add new text in the document, place the insertion point where you want to locate the new text and begin typing. As you type, Word inserts the characters and pushes the existing characters to the right or to the next line if necessary. Notice in the bottom example of Figure 2-5 how the added words "Albertson Beautiful Customizations" are inserted after the phrase "customer of," which makes some of the words in the top line drop down to the second line.

Inserted text   Text before deletion

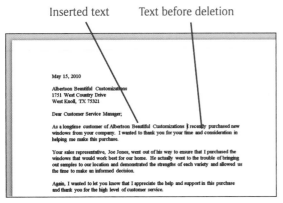

Figure 2-5
Insert additional text wherever you want.

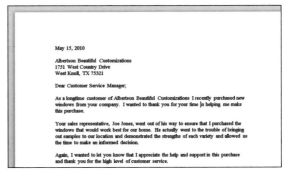

Figure 2-6
Deleting unwanted characters.

Overtype Mode

If you notice the existing text doesn't move over, but seems to disappear, you may have accidentally pressed the Insert key, which takes you out of Insert mode and into Overtype mode. Press the Insert key to return to Insert mode.

Deleting Existing Text

You can delete unwanted text one character, word, or paragraph at a time. Two common keys used to delete text are the Backspace and Delete keys. Pressing the Backspace key deletes one character at a time to the left of the insertion point, while pressing the Delete key deletes one character at a time to the right of the insertion point. In Figure 2-6, the words "and consideration" from Figure 2-5 were deleted by pressing the Delete key repeatedly until the words disappeared.

Backspace Key

On most keyboards, the Backspace key shows a left-pointing arrow, which makes it an easy way to remember which direction the Backspace key deletes.

Optionally, make a selection in your document and press either the Backspace or Delete key to delete the selection. See the next section for more on selecting text.

Selecting Text

Before you can make a change to existing text such as move, copy, delete, or change the formatting or placement of it, you must first identify the text you want to edit by selecting it. When text is selected, or *highlighted*, it appears on your screen as light type with a dark background—the reverse of unselected text. Word allows you to select contiguous or noncontiguous text for editing.

There are numerous ways to select text, either with the keyboard or the mouse. The following list shows a few of the different selection techniques.

▶ To select a single word, double-click the word.

▶ To select a sentence, hold down the Ctrl key and click anywhere in the sentence (see Figure 2-7).

Selected sentence   Selected word

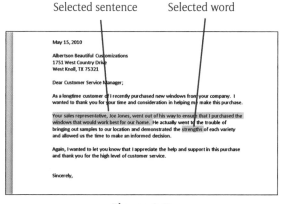

Figure 2-7
Selecting text to make additional changes.

▶ To select an entire paragraph, triple-click anywhere in the paragraph (see Figure 2-8).

▶ To select an entire document, hold down the Ctrl key and press the letter A.

Figure 2-8
Select an entire paragraph or the entire document.

Alternative Method

Another way to select the entire document is choose Home>Editing>Select>Select All.

▶ To select a single line of text, click once in the left margin with the mouse arrow pointing to the line you want selected.

▶ To select a contiguous text area, click at the beginning of the text you want selected, and then hold down the Shift key and click at the end of the text you want selected. Optionally, click and drag the mouse over the text you want to select.

▶ To select noncontiguous text areas, select the first area you want selected, and then hold down the Ctrl key and use the preceding techniques for each additional text area you want included (see Figure 2-9).

Figure 2-9
Selecting noncontiguous text in which to make changes.

Deselect Text

To deselect text, click once anywhere in the document or press one of the arrow keys.

Discovering AutoCorrect

Word includes a fabulous feature that makes us look like better typists than we really are! The feature is called AutoCorrect, and, in many cases, if you mistype a word or forget to capitalize a sentence, Word automatically corrects it. Or, if you type something like (c), Word automatically understands that what you really want is a copyright symbol, and it changes the (c) to ©.

To take full advantage of the automatic correction feature, you have to understand how it works and how to customize it to better fit your needs. Follow these steps to review the AutoCorrect options:

1. Click the File tab and choose Options, which displays the Word Options dialog box seen in Figure 2-10.

2. On the left side, choose Proofing.

Figure 2-10
Setting Word options.

3. Click the AutoCorrect Options button. The AutoCorrect dialog box opens (see Figure 2-11). On the AutoCorrect tab, you see the options Word automatically corrects for you.

But Wait! There's More!

Scroll down the list in the AutoCorrect dialog box to see hundreds of predefined AutoCorrect words and symbols.

Figure 2-11
Create your own AutoCorrect items.

4. If you want to add your own common mis-spellings to the list, type your common mistake in the Replace text box and then type the correction in the With box. Click the Add button to add the correction to the list.

Create Shortcuts

If you frequently use a lot of complex words such as chemical names or medical terms, enter an abbreviation for the term in the Replace box and put the complete term in the With box. After adding the term, when you need to add the term in your document, you need only type the abbreviation followed by a space, a period, or other character. For example, enter hctz to have Word replace it with Hydrochlorothiazide.

5. Click OK twice to close both the AutoCorrect and the Word Options dialog boxes.

Changing Text Case

As you just discovered, Word automatically corrects many text case errors. For example, if you type "Springtime," Word automatically changes it to "Springtime." If, however, you type the entire word in uppercase ("SPRINGTIME"), you can quickly change it to "Springtime" or "springtime." You can apply a text case change to a word, a phrase, or any amount of selected text. Just follow these steps:

1. Select the text you want to change. The text becomes highlighted.

2. Click Home>Font>Change Case. A drop-down menu of options appears as shown in Figure 2-12.

3. Select an option from the drop-down menu.

Figure 2-12
Quickly switch from lower- to uppercase lettering.

Moving and Copying Text

WITH WORD, YOU SHOULD NEVER have to type anything twice! Word provides a number of different methods with which you can copy and move text. Moving or copying text usually involves the Windows Clipboard, which temporarily holds text you place on it. You use the Windows Clipboard feature to move or copy text from one place to another, thereby avoiding the need to retype it.

Moving Text

When you want to remove text from one place and put it into another location, you select the text you want and then cut and paste the text. With cut and paste, Word deletes the selected text, holds it on the Windows Clipboard, and then places it into a new location. Just follow these steps:

1. Select to highlight the text you want to move.

2. Choose Home>Clipboard>Cut. The text disappears from the document, but Word stores it on the Windows Clipboard.

3. Click the mouse where you want to place the text. The blinking insertion point appears at the new location.

4. Choose Home>Clipboard>Paste, or press Ctrl+V. Word places the text at the new location. In Figure 2-13, the highlighted paragraph was originally the second paragraph, but through cutting and pasting, it is now the first paragraph.

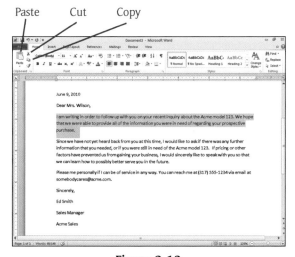

Figure 2-13
Save typing and editing time with Cut and Paste.

Paste Without Formatting

If you want to paste the text without the formatting, instead of clicking the Paste button directly, click the arrow beneath the Paste button and choose Paste Special. From the Paste Special dialog box (Figure 2-14), choose Unformatted Text and click OK.

Figure 2-14
Paste without any formatting included.

Copying Text

The Copy and Paste features leave the selected text at its existing location and duplicate it into a new location. Working similarly to the Cut and Paste functions, Copy and Paste use the Windows Clipboard to temporarily store the text. Use the following steps to copy text to a new location:

1. Select to highlight the text you want to duplicate.

2. Choose Home>Clipboard>Copy or right-click and choose Copy. The text remains in the document, but Word also stores it on the Windows Clipboard.

Keyboard Shortcut

Optionally, press Ctrl+C to copy selected text to the Clipboard.

3. Click the mouse where you want to place the text. The blinking insertion point appears at the new location.

4. Choose Home>Clipboard>Paste, or press Ctrl+V. Word places the text at the new location (see Figure 2-15). Notice that the first paragraph is repeated as the third paragraph.

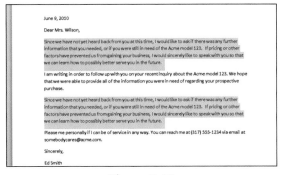

Figure 2-15
Duplicate text without retyping.

In some situations, when you paste text, you may see a small icon, called a Paste Options button, appear to the right of the pasted or moved text. See the section "Understanding Paste Options" later in this chapter.

Using Drag and Drop

Another, sometimes faster, method to move text from one location to another is to use the drag-and-drop editing function. The drag-and-drop feature works best for moving a relatively small amount of text a short distance. The following steps show you how to use drag and drop.

1. Select the text you want to move.

2. Position the mouse pointer on top of the highlighted text. The mouse arrow should point to the left.

3. Hold down the mouse button and drag the mouse pointer to the desired location. As you drag, a small box appears at the bottom of the mouse arrow and a gray line indicates the text position (see Figure 2-16).

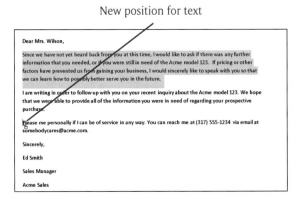

Figure 2-16
Select and drag text to a new location.

Copy Instead of Move

To copy text instead of moving it, hold down the Ctrl key before dragging the selected text. Then release the mouse button before releasing the Ctrl key.

4. Release the mouse button to finish the text move.

View Multiple Documents

If you want to move text from one document to another, open both documents and display them side-by-side by choosing View>Window>Arrange All. Then highlight and drag the desired text from one document window to another (see Figure 2-17). Hold down the Ctrl key if you want to copy the text to the second document.

If the pasted text is a different font, size, or style than the text near where you pasted, you'll see the Paste Options button, which provides the option to paste text with or without formatting. (You'll learn more about formatting in Chapter 3, "Making a Word Document Look Good.")

Click the arrow next to the Paste Options button, as seen in Figure 2-18, which displays the Paste Option Gallery and pick from the available choices:

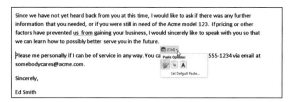

Figure 2-18
Select paste options.

Arrange All

Figure 2-17
Move or copy text easily between documents.

Understanding Paste Options

By default, when you paste text, Word includes any formatting contained in the original text along with the text. For example, if the original text is underlined, the pasted text is underlined as well.

▶ **Keep Source Formatting:** Leaves the pasted text formatted the same as the original text.

▶ **Merge Formatting:** Modifies the pasted text so it's formatted to match the closest existing text.

▶ **Keep Text Only:** Modifies the pasted text with the default document font.

Additional Options

After using the Ctrl+V shortcut to paste your text, just press the Ctrl key one more time to drop the new Paste Options gallery and change to a different Paste option.

Using Undo and Repeat

IF YOU MAKE A CHANGE and then decide you really don't want to make that change after all, use Word's Undo function. You can use Undo to restore text that you deleted, to delete text you just typed, or to reverse a recently taken action. Word keeps track of several steps you've recently taken, so you can also undo your actions back several steps if you prefer.

Save Cancels Undo

Be aware that once you save your document, you cannot use Undo to "unsave" it. Also, if you close the document, when you reopen it, you cannot undo changes made in your previous editing session.

▶ To reverse the last action you took, click the Undo button on the Quick Access Toolbar.

▶ To repeat a previous action, click the Repeat button on the Quick Access Toolbar. If you just used the Undo button, the repeat button allows you to undo the previous Undo action.

▶ To undo multiple actions at once, click the arrow next to the Undo button and choose how far back you want to reverse your actions (see Figure 2-19).

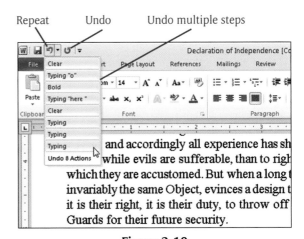

Figure 2-19
If you make a mistake, undo it!

Displaying Non-Printing Symbols

T O ASSIST YOU IN EDITING a document, Word can display hidden symbols it uses to indicate spaces, tabs, and hard returns, which are those created when you press the Enter key. These symbols do not print, but you can display them on your screen. You simply choose Home>Paragraph>Show/Hide. As shown in Figure 2-20, you see the paragraph symbol where a paragraph ends and you see dots that represent spaces and arrows that represent tabs.

Turn Off Display

To turn off the display of hidden characters, click the Show/Hide button again.

Paragraph symbol   Tab symbol   Show/Hide button

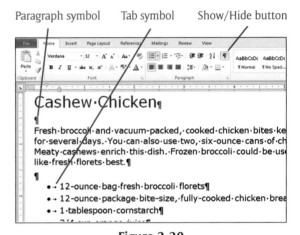

Figure 2-20

Viewing non-printing Word symbols.

Making a Word Document

Look Good

PICTURE YOURSELF GOING for an important job interview. You need to make a good impression, so you want to
look your best. So you make sure your clothes are clean
and coordinated, your hair is combed, and your shoes are shined.
You put on your best smile and go forward into the interview.

When you create a Word document, especially one that others
review, you want it to look the best. Besides making sure you've
dotted all the i's and crossed all the t's, the document should
have a clean, consistent, well defined appearance. You use
Word's formatting features when modifying your document's
appearance.

Selecting Text Attributes

WHEN YOU SPEAK, the tone of your voice conveys how you feel. You can convey your enthusiasm (or lack of it), be friendly, or be sarcastic. In a similar way, fonts, which are families of design styles for the numbers, letters, and symbols that make up text, can provide additional information to the readers. Fonts can, for example, make your document appear mature and businesslike or young and casual.

Choosing a suitable font size can make a document easier to read. Other text attributes you might use to set the document tone include style settings such as bold, underline, italics, or even color.

For many text attributes, Word offers a chance to "try before you buy" with its Live Preview feature. By pointing to various formatting choices you can see the effect the option has on your document before you actually choose the format choice. If you like it, you can simply click your mouse to choose the option. For example, if you hover your mouse over a font choice, the text appears deselected (it isn't) and displays with the font you are pointing to. Live Preview works with most font and paragraph formatting choices as well as styles and picture formatting changes.

Turn Off Live Preview

If you don't like the Live Preview option, you can turn it off. Click the File tab and choose Options. Click General and remove the check mark from Enable Live Preview. Then click OK.

Choosing a Font

In addition to the many fonts you already have on your machine, Word comes with additional fonts. The default font used with Word 2010 is called Calibri. Fonts generally fall into two categories: serif and sans serif. Serif fonts usually have details on the ends of some of the strokes that make up letters and symbols. A font that has serifs is called a serif font and a font without serifs is called sans serif, from the French word *sans*, meaning "without."

Changing fonts is a very simple process. Select the text you want to modify and choose Home>Font and from the Font drop-down menu select the font you want to use (see Figure 3-1).

Figure 3-1
Choose a font from the list.

Quickly Display Font

If you know the font name you want, you can quickly jump to that font by typing the first few characters of the font name. For example, if you want a Tahoma font, from the font list, type Ta, or for Arial, type Ari.

Selecting a Font Size

You can use any size for any font. Font sizes are measured in *points*, where a point is approximately 1/72 of an inch tall. Therefore, a 72-point font is approximately 1 inch tall.

Select the text you want to format and then choose Home>Font. Click the Font Size drop-down menu arrow. You see a drop-down menu of available sizes similar to those seen in Figure 3-2. Choose the size you want from the drop-down menu, or type your

own measurement in the Font Size box. And while you can enter a value between 1 and 1,638, don't expect to be able to read a one-point font, and a character as large as 1,638 points won't even begin to fit on a standard page!

Optionally, you can click the Grow Font or Shrink Font button to increase or decrease your font size. Figure 3-2 illustrates a document with a title font size of 24 points.

Font size   Grow font   Shrink font

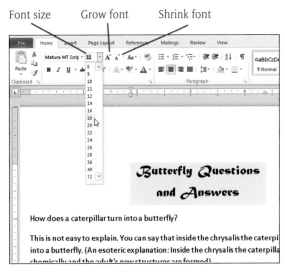

Figure 3-2
Changing font sizes.

Keyboard Shortcut

The keyboard shortcut for Grow Font is Ctrl+Shift+> and for Shrink Font it's Ctrl+Shift+<.

Applying Formatting Attributes

Applying formatting attributes such as **bold**, *italic*, or <u>underline</u> calls attention to particular parts of your text. Additionally, you can assign a superscript or subscript notation to any text that makes it appear above or below the standard text, such as a copyright or trademark symbol. You can easily access these choices and others with the Home tab of the Ribbon.

Insert Symbols

To insert a copyright, trademark, registered trademark, or any of hundreds of different symbols, choose Insert>Symbols>Symbols and make a selection from the Symbol gallery. Clicking More Symbols displays the Symbol dialog box, as seen in Figure 3-3.

Figure 3-3
Inserting special symbols and language characters.

Select the text you want modified and from the Home tab's Font group as shown in Figure 3-4, choose the attribute you want to apply.

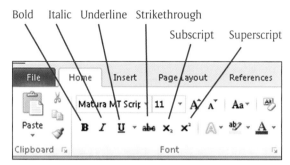

Figure 3-4
Applying special text attributes.

More Keyboard Shortcuts

Some formatting shortcuts include Ctrl+B for bold, Ctrl+I for italic, and Ctrl+U for single underline.

If you want your text underlined with something different from the single underline, you can click the down arrow next to the Underline button and select an underline style and color from the drop-down menu shown in Figure 3-5.

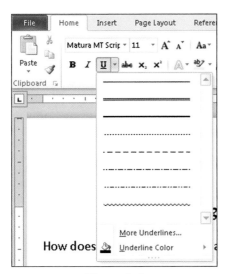

Figure 3-5
Choosing an underline style.

More Underline Choices

Choosing More Underlines displays the Font
dialog box where you can select even more
underline styles.

Adding Color

Another way to add impact to your document is by
adding color to your text. Color becomes very
effective when printing to a color printer or viewing your document onscreen. Follow these steps to
apply color to your text:

1. Select the text you want formatted.

2. Choose Home>Font>Font Color, or if you want
   to select a specific color, click the down arrow
   next to Font Color and make a choice from the
   resulting gallery as shown in Figure 3-6.

Font Color

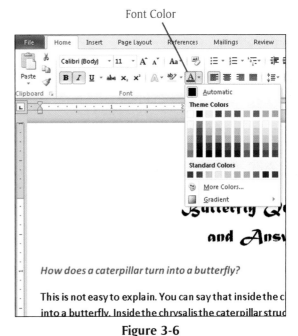

Figure 3-6
Add WOW to a document with color.

Do you notice how the gallery colors are grouped
together in themes? Office document themes,
available in Word, Excel, and PowerPoint, contain
colors, fonts, and other formatting options, all
designed to give your documents a polished, professional appearance. See "Working with Themes"
later in this chapter.

Highlighting Text

You can highlight text in your document in the same manner you highlight text with a marker in a book. You can even choose the color of highlighter you want to use. While on a monitor or with a color printer, you see the highlight color, on a black and white printer, highlighting prints as gray shading over the text. Highlighting calls attention to specific areas of your document.

Select the text you want to format with highlighting and then choose Home>Font>Text Highlight Color, or if you want to select a specific color, click the down arrow next to Text Highlight Color and make a choice from the resulting gallery. Word deselects the text and applies the highlighting. Figure 3-7 shows text with yellow highlighting.

Text Highlight Color

Figure 3-7
Call attention to special areas with highlighting.

Remove Highlighting

To remove highlighting, choose No Color from the available highlight color selections.

Adding Text Effects

New to Word 2010, you find the ability to add spectacular special effects to your text. With just a few mouse clicks, your text can illustrate shadows, glows, reflections, bevels, and many other great formatting features.

Select the text you want to work with, and then choose Home>Font>Text Effects. A gallery of text effects appears, as you can see in Figure 3-8. Select the effect you want, or click one of the options at the bottom for even more text enhancements.

Text Effects

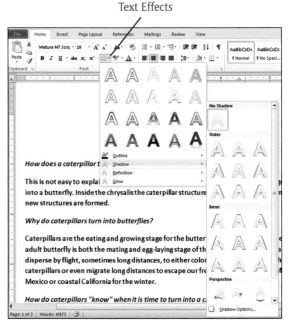

Figure 3-8
Add lots of pizzazz with text effects!

Using the Mini Toolbar

Word (along with Excel and PowerPoint) contains a semitransparent Mini Toolbar designed to provide quick access to many text and paragraph formatting features so you don't have to move your mouse so far to select the commands from the Ribbon.

The Mini Toolbar appears whenever you select some text. As your mouse points to the selected text, the transparent toolbar appears. As you move your mouse pointer so it rests on top of the toolbar, the Mini Toolbar appears in full opacity (see Figure 3-9).

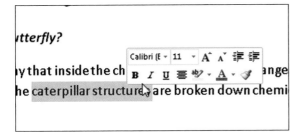

Figure 3-9
Save mouse movement by using the Mini Toolbar.

Available choices on the Mini Toolbar include:

▶ Font

▶ Font Size

▶ Grow Font

▶ Shrink Font

▶ Decrease Indent

▶ Increase Indent

▶ Bold

▶ Italic

▶ Underline

▶ Center

▶ Text Highlight Color

▶ Font Color

▶ Format Painter

Turn Off Mini Toolbar

If you find the Mini Toolbar distracting, you can turn it off. Click the File tab and choose Options. Click General and remove the check mark from Show Mini Toolbar on Selection. Click OK.

Using the Font Dialog Box

Another way to apply formatting to your selected text is through the Font dialog box, where you can make all your font choices via a single box. Also, you'll find that the Font dialog box offers additional attribute options not available on the Ribbon. Use the following steps to work with the Font dialog box:

1. Select the text you want formatted.

2. From the Home tab, click the Fonts group Dialog Box Launcher or press Ctrl+Shift+F. You see the Font dialog box displayed in Figure 3-10.

Figure 3-10
The Font dialog box.

3. Make any desired text attribute changes. The preview box at the bottom of the dialog box illustrates your choices. Live Preview isn't available from the Font dialog box.

4. Click the OK button.

Removing Formatting

If you decide you really liked the original formatting in your document, you can easily return it to the default document settings. After selecting the text from which you want to remove formatting, choose Home>Font>Clear Formatting. (See Figure 3-11.) All text and paragraph formatting choices return to the default setting with the exception of highlighting. Any applied highlighting remains on the selected text.

Clear Formatting

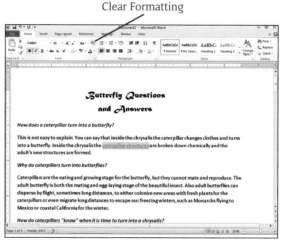

Figure 3-11
Easily remove unwanted formatting.

Changing the Default Font

As mentioned earlier in this chapter, Word 2010 begins with an 11-point Calibri font. If your company has a different font as its company standard or you just prefer a different font for most documents, you can change the default font for any new Word documents. Changing the default font does not affect any existing documents but will apply to all new documents.

Body Font

The document body font is actually determined by the theme you use. See "Working with Themes" later in this chapter.

You can set the default font from any blank document, or any currently open document. Just follow these steps:

1. From the Home tab, click the Fonts group Dialog Box Launcher or press Ctrl+Shift+F.

2. Select the font and size you want as your default.

3. Click the Default button. A confirmation message like the one seen in Figure 3-12 appears.

4. Click All documents based on the Normal template, and then click OK.

Figure 3-12
Confirm the Default font change.

Formatting Paragraphs

WORD INCLUDES MANY FEATURES designed to assist you in placing text on the page just the way you want it. You can align text left-to-right using tabs or alignment options, or you can adjust your text vertically using line spacing options. Take a look at some of the available paragraph formatting choices.

Aligning Text

Alignment arranges the text to line up at one or both margins, or centers it between the margins. Alignment applies to entire paragraphs. In other words, you can't center-align part of a paragraph and left-align another part of the same paragraph.

You can align text to the left, right, or center, or you can justify your text, which means that the text becomes evenly spaced across the page from the left margin to the right margin. Apply alignment options by selecting the text you want to align, then choosing Home>Paragraph and clicking one of the following alignment buttons:

▶ **Align Text Left:** The text aligns evenly at the left margin. This is the default choice.

▶ **Center:** The text centers evenly between the left and right margins.

▶ **Align Text Right:** The text aligns along the right document margin.

▶ **Justify:** The text fills with micro spaces so it aligns evenly on both the left and right margins.

Figure 3-13 illustrates a document with text matching each alignment option.

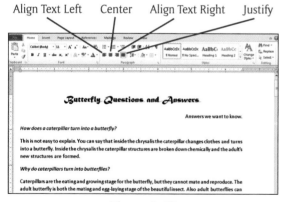

Figure 3-13
Changing alignment of selected text.

Adding Paragraph Borders

You can apply borders to any size block of text, which draws the reader's eye to specific areas for a "quick read." Use a border to place a frame around a word, phrase, paragraph, or group of paragraphs to frame the text and call specific attention to the areas. A border can encase the entire area or be any combination of lines around the text, such as above and/or below the text. Select the text you want bordered and choose Home>Paragraph. Click the drop-down arrow next to the Borders button, which displays a list of options like the one you see in Figure 3-14. Choose the border option you want.

Figure 3-14
Adding borders around text.

Automatic Border

Word automatically adds a thin single-line border if you type three dashes in a row and then press the Enter key. Typing three underscore characters in a row and pressing Enter automatically creates a thicker border line.

Shading Text

Shading helps you distinguish headlines and important passages such as sidebars by creating a screen, which is typically light gray shading against the standard black text. Screens can add contrast to and enhance the readability of your document. Shading especially looks good when used in combination with a border.

You may be wondering what's the difference between shading and highlighting. Highlighting only covers the selected text and not the entire paragraph. Also, you typically use a light color for highlighting so you can still see the black text through it. When you add shading, the shading covers the entire paragraph, and if you choose a darker color, Word automatically changes the text color to one that coordinates so you can still effectively read the text.

Add Black Shading

A great way to add enhancement is to use black or dark gray shading with white text.

Click anywhere in the paragraph you want shaded and choose Home>Paragraph and click the Shading arrow. Choose a color from the resulting Shading gallery as seen in Figure 3-15. In this figure, adding dark blue shading caused Word to change the font color to white.

Paragraph Shading

Figure 3-15
Adding shading to paragraphs.

Optionally, if you want to add a shading pattern ranging from a light 5% shade to patterns such as diagonal stripes or polka dots, you can choose Home>Paragraph, and then click the Borders drop-down arrow. From the list, select Borders and Shading, which then displays the Borders and Shading dialog box. Click the Shading tab then click the Fill drop-down arrow to select a fill color. Choices are available in themes or standard colors. You can then click the Style drop-down menu to select a pattern.

Patterns Are Distracting

Use caution with patterns. Using a busy pattern can make your text very difficult to read.

Indenting Text

Typically, text runs between the left and right margins, but you may want to indent particular paragraphs. Surprise! Word contains a tool for indenting. Click anywhere in the paragraph you want to indent and then choose Home>Paragraph>Increase Indent. Each click of the Increase Indent button indents the text one-half inch from the left margin. Click the Decrease Indent button to move the text back one-half inch.

If you want to indent the right margin or you want to manually set how much indentation Word applies, you can use the Format Paragraph dialog box. Click the Paragraph Dialog Box Launcher, which displays the Paragraph dialog box seen in Figure 3-16.

Click the spinner arrows for the Left or the Right text boxes to specify the number of inches to indent the left and right edge of the paragraph. The Preview box at the bottom shows the effects of your settings. Optionally, click the Special drop-down menu and select an indenting option:

▶ **First line:** This option indents only the first line of the paragraph and leaves the rest of the paragraph even with the left margin.

▶ **Hanging:** This option indents all lines except the first line of the paragraph.

Click OK after you finish making selections. Word applies the paragraph indentation settings you selected.

Another way to control indentation is by dragging the indentation icons on the ruler:

> ## View Ruler
>
> If you don't see the ruler, choose View>Show>Ruler.

▶ Left Indent

▶ Hanging Indent

▶ First Line Indent

▶ Right Indent

Figure 3-16
Set text apart by using indentation.

Working with Tabs

By default, each time you press the Tab key, Word moves the insertion point a half inch to the right. However, you can set tab stops at desired points along the ruler so that when you press the Tab key, the insertion point moves to that point automatically, instead of stopping every half inch.

Do not try to line up text by pressing the spacebar. Even if the text looks evenly aligned on the screen, it won't be lined up when printed. Use tabs instead.

The following steps show you how to set your own tab settings:

1. Click the mouse pointer at the location you want to create a tabbed paragraph.

Select Paragraphs

If you want to set tabs for multiple previously typed paragraphs, select the paragraphs before proceeding to Step 2.

---

2. Make sure the ruler display is turned on. If you don't see your rulers, choose View>Show>Ruler.

3. Click the Tab button located at the left end of the horizontal ruler as often as needed until you see your desired tab alignment icon (see Figure 3-17). Some tab choices include:

Tab button

Figure 3-17
Setting manual tabs.

▶ ⬛ **Left:** The Tab button defaults to the left tab symbol, which looks like an "L." When using a left tab, text appears with the left edge of the text at the tab.

▶ ⬛ **Center:** When you select a center tab symbol, the Tab button looks like an upside-down "T." When using a centered tab, text centers at the tab stop.

▶ ⬛ **Right:** When you select the right tab symbol, the tab button looks like a backward "L." When using a right tab, text appears with the right edge of the text at the tab stop.

▶ ⬛ **Decimal:** If you display the decimal tab, the Tab button appears as an upside-down "T" with a dot on the right. When writing out dollar and cent amounts, for example, decimal points align to the tab.

▶ ⬛ **Bar:** Bar tabs are very different from the previous four tabs. Text doesn't position around bar tabs. Instead, Word inserts a vertical bar at the top position and runs through the depth of the paragraph.

4. Click on the horizontal ruler to set the tab for the current paragraph or the currently selected paragraphs. Depending on the tab type you selected, a left, right, center, decimal, or bar tab symbol appears where you clicked the ruler.

5. Click in the paragraph and press the Tab key. Notice how the insertion point moves to the tab setting you created.

6. Type some text. The text you type appears on the page. In Figure 3-18, you see examples of left and right align tabs as you might use them in a document.

Figure 3-18
Line up text with tabs—not spaces.

Continue Tab Settings

Pressing Enter continues the tab settings to the next paragraph.

Moving a Tab

If you're not happy with the position of your tab stop, you can easily move it. Select to highlight the paragraphs that have a tab you want moved, and then drag the tab to a new location on the ruler bar. As you drag the tab, a vertical, dotted line like the one shown in Figure 3-19 illustrates the new tab position. When you release the mouse button, the text moves to the new tab position.

Figure 3-19
Easily move manual tabs to a different area.

Deleting a Tab

Like moving a tab, using the ruler makes deleting a tab a very simple process. Select the paragraphs that have a tab you want to delete and then drag the current tab setting off the ruler, into the body of the document. A vertical dotted line appears. When you release the mouse button, the tab disappears from the ruler and text realigns according to your new tab settings. If there is no previous manual tab stop, the default tab settings take effect.

Using the Tabs Dialog Box

If you want your tab stops at more precise positions than you get by clicking the ruler, or if you want a dot leader before the tab, use the Tabs dialog box. Select the text where you want to set the tab. From the Home tab, click the Paragraph Dialog Box Launcher and then click the Tabs button, or double-click any manual tab stop on the ruler. You see the Tabs dialog box shown in Figure 3-20.

Figure 3-20
The Tabs dialog box.

In the Tab stop position text box, type the location you want for the new tab and choose an Alignment and optional Leader style for the tab. Click the Set button. Repeat this action for each tab you want set. Click OK to close the Tabs dialog box.

Change Default Tab Setting

Optionally, use the Tabs dialog box to change the default tab stop setting from 0.5" to any desired amount.

Changing Line Spacing

Line spacing is the amount of vertical space between each line of text. You might want to change line spacing when you want to make a document such as a contract easier to read or to make room for changes when writing a document draft. Like text alignment, line spacing applies to complete paragraphs. Use the following steps to change line spacing:

Default Line Spacing

Word 2010 and 2007 use a default line spacing of 1.15. Earlier versions of Microsoft Word used single spacing (1.0) as the default setting.

1. Select the text you want to change.

2. Choose Home>Paragraph>Line and Paragraph Spacing. A list of options appears (see Figure 3-21).

3. Select a line spacing option. Word applies the spacing you select to the highlighted text.

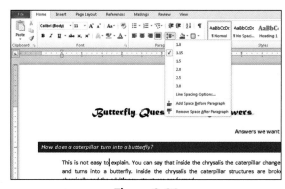

Figure 3-21
Choosing a line spacing option.

Changing Spacing Between Paragraphs

Paragraph spacing is the amount of vertical space between each paragraph of text. Remember that whenever you press the Enter key, you start a new paragraph. In early versions of Word, the default was no spacing between paragraphs, so, traditionally; you would press the Enter key a second time to leave space between two paragraphs. Word 2010 and Word 2007 use a different default setting. The default setting allows for 10 points of blank space at the bottom of every paragraph, thereby eliminating the need to press the extra Enter key.

However, you have complete control over how much spacing, if any, you want between two paragraphs. Similar to indentation, paragraph spacing is controlled through the Paragraph dialog box. From the Home tab, click the Paragraph Dialog Box Launcher, which displays the Paragraph dialog box (see Figure 3-22).

The Spacing section is where you determine the amount of space you want before or after each paragraph. Settings are measured in points and range from −1 to 1584.

Figure 3-22

Manually setting the desired amount of spacing between paragraphs.

Copying Formatting

IF YOU SPEND several minutes setting up just the right text and paragraph formatting, and you know you'll need the same formatting several more times in your document, you don't want to have to remember all your settings and repeat them over and over again. Instead, you can copy formatting from one area to others by using the Format Painter tool. Follow these easy steps to copy formatting:

1. Select some of the text containing the formatting you want to use elsewhere. Your selection could include just a few characters or an entire paragraph.

2. Choose Home>Clipboard>Format Painter. Your mouse pointer changes to the shape of a paintbrush.

3. Press and hold the mouse button and drag over the text you want formatted.

4. Release the mouse button. Notice, as shown in Figure 3-23, how the third paragraph takes on the formatting attributes of the first paragraph.

Keep Format Painter Active

To keep the Format Painter function active for repeated use, double-click the Format Painter button. When you finish using the Format Painter function, click the Format Painter button again, which turns it off.

Format Painter   Mouse pointer

Figure 3-23
Save formatting time by using the Format Painter tool.

Working with Lists

YOU CAN USE BULLETS or numbers to call attention to lists in your documents. Traditionally, you use bullets when the list items do not follow any particular order (such as a list of options), and you use numbers when you want the items to follow each other in numerical order (such as the steps in this book). Select the text for which you want to add bullets or numbers. Then, choose Home>Paragraph and click either the Bullets button or the Numbering button. Both items have a drop-down arrow from which you can select a bullet or number style (see Figure 3-24). You can preview the options with Live Preview by pausing your mouse over any option before selecting.

Bullets or Numbers?

If you choose bullets and then decide you want numbering, or vice-versa, select the text, and then choose the other option. If you decide you don't want a bulleted or numbered list, select the text and click the bullet or number button again, which removes the selected option.

Bullets   Numbering

Figure 3-24
Grab readers' attention by using bullets or numbering.

If you have not already typed your list, Word monitors your keystrokes and, depending on what you type, automatically converts a list to a bulleted or numbered list. If you type a 1 followed by a period and then either a space or tab, Word automatically converts the item to a numbered list. If you type an asterisk * followed by a space or a tab, Word automatically changes the asterisk into a bullet. When you finish typing and press the Enter key, Word creates the next numbered item, or adds another bullet.

Other features Word monitors and automatically changes include changing fractions to fractional characters like 1/2 to $\frac{1}{2}$ or applying ordinals such as changing 1st to 1st.

When Word formats the entry as a list, you see an AutoCorrect Options button next to the bullet or number (see Figure 3-25). If you don't want Word to change the list formatting, click the AutoCorrect Options button and choose Undo Automatic Numbering or Undo Automatic Bullets.

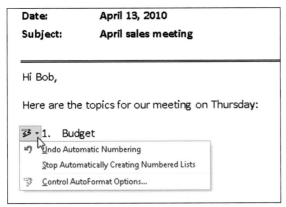

Date: April 13, 2010
Subject: April sales meeting

Hi Bob,

Here are the topics for our meeting on Thursday:

1. Budget
↻ Undo Automatic Numbering
Stop Automatically Creating Numbered Lists
⧉ Control AutoFormat Options...

Figure 3-25
Word's AutoFormat As You Type feature.

Turn Off Automatic Bullets and Numbers

To permanently turn off the automatic numbering or bullet formatting, choose File> Options. In the Proofing section, click AutoCorrect Options. Click the AutoFormat As You Type tab and turn off Automatic Bulleted Lists and Automatic Numbering. Click OK twice.

Working with Themes

YOU SPEND A LOT OF TIME preparing the content in your documents, making sure you are getting your point across to the recipient clearly. Throughout this chapter, you've seen how you can add a little extra "umph" to your document by adding formatting.

All Microsoft applications include a feature that saves you boatloads of time by providing expertly designed themes, which can give all of your Office documents a unified and professional appearance. Themes include a set of colors, fonts, and other formatting details that coordinate together and since the themes are shared across all the Office programs, all your Office documents can now have the same look.

By default, when you create a new Word (or Excel, PowerPoint and so forth) document, Office begins with the "Office" theme. As you've already seen, it starts with the Calibri 11 point font and you've also seen the default paragraph settings. Microsoft Office includes dozens of other themes with names such as Apex, Civic, and Metro. You can also download additional themes from Microsoft Office Online.

All of the document content links to the theme, so if you change the theme, a complete set of new colors, fonts, and effects is applied to your entire document. You can still, however, make any individual formatting changes to the document. Themes also save time when you need to add tables, charts or diagrams to your documents, because those elements can also include the matching theme settings.

To apply a different theme to your document, click Page Layout>Themes>Themes. A gallery of the themes seen in Figure 3-26 appears. As you hover your mouse over any theme, you can immediately see how the fonts and colors change in your document. Click the theme you want to use.

Themes and Colors

Theme colors have 12 color positions. The first four colors are for text and backgrounds. The next six are accent colors and the last two colors are used for hyperlinks. The folks at Microsoft built visibility rules into the themes so that usually you can switch colors at any time and all your content will remain legible and still look good.

Figure 3-26
Provide a unified appearance in documents by using Office themes.

Using Quick Styles

THIS ENTIRE CHAPTER is about making your document look good by using Word's many formatting tools. In the previous section, you discovered themes. You discovered that themes change the overall colors, fonts, and effects used in your document. However, there is a faster way to quickly apply formatting.

Quick Styles are predefined sets of font and paragraph formatting settings, each designed to coordinate with each other. For example, a Quick Style might include styles for headings, titles, body text, or even quotations. Some include color changes and some do not. Quick Styles change how the different colors, fonts, and effects are combined and which color, font, and effect is dominant.

Quick Styles are tied to themes and help maintain design and consistency in your document without actually changing the entire document theme. Use the following steps to work with Quick Styles:

1. Select the text to which you want to apply formatting.

2. Choose Home>Styles and click the More button next to the Styles scroll bar. A gallery of style options as you see in Figure 3-27 appears.

Figure 3-27
Choose from Word's predefined styles.

3. As you position your mouse over the styles, Live Preview shows you the effect on your selected text. Select the option that best suits your text.

View Additional Style Options

Optionally, choose Home>Styles>Change Styles>Style Set and view additional style options which are named after and originate from the different themes. (See Figure 3-28.)

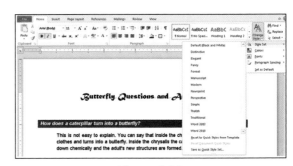

Figure 3-28
More Word predefined style formats.

4

Managing
Word Pages

PICTURE YOURSELF TAKING YOUR FAMILY to an amusement park. The older children want to go this way, and the younger children want to go another way. Grandma wants to browse through the shops and Grandpa just wants to sit and rest and watch. How will you manage everything? It makes your head spin just to think about it!

Managing a document's *whitespace*—the amount of blank space on a page—is an important aspect of designing professional-looking pages. You can increase or decrease whitespace by adjusting margins and the amount of text you place on a page. Additionally, Word provides the ability to work with multiple documents at the same time, as well as methods for quickly comparing information between two documents. When multiple windows are active, you'll need a way to manage them all. That's what this chapter is about…managing a Word document.

Creating Page Breaks

WORD AUTOMATICALLY INSERTS a page break when text fills the page. This page break sometimes doesn't fall where you want it to. You can override Word's automatic page break by creating your own page break. You can make a page break at a shorter position than Word chooses, but you cannot make a page longer.

A manual page break is sometimes called a hard page break because, unlike the page breaks that Word inserts, a manual page break doesn't move if you delete text above it, adjust the margins, or otherwise change the amount of text on the page. Insert a manual page break by positioning the insertion point where you want the new page to begin and choosing one of the following methods:

▶ Choose Insert>Pages>Page Break

▶ Choose Page Layout>Page Setup>Breaks>Page

▶ Choose Page Layout>Page Setup>Breaks>Page

If you are in the default Print Layout view, you see the text below the insertion point move down to the next page of the document. Between the pages, Word displays a gray bar as seen in Figure 4-1. (Document views are discussed later in this chapter.)

Show Hidden Characters

You can show or hide the hidden characters by choosing Home>Paragraph>Show/Hide ¶.

Figure 4-1
Manually starting a new page.

Word's automatic page breaks cannot be deleted, but the hard page breaks that you have inserted manually can be deleted at any time. Simply click the mouse pointer at the beginning of the text after the page break indication and then press the Backspace key. Word deletes the manual page break and the document text readjusts to fit on the pages correctly.

Using Section Breaks

WHEN YOU NEED TO APPLY different page formatting options to only a portion of the document, you need to break the document into *sections*. For example, when page 1 requires different margin settings from the rest of the document, you must break page 1 into its own section. If only pages 16–18 need to be printed in landscape orientation, you can break pages 16, 17, and 18 into a section.

Most section breaks involve entire pages; however, if you need different columns, they don't necessarily have to be on different pages. Word allows for four different types of section breaks:

▶ **Next page:** Inserts a section break and starts the new section on the next page.

▶ **Continuous:** Inserts a section break and starts the new section on the same page.

▶ **Odd page:** Inserts a section break and starts the new section on the next odd-numbered page.

▶ **Even page:** Inserts a section break and starts the new section on the next even-numbered page.

Section formatting options include the following, many of which are covered in this chapter:

▶ **Margins:** The amount of space between the text and the paper edge

▶ **Paper size:** The paper size you intend to use when printing

▶ **Paper orientation:** The direction the text prints on the paper edge

▶ **Paper source:** When printing, which paper tray the printer should pull paper from

▶ **Page borders:** Bordered lines that appear around the entire document page

▶ **Vertical alignment:** The placement of text between the top and bottom margins

▶ **Headers and footers:** Text that appears at the top or bottom of every document page

▶ **Columns:** How text in newsletter-style columns flows from one column to the next on the same page

▶ **Page numbering:** Sequential numbering for each document page

▶ **Line numbering:** How Word automatically counts the lines in a document and displays the appropriate number beside each line of text

▶ **Footnotes and endnotes:** A note of text placed at the bottom of a page or at the end of the document typically citing a reference used in the document

To insert a section break, position the mouse where you want the new section to begin and choose Page Layout>Page Setup>Breaks and select the desired section break type from the drop-down menu, as shown in Figure 4-2. A section break controls the formatting of the text that precedes it.

Figure 4-2
Types of page and section breaks.

Depending on the type of section break you choose, from the default Print Layout view, you see the text below the insertion point remain at the same location or move down to the next page of the document. However, if you are in Draft view or you have the Show/Hide characters active, you see the words "Section Break" and the type of section break in action, along with a dotted line, where the previous section ends (see Figure 4-3).

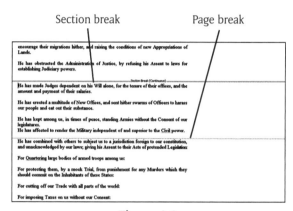

Figure 4-3
Section break indication.

Managing Page Layouts

SOMETIMES WORKING WITH a long document can feel a bit overwhelming. Fortunately, Word contains many features designed to assist you, such as those that allow you to set the page size and layout, mixing and matching them as needed.

Setting Margins

Margins are the spaces between the edges of the paper and where the text actually begins to appear. Word allows you to set margins for any of the four sides of the document and also allows you to mix and match margins for different pages. Word sets the default margins as 1 inch on each of the top, bottom, left, and right sides.

You can set the document margins before you begin entering text into a document, after you've completed the entire document, or at any time in between.

Choose Page Layout>Page Setup>Margins and select from the choices you see in Figure 4-4, or click Custom Margins, which displays the Page Setup dialog box where you can set your own choices. By default, Word applies the new settings to the entire document.

Figure 4-4
Choosing from standard margin options.

If you want to change margins for only part of the document, select the portion you want to change. From Page Layout>Page Setup>Margins, choose Custom Margins. Set the margins you want and,

from the Apply to drop-down menu, choose Selected Text (see Figure 4-5). Word creates section breaks and applies the new margin settings.

Figure 4-5
Applying margin settings to only part of a document.

Changing Document Orientation

Webster's dictionary describes *orientation* as a position in relation to a specific place or object. In word processing, orientation refers to how the text is positioned to the top of a page. Two orientations exist: Portrait, the default orientation, prints the text beginning along the short edge of the paper, and Landscape orientation prints along the long edge of the page.

Choose Page Layout>Page Setup>Orientation and choose Portrait or Landscape as seen in Figure 4-6.

Figure 4-6
Choosing a document orientation.

Different Orientation

Similar to margin settings, if you want to change the orientation for only part of the document, select the portion you want to change and, from the Page Setup dialog box, choose your orientation and from the Apply To section, choose Selected Text. Word creates section breaks and applies the new settings to the selected section.

Setting the Paper Size

Word assumes you want your document printed on standard paper 8.5 inches wide by 11 inches long, but you may want your document printed on a different paper size. Although Word can work with many different sizes of paper, often the selections available to you depend on the printer you have. In many situations, you can even create your own custom paper size.

Word provides a number of ways to manage document paper sizes.

▶ To change the paper size for the entire document, choose Page Layout>Page Setup>Size and select a size from the resulting drop-down menu (see Figure 4-7).

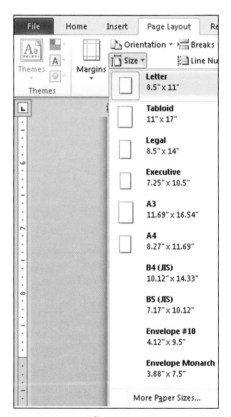

Figure 4-7
Selecting the desired paper size.

▶ To change the paper size from a certain location through the rest of the document, position the insertion point where you want the new paper size to take effect, and then choose Page Layout>Page Setup>Size and select More Paper Sizes. From the Paper tab of the Page Setup dialog box, select the paper size you want and then, in the Apply to drop-down menu, choose This Point Forward.

▶ To change the paper size for a particular section, create the section breaks where needed and click anywhere inside the section you want to change, or select the text area. Choose Page Layout>Page Setup>Size and select More Paper Sizes. From the Paper tab of the Page Setup dialog box, select the paper size you want and then, from the Apply to drop-down menu, choose This Section or Selected Sections.

Viewing a Document

WORD PROVIDES SEVERAL view perspectives to use when displaying a document, each having its own purpose. For each of the following views, except Print Preview, choose View>Document Views and choose an option.

View Icons

Word also displays View icons along the status bar that allow you to choose most of the view options.

▶ **Print Layout:** The default view, Print Layout, allows you to see how text, graphics, and other elements will be positioned on the printed page. This view is especially helpful if you are working with text columns or have graphic images in your document. In Print Layout view, you'll see the document's top and bottom margins, as well as the headers and footers. The top and bottom margins appear, and page breaks between pages are indicated by a darker area. See Figure 4-8.

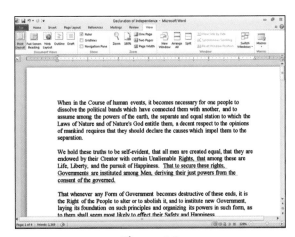

Figure 4-8
Print Layout view.

▶ **Full Screen Reading:** Using the Full Screen Reading view hides most of the Ribbon and other screen elements and displays your document two pages at a time, usually in a larger font size, scaling the contents of your document to pages that fit comfortably on your screen, making it easy to read. When in Full Screen Reading view, the page breaks are not necessarily the same page breaks as in the printed document. You can adjust the reading font size without actually affecting the document itself. (Choose View Options>Increase Text Size). See Figure 4-9 for an example of a document in Full Screen Reading view.

View Options

Figure 4-9
Full Screen Reading view.

Change Options

Use the View Options button to change Full Screen Reading view options. Click the Close button to return to the previously used view.

▶ **Web Layout:** When in Web Layout view you see how the document looks as viewed in a Web browser.

▶ **Outline:** Outline view displays your text in an outline format that includes the outlining tab from which you can display levels as well as promote and demote headings. (See Chapter 7, "Discovering Word Tools" for information on outlines.)

▶ **Draft:** Draft view is a text-only view used for typing, editing, and formatting text. It simplifies the layout of the page so that you can type and edit quickly. Page breaks are indicated by a dotted line, and headers, footers, page margins, backgrounds, and some other objects do not appear in Draft view. Figure 4-10 illustrates a document in Draft view.

Figure 4-10
Draft view.

Using the Zoom Feature

Using Word's ability to zoom in on a document allows you to examine your document more closely or in greater detail through a close-up view of your text. You can also zoom out to see more of the page, at a reduced size. Zoom settings do not affect the arrangement of text when you print the document. Choose View>Zoom, and you see that Word provides a number of ways that you can zoom in or out of your document:

Tip

Using the Zoom feature does not alter the size at which the document will print.

▶ Click the Zoom button to display the Zoom dialog box (see Figure 4-11) where you can choose the zoom percentage you want.

Figure 4-11
Choosing a Zoom percentage.

▶ Choose One Page to view the entire page (Figure 4-12).

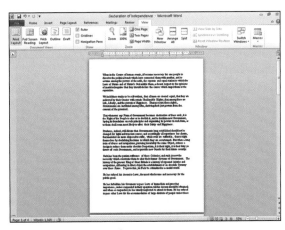

Figure 4-12
Viewing a single page.

▶ Choose Two Pages to view two pages side by side. Use the scroll bar to scroll down through the document two pages at a time.

▶ Choose Page Width to view the page by page width.

Zoom to Page Width

Setting the Zoom to Page Width can be very helpful if your document page orientation is set to landscape.

▶ Choose 100% to return to the normal zoom rate of 100%.

▶ Drag the zoom slider located on the status bar to zoom in and out as desired (see Figure 4-13). The current zoom rate appears next to the zoom slider.

Display the Zoom box

Decrease zoom   Zoom slider

Increase zoom

Figure 4-13
The zoom slider controls.

Use Mouse Scroll Button

If your mouse has a scroll button on top, you can use it to zoom in and out. Hold down the Ctrl key and move the scroll button forward to zoom in or backward to zoom out.

Working with Split Windows

If you want to see two parts of a document, but you can't get them on the screen at the same time, you can split a window. Doing so enables you to view part of a long document in the upper window while you view another part of the document in the lower window.

When you split a window, each window panel contains its own scroll bar. Choose View>Window>Split. A horizontal line with a double-headed arrow appears at the mouse pointer. Click the mouse where you want the window divided, which then locks in the split. The window divides into two sections with each section having its own scroll bar and rulers. Take a look at Figure 4-14 where you see page 1 in the top section and page 4 in the bottom section.

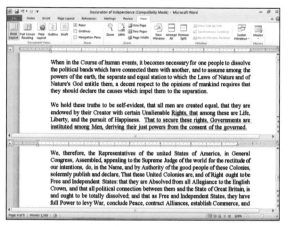

Figure 4-14
Viewing two different document areas.

Resize Windows

To resize the windows, position the mouse at the top of the bottom window until it becomes a double-headed arrow and then drag the line until the windows are the desired size.

When you want to remove the window split, choose View>Window>Remove Split. Your document reappears in a single window.

Comparing Documents Side by Side

Occasionally, you may want to view two documents side by side, perhaps to compare one version to another. Word provides the ability to view any two open Word document windows next to each other.

Choose View>Window>View Side by Side. If you have more than two Word documents open, Word first requests which window you want to compare to the top current window (see Figure 4-15). If you have only two open Word documents, you do not see this Compare Side by Side dialog box.

Figure 4-15
Viewing two different documents.

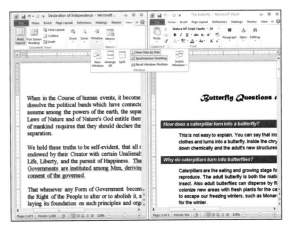

Figure 4-16
Managing Synchronous Scrolling.

To return to a single document window, deactivate the feature by choosing View>Window>View Side by Side.

Edit Document

To edit a document, click anywhere in the document window.

By default, the two windows are synchronized so that as you scroll through one window, the other one scrolls with it. If you want to scroll through the windows independently, you need to turn off Synchronous Scrolling. From either window, choose View>Window>Synchronous Scrolling (see Figure 4-16).

Using the Navigation Pane

If your document is quite lengthy, it can be difficult and time consuming to navigate through the document. However, if your document contains heading styles (see Chapter 3), you can use the Navigation Pane feature to ease navigation. The Navigation Pane also allows you to examine the document flow for completeness and ensure that formatting is consistent. Think of the Navigation Pane as a simple Table of Contents. Choose View>Show>Navigation Pane. A Navigation Pane, like the one seen in Figure 4-17, appears on the left side of the screen.

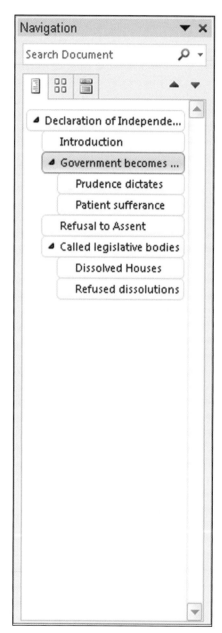

Figure 4-17
Working with a Navigation Pane.

Each item in the Navigation panel represents a heading in your document; you can click any item to move the insertion point to that place in the document. You can click the arrow to expand a heading or click the arrow again to hide subheadings.

To hide the Navigation Pane, choose View>Show> Navigation Pane, which removes the checkmark in Navigation Pane and closes the Navigation Pane.

Adding Headers and Footers

HEADERS AND FOOTERS are features used for placing information at the top or bottom of every page of a document. As you'd expect, a header prints at the top of every page, and a footer prints at the bottom. You can place any information in headers and footers, such as a company logo, the document title, page numbering, and so forth.

Using Header and Footer Styles

In keeping with the themed concept of Office 2010, the predefined headers and footers contain elements designed to make your document more visually appealing. Choose Insert>Header & Footer>Header (or Footer) which displays a gallery of 27 unique header (or footer) styles, as seen in Figure 4-18. If you were not already in Print Layout view, Word automatically switches you to it.

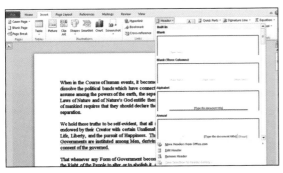

Figure 4-18
Creating a header or footer.

From the header or footer gallery, select the style you want. The document header area becomes visible, the body of the document fades, and Word dis-

plays an additional tab on the Ribbon. You can now use the Header & Footer Tools>Design tab for creating your personalized header or footer.

In the header example shown in Figure 4-19, Word inserts a placeholder for the document title. Click the placeholder and enter the desired text. Also in the same figure, you see a placeholder that says "Pick the Date." If you click the down arrow, Word displays a calendar from which you can select the date you want in the header. Optionally, you can just type a date in the date field. The actual choices you see depend on which header or footer style you select.

Placeholder   Design tab   Pick the date

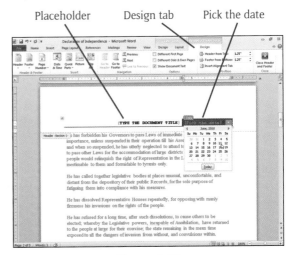

Figure 4-19
Working with text placeholders.

Now take a brief look at some of the tool groups on the Header & Footer Tools>Design tab, as seen in Figure 4-20.

Figure 4-20
The Header & Footer Tools Design tab.

Delete Placeholder

If you don't want the predefined placeholder, click the small tab above the placeholder and press the Delete key.

▶ **Header & Footer:** Use this group to change the header or footer style, or to insert the page number in the header or footer.

▶ **Insert:** From this group you can insert the current date or time, a picture, or a piece of clipart. You can also select from Quick Parts and choose one of the document properties shown in Figure 4-21.

Figure 4-21
Adding document Quick Parts.

▶ **Navigation:** Use the tools in this group to move between the document headers and footers.

▶ **Options:** The Options group allows you to choose whether the first page of your document should have a different header or footer from the rest of the document. You can also choose different headers for the odd or even numbered pages.

▶ **Position:** This group contains settings for exact header and footer placement in relation to the top or bottom of the document paper edges.

▶ **Close Header and Footer:** Use this button to close the header or footer and return to the document body. You can also double-click anywhere in the document body to close the header or footer.

Every page of the document displays the header and/or footer you created (see Figure 4-22). Remember, however, that documents displayed in Outline or Draft view do not show headers or footers.

Choose a Different One

If you don't like the header or footer you selected, double-click the header or footer and then, from the Header & Footer Tools>Design tab, click the Header or Footer button and choose a different header or footer.

Header

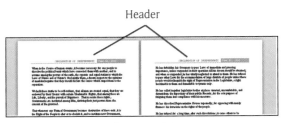

Figure 4-22
Viewing a document header.

More Header or Footer Choices

To further edit the header or footer, either double-click in the header or footer area, or choose Insert>Header & Footer>Header (or Footer)>Edit Header (or Footer). To remove the header or footer, choose Remove Header (or Footer) from the same menu.

Adding Page Numbering

Although Word automatically numbers your pages as you type them, it doesn't print the page numbers; it simply displays them in the screen status bar. You can easily tell Word you want to print them. Typically the page numbers appear in the header or footer area, but they don't have to. You can place them wherever you want. What you do need to remember though, is to use the Page Numbers feature provided by Word – don't try to type the page numbering yourself. If you type Page 1 of 6 in the footer; every page will say Page 1 of 6. If you use one of Word's Page Number features, the page numbering will change as needed, such as Page 2 of 6 or Page 3 of 6.

To insert a page number, choose Insert>Header & Footer>Page Number. A menu of placement options appears. You can put the page number at the top of the page in the Header, bottom of the page in the

Footer, in the page margins outside of the header or footer, or you can put the page numbering at the current document position of your cursor.

Choose the position you want, and then a gallery of prefabricated page number styles appears. (See Figure 4-23.) Select the page numbering style you want to use. Word adds the page numbering to your document as you see in Figure 4-24.

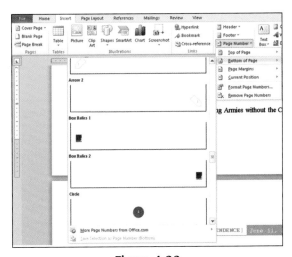

Figure 4-23
Select a page numbering style.

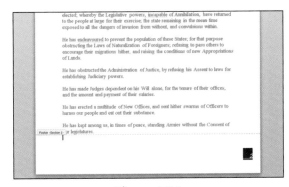

Figure 4-24
Page numbering added to the document.

Working with Columns
and Tables

PICTURE YOURSELF CRAWLING out of your warm bed after a good night's sleep. A luxurious aroma wafts through the house and you anticipate your first cup of hot coffee. You sit at the table and begin reading the morning paper, scanning the headlines and reading some articles in their entirety. You look at the financial section to check your stocks and you review the weather forecast for the next few days.

When you read a newspaper or magazine article, you read in columns. When you look at the financial page or the weather forecast, you're usually looking at a table, which is a grid consisting of rows and columns. That's what this chapter is all about...creating the type of document designed for reading large amounts of information quickly and easily.

Using Columns

NEWSPAPERS AND MAGAZINES are just a few of the documents that use columns to break up stories, with the text flowing from the bottom of one column to the top of the next. Of course, columns can be used for many other items, such as creating attractive newsletters, forms, or marketing materials.

Word applies columns to the entire document unless you first select the portion you want changed into columns, or you create section breaks and apply the column settings to the current section. You first discovered section breaks in Chapter 4.

Choose Page Layout>Page Setup>Columns. As shown in Figure 5-1, you see a drop-down menu of preset column options. Take a look at what each choice represents:

Figure 5-1
Choosing column settings.

▶ **One:** Use this choice to transform the document (or section) from multiple columns back to a single column.

▶ **Two:** Select this to divide the page into two equally spaced columns.

▶ **Three:** If you want three equally spaced columns on the page, choose this option.

▶ **Left:** The Left option divides the page into two columns, but the left column is smaller than the right (see Figure 5-2).

Figure 5-2
The left column is smaller than the right.

▶ **Right:** The Right option divides the page into two columns, but the right column is smaller than the left.

▶ **More Columns:** This option displays the Columns dialog box where you can customize your column settings.

For better column setting controls, choose the More Columns option. The Columns dialog box, as shown in Figure 5-3, provides a plethora of column options.

Figure 5-3
The Columns dialog box.

Use Section Breaks

Remember that if you want to make column changes to only a portion of the document, you must select that portion, or click in the section before choosing options from the Columns dialog box.

▶ Choose from any of the five preset column options.

▶ Manually set the number of columns, ranging from 1 column to 45 columns, by clicking the up/down arrows.

▶ Check the Line Between check box to add a solid line between the columns. Vertical lines between columns can make it easier to separate the columns when reading the text.

▶ Select a column and manually set the column width and the spacing between two columns. The whitespace between the columns is called the gutter. Each column can have its own width and gutter.

▶ Choose the Equal Column Width box if you want all columns equally spaced.

By default, text will flow down one column, then over to the next column. If you want the column to break at a particular point, you can insert a manual column break. Column breaks are similar to page breaks in that you cannot create a manual column break to make the column longer than the page margins, but you can make a column shorter. To create a manual column break, choose Page Layout>Page Setup>Breaks>Column.

Figure 5-4 illustrates a newsletter created in Word using columns, sections breaks and column breaks, page borders, shading, and a few graphics.

Figure 5-4
A finished newsletter.

Drop Caps

To create the large first letter, called a drop cap, select the first letter and choose Insert>Text>Drop Cap>Dropped.

Working with Tables

TABLES ARE GREAT for organizing information. A table is a grid of columns and rows, and the intersection of a column and row is called a cell. When you need to compare data or follow information across several columns, it's easier if the information is displayed in a table. You can use tables to place pieces of data side-by-side in a document—for example, in the various sections of an invoice or address list.

If you have used Microsoft Excel or another spread-sheet program, you will find working with tables in Word very similar. In fact, on a very small scale, Word tables are small spreadsheets.

Creating a Simple Table

When you create a table, all you need to do is esti-mate the number of rows and columns you need. Notice I said estimate. You'll find it easy to add or delete rows or columns after you create the table. Use the following steps to create a table:

1. Position the insertion point where you want the table to begin.

2. Choose Insert>Tables>Table, which displays a table grid like the one you see in Figure 5-5.

Figure 5-5
The table grid.

3. Drag the mouse across the squares that repre-sent the number of rows and columns you want in your table. Word's Live Preview feature draws a sample of the table in your document.

Alternate Method

If you don't want to drag across the table grid to set the table size, choose Insert Table. The Insert Table dialog box appears, in which you can type how many rows and columns you want in your table.

4. Click the square that represents the lower-right corner of your table. Word places the table into your document.

Notice in Figure 5-6 that the blinking insertion point is in the first table cell and that the Ribbon now con-tains two Table Tools tabs: Design and Layout.

Figure 5-6
Creating a table.

Tip

A table cell is a box that appears at the intersection of a row and column. Although the names don't display, each column takes an alphabetic letter, A, B, C, and so forth. Each row is indicated by a number. A cell, then, is referred to by both the column and row, such as A2 or B5. This is especially important if you create a formula in your table. (See "Creating Table Formulas" later in this chapter.)

Entering Text

Once you have your table in the document, you can start adding text to it. Click in the cell where you want to enter information and begin typing. If needed, Word automatically wraps the text and expands the row height to accommodate the text, as seen in Figure 5-7. You can press the Tab key to move to the next cell or press Shift+Tab to move to the previous cell. You can also use the up and down arrow keys to move up or down a row at a time.

Wrapped text

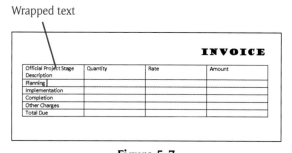

Figure 5-7
Table cells expand to accommodate entered text.

Converting Tables

Another method you can use to insert a Word table is by using existing text. If you already have a list where each column is separated by a tab, a comma, or other consistent character, you can easily convert that list to a table so you won't have to create the table and retype all the text. Conversely, if you put text into a table and then decide you would prefer it in tabular columns, you can convert the table into a list.

Be Consistent

In order for the conversion feature to work correctly, you must be consistent with the character you use to separate the items.

To convert a text list into a Word table, select the list and choose Insert>Tables>Table>Convert Text to Table. The Convert Text to Table dialog box shown in Figure 5-8 appears.

Other separation character

Figure 5-8
Converting an existing list into a Word table.

Based on the data you selected, Word guesses the number of columns you want. If you did not separate your columns with commas or tabs, in the Separate Text At section, choose Other and type the character you used, such as an asterisk or dash. Click OK and Word converts the list into a table. In Figure 5-8, I used the Tab character to separate the data.

If your text is already in a table, but you would prefer it in a list, click anywhere in the table and choose Table Tools>Layout>Data>Convert to Text. You see the Convert Table to Text dialog box seen in Figure 5-9. Choose the printing or non-printing character you want the text separated with and then click OK. The table disappears and the text remains.

Figure 5-10

Choosing a Quick Table style.

Figure 5-9

Converting a table back to standard text.

Creating a Quick Table

Another method for creating a table is using one of Word's Quick Tables. Quick Tables are nine predefined tables that include sample data and formatting. If you find a Quick Table close to what you actually need, you can save time by choosing the Quick Table and then changing the elements you want changed. Choose Insert>Tables> Table>Quick Tables and choose from one of the preformatted templates like you see in Figure 5-10.

> ### Save Table Styles
>
> If you create and format a table style you like and frequently use, select the table and choose Insert>Tables>Table>Quick Tables> Save Selection to Quick Tables Gallery. The next time you need that table you can select it from the Quick Tables gallery.

Okay…one more, rather fun way to create a Word table is by simply typing out a string of plus signs (+) and minus signs (-). Word uses its AutoCorrect feature to interpret your typing and convert it to a table. Type a plus sign and then type a series of minus signs until you have the first column width you want for your table. Type another plus sign, followed by more minus signs. Repeat these steps, placing a plus sign at the end of the series of minus signs (see Figure 5-11). When you press Enter, Word automatically converts it to a table.

Typing this....   Results in this...

Figure 5-11
Manually typing table boundaries.

Figure 5-12
Deleting unwanted table areas.

No matter which method you used to create your table, you enter the data as well as format or modify the table in the following ways.

Changing Table Size

Okay, now you have your table created, but it doesn't contain the right number of rows or columns. You can easily change the table size by adding or deleting rows or columns from your table. Table 5-1 illustrates some of the different ways you can change the table size.

Adjusting Column Width and Row Height

When you begin typing in a cell, you saw that as you type, the text wraps to the next line in the same cell. You may find that you don't want the data to wrap around, but the column is not wide enough to hold your data. You can easily change the width of columns or the height of rows. You can manage the task with the mouse or you can choose options in the Ribbon.

Table 5-1 Changing Table Size

To	Do This
Add rows to the table end	Click in the last table cell and press the Tab key or click in the last row and choose Table Tools Layout>Rows & Columns>Insert Below.
Add rows in the table middle	Click in a cell and choose Table Tools Layout>Rows & Columns>Insert Below (or Insert Above).
Add columns	Click in a cell and choose Table Tools Layout>Rows & Columns>Insert Left (or Insert Right).
Delete a column	Click in the column you want to delete and choose Table Tools Layout>Rows & Columns>Delete>Delete Columns (see Figure 5-12).
Delete a row	Click in the row you want to delete and choose Table Tools Layout>Rows & Columns>Delete>Delete Rows.
Delete an entire table	Click anywhere in the table and choose Table Tools Layout>Rows & Columns>Delete>Delete Table.

First, look at the methods you can use to change column width:

▶ Position the mouse over the edge of any cell in the column you want to adjust. Notice the mouse pointer changes to a bar with both left- and right-pointing arrows. Drag the edge of the cell until the column is the width you want (see Figure 5-13).

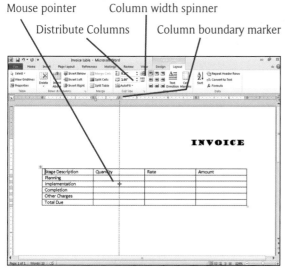

Figure 5-13
Drag to resize a column.

▶ Drag the column boundary marker on the ruler.

▶ Click in any cell of the column you want to adjust and choose Table Tools Layout>Cell Size>Table Column Width. Use the up/down arrows to set the desired column width.

▶ To force the column width so it's wide enough to fit the widest entry in the column, position the mouse pointer over the left edge of any cell in the column. When the mouse pointer changes to a bar with

the left- and right-pointing arrows, double-click the mouse. Word automatically expands the column to fit the widest entry.

▶ To force all columns to the same width, choose Table Tools Layout>Cell Size> Distribute Columns.

▶ To adjust the width of all of the table columns to fit their widest entry, choose Table Tools>Layout>Cell Size>AutoFit> AutoFit Contents.

The methods for modifying row height are very similar to those you use to change column width:

▶ Position the mouse over the bottom edge of any cell in the column you want to adjust. Notice the mouse pointer changes to a bar with both up and down arrows. Drag the bottom edge of the cell until the row is the height you want.

▶ Click in any cell of the row you want to adjust and choose Table Tools Layout>Cell Size>Table Row Height. Use the up/down arrows to set the desired row height.

▶ To adjust the height so it's tall enough to fit the tallest data entry, position the mouse pointer over the bottom edge of any cell in the row and double-click the mouse.

▶ To force each row to the same height, choose Table Tools Layout>Cell Size> Distribute Rows.

Changing Table Dimensions

If you find that your table dimensions don't quite provide the look you want, besides changing column widths and row heights, you can easily change the table size.

Just follow these steps:

1. Hover your mouse anywhere over the table until you see a sizing handle appear in the lower-right table corner. You must be in Print Layout view (View>Document Views>Print Layout) or Web Layout view (View>Document Views>Web Layout) to use this feature.

2. Position the mouse pointer over the handle until the pointer changes to a diagonal double-headed arrow.

Mouse pointer over sizing handle

Figure 5-14
Resizing a table.

3. Drag the sizing handle, which resizes the table. As you drag the handle you see a dashed line that represents the new table size. (See Figure 5-14.)

4. Release the mouse button to actually resize the table.

Moving a Table

The first step when creating a new table was to position the insertion point where you want the table. If you didn't have your insertion point in the right location, or you just decide you want to move the table, you can easily drag it to a different document area.

From Print Layout view or Web Layout view, as you move your mouse over the table, notice the upper-left table corner has a small box with a four-headed arrow in it. This is the Table Move handle. Position your mouse pointer over the Table Move handle until the mouse pointer changes to a four-headed arrow, and then drag the table to a new location. As you move the table, you see a dashed line which represents the new table position. See Figure 5-15 for an example.

Table Move handle

Figure 5-15
Moving a table.

> ## Copy Table
>
> If you want to copy the table instead of moving it, hold down the Ctrl key as you drag the table.

Selecting Table Areas

Often you want to make changes to an entire column or an entire row. Or perhaps you want to apply a certain formatting option to the entire table. Although you could make any desired changes one cell at a time, Word includes several methods you can use to select portions of the table so you can quickly apply any changes to the entire selection. The following list shows you several ways to select table cells:

▶ To select sequential cells, click in the first cell, then hold down the Shift key and select the last cell you want. Optionally, drag the mouse over a group of cells to select a sequential area. All cells in the selected area are highlighted.

▶ To select non-sequential cells, hold down the Ctrl key and click each additional cell you want to select. Figure 5-16 shows non-sequential cells selected and highlighted in blue.

▶ To select a single entire column, position the mouse pointer at the top of a column until the mouse turns into a down-pointing arrow, and then click.

▶ To select multiple columns, make sure the mouse pointer is the down-pointing arrow, and then drag across multiple columns.

▶ To select a single entire row, position the mouse pointer at the left of the row column until the mouse pointer turns into a white, right-pointing arrow, and then click.

▶ To select multiple rows, make sure the mouse is the right-pointing white arrow and then drag across multiple rows.

> ## Select Non-Sequential Cells
>
> When making non-sequential cell selections, you can include entire rows and entire columns along with individual cells or groups of cells.

▶ To select the entire table, click the table move handle which is the small box in the upper-left table corner.

▶ To clear any selection, click any nonselected cell or click outside of the table.

Stage Description	Quantity	Rate	Amount
Planning			
Implementation			
Completion			
Other Charges			
Total Due			

Figure 5-16
Selecting cells.

Formatting Cell Contents

If you want to change the appearance (formatting) of the table cells, you select the cells you want to modify and apply any of the standard formatting choices such as fonts, shading, and borders that you discovered in Chapter 3. However, Word also supplies a quick and easy way to format your table. By selecting from Word's large gallery of table styles you can apply attractive formatting with a click of the mouse. If needed, you then can make any additional adjustments to better meet your needs.

Take a look at the Design tab, shown in Figure 5-17. With the insertion point anywhere in your table, the Design tab displays a number of predefined themed formats. As you hover your mouse over any design option, Live Preview allows you to see the formatting as it would look in your actual document. When you find the style you want, click the mouse to actually accept the style.

More button

Figure 5-17
Use the Design tab to apply table styles.

Click the More button to display many more choices, such as seen in Figure 5-18.

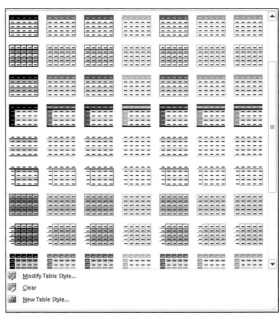

Figure 5-18
Choose from any of the many themed table styles.

Adjust Table Formatting

You can also easily adjust table formatting options by experimenting with the choices in the Table Style Options group.

Merging and Splitting Table Cells

By default, Word creates tables with each cell in a column the same width as the cell below it. Sometimes, however, especially if you are creating a form with your table, you may find some cells too small. Fortunately, you can combine adjacent cells to become larger cells. This is especially useful if you want to create a table header row such as the one seen in Figure 5-19.

Figure 5-20
Dividing a cell into multiple cells.

Figure 5-19
Merging multiple cells into one larger cell.

Drag across the two or more cells you want to merge and then choose Table Tools>Layout> Merge>Merge Cells. The highlighted cells combine into one larger cell.

If you want to split a cell into smaller cells, you need to tell Word into how many columns and rows you want the cell. Click anywhere in the cell you want to split and choose Table Tools>Layout> Merge>Split Cells. The Split Cells dialog box seen in Figure 5-20 appears. Choose how many columns and rows you want and then click the OK button.

Creating Table Formulas

If you have a complex table with lots of calculations, consider using Excel to perform the calculations and then inserting the spreadsheet into Word. The next section shows you how to accomplish that. But if you want a simple calculation such as adding a column of values, go ahead and let Word do the work for you.

There are two rules you must follow when creating Word calculations. One is that the entire calculation must be enclosed in a Word field. Word fields, which you'll see how to create shortly, are displayed with opening and closing curly brackets, { and }. The second rule is that all calculations must begin with an equals sign (=).

You create Word arithmetic formulas using operators to perform the calculation you want. Table 5-2 shows the mathematic operators used in Word tables along with an example of each.

Table 5-2
Mathematical Operators Used in Word

Name	Operator	Example	Result
Addition	+	{=6+3}	9
Subtraction	–	{=6-3}	3
Multiplication	*	{=6*3}	18
Division	/	{=6/3}	2
Percentage	%	{=6%}	.06
Exponentiation	^	{=6^3}	216

Figure 5-21
The Formula dialog box.

When creating a calculation, the power comes in to play in that you typically don't use the actual values; instead, you create a reference to them. Suppose cell B2 has a value of 6 and cell B3 has a value of 3. Now, suppose you want, in cell B4, to multiply those two values. In cell B4, you won't enter =6*3; instead, you'll enter =B2*B3. The advantage is that if you later change the value in cell B2 from 6 to 8, you won't have to retype the calculation—you'll simply tell Word to recalculate it. Look at how this is all accomplished:

1. First you must realize that calculations in Word tables are generated from formula fields. Click the cell in which you want a formula field and choose Table Tools>Layout> Data>Formula. You see the Formula dialog box shown in Figure 5-21.

2. Sometimes Word can detect the formula you want and automatically creates instructions. In the previous figure, Word assumes you want to add together (SUM) the cells above the current cell. Maybe you do, but to illustrate a formula, let's manually enter it. Highlight the existing text in the Formula text box and type an equals sign (=).

3. Type the rest of your formula such as you see in Figure 5-22. In this example, you want to multiply cells B3 and C3, which will give the total amount.

Figure 5-22
Creating a calculation.

4. Optionally, choose an option from the Number Format drop-down menu. This option determines the appearance of your answer such as whether to include a dollar sign, a percent symbol, or two decimal points.

5. Click OK. Word calculates the formula and displays the results.

If you later make a change to any of the table cells referenced in the formula, Word doesn't automatically update the formula answer. Right-click over the current answer and choose Update Field.

View the Formula

If you want to see the actual formula instead of the result, right-click over the answer and choose Toggle Field Codes. To view the answer again, repeat the action.

Word contains a number of predefined calculations, called functions, that you can plug into your formula fields. For example, if you simply want to add adjacent cells, use the SUM function, such as =SUM(ABOVE) or =SUM(LEFT). The ABOVE function tells Word to add all the non-blank cells directly above the answer cell. The LEFT function tells Word to add all the non-blank cells directly to the left of the answer cell. To use a function, choose Table Tools>Layout>Data>Formula. You can either accept the suggestion provided by Word, or click the Paste Function drop-down menu and choose a different function (see Figure 5-23).

Tip

Word cannot use a function to total the entire column or row if your column or row contains blank cells or cells with text instead of values.

Figure 5-23
Using calculation functions.

Take a look at the finished document as seen in Figure 5-24. The formatting tools along with the table tools enabled the creation of a nice-looking form.

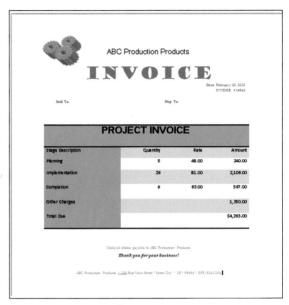

Figure 5-24
The final invoice created in Word.

Adding an Excel Table to a Word Document

IN THIS CHAPTER you've seen some of the power behind a Word table. As mentioned at the chapter beginning, a Word table is basically a small spreadsheet. You'll discover later in this book how to work with Excel worksheets, but you should also know that once you create an Excel worksheet, you can insert it into a Word document. Just follow these steps:

1. Position the insertion point where you want the Excel worksheet placed.

2. Choose Insert>Text>Object>Object. You see the Object dialog box.

3. Click the Create from File tab.

4. Click the Browse button. A Browse window opens.

5. Locate and double-click the file you want to insert. The Object dialog box reappears with the file name you selected (see Figure 5-25).

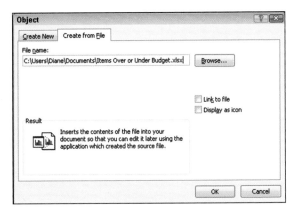

Figure 5-25
Select the Excel file you want to include.

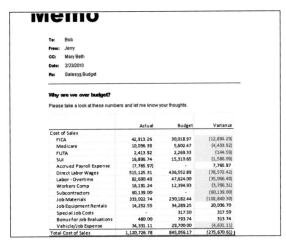

Figure 5-26
An Excel worksheet in a Word document.

6. Click OK. The Excel worksheet along with any formulas and formatting appears in your document. See the example in Figure 5-26.

Word considers the table an object in the document. To make any changes, double-click the inserted Excel worksheet where you will see the Excel worksheet Ribbon and options. Click outside the table to return to Word. Changes you make in the Word table do not affect the saved Excel worksheet.

Using Word for
Mail Merge

PICTURE YOURSELF OPENING THE MAIL. On the front of the envelope it says in big bold letters that "You have won TEN MILLION DOLLARS." Then, of course, in teeny tiny print it says "if you are the lucky winner." It has your name printed in big letters right there on the certificate! The funny thing is that each of your neighbors got exactly the same letter with their name on the envelope and certificate. Probably millions of exactly the same letter arrived in mailboxes all around the country.

Although our society has become a little more paperless than just a few years ago, realistically we still use snail mail for lots of things. We still rely on the postal service for delivery of our bills, catalogs, Christmas cards, and lots of other types of correspondence. And let's not forget the hard working trash collectors. They might be out of work if it weren't for all the junk mail we all receive!

This chapter is all about mail. Creating envelopes, labels, and mass mailings are all easy tasks when you use Word.

Generating a Single Envelope

ECAUSE OF THE AUTOMATION used by the post office when sorting mail, it's important to make sure the address is clear and concise. Hand addressed envelopes can easily be misread by both man and machine and, frankly, they often look very unprofessional.

By using Word to address your envelopes, you can create neat, accurate addresses for both the mailing address and the return address. You can even add a bar code that can often speed up delivery time or a graphic image to personalize your envelope.

Creating the Envelope

When you generate an envelope, Word displays an Envelopes and Labels dialog box. Obviously, for the envelope, you'll need a delivery address. First take a look at several methods Word uses to obtain a delivery address:

▶ If you have a letter or other document already on your screen, you can let Word automatically find the recipient address and fill it directly into the Delivery address box. By far, this is the fastest and easiest method! See Figure 6-1 for a sample letter that contains a recipient address.

▶ You can type the address directly into the Delivery address box in the Envelopes and Labels dialog box.

▶ From the Envelopes and Labels dialog box, you can choose an address from your Outlook contact list. (See Chapter 21 for information about the Outlook contact list.)

▶ You can copy the address from another source and then paste it into the Delivery address box. Use the Ctrl+V keyboard shortcut to paste the address.

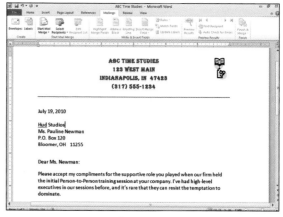

Figure 6-1
Word can pick up the mailing address from the current document.

Choose Mailings>Create>Envelopes. The Envelopes and Labels dialog box seen in Figure 6-2 appears. If your document contained the mailing address, the address already appears in the Delivery address area. If you don't see the delivery address in the dialog box, you need to enter the address using one of the previously listed methods.

Figure 6-2
Envelope settings.

Following are the other choices on the Envelopes tab:

▶ If you subscribe to an electronic postage service such as Stamps.com, check the Add Electronic Postage check box. You also should then click the E-Postage Properties button to set any desired options for your e-postage subscription.

▶ Enter your return address in the Return Address dialog box, or click the Address book button above it to extract your address from your Outlook contact list. When you exit the Envelopes and Labels dialog box, Word asks whether you want to save the return address as the default. If you choose Yes, the next time you open the Envelopes and Labels dialog box, your address will already be listed in the Return address section. You can change the default return address at any time.

▶ Click the Omit check box if you don't want Word to add a return address to the envelope.

▶ Click the Options button to display the Envelopes Options dialog box. From this dialog box you select the envelope size as well as the default font you want for the addresses.

▶ The Printing Options tab displays options for feeding envelopes, but I recommend you leave it at Automatically Select since Windows already knows how your current printer accepts envelope feeds.

Tip

Each printer model handles envelopes a little differently than the next one. Review your printer manual for envelope feed information.

Once you select the envelopes options, you now can either create or print the envelope. If you click the Print button, Word sends the printing information directly to your default printer. Make sure you have the printer on and the envelope inserted into the appropriate location. If you click the Add to Document button, Word adds a new page to the top of the document and displays the envelope (see Figure 6-3).

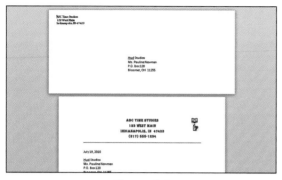

Figure 6-3
Adding an envelope to your document.

If you add the envelope to the document, you can, by using the Word tools you already know, edit the envelope addresses, change fonts, or even add a graphic to the envelopes. If you want to change the envelope options, click anywhere inside the envelope area and choose Mailings>Create>Envelopes again, which redisplays the Envelopes and Labels dialog box. Make any desired changes and then click Change Document.

Adding a US Bar Code

The computerized sorting equipment used by the United States Post Office relies on delivery point bar codes, which are also known as POSTNET bar codes. You can easily add a bar code to your envelope. Follow these steps:

Bulk Mailing

If you are processing a bulk mailing, you can save money by presorting the envelopes and including the POSTNET bar codes. Contact your post office for more information on bulk mail postal rates and requirements.

---

1. Add the envelope to your document. (See the previous section.)

2. Click the insertion point where you want the POSTNET bar code located, which is typically directly above or directly under the delivery address.

3. Choose Insert>Text>Quick Parts>Field. The Field dialog box appears.

4. In the Field names list, click once on BarCode. Bar code options appear on the right side of the dialog box, as shown in Figure 6-4.

Figure 6-4
Generating a bar code.

5. In the Field options section, click the "Bar Code Is US Zip Code" option.

6. Next to the "Bar Code Is US Zip Code" option, type the recipient's ZIP code and then click the OK button.

As you see in Figure 6-5, Word inserts the bar code at the insertion point.

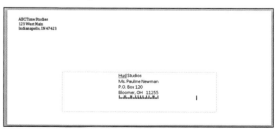

Figure 6-5
A POSTNET bar code.

Creating Labels

YOU CAN PURCHASE sheets of labels that feed easily into both inkjet and laser printers, making mailing labels easy to produce using Word's label function. Labels are especially useful if you have large quantities of letters to mail, and, of course, some envelopes are simply too big or bulky to fit into your printer. You can also use labels to create hundreds of items such as name tags, product information, file folder labels, or return address labels.

Similar to when you create an envelope, if you want Word to pick up the address automatically, create it in the form of a letter or document before you begin label creation. Otherwise, start with a blank document, and then follow these steps:

1. Choose Mailings>Create>Labels. The Envelopes and Labels dialog box appears with the Labels tab on top.

2. Click the Options button. The Label Options dialog box seen in Figure 6-6 appears.

3. Click the Tray drop-down menu and select the printer tray you plan on using for labels.

4. Click the Label Vendors drop-down menu and select the manufacturer of the labels you plan on using.

5. Click the label Product Number you want to use. A description of the selected label appears on the right side.

6. Click the OK button. You return to the Envelopes and Labels dialog box.

7. Choose Full Page of the Same Label. Select this option even if you want to enter different information on each label.

8. If you want a full page of the same label, enter or edit the label information in the Address section (see Figure 6-7) or click the Insert Address icon to choose from an Outlook contact.

For Individual Labels

If you want to type individual information on each label, leave the Address box blank.

Figure 6-6
Choosing a label size.

Figure 6-7
Enter address label information.

9. Click New Document. A screen full of labels or a label grid appears on your screen.

Labels Use Word Tables

Word uses tables when creating labels. If you don't see the gridlines indicating labels, click Table Tools Layout>Table>View Gridlines.

10. You can now optionally edit the individual labels and print them whenever you're ready (see Figure 6-8).

Figure 6-8
A full page of labels.

Move Label Edge

If you find that your labels are printing too close to the left edge of the label, press Ctrl+A to select all of the labels, and then drag the left indent mark a little to the right on the ruler.

Using Mail Merge

WHEN YOU PLAN on sending a group of recipients the same basic letter, that letter is called a form letter. A form letter results from merging a standard generic letter with personalized information. To create form letters in Word, you use the Mail Merge function.

You need two things to create a personalized mailing with a mail merge: a letter, which is called the main document and contains the information that doesn't change, and codes, called merge fields, that act as placeholders for the variable information. This variable information is usually a list of names and addresses, called the data source, and contains the information that does change for each letter. When you merge the two, the result is an individualized form letter, called the merge document.

Creating the Main Document

For the main document, you can use a letter that you've previously created or you can create a letter from scratch. Type your letter without filling in any of the information that will vary from recipient to recipient such as addresses, meeting dates, and such.

The following steps show you how to begin the mail merge process:

1. Open or type the letter you want as the main document.

2. Choose Mailings>Start Mail Merge>Start Mail Merge>Letters. If you were not already in Print Layout view, Word switches to Print Layout view (see Figure 6-9).

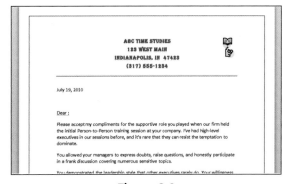

Figure 6-9

A mail merge main document.

Specifying Data for Your Mail Merge

Once you create your main document, you need to link the document to a file that contains your data. The data source could be in the form of a comma-separated value Word document or it could be in an Excel worksheet or an Access database. See Figure 6-10 for an example of each document type—Word, Excel, and Access.

Figure 6-10
Possible data sources.

Two terms commonly used with merge data files are fields and records. A field is an individual piece of information about someone or something such as a ZIP code, first name, or product description. A record is the complete picture of information with all the fields put together.

Selecting a Data Source

For the data source, you can select from a preexisting list or you can create a new one using Word. If you want to choose from an existing file, choose Mailings>Start Mail Merge>Select Recipients>Use Existing List (see Figure 6-11). The Select Data Source dialog box opens. Locate your data file and choose Open.

Figure 6-11
Selecting an existing data source.

If you have not already created a data source, you can create it with Word. Following are the steps for creating a data source in Word:

1. Choose Mailings>Start Mail Merge>Select Recipients>Type New List. The New Address List dialog box appears. Word tries to anticipate your needs by providing the most commonly used data fields. You'll soon see how you can add extra fields.

2. Enter the data for the first recipient. You do not need to enter data into every field as you see in Figure 6-12.

Figure 6-12
Adding records.

Moving Around Fields

Use the Tab key to move from one field to the next, or press Shift+Tab to return to a previous field.

---

3. Click the New Entry button, which creates a blank line for the next recipient. Optionally, as you press Tab after the last field, Word automatically adds a line for the next recipient.

4. Repeat steps 2 and 3 for each additional recipient.

Although Word includes commonly used data fields, you may need to add your own fields or remove the predefined fields you don't want. Click the Customize Columns button in the New Address List dialog box. The Customize Address List dialog box appears, like the one seen in Figure 6-13. Make any desired changes and then click OK. Here are the options available in the Customize Address List dialog box:

Figure 6-13
Customizing data fields.

▶ **Add:** To add additional fields, click the Add button. As seen in Figure 6-14, Word prompts you for a name for the new field. Type the name and click OK.

Figure 6-14
Adding a new data field.

▶ **Delete:** To delete an unwanted field, click a field name and then click the Delete button. A confirmation message appears. Click Yes to confirm the deletion.

▶ **Rename:** To rename a field, click the field name and then click the Rename button. Enter the new name in the resulting dialog box and click OK.

► **Move up:** To move a field farther up in the list, click the field name and click the Move Up button until the field is located where you want it.

► **Move down:** To move a field farther down in the list, click the field name and click the Move Down button until the field is located where you want it.

When you have all your entries in the New Address List, click the OK button.

Delete Record

If you want to delete a record, click anywhere in the record and click the Delete Entry button. Click Yes to the resulting confirmation message.

Word prompts you to save your address list. By default, Word attempts to save the file in the Documents>My Data Sources folder. Select a different folder if desired. Enter a file name and then click Save.

Data File Format

Word saves the data file as an MDB file, which is an Access database file.

Selecting Recipients

You may have a number of names in your data file, but perhaps you don't want to send the merged letter to everyone in the file. By default, Word assumes you want everyone in the data file, but you can pick and choose which recipients you want to use. Just follow these steps:

1. Choose Mailings>Start Mail Merge>Edit Recipient List. You see a Mail Merge Recipients list similar to the one displayed in Figure 6-15.

Figure 6-15
Deselect any recipient you don't want to include.

Sort Records

Click any column heading to sort the records by the selected column.

2. Click the check box to the left of the name for any recipient to whom you don't want to send the form letter. The check mark will be removed.

Edit Data

To edit recipient information, click the data source name, and then click the Edit button. The Edit Data Source dialog box appears, from which you can make any desired changes.

3. After determining that the desired recipients are checked, click the OK button.

Inserting Merge Fields

Now that you've created the main document and have selected a data source, the next step is to enter the merge fields (also called merge codes) into the main document, thereby instructing Word exactly where you want those data fields placed.

You have the option of placing a group of fields together or choosing the individual fields you want to enter. The field groups come in the two forms. The first group is for an Address Block which consists of the following fields: Title, First Name, Last Name, Company Name, Address Line 1, Address Line 2, City, State, and ZIP Code. The second group is for the Greeting Line, which includes a greeting such as "Dear" or "To," followed by the First Name and Last Name, and then a punctuation choice such as a comma.

Adding an Address Block

Begin by adding an Address Block. In the main document, click the insertion point where you want the recipient name and address. Choose Mailings>Write & Insert Fields>Address Block. The Insert Address Block dialog box appears, as seen in Figure 6-16.

Match Fields button

Figure 6-16
Setting options for an address block.

Since Word recognizes the individual fields—including name, address, city, state, and ZIP—as part of the address block, using the address block saves you the steps of inserting each of those fields individually. You can, however, choose the style of address block you prefer. Click on the various address formats and review in the preview panel just how your data looks with each format.

Match Up Fields

If the fields in your address block don't match your data, you can manually pair them together. For example, if you expect to see someone's first name, but instead you see their country, click the Match Fields button to identify and match the fields.

Click OK when you've decided on the format you want. Word returns to the main document and inserts a field <<AddressBlock>> at the insertion point. This is a hidden code to Microsoft Word. Don't try to just type <<AddressBlock>>.

Selecting a Greeting Line

Most form letters also include a personalized greeting. Use the Greeting Line field box to assist you. Begin by positioning the insertion point where you want the greeting line, usually two lines under the Address Block. Choose Mailings>Write & Insert Fields>Greeting Line. The Insert Greeting Line dialog box appears (see Figure 6-17).

Figure 6-17
Choosing a greeting line format.

Select a greeting from the first drop-down menu. Choices include "Dear," "To," or nothing at all. From the second drop-down menu, select the name format you like best and then from the third drop-down menu, choose a punctuation mark of a comma or a colon, or choose no punctuation.

In the event that one or more of your recipients doesn't have data in the first and last name fields, the Greeting line for invalid recipient names drop-down menu provides a couple of alternatives. Select the one you prefer for your document. Or you might have to click the Match Fields button and select the proper field.

Click the OK button, which returns you to the Word main document where you now see the <<Greeting Line>> field code.

Adding Individual Fields

If the field information you want to insert into your document doesn't fall into the Address Block or Greeting Line groups, you can manually insert fields into desired document areas. Just click the mouse pointer where you want the field to appear. Choose Mailings>Write & Insert Fields>Insert Merge Field and select the field you want in the letter.

Tip

It's not necessary to use all fields in a form letter, and you can use fields multiple times in the same document.

Figure 6-18 illustrates a sample form letter with an Address Block, Greeting Line, and an individual data field entered into the letter. To make it easier for you to see, I highlighted the fields in yellow.

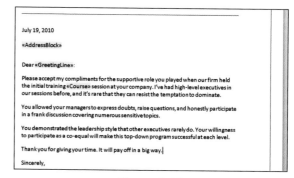

Figure 6-18
A sample form letter.

Finishing the Merge

Before you actually print all the records, you should preview them. Choose Mailings>Preview Results>Preview Results. You see your letter with data filled in from one of the records (see Figure 6-19). In the Preview mode, you can manually make any formatting or text changes, and the changes will appear for all recipients.

Use the Preview Results scroll buttons to browse between the previous and next records, or the first and last records. Again, in this figure, I left the fields highlighted in yellow to make it easier for you to see.

Preview Results scroll buttons

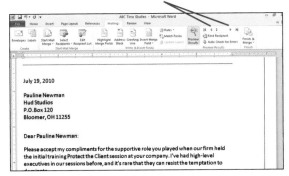

Figure 6-19
Previewing the merged letter.

When you are satisfied with the results, you're ready to finish the merge. Choose Mailings> Finish>Finish & Merge. A menu of options appears where you can edit the individual documents, print the documents, or send the documents via e-mail.

▶ **Edit the individual documents:** Choose this option if you want to personalize your letters. This option creates a new Word document where each letter is on its own page and any changes you make affect the individual current record only—not the other recipients. You have the option to merge all records, the current record, or a range of record numbers (see Figure 6-20).

Figure 6-20
Displaying the merged letters in a new Word document.

▶ **Print documents:** Choose this option if you don't need to make any individual changes and just want to print the merged documents. When you choose this option you can choose to merge all records, the current record, or a range of record numbers.

▶ **Send e-mail messages:** This option sends the document to the recipient via e-mail. The e-mail option only works if the individual record data includes e-mail addresses. When you choose this option, like the others, you can merge all records, the current record, or a range of record numbers. Additionally, as seen in Figure 6-21, you determine which field in your data source contains the e-mail address, and you can enter a subject line. Also, you determine if you want the letter sent as an attachment to the e-mail, in HTML format, in the e-mail, or in just a plain text with no formatting in the e-mail.

Don't Leave Subject Blank

Don't leave the subject line blank. Many e-mail filters will not display an e-mail without a subject.

Figure 6-21
Sending the merged letters via e-mail.

Discovering
Word Tools

PICTURE YOURSELF AS A SKILLED CRAFTSPERSON —a carpenter, for example. Whether you're building a bird house or a beach house, you know you need to use the right tools to get the job done. So it is with Microsoft Word. Different tasks require different tools, and it's important to use the right tool for the job.

Up to this point, you've used quite a few of the basic Word features. This chapter is sort of a hodgepodge of some additional tools provided with Word that can make your word-processing tasks easier and faster, and help improve the quality of your writing. Besides looking at tools for speed and quality, you'll also review features you might use to finish up a project such as printing or e-mailing a document. You'll also take a look at document security and how you can better protect your work.

As you work with Word, you may find you use some of the tools a lot and other tools very seldom, but as you proceed with your Word documents, at some time I'm sure you'll find yourself looking at your screen and thinking, "Aha! I can use the [*xxxx*] feature to accomplish this."

Employing Tools for Quality

WHETHER YOU ARE WRITING the great American novel, a standard business letter, or a résumé, spelling or grammatical errors can ruin the impression you're trying to create. Not only does Word have spelling and grammar checkers to correct document errors, it also has a thesaurus to help you find just the right word to convey your ideas.

Correcting Errors

Word has built-in dictionaries and grammatical rule sets that it uses to check your document. Word can identify possible problems as you type, and it also can run a special spelling and grammar check that provides you with more information about the problems and tools for fixing them. And although they have been greatly improved in Word 2010, these features aren't infallible; if you type "To *air* is human" instead of "To *err* is human," Word probably won't be able to tell you that you're wrong. However, combined with a good proofreading, these tools are very helpful.

Checking Spelling and Grammar as You Go

As you type your document, Word operates the spell checker tool in the background and identifies problems. Word tags potential spelling errors with a red wavy line under them. Right-click on an unrecognized word and you see a shortcut menu appear with possible suggestions for correction (see the example in Figure 7-1). Click on the correct spelling and the misspelled or unrecognized word is replaced with your selection. Occasionally Word cannot provide a suggestion. In those cases, you need to correct the error yourself.

Add to Dictionary

If Word interprets a word as a misspelling, but it is a word you use frequently, such as a name or business term, you can add it to your Dictionary so Word won't see it as a misspelling.

Add to Dictionary

Figure 7-1
Fixing errors as you type.

As with spelling errors, Word identifies potential grammatical errors by placing a green wavy line under the questionable text. Right-click on the questionable word or phrase to display a shortcut menu with suggested grammatical corrections. Click the appropriate option and Word replaces the incorrect word or phrase with your selection. Sometimes, however, Word cannot provide a suggestion; in those cases, you need to correct the error yourself.

Check for Yourself

Do not rely on Word's spell check and grammar features to catch all your errors. The tools are very helpful, but they are far from perfect and can miss many items. They can also flag items as errors that really are okay and can suggest wrong ways to fix both real problems and false errors. You alone are the one who knows what you want your document to say. Proofread it yourself!

Running a Spelling and Grammar Check

If you don't want to correct items as you type, Word can run a spelling and grammar check at the same time. Running the spell and grammar check also provides additional options for dealing with incorrect items. Use the following steps:

1. Position the insertion point at the beginning of the document to check the entire document. If you want to check only a portion of the text, select the text first.

2. Choose Review>Proofing>Spelling and Grammar. If there are no errors in the document, a message box appears advising you that the checks are complete; otherwise,

Word displays the Spelling and Grammar dialog box seen in Figure 7-2, referencing the first error, whether spelling or grammar.

Keyboard Shortcut

Optionally, press F7 to launch the Spelling and Grammar check.

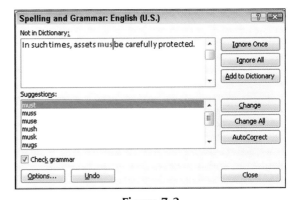

Figure 7-2
Using the Spelling and Grammar check to improve your document.

3. If the error is a spelling error, do one of the following:

   ▶ **Ignore Once:** Click this if you don't want to correct this instance of the spelling.

   ▶ **Ignore All:** Click this if you don't want to correct any instances of the spelling.

   ▶ **Add to Dictionary:** Choose this to add the word to the dictionary so that in the future Word won't flag it as an error.

   ▶ **Change:** Choose a word from the Suggestion list and then click Change, which changes just this incident of the spelling mistake.

▶ **Change All:** After selecting a replacement from the Suggestion list, choose Change All if you think you could have made the same mistake more than once.

▶ **AutoCorrect:** After making a selection from the Suggestion list, click this option to add the unknown word and the correction as an AutoCorrect entry. If you make the same misspelling in a future document, Word automatically changes it to the correction.

4. If the error is a grammatical error, such as you see in Figure 7-3, take one of these actions:

Don't Check Grammar

If you don't want Word to check grammar, remove the check mark from the Check Grammar option.

Check Grammar

Figure 7-3
Catching grammatical mishaps.

▶ **Ignore Once:** Click this option if you don't want to change this instance of the grammatical problem.

▶ **Ignore Rule:** Click this option to ignore all instances of the same grammatical problem type.

▶ **Next Sentence:** Click this option to skip the error and continue the check. All instances of the same error are ignored.

▶ **Change:** Choose an option from the Suggestion list and then click Change, which changes just this incident of the grammatical mistake.

▶ **Explain:** Click this option to launch an article that explains the error and offers suggestions for avoiding the error.

5. When all potential mistakes are identified, Word notifies you that the spelling and grammar check is complete. Click the OK button.

Changing Spelling Options
Word provides quite a few options for both the spelling and grammar correction features. For example, if you don't want Word to check your spelling or your grammar as you type, you can turn off the feature. Click the File tab and choose Options. Click the Proofing option.

From the Proofing section, as seen in Figure 7-4, you can set or turn off any desired proofing options. Some of the options apply to all Office 2010 applications and some apply only to Microsoft Word. There are even a few options that apply only to the current document.

Show readability statistics

Figure 7-4
Setting proofing options.

Readability Statistics

From the Options window, click the Show Readability Statistics check box, and after running a Spelling and Grammar check, Word displays statistics such as the number of words, characters, paragraphs, and sentences, as well as average words per sentences or the readability grade level. See Figure 7-5 for an example.

Figure 7-5
Viewing document statistics.

Finding Elusive Words with the Thesaurus

A key to good writing is using words that add interest and flair. However, remember that you need words appropriate for your audience. If you are addressing a group of grade school children, you'll use simpler words than if you are writing your college thesis. If you need a little help finding just the right word, try using Word's thesaurus.

Click anywhere in the word you want replaced and then choose Review>Proofing>Thesaurus. Optionally, press Shift+F7 to launch the thesaurus. A Research pane similar to the one seen in Figure 7-6 appears on the right side of the screen and displays various meanings of the current word and possible replacements. If you don't see the exact word you want, click a similar word, which displays its synonyms. Click the Back button to return to the previous word. When you locate the word that best fits your document, click the arrow next to it and choose Insert. Word replaces the current word with your selection.

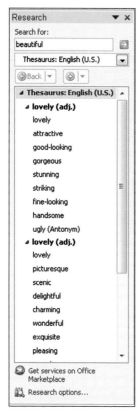

Figure 7-6
Locating synonyms with the thesaurus.

Click the Research close box to close the Research pane.

Using Find and Replace

Word's Find and Replace features are real time savers. For example, you can quickly find out if you covered a particular topic in a lengthy report, or you can change names, dates, and prices throughout documents with just a few keystrokes.

Using Find

Word's Find command is useful when you want to seek out text that you may have trouble visually

locating in a document. The Find command doesn't change any text; it simply locates and highlights the specified text for you. Follow these steps:

1. Choose Home>Editing>Find, or press Ctrl+F. The Navigation Pane appears on the left side of the screen (see Figure 7-7).

2. In the text box, type the word or phrase that you want to search for. As you type, Word automatically highlights and displays each occurrence of the word or phrase you're looking for.

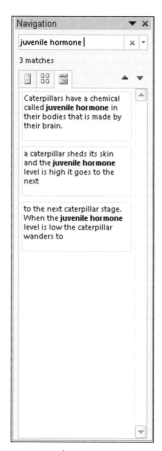

Figure 7-7
Finding document text.

Starting Point

The Find command begins its search at the location of the insertion point.

3. The Navigation Pane also lists the other occurrences of the searched text. Click any occurrence to instantly jump to the text. If you want to discontinue the search, simply close the Navigation Pane.

Exact Find

Unless you specify whole words (see the next section), Word locates any instance containing the letters you specify. For example, if you enter read in the Find box, Word also locates words like bread or reading.

Extending Search Options

If you need to be a little more specific about what you're searching for, Word provides a number of extended options to assist you.

Open the Navigation Pane by choosing Home>Editing>Find, or press the Ctrl+F keys and in the search text box, type the word or phrase for which you want to search. Click the Find Options arrow next to the text box which displays a menu like the one you see in Figure 7-8. Choose Options which displays the Find Options dialog box you also see in Figure 7-8, and then selecting the options you want. Click OK when you are finished and Word continues the search using the options you selected.

Find Options arrow

Figure 7-8
Specifying search options.

Take a brief look at the most commonly used options:

▶ **Match Case:** Check this to locate instances that match the upper- and lowercase letters as you entered in the Find box. For example, if you typed Go, Word will not locate go or GO.

▶ **Find Whole Words Only:** Check this to locate instances of the entire words only. For example, if you enter read in the Find box, Word will ignore words like bread or reading.

▶ **Use Wildcards:** Check this to use the wildcards ? or * in your search. The ? character matches any single character and the * character matches any number of characters. For example, if you enter b?d in the Find box, Word finds bad, bed, or bidding, but not bread. If you enter b*d, Word locates words like bad, bed, abide, bidding, bread, bored, and so forth.

▶ **Sounds Like:** Check this to locate instances that are phonetically the same as the text in the Find box. For example, if you entered *foul*, Word also locates *fowl*.

▶ **Find All Word Forms:** Check this to locate all grammatical forms of the search word. For example, if you enter *they*, Word also locates *their*, *theirs*, *them*, and *themselves*.

▶ **Highlight All:** Checked by default, this option tells Word to highlight all occurrences of the found text.

▶ **Incremental Find:** Also checked by default, the Incremental find allows Word to start searching as soon as you start typing in the Find box.

▶ **Match Prefix:** Check this to locate words that only begin, not contain or end, with the search word. For example, if you enter mini, Word also locates *minimum* or *miniature*, but not *administration*.

▶ **Match Suffix:** Check this to locate words that only end, not contain or begin, with the search word. For example, if you enter *ration*, Word also locates demonstration but not *rational*.

▶ **Ignore Punctuation Characters:** Check this to ignore punctuation marks such as '?-"!;:,. and /. For example, if you entered *1478*, Word also locates *1,478* and *14.78*.

▶ **Ignore Whitespace Characters:** Check this to ignore spaces and tabs. For example, if you enter *lonestar*, Word also locates lone star.

Finding Formatted Text

You can also locate text that contains a specified type of formatting. For example, you want to locate the word apple but only if you underlined the word. Follow these steps:

1. From the Navigation Pane, click the drop-down arrow next to the text box and choose Advanced Find. The Find and Replace dialog box opens.

2. Click the More button, which expands the Find options as seen in Figure 7-9. The More button turns into a Less button. Some of the options here are similar to those you viewed in the previous section.

Less button

Figure 7-9
Expand the search options.

3. Click the Format button. You see a list of formatting options.

4. Click the formatting type you want to locate. Choices include Font, Paragraph, Tabs, Language, Frame, Style, and Highlight. A dialog box appropriate to your selection appears. In Figure 7-10 you see the Find Font dialog box.

Figure 7-10
Searching for formatting.

5. Select the formatting you want to search for and then click OK which returns you to the Find and Replace dialog box.

Formatting Shortcuts Accepted

Instead of choosing font options from a dialog box, you can press a formatting shortcut key such as Ctrl+B for bold.

6. In the Find What text box, enter the text you want to search for, or, if you want to find the formatting only, regardless of the text, leave the Find What box empty.

7. Specify any other search options and click Find Next to begin your search. Click the Cancel button when you are finished.

Remove Formatting Specifications

Click the No Formatting button to remove any formatting specifications.

Finding Special Characters

In Chapter 2, you discovered that Word hides many characters such as the dots used for spaces, or an arrow for tabs, or even the paragraph mark ¶ at the end of a paragraph. You can have Word search for a number of special characters.

From the expanded Find and Replace dialog box, click the Special button. You see a list of formatting options as shown in Figure 7-11. Choose the special character for which you want to search. Word places a code for the character in the Find What text box. Specify any other search options and click Find Next to begin your search.

Figure 7-11
Searching for special characters.

Figure 7-12
Entering Find and Replace text.

Using Replace

If you want to locate some particular text and change it to something else, let Word do it for you with the Replace feature. The Replace feature is very similar to the Find function you just discovered. You can locate text and replace it with different text, or you can locate text and replace it with the same or different text, but perhaps with different formatting. Follow these simple steps:

1. Choose Home>Editing>Replace, or press Ctrl+H. The Find and Replace dialog box appears with the Replace tab on top.

2. In the Find What text box, enter the text you want to search for.

3. Click in the Replace With text box and type a replacement word or phrase (see Figure 7-12).

Replace with Nothing

To delete the "found" text, leave the Replace With text box empty. Word will replace the found text with nothing.

4. Specify any additional search or replace options such as matching case or a particular format.

5. Click Find Next. Word locates the first match.

6. Choose one of the following:

   ▶ Click Replace if this is the text you want to change. Word replaces the text and locates the next occurrence.

   ▶ Click Replace All to replace all occurrences of the found text with the replacement text. Word displays a dialog box indicating how many occurrences it replaced. (See Figure 7-13.)

Figure 7-13
Using the Replace All command.

Use with Caution

Use the Replace All button cautiously. Remember that Word takes you very literally. Make sure the Find and Replace options are exactly as you want them.

▶ Click Find Next to skip making changes on this occurrence and locate the next match.

7. Word notifies you when no more occurrences of the search text exist. Click OK to close the message box and click Cancel to close the Find and Replace dialog box.

Applying Tools for Speed

WORD INCLUDES A NUMBER of tools that help speed up the process of creating and editing documents—tools that can locate mistakes and correct them automatically, tools that do your typing for you, and tools that let you quickly make changes in your document.

Creating Bookmarks

Just like you use a bookmark to mark a certain place in a book, electronic bookmarks identify specified text locations for future reference. As an example, you might use a bookmark to help you quickly jump to certain topics in your document.

Tip

Bookmarks are useful for electronic reading only and do not affect a printed document.

Place the insertion point where you want to create a bookmark and choose Insert>Links>Bookmark. The Bookmark dialog box seen in Figure 7-14 appears.

Figure 7-14
Creating a bookmark.

Type a name for the bookmark and click Add. Word saves the bookmark and closes the Bookmark dialog box.

Tip

Bookmark names cannot include spaces or special characters except the underscore character (_).

Now instead of scrolling through the document to locate the text, you can quickly jump to it. Click Insert>Links>Bookmark which displays the Bookmark dialog box along with a list of all the bookmarks in your document. Select the bookmark you want and click Go To.

Optionally, you can get to a bookmark by using the Go To option, found on the Find and Replace dialog box. Choose Home>Editing and then click the down arrow next to the Find option. Choose Go To. The Find and Replace dialog box appears with the Go To tab on top (See Figure 7-15).

Shortcuts

Two alternative methods of displaying the Go To option are pressing F5 or pressing Ctrl+G.

Click Bookmark and then from the Enter Bookmark Name drop-down menu, choose the bookmark you want. Click Go To and Word instantly jumps to the bookmark location.

Figure 7-15
Locating a bookmark.

Specifying Hyperlinks

Hyperlinks, similar to bookmarks, take you to a specific location. However, not only can hyperlinks jump to a location in your document, they can also jump to another file on your computer, on your network, or to a Web page. Like bookmarks, hyperlinks are useful for electronic reading only and do not affect a printed document.

Word automatically creates some hyperlinks for you. For example, if you type a Web address or e-mail address, as soon as you press Enter or the spacebar, Word underlines the area and creates the link. The AutoFormat As You Type function is what controls the automatic link creation behavior.

If you want to manually create a link, first select the text or graphic you want the reader to click to launch the hyperlink. Choose Insert>Links>Hyperlink, which displays the Insert Hyperlink dialog box. The Insert Hyperlink dialog box offers several options from which you can select:

▶ If you want to link to a different file or to a Website, choose Existing File or Web Page. For a different file, locate and select the file name so when the user clicks the link, the referenced file will open. However, if you want to link to a Website, enter the Web address in the Address text box. When the user clicks the link, the Web browser will open to the referenced Web page. Figure 7-16 illustrates a link to a Website.

Figure 7-16
Creating a hyperlink to a Website.

▶ If you want to link to a different location in the current document, click the Place in This Document button, then specify which heading or bookmark you want to reference. When users click on this link they will be redirected to the specified location.

▶ If you want, when the hyperlink is clicked, to create a new document, choose Create New Document and then enter a name and folder for the new document.

▶ If you want to send an e-mail when the link is selected, click the E-mail Address button, then enter the recipient's e-mail address and a subject. When the user clicks the link, the user's e-mail program starts. Figure 7-17 illustrates the e-mail link options.

Figure 7-17
Creating an e-mail hyperlink.

Word displays hyperlinks in a different color text and with an underline. Press Ctrl and click any link to jump to the specified location. As you hover your mouse over the link, a tip appears with instructions for following the link and a notation to where the link will take you (see Figure 7-18).

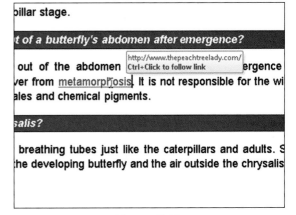

Figure 7-18
Hold down the Ctrl key and click the link.

Generating Text with Building Blocks

Are you tired of typing your address over and over when composing letters? Or, do you have a standard phrase that you need to frequently add to your documents? Word provides a couple of methods you can use to quickly add the text into your document.

The first method is using Word's AutoCorrect function, which you discovered in Chapter 2, "Getting Started with Word." Not only can you add words and symbols, you can generate a text paragraph or even a graphic with your signature. The only problem is that the AutoCorrect function limits each entry to 255 characters.

Office 2010 is designed to be modular, so it uses a function called Building Blocks that are divided into 14 galleries. Think of building blocks as recycled material. You've already been introduced to some of the building blocks when you discovered some of the built-in options in Headers, Footers, Page Numbering, and Quick Tables. Take a brief look at some of the different building block galleries and what type of element each gallery holds:

- ▶ **AutoText:** Holds small text entries or graphics that you want to use again, such as a standard contract clause or a mission statement.

- ▶ **Bibliography:** Holds text in the form of a reference list of works by author, subject, or other relevant information.

- ▶ **Cover Pages:** Holds preformatted cover pages such as those you might use for reports. Figure 7-19 illustrates one of the sample Cover Page building blocks.

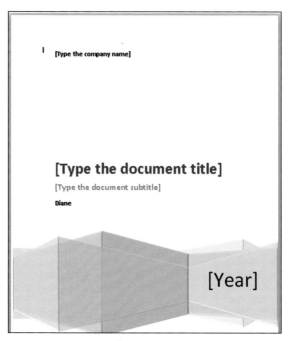

Figure 7-19
The Cubicles cover page.

- ▶ **Quick Parts:** Holds miscellaneous building blocks that don't fit any other gallery.

- ▶ **Equations:** Holds predefined equations objects.

- ▶ **Footers:** Holds a number of predefined footers that appear at the bottom of the page.

- ▶ **Headers:** Holds a number of predefined headers that appear at the top of the page.

- ▶ **Page Numbers:** There are four page number galleries that hold predefined page numbers—some at the current location, some at the bottom or top of the page, and some in the margins.

- ▶ **Table of Contents:** Holds predefined tables of contents that are created based on heading styles in the document.

- ▶ **Tables:** Holds a series of predefined tables such as those in the Quick Tables.

▶ **Text Box:** Holds predefined text box layouts and formatting.

▶ **Watermarks:** Holds several predefined watermarks such as Draft, Do Not Copy, or Confidential. Watermarks are in light gray shading and appear in the background of a document such as you see in Figure 7-20.

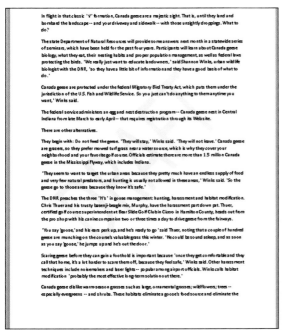

Figure 7-20

A watermark building block.

Inserting Building Blocks

Now that you see all the different types of building blocks, take a look at how to insert any of the existing blocks into your document. Just follow these steps:

1. Position the insertion point where you want to insert the building block.

2. Choose Insert>Text>Quick Parts>Building Blocks Organizer. The Building Blocks Organizer appears.

3. Click a building block to display a preview on the right side, such as you see in Figure 7-21.

Figure 7-21

Click the Building Block Organizer to see a preview.

Sorting Building Blocks

Click any building block column heading to sort the building blocks by that column.

4. Click the Insert button. Word inserts the building block into your document.

Placeholders

Some building blocks prompt you to insert text such as your company name or a document title. Click the placeholder and type the appropriate text.

Creating Custom Building Blocks

If none of the predefined building blocks suit your needs, you can create your own custom building block. Additionally, you can start with one of the existing building blocks and customize it to a better fit and then save it for future use. Just follow these simple steps:

1. Create the text and formatting for the new building block.

2. Select the area you want to save as a building block.

3. Choose Insert>Text>Quick Parts>Save Selection to Quick Part Gallery. The Create New Building Block dialog box appears.

4. Fill in the appropriate information as seen in Figure 7-22.

Figure 7-22
Naming a custom building block.

▶ **Name:** By default, Word picks up the first few characters of the text you selected; however, you can give the building block a short, more descriptive name.

▶ **Gallery:** Select which of the Gallery types you want. Most likely, you'll want to use the Quick Parts gallery.

▶ **Category:** You can further differentiate the items in the gallery by creating and assigning categories.

▶ **Description:** Enter a longer description to help you identify the building block and its purpose.

▶ **Save in:** Select whether to save the new item under the Building Block area, which makes it available no matter which template you use, or choose to save it only if you are using the Normal template. (Templates are discussed later in this chapter.)

▶ **Options:** Choices include whether to insert the building block at the current cursor position, start a new paragraph and then insert the building block, or to start a new page and then insert the building block.

5. Click OK. Now when you open the Building Blocks Organizer, you'll see your custom building block.

When you exit Word, you see the message box seen in Figure 7-23. Choose Save to save the changes.

Figure 7-23
Saving building blocks for future use.

Delete Building Blocks

If you no longer want a custom building block, display the Building Blocks Organizer, select the building block you want to delete, and click the Delete button. Click Yes to the confirmation message that appears.

Adding Automatic Date Codes

When you create a document and you type in a date, the date is said to be static, meaning it doesn't change when the date changes. So if you type September 16, 2010, the document will always read September 16, 2010. If, however, you want the date or time to change with the calendar, you need to insert a dynamic date or time. Word handles these in the form of a field code. Just follow these steps:

1. Position the insertion point where you want the date.

2. Choose Insert>Text>Date and Time. The Date and Time dialog box appears (see Figure 7-24).

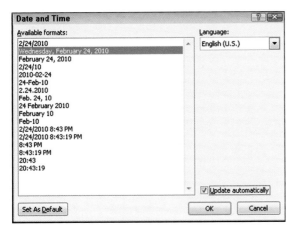

Figure 7-24
Adding an automatic date in the format you need.

3. Click the date format you want to use.

4. Click the Update Automatically check box and then click OK.

Static Date

If you only want the current static date and not a dynamic date, do not select the Update Automatically option.

Word inserts the current date field into the document. As you hover your mouse over the date, the field becomes shaded and if you click the field, the field placeholder appears (see Figure 7-25). Fields update automatically each time you open the document, but if you want to update a field manually, click the Update button at the top of the field placeholder.

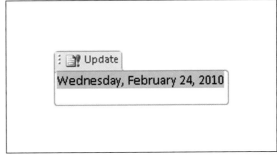

Figure 7-25
Word fields appear with shading.

Inserting Another File

If you have already created a file and need to insert it into the current document, you *could* open the document you want to insert, select the entire document, copy it, and then paste it into the new document.

Another method, however, is to position the insertion point where you want the file to begin and then choose Insert>Text. Click the Object arrow and choose Text from File. The Insert File dialog box seen in Figure 7-26 appears.

Figure 7-26
Inserting an existing file.

Locate and click the file you want and then choose Insert. The entire file appears in the current document.

Selecting a Template

Templates are another time-saving feature. Every Microsoft document is based on a template, which determines the basic structure for a document and contains settings such as styles, AutoText, fonts, macros, menus, page layout, and any special formatting. Templates appear as untitled documents with text, graphics, formatting, and other attributes applicable to that template. The advantage of a template is that you cannot easily permanently overwrite it. When you create a document based on a template, Word prompts you to save the document with its own name.

Most new documents are based on the default Normal template. However, you can create documents based on templates for memos, faxes, and lots of other types of documents. Word provides a variety of ready-to-use document templates. Just follow these steps to create a new document based on a template.

1. Click the File tab and choose New. The Word Backstage view displays the New document options shown in Figure 7-27.

Create button

Figure 7-27
Choosing a template category.

2. Chose a category. Word displays thumbnail representations from the hundreds of templates available from Microsoft Office Online. (See Figure 7-28.)

Download button

Figure 7-28
A Conference Agenda template.

Tip

You cannot access the Word templates by pressing Ctrl+N. The Ctrl+N keystroke shortcut automatically creates a new document based on the Normal template.

3. Click the template you want and then click Download. Word then downloads the template and displays it on your screen. In many templates, Word places prompt fields in the areas where you probably want to enter information.

Previously Installed Templates

If you want one of the already installed templates, choose Installed Templates or My Templates, click the template you want, and then click the Create button.

Downloaded Templates

You only have to download a template once. The next time you want the template, you see it listed under the Blank and Recent category or under My Templates.

Creating Footnotes and Endnotes

OFTEN REPORTS PRESENT material that requires notes set off from the regular text—for example, when you credit material from another source. You can use the Word Footnote or Endnote feature to add these explanatory or source notes to your document.

Generating a Footnote or Endnote

To give credit where credit is due, you can use the Word Footnote or Endnote feature. Word places footnotes at the bottom of the page where the note reference mark appears, and places endnotes at the end of the document.

When creating a footnote, Word automatically adds a number or a character to mark the reference as well as a separating line. If you have both footnotes and endnotes in a document, Word numbers them independently.

Position the insertion point where you want the note reference mark to appear and choose References>Footnotes>Insert Footnote. The insertion point drops to the bottom of the screen where you can cite the actual reference (see Figure 7-29). As you create additional notes, Word numbers the references sequentially. In this example, I highlighted the reference mark and the citation to make it easier for you to see.

Footnote reference mark

Figure 7-29
Creating footnotes.

Copying Notes

Sometimes you will refer to a source more than once in a document. Fortunately, as another time-saving measure, you don't have to retype the text for the footnote; you can copy and paste it into a new location. Word will renumber all the notes affected by the change. Follow these steps:

1. Select the note reference mark of the footnote or endnote that you plan to copy. The reference mark is highlighted.

2. Choose Home>Clipboard>Copy. It won't look like anything happened, but Word is keeping track for you.

3. Position the insertion point at the location for the duplicated note.

4. Choose Home>Clipboard>Paste. The note reference mark of the copied footnote or endnote appears in the original and new location, and the footnote or endnote appears in the footnote or endnote text area with the correct numbering. In Figure 7-30, footnote number 2 was duplicated and now also appears as footnote number 4.

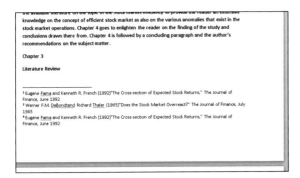

Figure 7-30
Duplicate footnotes without retyping them.

Moving Notes

You can move a footnote or endnote to a new location, and Word will renumber all of the notes affected by the move. Select the note reference mark of the note that you plan to move. If you want to move any surrounding document text along with the reference number, highlight it as well. Choose Home>Clipboard>Cut and then position the insertion point at the location for the duplicated note. Choose Home>Clipboard>Paste. The note reference mark of the copied footnote or endnote appears in the new location, and the footnote or endnote appears in the footnote or endnote text area with the correct numbering.

Delete Notes

Delete a footnote or endnote by highlighting and deleting the note reference mark, not by deleting the footnote or endnote. After pressing the Delete key, Word deletes the note reference mark and the footnote or endnote in the text area and then renumbers all the notes affected by the deletion.

Converting a Footnote to an Endnote

What happens if you create footnotes throughout your report and then decide that you should have used endnotes? Word can convert footnotes to endnotes and endnotes to footnotes, thereby saving you the headache of retyping each entry.

In the reference area at the bottom of the page or at the bottom of the document, locate and highlight the reference you want to change. Right-click the reference and choose Convert to Endnote or Convert to Footnote, depending on which reference you currently selected (see Figure 7-31).

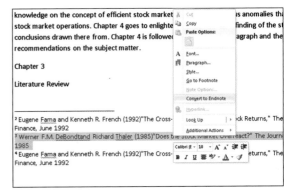

Figure 7-31
Converting a footnote to an endnote.

Working with Outlines

A GREAT ORGANIZATIONAL TOOL, Word outlines assist you by using headings and subtopics to categorize a task and its sub tasks. The easiest way to create an outline is by beginning in the Outline view. Choose View> Document Views>Outline or, optionally, just click the Outline view button located on the status bar.

While in Outline view, you see a new tab at the beginning of the Ribbon. The Outlining tab is designed to assist you in creating your outline (see Figure 7-32).

Figure 7-32

The Outlining Ribbon.

Generating Headings

Word considers the first line of text you type in an outline to be a Level 1 heading, the top-most level. Word uses styles to track outline headings and sub-headings, and a Level 1 heading is a style. You use the Tab key to demote your headings and the Shift+Tab keys to promote your headings.

Type the first line of your outline and then press the Enter key, which moves the insertion point to the next line. Type the second line of your outline. Notice that the text still appears as a Level 1 heading. When you want to create subheadings, use the Tab key to indent the text. Word automatically assigns a Level 2 heading. Each time you press the Tab key, Word creates a lower-level subheading. A Word outline can contain up to nine heading levels.

When you need to return to a higher level, press the Shift+Tab keys. Figure 7-33 illustrates a sample document outline with several heading levels.

Figure 7-33

A sample outline.

Body Text

If you want to add text to your outline that isn't really an outline heading, you create body text. Typically, body text elaborates more on the outline level heading directly above it. You create body text by using the Outlining tab. Type the text you want as body text and click Outlining>Outline Tools>Demote to Body Text.

As you organize your thoughts and ideas in an outline, you might change your mind and want to cover a topic earlier than originally planned. You can move selected headings along with any associated subheadings and body text up or down to any location in your outline. Click the Heading icon of the section you want to move and either click the Move Up button or click the Move Down button. The selected section moves up or down one line with each click of the button.

Promoting or Demoting Headings

A Level 1 heading is the highest level in an outline and a Level 9 heading is the lowest. To change the heading level of existing text, place the insertion point anywhere in the line you want to promote and press the Tab key, or use the Shift+Tab key to demote or promote the text. Optionally, you can use the Outlining tab on the Ribbon to demote or promote your text.

Click anywhere in the line you want to change and click the promote or demote button, or you can click the current Outline Level drop-down menu and choose from the resulting list seen in Figure 7-34.

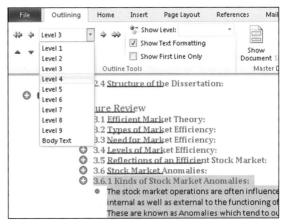

Figure 7-34
Choosing a new level.

Promote Heading

The Outlining tab on the Ribbon also contains a button with double arrowheads pointing left. Click that button to quickly promote the current line to a Heading 1, the highest level.

Viewing the Outline

While in Outline view, you can expand or collapse the various levels to view only the portions you want to see. For example, you can view headings only to get an overview of the entire document, thereby helping you further organize your thoughts. Additionally, you can turn the formatting display on or off. Word includes several areas on the Outlining tab to assist you with viewing your outline.

▶ **On the outline body, double-click the Heading button that looks like a circle with a plus sign in it.** If the Heading button has a minus sign, there are no subheadings or body text under that heading; however, a plus sign indicates additional items. Word collapses the body text and subheadings of the first level below the currently selected heading, or, if the heading is already collapsed, Word expands the first heading level below the currently selected heading. Each double-click will collapse or expand additional headings.

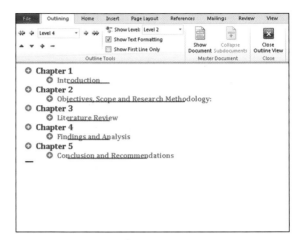

Figure 7-35
Displaying only the levels you want to view.

Open Headings

Optionally, double-click a Collapse and Expand icon to fully open the selected heading.

▶ **From the Outlining tab on the Ribbon, the Outline Tools group, click the Show Level down arrow, which displays a drop-down menu of heading options.** Select a level and Word displays only the headings at the level you chose and those that are higher. For example, as shown in Figure 7-35, if you select Show Level 2, both Level 1 and Level 2 headings appear but not Level 3 headings.

Show All

Click Show All Levels to view the entire outline.

▶ **Choose Outlining>Outline Tools>Show First Line Only.** The outline display toggles between displaying all the body text or only the first line of each body text paragraph.

▶ **Choose Outlining>Outline Tools>Show Text Formatting.** The outline view toggles between displaying the outline with or without character formatting. Figure 7-36 illustrates the outline without text formatting.

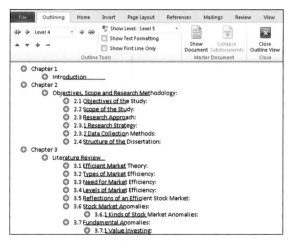

Figure 7-36
Viewing an unformatted outline.

Tip

When you print an outline, Word prints the outline in its entirety as it displays in Print Layout view, without the indentation you see in Outline view.

Keeping Documents Secure

MANY DOCUMENTS CONTAIN DATA that is confidential in nature, such as business plans or personal diaries. In today's world of electronic snooping, it's up to you to protect your work against prying eyes. Even if you allow others to view your documents, you may want to prevent accidental or intentional changes. Fortunately, Word provides several security tools including password protection.

Inspecting for Personal Information

Many Word documents contain *metadata*, which is somewhat hidden information that others could see—data such as the names of people who have previously edited the document, file locations, and even e-mail addresses. You may not want others to have access to this information. Fortunately, you can eliminate the metadata by using the Document Inspector.

If you are collaborating with others using features such as comments or tracked changes, you may not want to remove the metadata until the collaboration is complete. Typically, you run the Document Inspector just prior to publication.

First save your file and then click the File tab and from the Info document panel, choose Check for Issues. From the drop-down menu that appears, choose Inspect Document. You see the Document Inspector dialog box shown in Figure 7-37.

Figure 7-37
Inspecting your document for personal information.

Deselect any options you do not want to check and click the Inspect button. Word inspects the document for various types of potential personal information. When the inspection is complete, the Document Inspector reappears with information as seen in Figure 7-38.

Click the Remove All button next to any option you want removed. Word removes the selected information and the Remove All button next to the option disappears. Repeat this for any additional items you want to remove. When finished, click the Close button and resave your file.

Figure 7-38
The Document Inspector reveals potential problem areas.

Restricting Formatting Changes

If you apply a file password (which you'll see how to do later in this chapter), with the right password you or others can open or modify the document. If you can modify a document, you can modify any portion of it—content or formatting. One method of protection you can apply is to protect the document against formatting changes. Then, before someone can change the document appearance, they must first enter a password. Follow these steps to lock-in document formatting:

1. Choose Review>Protect>Restrict Editing. A Restrict Formatting and Editing pane opens on the right side of the screen as seen in Figure 7-39.

Settings

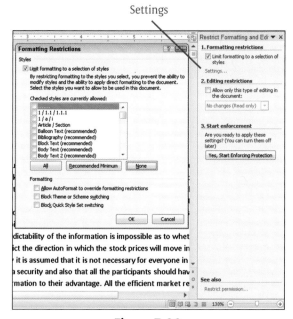

Figure 7-39
Stop unwanted formatting changes.

2. Click the Limit Formatting to a Selection of Styles check box.

3. Click the Settings link. The Formatting Restrictions dialog box appears (also seen in Figure 7-39). By default, changes to any styles are allowed.

4. Click the None button. All choices are deselected; however, if you do want to allow formatting changes to a particular style, you can recheck that style name.

5. Click the OK button. If you get a message box saying "This document may contain formatting or styles that aren't allowed. Do you want to remove them?" click No.

6. From the Restrict Formatting and Editing pane, click the third option: Yes, Start Enforcing Protection. The Start Enforcing Protection dialog box appears.

7. Enter an optional password and then reenter the password to confirm it. The password you type appears as a series of black dots.

8. Click OK. Notice how any Ribbon option that affects formatting becomes unavailable.

If you want to make any formatting changes, you must first, from the Restrict Formatting and Editing pane, click the Stop Protection button. If you don't see the Restrict Formatting and Editing pane, choose Review>Protect>Protect Document. You must then enter the password to stop the protection and allow formatting changes.

Marking a Document as Final

To protect your document against accidental changes, Word includes a feature called Mark as Final. After choosing the option, the document cannot be changed unless you choose the Mark as Final option again, which then allows document changes.

Click the File tab and from the Info document panel, in the first section, click the Protect Document button. From the resulting drop-down menu, choose Mark as Final. A confirmation message appears. Click OK. Next, another confirmation message appears as you see in Figure 7-40. Click OK to that message also.

Figure 7-40
Disable editing by marking a document as final.

133

Marking a document as final disables every option in the Ribbon that could change the document in any way. A bar appears across the top of the window (see Figure 7-41) indicating the document is marked as final and if you attempt to make any changes, Word simply ignores you. The document title bar also shows the document as (Read-Only).

Edit Anyway button

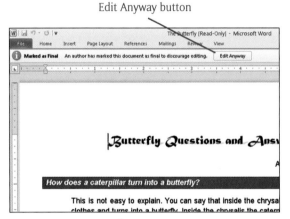

Figure 7-41
Opening a document marked as final.

This feature is easily bypassed. Suppose you need to change a date in the document or you forgot to list a particular item. You can "unmark" the document from being final by simply clicking the Edit Anyway button.

Saving a File as Read-Only

If your goal is to prevent accidental changes either by you or others, one of the easiest methods is to save the file with a read-only recommendation. When a file is read-only, you can still make changes to the document, but the only way you can save those changes is to save the file to a different file name or folder.

1. Click the File tab and choose Save As.

2. Optionally, select a different folder in which to save the file.

3. Enter a file name if you haven't already assigned a name.

4. Choose Tools>General Options (see Figure 7-42).

Figure 7-42
Choosing general file options.

5. From the General Options dialog box, click the Read-Only recommended check box

6. Click the OK button, which returns you to the Save As dialog box.

7. Click the Save button.

When you or another user attempts to re-open the file, the message shown in Figure 7-43 is displayed. Click Yes to open the File as a Read-Only file. If you choose No, the file opens as a standard file where changes can be made.

Figure 7-43

The read-only recommendation box.

Assigning a File Password

Another method to protect your documents, and probably one of the safest methods, is to assign a password. When you assign a file password, the application uses a key to encrypt the document's contents. Word, Excel, and PowerPoint all allow you to assign passwords. There are two levels of password protection you can use. One forces any-one who attempts to even open the file to supply a password. Of course, if they cannot open the file, they cannot view it or modify it. The second level is where you could allow others (with or without password protection) to open the file and view it, but not allow them to edit the file in any way with-out first providing another password.

To create file passwords, click the File tab and choose Save As. Select a folder for your file and enter a file name. Choose Tools>General Options. The General Options dialog box appears. Type a password in the Password to Open text box if you want users to enter a password before they can open and view the document. Word displays pass-words with a black dot for each character, like those shown in Figure 7-44.

Figure 7-44

Assigning a file password.

Password Etiquette

Good passwords should be at least eight characters and should contain a mixture of numbers as well as upper- and lowercase let-ters. Passwords are case sensitive. Don't, how-ever, make your passwords so difficult you can't remember them. If you lose the pass-word to your Word, Excel, or PowerPoint doc-ument, it cannot be recovered!

Optionally, you can leave the Password to Open box empty and enter a password in the Password to Modify text box. Using this option allows others to open the file, but they cannot make any changes without keying in the password. Click OK and a message box appears prompting you to reenter the passwords just in case you typed them incorrectly the first time. Reenter the passwords as prompted and click OK; then, click the Save button to save the password security.

Figure 7-45

Enter the required password to open the file.

Use Separate Passwords

If you want to use both a password to open and a password to modify, it's a good idea to use different passwords for each function.

Remove Passwords

To remove file passwords, from the General Options dialog box, delete the characters from the Password to Open or Password to Modify text box and resave the file.

When you or anyone opens the file, they are prompted to enter the password (see Figure 7-45).

Printing and Publishing

YOU DID IT! You created a great document, and now it's time to use it. With the adoption of e-mail within most corporations and homes, many documents today might never be printed on paper—they may only ever exist in an electronic form; however, there may still be times when you need a paper copy. This section shows you how to distribute your document both on paper and electronically.

Using Print Preview

Before you print your document, you should preview it on the screen so you can sit back and look at how document layout settings such as the margins will look in the printed document. In Print Preview, although you can only view the document and cannot edit it, you can tell quite a bit about it from a different perspective. The following steps walk you through the Print Preview process:

1. Click the File tab and, from the Backstage view that appears, choose Print. A print settings section appears on the left and a preview of the worksheet appears on the right.

2. From the preview area (shown in Figure 7-46), select from the following options:

   ▶ If you have multiple pages, click in the page number box, then click the Next Page or Previous Page buttons to view additional pages.

   ▶ Use the Zoom controls in the lower-right to enlarge or reduce the view or click anywhere in the Preview window to zoom in or out.

Page number box   Next Page   Zoom controls

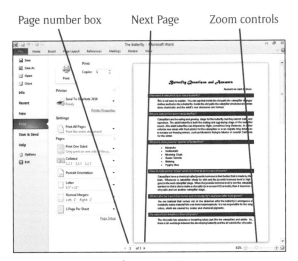

Figure 7-46
Previewing your document before printing it.

If you're ready to print your document, continue to the next section, but if you want to return to the document, click the File tab.

Printing a Document

When your document is complete and you've reviewed it for any changes, you may want to make a hard copy of it to file away or to share with others. Click the File tab and, from the Backstage view that appears, choose Print. A Print Settings section appears on the left and a preview of the worksheet appears on the right. The Print Settings section seen in Figure 7-47 illustrates the many printing options.

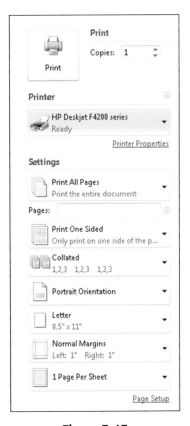

Figure 7-47
Print Settings.

Take a look at a few of the printing options:

▶ **Copies**: Select the number of copies you want to print.

▶ **Printer:** If you are connected to more than one printer, you can select which printer you want to use from the Name drop-down menu.

▶ **Settings:** Determine which pages you want to print. If you highlight a document area before you display the Print dialog box, you can choose Selection to print only that area. If you want to print only selected pages, enter into the Pages text box the page numbers separated by a comma or a dash. For example to print only the first three document pages, enter 1, 2, 3 or 1-3. Other settings include options such as margins, paper size, or collating options. The last option (pages per sheet) determines how many document pages you want to print on a single sheet of paper. The formatting and document page layouts do not change; Word simply reduces the size of each printed page to fit the number of pages that you select. This feature is helpful as an overview or handout document.

Choose any desired options and then click the Print button to begin printing.

E-Mailing a Document

If you have e-mail access, you can send a document directly to another person. Word copies the content of the document as an attachment to an e-mail message. Although many e-mail applications work fine with this feature, Office works best with Outlook and Outlook Express.

With the document open and ready to send, click the File tab and choose Save & Send>Send Using E-Mail. Then click the Send as Attachment button. Word launches your e-mail application with the file listed as an attachment. Type the recipient's e-mail address or click the To button to select from your Outlook Contact List (see Chapter 21, "Working with Outlook Contacts"). Word automatically adds the document name as the subject, but you can click the Subject text box and change the subject. Optionally, type a message in the message body (see Figure 7-48). Click the Send button when you are finished.

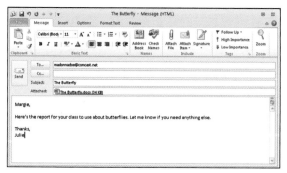

Figure 7-48
E-mailing a Word document as an attachment.

Part III
Excel

When it comes to software for crunching numbers, there is nothing better than Microsoft Excel. You can use the application for tasks such as balancing your checkbook, projecting company profits, tracking your CD collection, or tallying up your recent trip expenses. Excel performs the math for you quickly and accurately. This section explains the fundamentals of working with the Excel workbook. Even if you have worked with spreadsheets before, I'm sure you will pick up a few tips and tricks along the way.

Creating a Basic
Worksheet

PICTURE YOURSELF STARING OUT across the horizon. As you view the sun reflecting on the crystalline water, you are contemplating a decision you must make. You're probably making a mental list about the decision, listing the pros in one column and the cons in another column.

Welcome to Excel, the most powerful and popular spreadsheet program in the world. "What is a spreadsheet program?" you may ask. Well, it's a computer program that features a huge grid designed to display data in rows and columns. You use it to perform calculations, sort large amounts of data, and extract information that meets criteria you specify, all of which can help you make better decisions. Whether you need a list of names and addresses or a document to calculate next year's sales revenue based on prior years' performance, Excel is the application you want to use.

But every Excel task you tackle begins with a blank sheet. And that's where this chapter begins—with a blank sheet. This chapter begins with the basics of Excel.

Exploring the Excel Window

PREVIOUSLY, YOU MAY HAVE used a paper, pencil, and calculator to track information, whether to figure a simple calculation or track a list of items in alphabetical order. Excel handles those tasks and many more, including complex calculations. At first glance, however, the Excel opening screen can appear very intimidating with all its buttons, options, rows, and columns. Once you understand the purpose for those options, you will feel much more comfortable with the Excel screen.

Identifying Screen Elements

As mentioned in Chapter 1, many items that you see when you open a new worksheet (also called a spreadsheet) are standard to most Microsoft Office programs. You see the Ribbon with its tabs and groups, and you see the status bar at the bottom of the window. However, the following list illustrates a few elements that are specific to Excel (see Figure 8-1).

Name box   Current cell   Formula bar

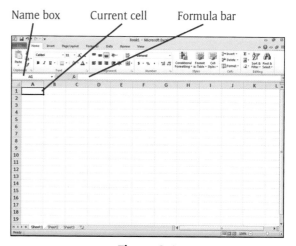

Figure 8-1
The Excel screen.

▶ **Worksheet area:** A rectangular grid consisting of rows and columns. Columns are labels with letters across the top, and rows are indicated by numbers.

▶ **Cell:** The intersection of a row and a column, also known as a cell address. When referring to a cell address, Excel references the column letter first, then the row number. For example, Excel refers to a cell address as C13 not 13C. The current cell has a heavy border around it.

▶ **Edit line:** The edit line consists of three parts: the Name box, the Insert Function button, and the Formula bar.

▶ **Selection indicator:** Shows the address or name of the currently selected cell. You can also use this area to create or use a range name. (See "Working with Range Names" later in this chapter).

▶ **Insert Function button:** Provides a means to insert Excel functions. (See Chapter 9, "Working with Formulas and Functions").

▶ **Formula bar:** Displays the contents of the currently selected cell.

▶ **Scroll bars:** The screen has both horizontal and vertical scroll bars.

▶ **Sheet tabs:** Each Excel file begins with three worksheets.

Moving Around the Screen

Each worksheet has 16,384 columns, beginning at column A and extending to column XFD, and 1,048,576 rows. That gives you over seventeen *billion* cells in a single worksheet in which you can enter information! Because of the large size of an Excel worksheet, you need ways to move around quickly. You can use your mouse or keyboard to move around a worksheet.

Using the Mouse

Because there are over 17 billion possible cells in a single worksheet, you may find that using the mouse is an easy way to move around in the worksheet.

Click the mouse pointer on any cell to move the active cell location to that cell. You can use the scroll bars to see more of the worksheet. Both the horizontal and vertical scroll bars have arrows at each end to extend the worksheet scroll amount (see Figure 8-2).

Horizontal scroll bar   Vertical scroll bar

Figure 8-2
The worksheet scrollbars.

Also, by default, Excel displays three worksheets, labeled Sheet1, Sheet2, and Sheet3. Clicking any worksheet tab makes that Sheet appear on top of the other worksheets (see Figure 8-3). You'll learn more about working with multiple worksheets in Chapter 11, "Managing Large Amounts of Data."

Using the Keyboard

As you have just discovered, you can use your mouse to move around an Excel worksheet; however, you may like using the keyboard better. Table 8-1 describes keyboard methods for moving around a worksheet.

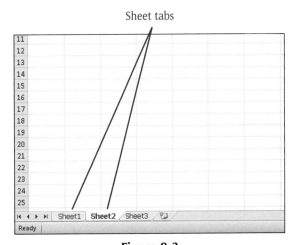

Sheet tabs

Figure 8-3
Viewing Sheet2.

Table 8-1 Excel Movement Keystrokes

Keystroke	Result
Arrow keys	Moves one cell at a time up, down, left, or right
Page Down	Moves one screen down
Page Up	Moves one screen up
Home	Moves to column A of the current row
Ctrl+Home	Moves to cell A1
Ctrl+End	Moves to the lower-right cell of the worksheet that contains formatting or data
Ctrl+Arrow key	Moves to the beginning or end of a row or column
Ctrl+Page Down	Moves to the next worksheet (see Figure 8-3)
Ctrl+Page Up	Moves to the previous worksheet
F5	Displays the Go To dialog box

Using the Go To Command

You just discovered that you can press the F5 key to display the Go To dialog box. You can use the Go To command to jump to a specific cell or area of the worksheet. The Ribbon command for executing the Go To command is Home>Editing>Find & Select>Go To. The Go To dialog box is displayed. In the Reference box, enter the address of the cell you want to go to and then click the OK button (see Figure 8-4). The Go To box also displays any recently accessed cells and range names in the current workbook.

Figure 8-4
The Go To dialog box.

Case Doesn't Matter

Cell addresses are not case sensitive.

Entering Excel Data

THERE'S AN OLD ADAGE that says "You have to crawl before you can walk." That saying applies to Excel worksheets as well. You need to learn the basics before you learn the more complex Excel features. This section shows you how to get the basic data into your worksheet.

Worksheet data is made up of three components: labels, values, and formulas. This section discusses entering labels and values, and you'll learn about creating and entering formulas in Chapter 9, "Working with Formulas and Functions." When you are ready to enter data into a worksheet cell, you must first click on the cell in which you want the information.

Entering Labels

Labels are traditionally descriptive pieces of information, such as names, months, or other identifying information. Excel automatically recognizes information as a label if it contains alphabetic characters. Don't worry if the entire label does not appear to fit into a cell width. If needed, Excel automatically extends the data past the cell width, and you'll soon discover how you can manually widen a cell.

Excel aligns the data to the left side of the cell. If the descriptive information is too wide to fit in a cell, Excel extends that data past the cell width as long as the next cell is blank. If the next cell is not blank, Excel displays only enough text to fit in the current cell. Widening the column displays the additional text.

Click the cell in which you want to place the label and type the text. Press the Enter key and Excel accepts the label and aligns the data along the left edge of the cell. After pressing Enter, the cell below the one in which you just entered data becomes the current cell. If you make a mistake and have not yet pressed the Enter key, press the Backspace key to delete characters and type a correction, or press the Escape key to cancel typing in the selected cell.

Movement Key Option

Optionally, instead of pressing the Enter key, press the Tab key, which makes Excel move to the right instead of down. Or, you can press an arrow key instead of the Enter key, which moves the next selection in the direction of the arrow key.

Figure 8-5 illustrates a worksheet with several labels. Also notice that Excel displays the contents of the current cell in the Formula bar.

Current cell contents

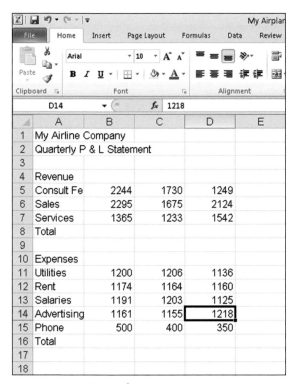

Figure 8-5
Labels appear aligned to the left side of the cell.

Entering Values

Values are the raw numbers that you track in a worksheet. When you enter a value, you don't need to enter commas or dollar signs. In Chapter 10, "Making Your Worksheet Look Good," you'll learn how to let Excel do that for you.

Click on the cell in which you want to place the value and type the numerical values. Press Enter to accept the value. Excel enters the value into the cell and aligns it along the right cell edge (see Figure 8-6).

Figure 8-6
Entering values.

As you can see, Excel drops the leading and trailing zeros. For example, if you enter the value of 0123, Excel sees it as 123. If you enter 123.40, Excel displays it as 123.4. The trailing zero is not lost; it simply doesn't display.

Enter Value as Label

To enter a value as a label, type an apostrophe (') character before the number. The apostrophe character tells Excel to treat the information as a label instead of a value.

If your value is too large to fit into the cell width, Excel may display a series of number signs (####), or it may round the value display. Don't worry about the appearance that displays in Excel. You'll discover how to change the display of your data in Chapter 10. Table 8-2 illustrates some of the ways that Excel, by default, displays numeric data.

Table 8-2 Excel Value Appearances

Keystroke	Result
1074	1074
0174	174
'0174	0174
39.95	39.95
39.50	39.5
39.501	39.501
4789547.365	4789547.37

Entering Dates

Although dates contain characters, and look like a label, Excel technically considers them values, because Excel can calculate the time between dates, which you will learn about in Chapter 9, "Working with Formulas and Functions." For example, day 1 is January 1st, 1900, day 2 is January 2nd, 1900, and so forth.

Entering Today's Date

To enter today's date as a static entry, press Ctrl+Shift+; (semicolon). To enter the current time as a static value, press Ctrl+Shift+: (colon).

When you enter a date, by default Excel may not display it on the screen in the same way that you type it. You will discover how to format dates in different arrangements in Chapter 10, "Making Your Worksheet Look Good." Table 8-3 and Figure 8-7 show how Excel automatically displays dates.

Figure 8-7
Entering dates into the worksheet.

Table 8-3 Entering Dates

You Type	Excel Displays
January 23, 2010	23-Jan-10
January 23	23-Jan
Jan 23	23-Jan
1/23	23-Jan
1-23	23-Jan
1-23-10	1/23/2010
1/23/10	1/23/2010

Tip

Depending on the Regional and International settings of your computer, your system may display differently, such as displaying only the last two digits of a year.

Extending a Series with AutoFill

Excel includes a great built-in, time-saving feature called AutoFill. If you provide Excel the beginning pattern, such as a month, day, or numbers, Excel can fill in the rest of the pattern for you. For example, if you type January, Excel fills in February, March, April, and so on. AutoFill works with days of the week, months of the year, or yearly quarters such as 2nd Qtr. You can enter the entire word or you can enter the abbreviated form such as Wed or Sep. The following steps show you how to use the AutoFill feature:

1. Fill the first cell with data (for example, a day or month, such as Monday or August).

2. Press Enter, which accepts the data entry.

3. Select the cell in which you just entered the data.

4. Position the mouse pointer on the small black box at the lower-right corner of the data cell (fill handle). Your mouse pointer turns into a small black cross.

5. Drag the small black box across the cells you want to fill. You can drag the cells right, left, up, or down.

6. Release the mouse. Excel fills in the cells with a continuation of your data. Figure 8-8 shows how Excel fills in the cells with a continuation of the months.

Figure 8-8
Using AutoFill for calendar months.

AutoFill Series

To AutoFill a series of numbers, enter two values in two adjacent cells, such as 1 and 2 or 5 and 10. Select both cells, and then use the AutoFill box to highlight cells. Excel continues the series as 3, 4, 5, or 5, 10, 15 and so forth.

If you use AutoFill on a text word or a single value, Excel duplicates it. For example, if you use AutoFill on a cell with the word Michael, all filled cells contain Michael.

Learning Selection Techniques

TO MOVE, COPY, DELETE, OR CHANGE the formatting of data in a worksheet, you must first select the cells you want to modify. Selected cells appear darker onscreen—just the reverse of unselected text, with the exception of the first cell. The first cell does not appear darker; it just has a dark border around it.

Look at the Mouse

Make sure the mouse pointer is a white cross before attempting to select cells.

To select more than one cell, perform one of the following actions:

▶ **To select a single entire row, click the row number.** As the mouse is on the row number it appears as a black arrow pointing right.

▶ **To select multiple rows, drag across multiple row numbers, as seen in Figure 8-9.**

▶ **To select a single entire column, click a column heading.** As the mouse is on the column heading, it appears as a black arrow pointing down.

▶ **To select multiple columns, drag across multiple column headings.**

	A	B	C	D	E	F
1	My Airline Company					
2	Quarterly P & L Statement					
3						
4	Revenue	January	February	March		
5	Consult Fe	2244	1730	1249		
6	Sales	2295	1675	2124		
7	Services	1365	1233	1542		
8	Total					
9						
10	Expenses					
11	Utilities	1200	1206	1136		
12	Rent	1174	1164	1160		
13	Salaries	1191	1203	1125		
14	Advertising	1161	1155	1218		
15	Phone	500	400	350		
16	Total					
17						
18						
19						
20						

Figure 8-9
Selecting multiple rows.

▶ **To select contiguous cells, click the first cell, hold down the Shift key and select the last cell you want to select.** Excel designates a contiguous cell range with a colon dividing the beginning and end. For example, B1:C3 means cells B1, B2, B3,C1, C2 and C3 are included.

Select a Contiguous Area

Optionally, drag the mouse over a group of cells to select a contiguous area.

▶ **To select non-contiguous cells, click the first cell, hold down the Ctrl key and click each additional cell you want to select.** Figure 8-10 shows the non-contiguous cells A3, A13, D1, and D4 through D12 selected. When making non-contiguous cell selections, you can include entire rows and entire columns along with individual cells or groups of cells.

	A	B	C	D	E	F
1	My Airline Company					
2	Quarterly P & L Statement					
3						
4	Revenue	January	February	March		
5	Consult Fe	2244	1730	1249		
6	Sales	2295	1675	2124		
7	Services	1365	1233	1542		
8	Total					
9						
10	Expenses					
11	Utilities	1200	1206	1136		
12	Rent	1174	1164	1160		
13	Salaries	1191	1203	1125		
14	Advertising	1161	1155	1218		
15	Phone	500	400	350		
16	Total					
17						
18						
19						
20						

Figure 8-10
Selected non-contiguous cells.

▶ To select the entire worksheet, press Ctrl+A or click the small gray box located to the left of column A and above row 1.

Clear Selection

Click any single cell to clear the selection.

If you are inputting data, you can save time by leaving your hands on the keyboard, so Excel also provides ways you can make many selections with your keyboard, instead of the mouse. Here are a few of the methods you can use:

▶ Select a contiguous range by using an arrow key to move to the beginning of the range you want and then hold the Shift key while you arrow-key to the last cell of the range.

▶ Select an entire column by pressing Ctrl+spacebar.

▶ Select multiple adjacent columns by first selecting a cell in each column and then pressing Ctrl+spacebar.

▶ Select an entire row by pressing Shift+spacebar.

▶ Select multiple adjacent rows by first selecting a cell in each row and then pressing Shift+spacebar.

▶ Select all data filled cells adjacent to the current cell by pressing Ctrl+Shift+* (asterisk). (See Figure 8-11.) The current cell does not have to be at the beginning of the range.

	A	B	C	D	E	F
1	My Airline Company					
2	Quarterly P & L Statement					
3						
4	Revenue	January	February	March		
5	Consult Fe	2244	1730	1249		
6	Sales	2295	1675	2124		
7	Services	1365	1233	1542		
8	Total					
9						
10	Expenses					
11	Utilities	1200	1206	1136		
12	Rent	1174	1164	1160		
13	Salaries	1191	1203	1125		
14	Advertising	1161	1155	1218		
15	Phone	500	400	350		
16	Total					
17						
18						
19						
20						

Figure 8-11
Selected contiguous cells with data.

Editing a Worksheet

WHEN YOU CREATE A WORKSHEET, a lot of data entry is usually involved. Excel has features to assist you with some of the repetitive work, but unfortunately you'll probably still make mistakes. You may need to edit the entries you made in some cells, and you may want to make changes to the construction of your worksheet. Excel includes the ability to reorganize your worksheet without having to reenter any data.

Editing Cell Data

You can edit your data in a variety of ways. You might need to change the contents of a cell or delete its current content. If you enter data into a cell and later decide you do not want the information in the worksheet, you can delete the entire contents of a cell by pressing the Delete key or by choosing Home>Editing>Clear>Clear Contents.

There are several methods you can use to edit cell data. One simple method of changing cell content is to select the cell and type the new data. When you type the new data and press Enter, it replaces the current cell content. Optionally, you can use the Edit feature. You'll find the Edit feature very useful if your cell has a lot of information in it and you need only to change a few characters. In some situations, editing may be faster than retyping the entire cell contents. Follow these steps to edit the cell contents:

1. Double-click the cell you want to edit. The insertion point blinks within the cell and the status bar indicates you are in Edit mode (see Figure 8-12).

Insertion point

◢	A	B	C	D	E
1	My Airline Company				
2	Quarterly Profit & Loss		Statement		
3					
4	Revenue	January	February	March	
5	Consult Fe	2244	1730	1249	
6	Sales	2295	1675	2124	
7	Services	1365	1233	1542	
8	Total				
9					
10	Expenses				
11	Utilities	1200	1206	1136	
12	Rent	1174	1164	1160	
13	Salaries	1191	1203	1125	
14	Advertising	1161	1155	1218	
15	Phone	500	400	350	
16	Total				
17					
18					

Figure 8-12
Edit cell contents without having to start over.

Keyboard Shortcut

Optionally, press F2 to launch the Edit mode.

2. Press the arrow key until the insertion point is located where you need to make a change.

3. Type the changes, whether adding new characters or pressing Backspace or Delete to remove existing characters. As you type, the changes appear in the current cell.

4. Press the Enter key to accept the changes.

Using Undo and Redo

If you make a change and then determine you really didn't want to make that change, Excel provides an Undo feature. You can use Undo to restore text that you deleted, delete text you just typed, or reverse a recently taken action. An exception to the Undo function is that if you save your worksheet, you cannot "unsave" it. Also, if you close the worksheet, you cannot undo changes made in the previous editing session when you reopen the worksheet.

To undo any actions or correct any mistakes you make when entering data, perform one of the following options:

▶ Choose Undo from the Quick Access Toolbar.

▶ Press Ctrl+Z.

▶ To undo several steps at once, click the arrow on the Undo button and select the step from which you want to begin the Undo action (see Figure 8-13).

To repeat your last action, click the Redo button on the Quick Access Toolbar or press Ctrl+Y.

Tip

There are some actions that Excel cannot repeat.

Figure 8-13
Select the steps you want to reverse.

Inserting Areas

Occasionally you need to insert a column, row, or a single cell in the middle of existing information. Inserting columns, rows, or cells moves existing data to make room for new rows or columns.

You can insert a column or row anywhere you need it by first selecting a cell where you want the new column or row located. Choose Home>Cells>Insert (arrow) and choose Insert Sheet Rows or Insert Sheet Columns. Figure 8-14 illustrates a newly inserted column C.

Figure 8-14
Inserting additional columns.

Inserting Multiple Columns or Rows

To insert multiple columns or rows, select headings or row numbers across multiple columns or rows.

If you insert a column, Excel moves information in the current column (and all columns to the right of the current column) to the right. If you insert a row, Excel moves information in the current cell and all cells below the current row down.

Tip

No matter how many rows or columns you insert, Excel does not exceed its original worksheet size of 16,384 columns and 1,048,576 rows.

Instead of inserting an entire column or an entire row, you can also insert just a single cell or even a group of cells. Excel then moves existing data down or to the right, depending on an option you specify. Begin by selecting the cells where you want new cells. Then choose Home>Cells>Insert (arrow) and choose Insert Cells. You see the Insert dialog box seen in Figure 8-15.

Figure 8-15
Choose the direction you want existing cells to move.

Click the desired insert option and then click OK. Excel shifts existing data according to your selection. In Figure 8-16, a blank cell was inserted in cell C13.

Bypass Dialog Box

To bypass the Insert dialog box and just insert a cell, choose Home>Cells>Insert.

	A	B	C	D	E
1	My Airline Company				
2	Quarterly P & L Statement				
3					
4	Revenue				
5	Consult Fe	2244	1730	1249	
6	Sales	2295	1675	2124	
7	Services	1365	1233	1542	
8	Total				
9					
10	Expenses				
11	Utilities	1200	1206	1136	
12	Rent	1174	1164	1160	
13	Salaries	1191		1125	
14	Advertising	1161	1203	1218	
15	Phone	500	1155	350	
16	Total		400		
17					
18					

Figure 8-16
Inserting cells where needed.

Deleting Areas

Like inserting areas, you can delete unwanted columns, rows, or cells. Excel moves existing data to take up the room made by the deletion. Use caution when deleting entire rows or columns. Excel deletes the entire row of sixteen thousand plus columns or one million plus rows. Any data in the selected row or column gets deleted as well. No confirmation appears before Excel actually deletes the area.

When you delete columns, Excel pulls the remaining columns to the left; when you delete rows, Excel pulls the remaining rows up. You can delete multiple rows or multiple columns, whether contiguous or non-contiguous; however, you cannot delete both rows and columns at the same time. Choose Home>Cells>Delete (arrow) and choose Delete Sheet Rows or Delete Sheet Columns (see Figure 8-17).

Figure 8-17
Deleting unnecessary columns or rows.

You can also delete a single cell by choosing Home>Cells>Delete or Home>Cells>Delete (arrow) and choosing Delete Cells. You may be prompted which direction to move the remaining cells.

Moving Data

If you're not happy with the placement of data, you don't have to delete it and retype it. Excel makes it easy for you to move it around. In fact, Excel provides several methods to move data. You can cut and paste it or you can use the drag-and-drop method.

Using Cut and Paste

Excel uses the Windows Clipboard, which allows you to collect text and other items from Excel or any Office document or even other programs, and then paste them into an Excel worksheet. If you want to move cells from one place to another, the Clipboard is a great tool to assist you. The process involves selecting cells and either cutting (moving) or copying (duplicating) them to the Clipboard, and then telling Excel where to paste (place) them.

1. Select the area of data you want to move.

2. Choose Home>Clipboard>Cut. A marquee (which looks like marching ants) surrounds the cells (see Figure 8-18).

Figure 8-18
A marquee ("marching ants") forms around a cut or copied area.

Duplicate Cell Contents

To duplicate (instead of move) the selected cells to a new location, choose Home>Clipboard>Copy.

3. Click the cell to which you want to move the selected area.

4. Choose Home>Clipboard>Paste. The selected cells are pasted into the new location.

Paste Overwrites

Make sure the cells you paste into are empty. Pasting overwrites any existing data.

5. Paste the cells into another location or press Esc to cancel the marquee.

Keyboard Shortcuts

Optionally, press Ctrl+C to copy the selected cells, Ctrl+X to cut the selected cells, or Ctrl+V to paste the selected cells.

Dragging and Dropping Data

Drag and drop is another method often used to move data from one location to another. The drag-and-drop method works best when moving a few cells of data a short distance. Just follow these steps:

1. Select the cells you want to move.

2. Position the mouse pointer on the border edge of the highlighted cells. The mouse pointer must appear as a white arrow pointed to the left with four black arrowheads.

Mouse pointer

Figure 8-19
Pay attention to the mouse pointer before dragging cells.

3. Hold the mouse button down and drag the mouse to the desired location (see Figure 8-19). A gray border appears around the cells you point to. Additionally, a ScreenTip appears confirming the cell location.

Copy by Dragging

To copy text with drag and drop, hold down the Ctrl key before dragging the selected cells. Release the mouse button before releasing the Ctrl key.

4. Release the mouse button to move the cell data to the new location.

Transposing Data

If you have data you originally entered across a row and then decide it would be better placed in a column, you can tell Excel to transpose the data. The same is true if you have data in a column that you want moved to a row. Use these steps:

1. Select the cells you want to transpose.

2. Choose Home>Clipboard>Copy (or press Ctrl+C).

Tip

The Transpose feature will not work if you choose Cut instead of Copy.

3. Click the cell where you want the transposed cells to begin.

4. Choose Home>Clipboard and click the down arrow below Paste.

5. Choose Transpose. As you see in Figure 8-20, Excel copies the selected cells into the new area, transposing rows into columns or columns into rows.

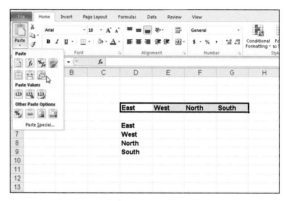

Figure 8-20
Reverse the flow of data by transposing cells.

Working with Range Names

IF YOUR WORKSHEET DOESN'T contain massive amounts of data, then working with individual cells is generally quick and easy. However, as your worksheet data expands, performing operations cell by cell can become tedious and can allow for more human error. Instead, you can work with a group of cells in a single operation. You have already experienced working with ranges if you selected more than once cell at a time to move, copy, or delete. Let's take that to the next level. If you repeatedly go to or use in a formula a specific cell or group of cells, it will help you to assign those cells a range name.

A *range name* is basically a descriptive name for a specified worksheet area, making them much easier to remember than actual cell addresses. Formulas can use range names, and the Go To dialog box can recognize range names.

Naming a Range of Cells

Giving cells intuitive names makes locating data easier. It also can help make formulas more logical and easier to understand. (You'll work with formulas in Chapter 9.) Ranges can be a single cell, a contiguous group of cells, entire rows, or entire columns. Use the following steps to assign a range name:

1. Select the cells you want to name.

2. Choose Formulas>Defined Names>Define Name. The New Name dialog box appears.

3. In the Name text box, type a name for the range (see Figure 8-21). Name the range something that clearly identifies the area, such as Income or Grades. Range names are not case sensitive; however, range names must follow these conventions:

Selected cells

Figure 8-21
Creating a range name.

▶ Range names must begin with a letter, an underscore, or a backslash.

▶ Range names cannot include spaces.

▶ Range names cannot include operator symbols (+, -, *, /, <, >, or &).

▶ Range names can be up to 255 characters; however, shorter is better.

▶ Range names cannot be the same as a cell address. For example, you can't name a range AB32.

4. Click OK.

Using Named Ranges

Jumping to a remote area in the worksheet is only a mouse click away when you use range names, because Excel provides a convenient drop-down menu that you can use to move around quickly.

Click the down arrow in the Name box which displays a list of named ranges such as you see in Figure 8-22. Select the range name you want to access and Excel immediately highlights the named cells.

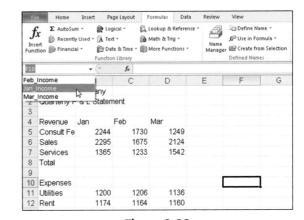

Figure 8-22
Quickly locate an area by choosing a range name.

Managing Range Names

Excel worksheets can accommodate an almost unlimited number of range names. However, if your workbook has quite a few, it can be difficult to manage or remember what each range represents. To assist you with range names, Excel includes the range Name Manager feature.

Choose Formulas>Defined Names>Name Manager which displays the Name Manager dialog box shown in Figure 8-23. You can select from the following options:

Figure 8-23
Use the Name Manager to add, edit, or delete range names.

▶ Click the New button, which displays the New Name dialog box in which you can enter a range name and enter the cell location it refers to. Instead of typing the range cell locations, click the Collapse button, which moves aside the New Name dialog box. You can then use your mouse to select the desired cells. Press Enter or click the Collapse button again to return to the New Name dialog box. Click OK when you are finished.

▶ Click an existing range name and then click the Edit button, which displays the Edit Name dialog box shown in Figure 8-24. Use this dialog box to change the range name or the range cell location reference, and click OK to apply your changes.

Collapse button

Figure 8-24
Editing a range name or cell location.

▶ Click an existing range name and then click the Delete button. A confirmation message appears making sure you want to delete the range name; click OK to do so.

Filter Range Names

If you have a lot of range names, you can click the Filter button and elect to display only the items meeting selected criteria.

Click the Close button to close the Name Manager dialog box.

Using Data Validation

WHEN YOU CREATE a worksheet, you want the data you or others input to be accurate. Typos can destroy the integrity of your collected data. Fortunately, Excel provides a Data Validation feature that can restrict what is entered into a cell. For example, if you were entering student grades, which usually have values that range from A through F, you would want Excel to stop the input if someone entered H or 6. Another example might be that you want all State designations to comply with the two-character postal code, such as CA or IN. You can tell Excel to stop (or warn) you if someone enters IND or Indiana.

The following steps show you how to create cells with data validation.

1. Select the cell or cells you want Excel to validate.

2. Choose Data>Data Tools>Data Validation. The Data Validation dialog box displays with three tabs.

3. In the Settings tab, open the Allow drop-down menu and choose the type of validation, such as:

   ▶ Values such as Whole Number or Decimal where you specify the upper and lower limits of allowable data values.

   ▶ Lists such as a list you define, a range of cells in the existing worksheet, or a named range (see Figure 8-25).

List location

Figure 8-25
Create a list of acceptable options or select one from the worksheet.

Drop-Down Menu

When creating a list, if you want the available choices to appear when the cell is selected, make sure to select the In-Cell drop-down check box.

   ▶ Dates or Times, where you specify ranges or limitations such as greater than or less than, or even a specific date.

   ▶ Text Length, where the number of characters in the data must be within the limits that you specify.

4. If necessary, display the Data drop-down menu and select criteria such as Between, Greater Than, and so on.

5. Select criteria such as maximum and minimum values, or specify a data location. Enter values or cell addresses. Precede a value with an equals sign (=) to specify a range name.

6. From the Input Message tab, optionally enter a comment to display whenever someone clicks on the validated cell. Think of it as a help message.

7. On the Error Alert tab, choose from the Style drop-down menu whether you want Excel to warn you or completely stop you from entering an invalid entry (see Figure 8-26).

Customized error message

Figure 8-26
Determining the action to take when invalid data entry occurs.

Customize Error Message

On the Error Alert tab of the Data Validation dialog box, you can customize the error message Excel displays when an invalid entry is entered.

8. Click OK.

When you enter data into a cell that has a validation requirement, one of two things happens:

▶ If the data meets the validation rules, Excel accepts the entry and moves to the next cell down.

▶ If the data does not meet the validation rules, Excel displays an error message similar to the one you see in Figure 8-27.

Figure 8-27
Entering invalid data into validated cells.

Depending on the setting chosen when the data validation rule was set, choose an option:

▶ **Stop:** Choose Retry or Cancel. You cannot leave invalid data in the cell. Retry returns you to the cell where you can change the value. Cancel deletes your entry and returns the cell to its previous value.

▶ **Warning:** Choose Yes or No or Cancel. Choosing Yes retains the value you entered, choosing No goes back to the cell where you can change the value, and choosing Cancel deletes your entry and returns the cell to its previous value.

▶ **Information:** Choose OK or Cancel. Choosing OK retains the value you entered, and choosing Cancel deletes your entry and returns the cell to its previous values.

Figure 8-28 shows a cell where, due to data validation options, you pick from a list.

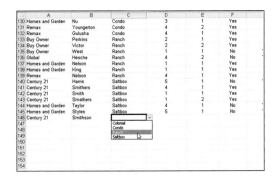

Figure 8-28
Picking from a data validation list.

Tip

Cells that contain invalid data may display a small green triangle in the upper-left corner.

If you need to locate which cells in the worksheet contain data validation, you can tell Excel to show you which ones. You can also tell Excel to show you only the cells that contain invalid data. Remember that when setting the validation, you can tell Excel to warn you of an invalid entry or to go ahead and accept it.

To have Excel show you all cells that have validation, choose Home>Editing>Find & Select>Data Validation. Cells with validation restrictions become highlighted, as seen in Figure 8-29.

Figure 8-29
Locating cells with data validation restrictions.

To have Excel show you cells that contain invalid data, choose Data>Data Tools and click the arrow next to Data Validation. Choose Circle Invalid Data. Excel places circles around any invalid data (see Figure 8-30).

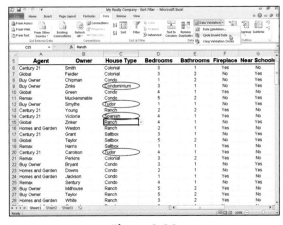

Figure 8-30
Indicating cells with invalid data.

Validation circles do not print. To remove the circles, repeat the previous step but choose Clear Validation Circles.

Remove Data Validation

To remove data validation, select the cells for which you want to remove validation and then choose Data>Data Tools>Data Validation. From the Data Validation dialog box, click the Clear All button and then click the OK button.

Working with Formulas and
Functions

PICTURE YOURSELF AT TAX TIME without a computer, a calculator, or a nearby tax firm or accountant. Can you imagine all the figuring that occurs? Calculate your wages less deductions times the tax percentage. Now take that amount and do a hundred other calculations around it. Sound daunting? It is. And you thought that math was never your strong point in school anyway! Fortunately, in today's age, people have accountants, calculators, and computers readily accessible, so they don't have to do all that manual calculating.

One of Excel's best strengths is its ability to perform almost any type of calculation. Excel performs everything from simple addition to complex scientific and calculus notations with ease and, most importantly, with accuracy. This chapter introduces you to Excel formula generation. You'll also become acquainted with the more complex formulas called *functions*, all of which are designed to provide you with accurate information so you can make more informed decisions about the task at hand.

Working with Formulas

MANY PEOPLE USE A WORKSHEET to perform mathematical calculations. By using formulas, if a value in a referenced cell changes, any formula based on the cell automatically adjusts to accommodate the new value. Excel can accommodate both simple formulas, such as adding two values together, and complex formulas, such as adding two values together and multiplying the result by another number. In addition, Excel can include the values from many different worksheet cells.

Creating Formulas

All formulas must begin with the equals (=) sign, regardless of whether the formula consists of adding, subtracting, multiplying, or dividing. Formulas can reference either a static value or the value in a referenced cell.

Creating a Simple Formula

An example of a simple formula is to add two cell values together. For example, you could choose to add the values of B5 and C5. Just follow these steps:

1. Click the cell in which you want to place the result.

2. Type an equals (=) sign to begin the formula.

3. Type the cell address of the first cell to be included in the formula. This is called the cell reference. Excel references the cell

address in color and places a matching color box around the referenced address (see Figure 9-1).

Tip

Worksheet cell references in formulas are not case sensitive. For example, F2 is the same as f2.

Figure 9-1
Referenced cells are bounded by a colored box.

4. A formula needs an operator to state the next action to be performed. Operators are plus (+), minus (-), multiply (*), or divide (/) symbols. Type the operator.

5. Type the reference to the second cell of the formula. Excel references the second cell address in a different color and places a matching color box around the referenced address.

6. Press the Enter key. The result of the calculation appears in the cell (see Figure 9-2).

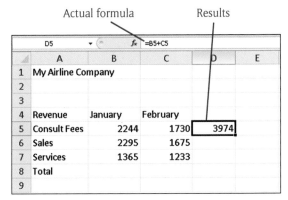

Figure 9-2

The calculation results.

Tip

Notice how the result appears in the cell, but the actual formula, =B5+C5, appears in the Contents box of the Edit line.

Creating a Compound Formula

You use compound formulas when you need more than one operator. Examples of a compound formula might be =B7+B8+B9+B10 or =G4*H2+A16.

Tip

When you have a compound formula, Excel will do the multiplication and division first, and then the addition and subtraction. If you want a certain portion of the formula to be calculated first, put it in parentheses. Excel will do whatever is in the parentheses before the rest of the formula. For example, the formula =B11-B19*A23 will give a different answer than =(B11-B19)*A23. It's the old school rule called "Rule of Priorities" or "Order of Precedence".

In the cell where you want the formula answer, type an equals sign (=) to begin the formula and type the reference to the first cell of the formula. Next, type the operator and then type the reference to the second cell of the formula. Type the next operator and then the reference to the third cell of the formula. Repeat adding operators and references until the formula is complete, adding parentheses wherever necessary. Press Enter to accept the formula. Figure 9-3 illustrates a cell with a compound formula.

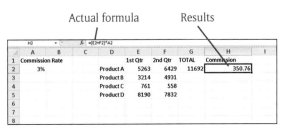

Figure 9-3

A compound formula.

If you are following the examples in this book, try changing one of the values you originally typed in the worksheet and watch the answer to the formula change.

You edit formulas in the same way you edit any other Excel data, either by retyping the formula or double-clicking the cell and making corrections. When editing formulas, Excel color codes each cell address to its corresponding cell. When you press the Enter key, Excel recalculates the formula.

Copying Formulas

Now that you've created a formula, there's no reason to type it repeatedly for subsequent cells. Let Excel copy the formula for you! When you copy a formula, the formula changes depending on where you put it. It is said, therefore, to be relative—relative to the position of the original formula.

Copying with AutoFill

If you're going to copy a formula to surrounding cells, you can use the AutoFill method. You first learned about the AutoFill command in Chapter 8, "Creating a Basic Worksheet." Follow these steps to copy a formula:

1. Click the cell that has the formula.

2. Position the mouse pointer on the lower-right corner of the beginning cell. Make sure the mouse pointer turns into a black cross.

3. Press and hold the mouse button and drag to select the next cells to be filled in.

4. Release the mouse button. Excel copies the formula.

When Excel copies a formula, the references change as the formula is copied. If the original formula was =E2+F2 and you copied it to the next cell down, the formula would read =E3+F3. Then, if you copied it down again it would be =E4+F4, and so on. Take a look at the copied formula in Figure 9-4.

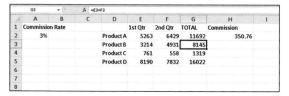

Figure 9-4

Copying a formula changes the formula references.

Copying with Copy and Paste

If the originating cells and the recipient cells are not sequential, you will find it easier to use the Copy and Paste commands. You first learned about the Windows copy and paste functions in Chapter 2, "Getting Started with Word."

1. Select the cell with the formula that you want to duplicate.

2. Press Ctrl+C or choose Home>Clipboard> Copy. A marquee appears around the copied cells.

3. Highlight the cells in which you want to place the duplicated formula and either press Ctrl+V or choose Home>Clipboard>Paste.

Cancel Marquee

If necessary, press the Escape key to cancel the "marching ants" marquee.

Copying Values Instead of Formulas

As you've seen when you copy a formula, you don't copy the formula results, you copy the formula's underlying mathematical expression. What about those times where you just want the resulting value, but not the formula? Fortunately, Excel includes a tool that provides the value only. Copy the cells containing the values you want and then in the cell where you want the answers, click the arrow below the Paste button shown in Figure 9-5 and choose Paste Values. Excel then pastes in only the results, not the formula.

Figure 9-5
Pasting in values.

Creating an Absolute Formula Reference

Occasionally when you copy a formula, you do not want one of the cell references to change. That's when you need to create an *absolute reference*. To indicate an absolute reference, you use the dollar sign ($).

It's called an absolute reference because when you copy it, it absolutely and positively stays that cell reference and never changes. An example of a formula with an absolute reference might be =B22*B24. The reference to cell B24 will not change when copied.

Figure 9-6 shows a formula that is supposed to take the cost of an item and multiply it to the mark-up rate. The result is the retail cost of the item. The first formula is fine, but, as you can see, when the formula is copied or filled down, the other products display

an erroneous retail price of 0. The original formula was =E2*A2, where A2 is the mark-up percentage rate. When the formula is copied down to the next cell, it becomes =E3*A3, and the cell in A3 is not the mark-up percentage rate cell. Use the following steps to create an absolute reference:

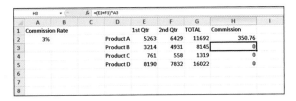

Figure 9-6
Not using an absolute reference creates an incorrect answer.

1. Click the cell in which you want to place the formula answer.

2. Type the formula. If any references are to be an absolute reference, add dollar signs ($) in front of both the column reference and the row reference.

Keyboard Shortcut

When typing the cell reference, press F4 to automatically create the absolute reference.

---

3. Press the Enter key. Excel displays the answer in the cell.

Tip

Compound formulas can also have absolute references.

4. Copy the formula to other cells using one of the methods you discovered earlier in this chapter.

Using Excel Functions

WHILE CREATING A FORMULA provides mathematical calculations, Excel includes a much more powerful feature called *functions*. Functions are basically a fast way to enter a complex formula. Excel has hundreds of functions you can use, and it groups them together by categories, such as mathematical, statistical, logical, or date and time. Using functions can save considerable room in the Formula bar and cuts down on typographical errors that are so easy to make when typing formulas.

Understanding Function Syntax

Functions consist of several different parts. Like a formula, a function begins with an equals (=) sign. The next part is the function name, which might be abbreviated to indicate what the function does. Examples of a function name include SUM, AVERAGE, or COUNT. After the name, you enter a set of parentheses and enter arguments within those parentheses. For every open parenthesis there must be a closing parenthesis.

Arguments are additional pieces of information that clarify how you want the function to behave. Arguments can consist of one or more components, ranging from cell addresses such as D13 or a range of cell addresses like D13:D25, to other variables such as a number of digits you want Excel to do something to. With only a few exceptions, all functions in Excel must follow that pattern. This function structure is called the *syntax*. Following are a few examples of function syntax. You'll learn throughout this section what these functions do.

► =SUM(B3:B21)

► =AVERAGE(F1:G6)

► =IF(B3>B4,"yes", "no")

Creating a Total with the SUM Function

The most commonly used function in Excel is the SUM function, which adds two or more values together and displays the total in the current cell. If any of the values change, the SUM total will automatically update. There are a number of methods to enter the SUM function, but this section describes two of the most common ways. The syntax for the SUM function is =SUM(*range of values to total*).

Entering a SUM Function

One way to enter a SUM function is to type the function in its syntax directly into a cell where you want the answer. Like other formulas, Excel displays the answer in the current cell, but displays the actual function in the Formula bar (see Figure 9- 7).

Function results   Function

Figure 9-7
Using the SUM function.

The following steps show you how to enter a SUM function:

1. Click in the cell where you want the total of the values to display. Type an equals sign (=). The blinking insertion point appears after the equals sign, but do not press the Enter key until the function is complete. Type the word SUM and then type an opening parenthesis.

   The arguments for a SUM function require that you enter the cell addresses you want to add. When you enter function arguments, you type the cell addresses you want to add. If the cell addresses are adjacent to each other, you separate them with a colon (:). For example, typing B2:B5 will add the values in B2 plus B3 plus B4 plus B5. If the cell addresses you want to add are not adjacent, you separate them with a comma. For example, entering B2, B5, B13 will add the values in cells B2 and B5 and B13 but not the value of any cells in between. You can also combine adjacent and non-adjacent cells, such as B2, B5, B13:B15, which would add the values in cells B2 and B5 and B13, B14, and B15.

Selecting Cells with the Mouse

Instead of typing cell addresses, you can use your mouse to select the desired cells. Highlighting the cells with the mouse instead of typing them makes it easier to see that you have selected the correct cells.

2. Type the cell addresses you want to add together, using a colon or comma to separate the addresses. As you type the cell addresses, Excel puts a border around the cells so you can quickly see if you typed the correct cell address.

3. Type a closing parenthesis and then press the Enter key. The resulting value appears in the cell, but the Formula bar still reflects the function and its arguments.

Using the AutoSum Button

Since the SUM function is the function used most, Microsoft includes a button for it on the Ribbon. In fact, you'll find the AutoSum button on the Ribbon twice—once on the Home tab and again on the Formulas tab. The AutoSum button looks like this Σ (a Sigma). Using the AutoSum button makes creating a simple addition formula a mouse click away! Begin with these steps:

1. Click the cell below or to the right of the values you want to total.

2. Choose Home>Editing>AutoSum or Formulas>Function Library>AutoSum. The cells to be totaled are highlighted. Excel first suggests the values in the cells directly above it (see Figure 9-8), but if no values are directly above the current cell, Excel looks for values in the cells to the left.

Figure 9-8
The AutoSum feature in action.

Select Different Cells

If you want to total different cells than Excel has chosen, select them with your mouse.

3. Click the AutoSum button again or press the Enter key. Excel enters the total value of the selected cells.

Using Other Functions

As mentioned at the beginning of this section, Excel includes hundreds of built-in functions that are divided into categories according to their purpose. The SUM function, for example, is considered a mathematical function.

This section shows you some of the function categories. Don't get discouraged when viewing the functions and their arguments. Excel provides a great tool to assist you with them. You'll learn about that tool shortly.

Tip

In the following examples, I list for you the function syntax. However, in many cases the descriptions of the arguments are my interpretation of them—not necessarily the complex terms sometimes used by Excel.

Calculating with Mathematical Functions

One category of functions is comprised of mathematical and trigonometric functions. You find the mathematical and trigonometry functions by choosing Formulas>Function Library>Math & Trig and then choosing the function you want. Following are some common mathematical functions.

▶ **INT:** The INT function rounds a number down to the nearest integer. The number can be a specific number you type or, more commonly, the reference to a specific cell. The syntax is =INT(*cell address or number*). For example, to find the integer of cell B3, you would enter =INT(B3).

Nested Functions

Functions can be nested. For example, to find the integer of the SUM of a range of cells, you might type =INT(=SUM(B3:B10)). Excel will add each cell and round down the total.

▶ **ROUND:** Whereas the INT function displays whole numbers for you, the ROUND function takes a value and rounds it to a specified number of digits. The ROUND function contains two arguments—one to specify which cell you want to round and the second to tell Excel how many decimal places you want to display. The syntax is =ROUND(*cell address or number,num of digits*). For example, if cell C2 has a value of 27.63578 and you want it rounded to two decimal places, you would enter =ROUND(D1,2); then Excel would display the answer of 27.64. Excel also includes the ROUNDUP and ROUNDDOWN functions, which specifically round the answer up or down the number of digits you specify. See Figure 9-9 for an example.

	f_x	=ROUND(C2,2)	
B	C	D	E
	27.6358	27.64	

Figure 9-9
Rounding a value.

► **SQRT:** Finds the square root of a cell or cell range total. The syntax is =SQRT(*cell range*).

► **RAND:** The RAND function simply provides a random decimal value in a cell. The value is always greater than 0 but less than 1, and every time the worksheet recalculates any other value, the random value changes. The RAND function has no arguments, so the syntax is =RAND(). There is also a similar RANDBETWEEN function that lets you specify a low and high value range. =RANDBETWEEN(2,50) extracts a random whole number between 2 and 50.

► **POWER:** Raises a number exponentially. There are two arguments in this function. The first argument refers to the number (or cell address) you want to raise and the second argument is to what power. The syntax is =POWER(*number or cell, power*). Entering =POWER(5,3) results in 125.

► **ROMAN:** Displays the Roman numeral value of a cell. The syntax is =ROMAN(*number or cell*). So if in cell B3, you had a value of 17 and in cell B4 you entered =ROMAN(B3), the result is XVII. Using negative values or values greater than 3999 results in an error. Figure 9-10 illustrates an example where several years are converted to Roman numerals.

B	C	D	E
	1968	MCMLXVIII	
	2009	MMIX	
	2010	MMX	

Figure 9-10
Converting a value to Roman numerals.

Analyzing with Statistical Functions

Statistical-based functions provide a means for analysis of data. Statistical analysis helps you explore, understand, and visualize your data. You access statistical functions from Formulas> Function Library>More Functions>Statistical. Here are just a few of the statistical functions:

► **AVERAGE:** The AVERAGE function finds an average of a range of values. The syntax for this function is =AVERAGE(*range of cells or values to average*). An example might be =AVERAGE(B7:D7), which would add the values in the three cells B7, C7, and D7, then divide that total by three to get the average value. Figure 9-11 shows the average value of a range of cells.

G5	▾		f_x	=AVERAGE(B5:F5)		
	A	B	C	D	E	F	G
1	City Temperatures						
2							
3							
4	City	Mon	Tue	Wed	Thu	Fri	Average
5	Orlando	67	74	66	65	73	69
6	Tampa	71	66	65	72	69	
7	Boston	69	73	71	68	67	
8	LA	66	65	70	71	74	
9	Seattle	69	73	66	74	73	
10							

Figure 9-11
Finding the average value of a cell range.

▶ **MAX and MIN:** Two other common statistical functions are the MAX and MIN functions. The MAX function will display the largest value in a range of cells, whereas the MIN function will display the smallest value in a range of cells. The syntax is =MAX(*range of values*) or =MIN(*range of values*).

▶ **COUNT:** The COUNT function is handy for finding out how many numerical entries are in a specified area. The syntax is very simple: =COUNT(*range of cells to count*).

▶ **COUNTA:** The COUNTA function is similar to COUNT except it is not limited to numerical entries; it will count any non-blank cell, no matter what type of information the cell contains. The syntax is =COUNTA(*range of cells*).

▶ **COUNTBLANK:** The COUNTBLANK function determines the number of blank, or empty, cells in a range. The syntax is =COUNTBLANK(*range of cells*).

Additional Functions Under AutoSum Button

Choose Formulas>Function Library or Home>Editing and click the arrow next to the AutoSum button to quickly select the commonly used SUM, AVERAGE, MAX, MIN, and COUNT NUMBERS (which is the COUNT) commands (see Figure 9-12).

Figure 9-12
Save time by choosing from the AutoSum functions list.

Using Date Functions

Date functions are commonly used to enter the current date into a worksheet, or to calculate the difference between two or more dates. Excel stores dates as sequential serial numbers so they can be used in calculations. By default, January 1, 1900 is serial number 1, and July 20, 2005 is serial number 38553, because it is 38,553 days after January 1, 1900. When you type a date in Excel, it displays the date in a regular date format, such as 20-Jul-05, but behind the scenes Excel still considers that date a serial number. You will discover in Chapter 10, "Making Your Worksheet Look Good," how to format dates into a more understandable format. Access the date or time function by choosing Formulas>Function Library>Date & Time.

Use Dates and Times in Calculations

Because dates and times are values (date serial numbers), they can be added, subtracted, and included in other calculations.

▶ **NOW:** If you enter the NOW function in a cell, Excel will display the current date and time. The date and time are dynamic in that the current date and time will change whenever you recalculate anything in the worksheet. By default, Excel recalculates the worksheet whenever any changes, additions, or deletions are made. The NOW function does not contain any arguments, so the syntax is =NOW().

▶ **MONTH:** The MONTH function returns the month number of a date serial number or a date in a cell. The syntax is =MONTH(*serial number or cell address*). If you have a date of 19-May-99 in cell C16 and you enter =MONTH(C16), Excel returns the value of 5 since May is the 5th month in the calendar year.

▶ **NETWORKDAYS:** The NETWORKDAYS function returns the number of working days between two dates. Working days exclude weekends and identified holidays. The syntax also includes an optional argument where you can enter any additional number of days to exclude. The syntax is =NETWORKDAYS(*StartDate, EndDate, optional holidays*). For example, if you enter a start date of August 15, 1985 and an end date of March 23, 2007 and using the standard number of holidays, Excel returns a result of 5,637. See Figure 9-13 for another example.

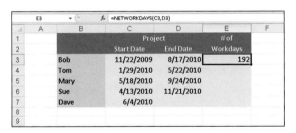

Figure 9-13
Calculating days worked.

Today's Date

A quick way to calculate the number of days between two dates is to enter =NOW() or =TODAY()in one cell and another date in another cell. Then create a formula to subtract the older date from the newer date. Excel displays the difference in a date format, so you'll need to format the value as a number.

Figuring with Financial Functions

Financial functions perform elaborate calculations such as returns on investments or cumulative principal or interest on loans. Functions exist for calculating future values or net present values on investments and for calculating amortization. Take a look at the PMT function and how you can use it.

The PMT function calculates the payment for a loan based on a constant interest rate. You will need to enter the interest rate, the number of payments, and the amount of the loan. The syntax is =PMT(*rate,nper,pv,fv,type*) where rate is the interest rate, *nper* is the number of payments and pv is the loan amount. There are two other optional arguments, including *fv* (future value), which Excel assumes to be zero unless you enter a *fv*, and *type*, which refers to when the payment is due. The following steps show you how you enter this function.

1. In separate cells, enter a loan amount, an interest rate, and the number of payments you intend to make. See Figure 9-14 for an example.

Figure 9-14
Preparing to calculate payments.

Uniform Units

Be uniform about the units you use for specifying *rate* and *nper*. If you make monthly payments on a six-year loan at an annual interest rate of 8 percent, use 8%/12 for *rate* and 6*12 for *nper*. If you make annual payments on the same loan, use 8 percent for *rate* and 6 for *nper*.

2. Type =PMT(in the cell where you want to display the payment amount. Excel will immediately identify the entry as a function and display a function ScreenTip with the function syntax.

3. Click or type the cell address you entered for the interest rate. The referenced cell will have a border around it.

4. Type a comma to separate the arguments.

5. Click or type the cell address you entered for the number of payments and then type another comma.

6. Click or type the cell address you entered for the value of the loan and then type the closing parenthesis.

7. Press the Enter key. Excel calculates and displays the payment amount as you see in Figure 9-15.

Figure 9-15
The net payment amount.

Tip

The payment amount returned by PMT includes principal and interest only.

Understanding Logical Functions

You have seen that most functions work basically the same way. You enter the equals sign, enter the function name, and then tell the function which data to use. Most functions involve some sort of mathematical calculation. Logical functions are different in that they use operators such as equal to (=), greater than (>), less than (<), greater than or equal to (>=), less than or equal to (<=), and not equal to (<>).

One of the most commonly used and most powerful logical functions is the IF function. IF evaluates a condition and returns one of two answers, depending on the result of the evaluation. The IF function has three parts. The first part determines if a situation is true or false; the second part determines the result to display if the first part is true; and the third part determines the result to display if the first part is false. It's really not as confusing as it may sound. The syntax is =IF(*item to test, value if true, value if false*).

For example, suppose in cell C1 you want to find out if the value in cell B5 is greater than the value in cell B6. If B5 is larger than B6 (true), you want to enter "Yes" in cell C1; if B5 is not larger than B6 (false), you want the answer "No" in cell C1. You would enter the function as =IF(B5>B6,"Yes","No"). Look at the steps needed to create an IF function and its arguments:

1. Type =IF(in the cell in which you want to display the answer. Excel will immediately identify the entry as a function and display a tip box with the function syntax.

2. Type the first argument including an operator. This is the condition you want Excel to evaluate.

3. Type a comma to begin the second argument and then type the result you want if the evaluation is true. The true result can be a value, a calculation, or text.

Enclose Text in Quotes

If you want the result to be text, the result's argument must be enclosed in quotation marks. The quotation marks will not be displayed in the answer. No quotation marks are needed if the result is numeric.

---

4. Type a comma to begin the third argument and type the result you want if the evaluation is false. The false result can also be a value, a calculation, or text.

5. Type the closing parenthesis and then press the Enter key. Excel calculates and displays the evaluation result.

In the example you see in Figure 9-16, the IF function checks whether the total project days is less than the goal of 125 days. If it is, Yes! is displayed; if not, No is displayed.

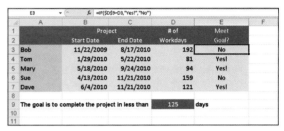

Figure 9-16
Using the IF function.

Looking Up with Lookup Functions

The Lookup category contains functions designed to save you time by finding related data. If you work with large lists in Excel, you can use lookup functions to retrieve individual records from those lists quickly. Two commonly used lookup functions are the VLOOKUP and the HLOOKUP.

The V stands for vertical and the H stands for horizontal. You use VLOOKUP when you need to search through columns of information, and you use HLOOKUP when you need to search through rows of information.

The VLOOKUP actual syntax is VLOOKUP(*lookup_value,table_array,col_index_num*), but let's see if I can translate that into something a little simpler. To understand this formula, take a look at the table in Figure 9-17. You'll use it to illustrate the VLOOKUP function.

The first argument *lookup_value* is really asking for where Excel finds the value you want to match, so let's rename it lookup cell. In this example, you want to know how many calls were made to a specific city, which you will enter in cell E3, so the first argument is in cell E3.

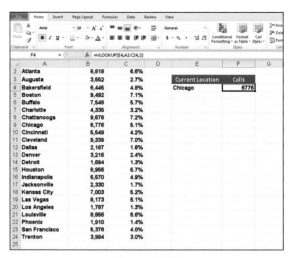

	A	B	C	D	E	F	G	H	I	J
1	CITY	CALLS	% OF TOTAL							
2	Atlanta	8,818	6.6%							
3	Augusta	3,552	2.7%							
4	Bakersfield	6,445	4.8%							
5	Boston	9,492	7.1%							
6	Buffalo	7,548	5.7%							
7	Charlotte	4,335	3.2%							
8	Chattanooga	9,678	7.2%							
9	Chicago	6,776	5.1%							
10	Cincinnati	5,549	4.2%							
11	Cleveland	9,339	7.0%							
12	Dallas	2,187	1.6%							
13	Denver	3,216	2.4%							
14	Detroit	1,694	1.3%							
15	Houston	8,956	6.7%							
16	Indianapolis	6,570	4.9%							
17	Jacksonville	2,330	1.7%							
18	Kansas City	7,003	5.2%							
19	Las Vegas	8,173	6.1%							
20	Los Angeles	1,787	1.3%							
21	Louisville	8,956	6.6%							
22	Phoenix	1,910	1.4%							
23	San Francisco	5,378	4.0%							
24	Trenton	3,994	3.0%							

Figure 9-17
A typical lookup table.

Sort First

One important factor with VLOOKUP (and HLOOKUP) is that the first column (or first row) MUST be in alphabetical order. See Chapter 11, "Managing Large Amounts of Data," for instructions on sorting your data.

The second argument *table_array* is prompting you to specify where you have your list. Let's call it *list area*. You can enter a range name or you can specify the range of cells. Do not include column headings. In this example, the list is in cells A2 through C24, which you would specify as A2:C24.

The third argument asks which column of the list do you want to extract. Again referring to the example, since you want the number of calls, you need the second column.

So after translating the VLOOKUP to read =VLOOKUP(*lookup cell, list area, column number*), you need to enter =VLOOKUP(E3,A2:C31,2), which gives you a result of 6,776. If you type another city in cell E3—Boston, for example—you get a different result of 9,492. You can verify those results by manually looking up Chicago or Boston in the list (see Figure 9-18).

Figure 9-18
VLOOKUP results.

The steps in the previous section used the VLOOKUP function because the data resided in columns. In an HLOOKUP the data resides in rows. HLOOKUP works just like the VLOOKUP except it looks in the top row of the list and returns the value of the indicated cell.

The HLOOKUP syntax is HLOOKUP(*lookup_value, table_array,row_index_num*) or as translated earlier, =HLOOKUP(*lookup cell, list area, row number*). Figure 9-19 illustrates the HLOOKUP function in action.

Figure 9-19
HLOOKUP results.

176

Writing Text Functions

The text category typically works with the text in a cell. The cell could have numbers, but the function in the category doesn't handle them as values in that it doesn't add values such as 2+3 to equal 5. Depending on the text function it might add them together as cells so that a cell with 2 and a cell with 3 becomes 23, or APPLE and PIE become APPLE PIE. Other functions reveal only a specified number of characters such as the 3 characters on the left side of the cell (YORKSHIRE becomes YOR) or the right four characters (YORKSHIRE becomes HIRE). Take a look at a few of the text functions:

▶ **CONCATENATE:** This function joins together several text cell strings into a single text string. For example, if in cell A2 you had Mary and in cell B2 you had Jones, if you concatenate them you end up with Mary Jones. The syntax is =CONCATENATE (*cell address or value or text1, cell address or value or text2, cell address or value or text 3*). You can add together up to 255 different text strings, numbers, or cell references. Let's look at the above example. If you simply entered the function as =CONCATENATE(A2,B2) you end up with MaryJones. You need to enter =CONCATENATE(a2, " ",B2), like you see in Figure 9-20, which provides Mary Jones. The second argument was a space, and all manually entered text must be enclosed in quotes.

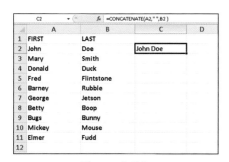

Figure 9-20
Adding several text cells together.

▶ **RIGHT:** Displays a specified number of characters from the right side of a cell. (There's also a LEFT function that provides a specified number of characters from the left side of a cell.) As an example, beginning at cell A2, you have a list of inventory items that begin with a two-digit vendor code and then a three-digit part number such as 63174. For your purpose you need only the part number, which is the three characters on the right. The syntax is =RIGHT(*cell address, number of characters*), so you would enter =RIGHT(B2,3), which returns the value 174 (see Figure 9-21).

Figure 9-21
Extracting characters.

▶ **PROPER:** The PROPER function capitalizes the first letter in each word of the cell text. If you have The *dog is gone* in cell G5, using the PROPER command results in *The Dog Is Gone*. The syntax is =PROPER(*cell address*).

▶ **UPPER:** Converts cell text to all uppercase letters. The syntax is =UPPER(*cell address*). If the value of cell C3 is John Smith, entering UPPER(C3) results in JOHN SMITH. There is also a LOWER command that uses the same command to convert cell text to all lowercase letters.

▶ **TRIM:** The TRIM function removes any extra spaces but leaves one space between each word. The syntax is =TRIM(*cell address*).

▶ **REPT:** The REPT function allows you to repeat characters a specified number of times. The syntax is =REPT(*what characters, number of times to repeat*). If cell G5 had a value of 12, then if you enter =REPT("*", G5) the answer cell would show 12 asterisks. You can specify more than one character such as */ or <>.

Getting Help with Excel Functions

With each Excel function having a different syntax, it becomes almost impossible to remember the syntax of each function. You've already seen that when you begin typing the function and the open parenthesis, Excel displays a function ScreenTip to help you, but you can get even more help with functions by using the Insert Function feature. Just follow these steps:

1. Click the cell where you want to enter a function.

2. Choose Formulas>Function Library>Insert Function. Excel automatically inserts the equals (=) sign in your selected cell and the Insert Function dialog box opens.

3. Click the Or Select a Category arrow and choose a function category. If you don't know the category, choose All (see Figure 9-22).

4. Choose the function you want. The function syntax and a description of the function display under the function list.

Figure 9-22
Selecting a function from the Insert Function box.

Enter Function Description

If you don't know the name of the function you want, in the search box, type a description of what you want to do, then click Go. Excel displays a list of possible functions to meet your needs.

5. Click OK, which opens the Function Arguments dialog box. In the selected cell, Excel inserts the Function name and the parentheses.

Optional Arguments

Since some function arguments are optional, in the Function Arguments dialog box, Excel lists the required arguments in bold.

6. In the first argument box, type the cell address, actual value, or click on the cell that contains the argument.

7. Click in the next argument box and repeat the previous step. As you click in each argument, Excel displays a description. Repeat until all required arguments have a cell reference or a value. Figure 9-23 illustrates the IF function arguments dialog box and Figure 9-24 illustrates the VLOOKUP arguments dialog box.

8. Click on OK. The Function Arguments dialog box will close and Excel displays the function result in the selected cell.

Figure 9-23
The IF function and its arguments.

Figure 9-24
The VLOOKUP function and its arguments.

Troubleshooting Errors

GIGO: GARBAGE IN, GARBAGE OUT. That's what happens if you enter incorrect data into your worksheet. The answers become garbage and are useless. To help you locate potential problems, Excel provides a number of tools.

Viewing Formulas

As you've already seen, when you create formulas, the result of the formulas is what Excel displays in the worksheet. Although the Edit line displays the actual formula, you can view only one formula at a time. Excel provides a method to view the formulas in the cells. Having the formulas display is a wonderful tool for proofing and troubleshooting formula errors in your worksheet.

Choose Formulas>Formula Auditing>Show Formulas. Excel displays the formulas in each cell (see Figure 9-25) instead of the formula result. Each cell reference in a formula is assigned a color and a corresponding colored box surrounds the referenced cell whenever you click a cell with a formula. If you print the worksheet while the formulas are displayed, the formulas will print, not the formula results.

![Figure 9-25 screenshot showing Excel worksheet with formulas displayed]

Figure 9-25
Displaying the actual formulas.

Understanding Common Formula Error Messages

There are a number of error messages that may appear when you type a formula. Some are typing mistakes and some may be a result of a cell value.

Other errors may appear in the formula result cell. Following are a few of the more common error messages.

180

▶ **#DIV/0!:** This means that the formula is trying to divide by either an empty cell or one with a value of zero (see Figure 9-26). Make sure all cells in the division have a non-zero value.

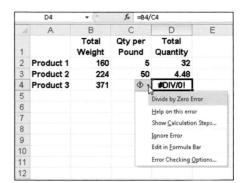

Figure 9-26
Divide by zero error.

▶ **#REF!:** This may mean that the formula includes an invalid cell reference.

▶ **#VALUE!:** This error means the formula references an invalid cell address. For example, the cell you reference contains text but the formula expects to find a value. You might also see this error if you delete a value in a cell that was used in a formula. Locate and correct the invalid cell reference.

▶ **#NAME?:** This error occurs when Excel doesn't recognize text in a formula, often because of a range name or function name misspelling.

► **Formula Omits Adjacent Cells:** This error means a formula refers to a group of cells that have numbers adjacent to it. Study the formula to make sure you didn't forget to include additional cell references in the formula.

► **Number Stored as Text:** This means a cell contains what looks like a value, but the content is stored as text. Simply verify that you intend to store the entry as a text entry not as a value.

► **Circular:** This means that a formula in a cell refers to the same cell. Excel displays a circular reference notation in the status bar. Excel may also display an error box and display a Circular Reference help window to assist you in locating the erroneous formula. In Figure 9-27, the formula in B7 is trying to add itself to the total, thereby creating the circular reference.

Figure 9-27
Circular reference error.

Identifying Formula Precedents and Dependents

The Formula Auditing features can assist you in tracing through formulas such as when resolving worksheet errors. The Formula Auditing features display tracer arrows, which are arrows that show the relationship between the active cell and its related cells. It traces *dependents*, which are other cells that are affected by the current cell, and *precedents*, which are other cells that affect the current cell.

Select a cell that contains a formula or one that is referenced in one or more formulas and choose Formulas>Formula Auditing>Trace Precedents, or choose Formulas>Formula Auditing>Trace Dependents. As you see in Figure 9-28, Excel displays one or more blue arrows pointing out dependents or precedents. You see where cell B2 is a precedent for cells G2, H2, I2, B7, B8, and B9.

Figure 9-28
Viewing formula precedents.

To remove the dependent or precedent tracings, click Formulas>Formula Auditing>Remove Arrows.

Making Your Worksheet
Look Good

PICTURE YOURSELF GROWING a bonsai tree. It begins as a small root and through careful shaping and care becomes a beautiful work of art. The overall artistic effect is of great significance in growing the trees. Everything must be proportional: the size of the tree, its leaves or needles, its flowers or fruit, and the container in which it grows. The container, especially, must be chosen to harmonize with the tree in size, shape, and color.

In Excel, you begin with a blank worksheet, add in your data, and then you find that columns often aren't wide enough, fonts are too small to read, dates display in an unusual manner, and when you have columns of data stacked next to each other, sometimes the information begins to overlap. It just plain looks boring.

Fortunately, Excel includes a plethora of features with which you can make the worksheet more interesting and easier to read. Change the fonts, or make the numbers easier to read by adding numeric formatting. Liven up your worksheet with effective use of borders, lines, and color. Whoever said "Looks aren't everything" wasn't staring at an unformatted Excel spreadsheet. This chapter is about shaping your worksheet into its own work of art.

Changing Cell Formats

YOU CAN CHANGE the size or appearance of any cell regardless of content. For example, by default, values are displayed as general numbers; however, you can choose to display values as currency, percentages, fractions, dates, and many other formats. You can make your titles large and bold so they are quickly noticed.

Formatting Values

The Excel Ribbon provides several methods you can use for formatting values. First, there are buttons on the Home tab of the Ribbon that include several popular number styles: accounting, percentages, and commas. You can also choose from the Number Format drop-down menu, or you can open the Format Cells dialog box where you'll see all available options.

Select the cells you want formatted. You can select a few cells, entire rows, entire columns, or the entire worksheet. Choose Home>Number and select from the following options (see Figure 10-1):

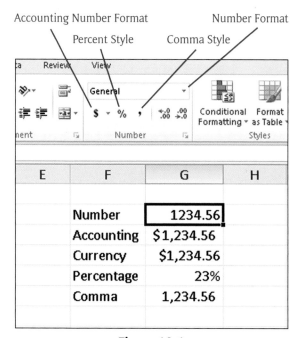

Figure 10-1
Numeric values formatted with different styles.

▶ **Accounting Number Format:** The Accounting option has a drop-down menu from which you can select international currency symbols.

▶ **Percent Style:** When changing numbers to display as a percentage, Excel automatically multiplies the cell value by 100 and displays the result with a percent symbol and no decimal points. For example, if the cell has a value of 15, Excel displays 1500%; however, if the cell has a value of 0.15, Excel displays 15%.

▶ **Comma Style:** When you apply a comma style to selected values, Excel separates the thousands, making the data easier to read. The Comma option also automatically adds two decimal places but does not include a dollar sign.

▶ **Number Format:** Choose the drop-down arrow to display a list of options such as seen in Figure 10-2. This figure illustrates values formatted in various Excel styles. Accounting and Currency format may appear the same, but they really are different. The difference is in the placement of the dollar sign. In currency style, the dollar sign is right next to the numbers, but in accounting style, the dollar sign is on the left edge of the cell.

Figure 10-2

Choose from several format options.

Another method for selecting number formatting is using the Number group Dialog Box Launcher, which displays the Format Cells dialog box seen in Figure 10-3. Number format selections are on the Number tab.

Automatic Format

If you type the dollar sign ($) along with the cell value, Excel automatically formats the cell into a currency format. If you type a comma (,) to separate thousands, Excel automatically formats the cell to a number. If you type the percent symbol (%), Excel automatically formats the cell as a percentage.

Figure 10-3
The Format Cells dialog box.

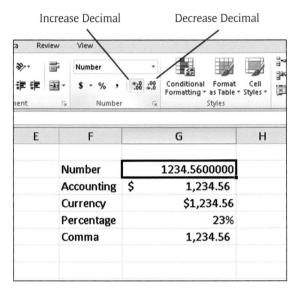

Figure 10-4
Easily add or remove decimal places.

The Format Cells dialog box allows you to select from several number formatting styles, including choosing whether to display negative numbers in red, choosing the number of decimal points, and even selecting the desired type of currency symbol. There is also a Special category where you can format numbers to match the pattern for telephone numbers or social security numbers.

As mentioned earlier, by default, the Comma and Currency styles include two decimal places, and percentages don't include decimal points. If you have a number in a formatted cell with more than the two decimal points, Excel rounds up the number. So if you enter 75.257 in a cell, then format that cell to comma or currency, Excel displays $75.26. There are Ribbon buttons, however, that allow you to increase or decrease the number of decimal places. Excel numbers can display up to 30 decimal places.

Select the cells you want formatted and choose Home>Number>Increase Decimal. Each click of the button adds another decimal digit to the right of the decimal point (see Figure 10-4).

Column Too Narrow

If a formatted value cannot fit within the width of a cell, Excel may display a series of ### or it may automatically round the value. You discover how to widen a column later in this chapter.

To remove digits to the right of the decimal point, choose Home>Number>Decrease Decimal. Each click removes a number from the far right of the decimal point and rounds the value in the cell.

Designing with Fonts

Excel uses a default font of Calibri, but from the Home tab of the Ribbon you can easily change the font typeface, size, and style. *Fonts* are typefaces in different styles that give your text character and impact. Your selection of fonts varies depending on the software installed on your computer.

The default font size in an Excel worksheet is 11 points. There are approximately 72 points in an inch, so a 10-point font is slightly less than one-seventh of an inch tall.

Additionally, Excel includes three font styles you can select from the Ribbon. Font styles include **bold**, <u>underline</u>, and *italics*. Here are the steps you take to change fonts and font attributes:

1. Select the cells you want to format.

2. On the Home tab, open the Font drop-down menu and select a font. If you hover your mouse over a font before clicking it, Excel displays the selected cells in the different fonts (see Figure 10-5).

Font Size arrow   Decrease Font Size

Increase Font Size

Figure 10-5
Direct attention to cells by changing the font face.

3. From the Home>Font group, click the Font Size arrow and select a font size.

Increase or Decrease Font Size

Optionally, click the Increase Font Size or the Decrease Font Size button to increment or decrease the font size one step at a time.

---

4. From the Home>Font group, click an attribute such as Bold, Italic, or Underline (see Figure 10-6). The Bold, Italic, and Underline buttons are toggle switches, meaning that one click turns them on, but if you click again Excel turns them off.

Bold   Italic   Underline

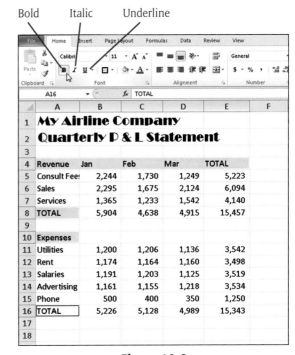

Figure 10-6
Enhance cell data with text attributes.

Keyboard Shortcuts

Shortcut keys for Bold, Italic, and Underline are Ctrl+B, Ctrl+I, and Ctrl+U, respectively.

Underlining is not the same as a cell border. (Cell borders are discussed later in this chapter.) The default underline style is a single underline. Click the Underline button down arrow to select Double Underline. Or, choose additional underline options through the Font group Dialog Box Launcher, which displays the Format Cells dialog box. Underline options appear on the Font tab, as you see in Figure 10-7.

Figure 10-7
Choose from these underline options.

Change Default Font

To change the default Excel font, choose File>Options. From the General section, click the Use This Font drop-down menu and select the font you want in all new workbooks. Click OK twice.

Changing Data Color

If you want to add color to your worksheet, try changing the font color. Select the cells you want to format and choose Home>Font and click the Font Color drop-down arrow to select a color. Excel's Live Preview feature, as you see in Figure 10-8, shows you the selected cells in the new font colors.

Tip

The colors you see depend on which theme you are using. See "Working with Themes," later in this chapter.

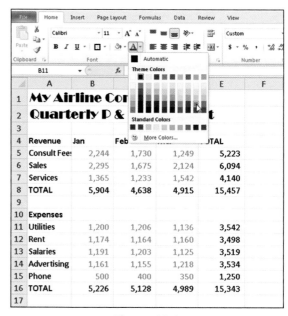

Figure 10-8
Choosing a color for your text.

Alternative Method

Another method to select Font color is through the Font group Dialog Box Launcher, which displays the Format Cells dialog box. Font color selection is on the Font tab.

Working with Date Formats

As you learned in Chapter 8, "Creating a Basic Worksheet," Excel may not display a date in the same format as you entered the data. A couple of date format options are accessible through the Number Format drop-down menu, but more extensive options are offered in the Format Cells dialog box.

Select the cell that has a date you want formatted and then, from the Home tab, click the Number group Dialog Box Launcher, which displays the

Format Cells dialog box. Click the Date category, as seen in Figure 10-9, which displays a variety of date formats. Select a format for the selected cells and click the OK button.

Figure 10-9
A few of the available Excel date formats.

Working with Alignment and Spacing

I N THE PREVIOUS SECTION, you worked with the appearance of cells as to their font face, size, color, and so forth. In this section, you discover how to change the worksheet itself so you can see more (or less) of the information in the individual cells, and especially how the cell contents line up with the cell edges.

Adjusting Column Width

By default, Excel columns are 8.43 characters wide. When the content of a cell is too long to fit into its cell, depending on the type of data, Excel may automatically widen the column or display the information in a different format. You can manually resize a column so all data displays correctly.

If a label does not fit into the cell, the contents spill into the next cell to the right, if the next cell is empty. If the next cell is not empty, Excel displays only the amount of text that fits into the cell. The extra text is not cut off, it's just not displayed.

If a value is too wide, Excel may do one of several things:

▶ Display the number in scientific notation so it displays in fewer characters.

▶ Automatically widen the cell.

▶ Round the value's decimal points.

▶ Display the data as a series of number signs (#).

The following steps show you how you can widen a column:

1. To adjust the width of columns headings, select the headings of the columns you want widened. If you want to adjust a single column, click any cell in that column or select the column heading.

2. Choose a method to adjust column width:

▶ To manually change the width of columns, position the mouse pointer on the right boundary of the column heading until it turns into a double-ended arrow. Drag until the column is the width that you want. As you move the pointer, a ScreenTip displays the new width. In Figure 10-10 you see the expansion of column A.

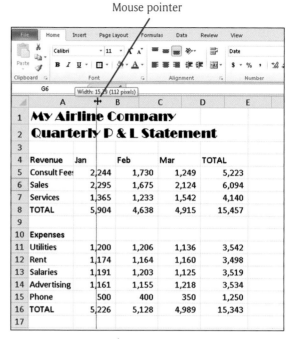

Mouse pointer

Figure 10-10
Manually changing column width.

Display Measurement

Excel displays cell width in characters and pixels instead of inches. The minimum column width is 0 characters, and the maximum is 255 characters.

▶ To set column width to a specific setting, choose Home>Cells>Format> Column Width. The Column Width dialog box, shown in Figure 10-11, appears. Type the exact width you want; then click OK.

Figure 10-11
The Column Width dialog box.

▶ To automatically change the column width so it fits the widest entry, double-click the boundary on the right side of the column heading or choose Home>Cells>Format>AutoFit Column Width. The column automatically expands to fit the widest entry in the column.

Default Column Width

The default column width is 8.43 based on the default 11-point Calibri font. If you change the default font type or size, Excel may also change the standard column width. You can manually set a default column width by choosing Home>Cells>Format>Default Width.

Changing Row Height

When you change to a larger font, Excel usually enlarges the row height to accommodate the larger font size. You can also manually resize the row height. Highlight the row headings whose height you want to adjust and do one of the following:

Display Measurement

Excel displays row height in points instead of in inches.

▶ Manually change the row height. Position the mouse pointer on the bottom boundary of the row heading until it turns into a double-ended arrow. Drag until the row is the height that you want. As you move the pointer, a ScreenTip displays the new height. In Figure 10-12, you see the height of row 2 increasing.

Mouse pointer

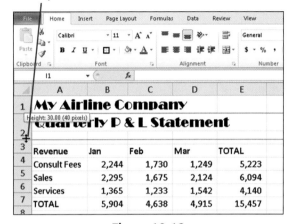

Figure 10-12
Increasing row height manually.

▶ Set row height to a specific setting by choosing Home>Cells>Format>Row Height. The Row Height dialog box appears. Type the exact height you want, and then click OK.

▶ To automatically change the height of the row so it fits the tallest entry in the row, double-click the boundary on the bottom of the row heading or choose Home>Cells>Format>AutoFit Row Height. Excel examines the rows contents and sets the height slightly larger than the tallest entry.

Default Row Height

The default row height is 15 based on the default 11-point Calibri font. If you change the default font type or size, Excel may also change the standard row height. You cannot manually set a default row height.

Figure 10-13
Aligning cell contents horizontally.

Aligning Data

By default, Excel makes labels left-aligned and values right-aligned to their cells. You can change the alignment of cells individually or in a block so they are aligned left, right, centered, or full justified. You can also wrap text in the cells when the text is too long to fit in one cell and you don't want it to overlap to the next cell. Additionally, Excel aligns text vertically to the bottom of the row, but you can also center it or align it to the top of the cell.

Begin by selecting the cells you want to align and choosing Home>Alignment. Then, select one of these alignment buttons:

- ▶ **Align Text Left:** Horizontally aligns the data along the left edge of the cell.
- ▶ **Center:** Centers the data horizontally in the middle of the cell. If you change the column width, the data remains centered to the new column width. In Figure 10-13, cells C2 through E2 are left-, center- and right-aligned respectively.
- ▶ **Align Text Right:** Horizontally aligns the data along the right edge of the cell.

Accounting Alignment

Values formatted as Accounting display only as right-aligned. You can change alignment on all other formatting styles.

- ▶ **Top Align:** Aligns the data vertically along the top edge of the cell.
- ▶ **Middle Align:** Centers the data vertically in the cell.
- ▶ **Bottom Align:** This is the default option and aligns the data along the bottom edge of the cell. Notice the heading in Figure 10-14. Cell A2 shows a top alignment whereas cell A1 shows the default bottom alignment.

Additional Alignment Options

Optionally, you can view additional alignment options using the Format Cells dialog box. From the Home tab, click the Alignment group Dialog Box Launcher. If necessary, click the Alignment tab, set any desired alignment options, and then click OK.

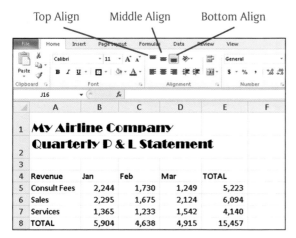

Figure 10-14
Vertical cell alignment.

Merging Cells

Sometimes the rectangular grid can get in the way of your design creativity. Perhaps just one cell in the worksheet is too small, or you want to center text across a group of columns to create attractive headings. Fortunately, you can merge multiple cells. Select the cell containing the data you want to merge and the cells you want to include in the merge. The data cell must be in the left cell of the selection and the other cells cannot contain data, as shown in Figure 10-15.

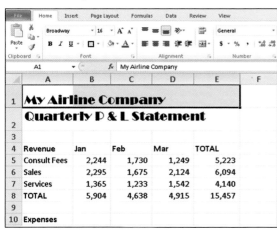

Figure 10-15
Selecting the cells you want to merge.

Choose Home>Alignment>Merge & Center. All the selected cells merge into one larger cell, and the data is centered horizontally. If you select cells vertically and choose the Merge and Center command, Excel merges the cells and vertically bottom-aligns the data. See Figure 10-16, which shows cells A1 through E1 merged horizontally as well as cells A2 through E2.

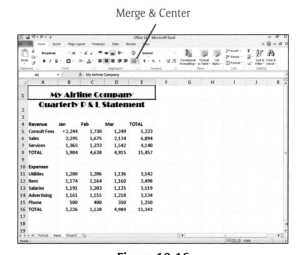

Figure 10-16
Merging cells can create a title for the worksheet.

Tip

In this example, it appears that the heading is located in Columns A through E; however, the text is still in Column A. If you need to change the text, be sure to select Column A, not Column B, C, or D.

After clicking Merge & Center, you can change the alignment. Click the Merge & Center button again to unmerge the cells from each other.

Indenting Cell Data

What about those cells that you want left-aligned, but not all the way to the edge? You could insert some spaces in front of the text, but because of font styles, the text doesn't line up evenly. If you insert spaces in front of values, Excel simply ignores them. So what can you do? You can use the Indent buttons. Just follow these steps:

1. Select the cells you want to indent.

2. Choose Home>Alignment>Increase Indent. Each Increase Indent click adds a small amount of space between the cell border and the data itself. See Figure 10-17, where cells A5 through A7 and cells A11 through A15 are indented. How Excel indents depends on how you format the cell:

▶ If the data is left-aligned, Excel indents to the left.

▶ If the data is right-aligned, Excel indents to the right.

▶ If the data is centered, with the first click Excel indents to the right, but subsequent clicks cause Excel to move the data to the left.

Remove Indent

Click the Decrease Indent button to remove indentation.

Wrapping Text in a Cell

The Wrap Text feature treats each cell like a miniature word processor, with text wrapping around in the cell.

1. Select the cells you want to format.

2. Choose Home>Alignment>Wrap Text. As in Figure 10-18, if the selected text cells contain more text than will fit the width of the cell, Excel displays it on multiple lines. Notice that Excel automatically increases row height to accommodate the additional text lines.

New Line

To force a new line of text in a wrapped cell, press Alt+Enter where you want the new line to begin.

Decrease Indent   Increase Indent

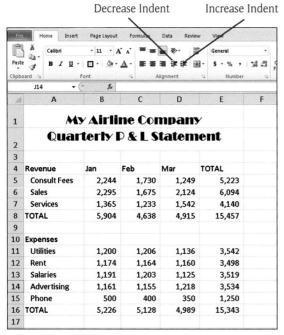

Figure 10-17

Indenting helps set data apart from other cells.

Wrap Text button

Figure 10-18
A worksheet cell with wrapped text.

Shrink to Fit

If you open the Format Cells dialog box, you see a Shrink to Fit option on the Alignment tab. This option allows Excel to automatically change the font size in the selected cell to force the data to fit within the cell's current width. Use caution with this option; the text may become so small that it's unreadable.

Rotating Cell Text

Another feature you can use to dress up your worksheet is to rotate the text. Rotating text is often helpful for headings, but I wouldn't recommend it for your actual data. It can be a little difficult to read. The following steps show you how to rotate text:

1. Select the cells you want to format.

2. Choose Home>Alignment>Orientation. A list of options appears:

   ▶ **Angle Counterclockwise:** Angles the text in the cell from left bottom to right top.

▶ **Angle Clockwise:** Angles the text in the cell from left top to right bottom.

▶ **Vertical Text:** Centers the text and places one letter on top of the other.

▶ **Rotate Text Up:** Places the text on the lower-right side of the cell and runs it vertically up the cell.

▶ **Rotate Text Down:** Places the text on the lower-left side of the cell and runs it vertically down the cell.

Specific Rotation

Click the Alignment group Dialog Box Launcher to open the Format Cells dialog box where you can select a specific degree of rotation.

3. Choose an option. The selected cells take the rotation you choose. In Figure 10-19, you see heading cells angled counterclockwise.

Orientation button

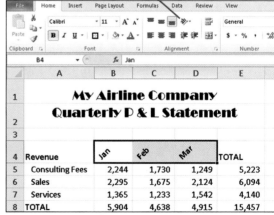

Figure 10-19
Rotating cell data to add a special effect.

Adding Borders and Shading

O N THE SCREEN, each cell has a light gray border around it, but those borders do not print by default. That's called the *grid*, and it is there for the ease of viewing each cell independently. In fact, you can turn the grid display off and on by clicking View>Show>Gridlines. If you want borders around your cells, whether around the entire cell, or just on a part of the cell, Excel provides a tool to easily create printable lines. You can also add pizzazz to your worksheet by adding backgrounds and patterns.

Placing Borders Around Cells

You can add border lines to individual cells and groups of cells. A border can appear around all sides of the cell or only on certain sides, such as the top or bottom. Different from an underline, which runs directly under letters and numbers, a border flows across the entire width or height of a cell.

To add a border, select the appropriate cells. Choose Home>Font and then click the arrow next to the Borders button. A variety of border options appears, as you see in Figure 10-20.

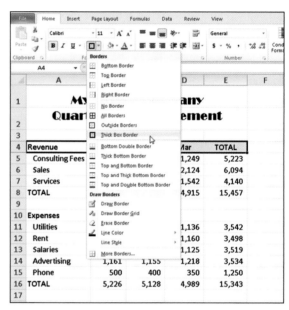

Figure 10-20
Creating cell border lines.

Select the border you want. Excel applies the border to the selected cells. Optionally, click the More Borders option, which opens the Format Cells dialog box. From there you can select even more border styles, colors, and options.

Applying Cell Background Colors

Adding a background color to a cell or group of cells can make your worksheet more interesting and can call attention to specific areas of the worksheet. Excel calls the background color the Fill color.

Last Used Border

The Borders button ScreenTip may display Bottom Border, Top Border, or whatever border was last used.

Select the cells to which you want to add background color. From the Home tab, in the Font group, click the down arrow next to the Fill Color icon. A gallery of colors appears (see Figure 10-21).

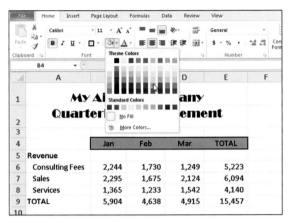

Figure 10-21
Choosing a color for cell background shading.

Select the cell background color you want or choose More Colors to create your own shading color. To remove cell background shading, choose No Fill.

> ## Reverse Colors
>
> A good combination to use with a black and white printer is a black background and a light font color.

Adding Cell Patterns

You can use a pattern instead of a single color as a background to your cells. A pattern uses two colors, arranged in some design, such as stripes or

dots. Each pattern has both a background and a foreground color. The background color is the base color, whereas the foreground color is the color of the stripes or dots. Be careful using patterns because they can be distracting to the reader.

The following steps show you how to add fill patterns:

1. Select the cells you want formatted.

2. Choose Home>Cells>Format>Format Cells as you see in Figure 10-22, which launches the Format Cells dialog box.

Figure 10-22
Format Cells options.

> ## Alternative Method
>
> Optionally, click the Dialog Box Launcher from the Font, Alignment, or Number group.

3. From the Fill tab, click the down arrow next to Pattern Style and select a pattern of your choosing (see Figure 10-23).

4. From the Pattern Color drop-down menu, optionally choose a color for your pattern.

5. Click the OK button.

Figure 10-23
Choosing a cell pattern.

Discovering Formatting Shortcuts

S O FAR YOU'VE LEARNED quite a few ways to dress up your worksheet. There appears to be a button for just about anything. Now, however, you need to speed up the process of formatting worksheets. Fortunately, Excel includes several features to assist you.

Using the Mini Toolbar

In Chapter 3, "Making a Word Document Look Good," you discovered that while formatting text in Word, you could use the Mini Toolbar to provide quick access to commonly used formatting features. Excel also provides a Mini Toolbar which contains many of the formatting commands available on the Home tab, making it unnecessary for you to actually switch to the Home tab. The usefulness of the Mini Toolbar comes from the fact that you don't have to move your mouse so far to select the commands from the Ribbon.

Along with a context-sensitive shortcut menu, the Mini Toolbar appears whenever you right-click on a cell or group of cells (see Figure 10-24). Choose the formatting attribute you want to apply. The cells take the selected attributes and the Mini Toolbar remains open for you to make additional selections. Click any cell to close the Mini Toolbar.

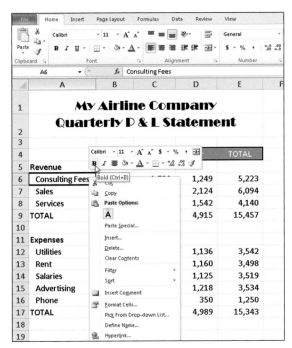

Figure 10-24
Save mouse movement by using the Mini Toolbar.

Copy Formatting

Sometimes it takes a lot of time and effort to get the formatting of a cell just the way you want it. Rather than duplicate all those steps for another cell, Excel includes a Format Painter feature that copies formatting from one cell to another. Copied formatting includes font size, color, style attributes, shading, and alignment. When you copy the formatting, the values in the cells are not affected.

1. Click a cell containing formatting you want to copy.

2. Choose Home>Clipboard>Format Painter. The mouse pointer is a white plus sign along with a paint brush like the one you see in Figure 10-25.

Lock Format Painter Tool

Double-click the Format Painter tool to lock it in so you can paint additional cells without having to reselect the tool. Click the Format Painter tool again to unlock it.

Format Painter   Mouse pointer

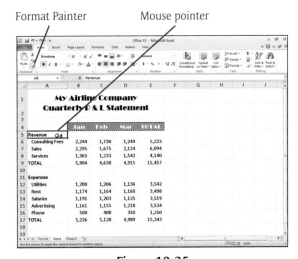

Figure 10-25
Use the Format Painter tool to duplicate formatting selections.

3. Click or drag across the cells you want to format. Excel immediately applies formats such as font, size, colors, borders, and alignment.

Copy Column Width

To quickly copy the width of one column to another column, select the heading of the first column, click the Format Painter tool, and then click the heading of the column where you want to apply the column width.

Working with Themes

In Chapter 3, you discovered that you could use Office themes, which are professionally designed predefined sets of colors, fonts, and other effects that you can apply to your Office documents. Themes are consistent throughout all Office documents, so using them brings continuity to your work. The default theme used by Excel is called the Office theme, but there are quite a few others. Take a brief look at how changing a theme changes the options Excel provides.

Tip

Themes are available in Word, Excel, PowerPoint, and Outlook. In Publisher, themes are called Schemes.

In Figure 10-26, which has the standard Office theme, you see that the default font is Calibri 11 point and you see some of the coordinating colors available from the Fill Color drop-down menu.

Now look at Figure 10-27, which is the Waveform theme. The default font is Candera and the theme colors available under the Fill Color drop-down menu are entirely different, much more vibrant, than the ones available with the standard Office theme.

To choose a different theme for your Excel Worksheet, choose Page Layout>Themes>Themes. A variety of theme choices from which you can select appears, as you see in Figure 10-28.

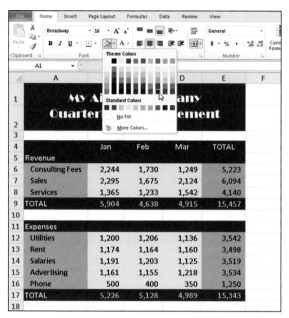

Figure 10-26
Office theme options.

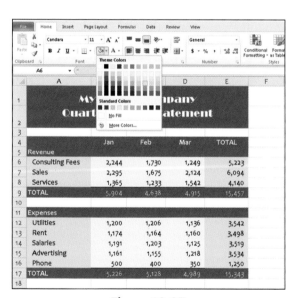

Figure 10-27
Waveform theme options.

Figure 10-28
Choose your favorite theme.

Using Cell Styles

Based on themes, Cell Styles let you quickly apply a group of formatting options to a selected group of cells. The choices you have available depend on the theme you choose for your document. The following steps show you how to apply Cell Styles.

1. Select the cells you want to format.

2. Choose Home>Styles>Cell Styles. In Figure 10-29, you see that Excel displays a gallery of predefined styles. This worksheet is using the Composite theme.

Figure 10-29
Select from many cell styles.

Excel Styles

Excel styles include Normal (the default style for regular cell text), Heading 1 through Heading 4 (suitable for worksheet headings), Accent1 through Accent6 (font and fill effects to make text stand out), and several data model styles (Calculation, Input, Output, and so on).

3. Excel's Live Preview shows your choice before you actually apply it. Select the style you want to use.

Conditional Formatting

WHEN YOU USE conditional formatting, you can instruct Excel to change the formatting for a cell if the cell's value meets a certain criteria. You use conditional formatting to visually annotate your data for both analytical and presentation purposes or to easily find exceptions and to spot important trends in your data. For example, if sales for any salesperson fall beneath their quota, you could have Excel automatically format it in red or with shading or borders. Follow these simple steps:

1. Select the cells to which you want to apply conditional formatting.

Conditional Formatting

Reasons for using conditional formatting might include locating dates that meet a certain condition (such as falling on a Saturday or Sunday), specifying highest or lowest values in a range, or indicating values that fall under or over a specified amount.

2. Choose Home>Styles>Conditional Formatting>Highlight Cell Rules.

3. Select the criteria you want to use. Criteria options include Greater Than, Less Than, Between, Equal To, Text That Contains, A Date Occurring, and Duplicate Values. A dialog box opens where you can specify the value. In Figure 10-30, in order to see which grade averages were over 75%, you use the Greater Than criteria.

Figure 10-30
Specifying conditions for formatting.

4. Enter the values you want to reference in the text box. The number of boxes depends on the criteria you selected in Step 3. You can

type a value here, such as 500, or you can reference a cell address such as F13.

5. Click the drop-down arrow next to the format options so you can specify the format options to employ if the condition you specified is true. Live Preview shows you what your data will look like.

Custom Format

Click the Custom Format option where you can create your own format, selecting from font styles and color, numeric and other formats, borders, patterns, or background color.

6. Click OK. (In Figure 10-31, you see formatting options applied to seven cells that meet the specified criteria of being greater than the average.)

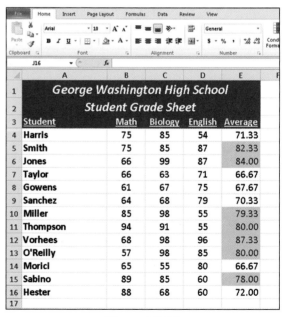

Figure 10-31
Cells with conditional formatting applied.

7. Repeat Steps 2 through 6 to apply any additional conditions.

Clear Conditional Formatting

To clear conditional formats, go to the Home tab and choose Styles>Conditional Formatting>Clear Rules>Clear Rules from Selected Cells.

Another form of conditional formatting is the Data Visualization. With Data Visualizations, you see your data conditions even better in the form of gradient colors, data bars, and icon sets.

Select the cells to which you want to apply formatting and choose Home>Styles>Conditional Formatting. Select from the following options. (Figure 10-32 shows an example of all three data visualizations.)

Figure 10-32
Using data visualizations.

▶ **Data Bars:** A gradient-style bar helps you see the value of a cell relative to other cells. The length of the data bar represents the value in the cell, so a longer bar represents a higher value and a shorter bar represents a lower value. The data bars have six color options designed to match Excel themes.

▶ **Color Scales:** Designed to visually help you understand your data, color scales compare a range of cells by using two colors representing higher or lower values or three colors representing higher, middle, or lower values. The color scale bars come in eight color themes, including red, yellow, and green. You can also create your own scheme by choosing More Rules under the Color Scales options.

▶ **Icon Sets:** Icon sets help you classify data into three, four, or five categories with each icon representing a range of values such as higher, middle, and lower. As shown in Figure 10-33, icon sets include arrows, traffic lights, clocks, and even flags.

Figure 10-33
Select the icon symbol you want to use to represent your data.

Icon Size

The icon size you see depends on the cell font size. You may need to adjust the column width to accommodate the icon.

Managing Large Amounts
of Data

PICTURE YOURSELF ON A WARM SUMMER EVENING, staring up into the constellation, feeling awed at the sheer vastness and the abundance of shining stars you see. Can you count them? Of course, the actual number of stars in the sky remains a great unknown, but we do know they are a seemingly endless bounty like the number of grains of sand on the beach.

Sometimes working with large amounts of data can make you feel like you'll never find your way through it. Fortunately, Excel contains quite a few tools specifically designed to manage volumes of information.

This chapter is about the volume and how you can easily manage all the data whether on a single sheet, on multiple worksheets, or even in multiple workbooks.

Working with Multiple Worksheets

FIRST LET ME CLARIFY a couple of terms. A *worksheet*, sometimes called a spreadsheet, is a collection of cells that can have more than one million rows down and over sixteen thousand rows across. Each cell of each sheet can contain over 32,000 characters.

By default, each time you create a new Excel file, it contains three worksheets. Technically, Excel calls files with multiple sheets workbooks. Think of a workbook as a three-dimensional worksheet. Each workbook, however, can have an almost unlimited number of worksheets, limited only by your computer's memory. The resulting possible number of cells in a single workbook is too huge to even dream about, but the fact remains that you could create a single huge workbook. Realistically, however, you'll probably have a number of different workbooks, each with a number of worksheets.

Excel makes it easy to work with multiple worksheets. You can easily maneuver between the worksheets; insert, delete, move, and copy worksheets; rename the tabs that reference them; and create formulas that reference other worksheets or workbooks.

Moving Between Worksheets

By default, a new blank workbook includes three worksheets named Sheet1, Sheet2, and Sheet3. You can move from worksheet to worksheet using the mouse or the keyboard. With the mouse, click on any desired tab.

If your workbook has more worksheets than you can see at the bottom, click the First, Previous, Next, or Last navigation buttons in the bottom-left corner of the workbook.

You also can use the keyboard to move from worksheet to worksheet. Press Ctrl+Page Up to move to the previous sheet or press Ctrl+Page Down to move to the next sheet.

Inserting Additional Worksheets

If you need extra worksheets in your workbook, you can easily add them. Whenever you save the Excel file, all worksheets in the workbook are saved. Excel provides several methods to insert additional worksheets:

▶ **Choose Home>Cells>Insert (arrow)> Insert Sheet.** Excel automatically inserts a new blank worksheet on top of the currently selected sheet. Excel automatically assigns the next number, such as Sheet4.

▶ **Click the Insert Worksheet tab. It's located after the last named worksheet tab.** (See Figure 11-1.)

▶ **Right-click a worksheet tab and select Insert from the resulting shortcut menu.** The Insert dialog box opens. Choose Worksheet and then click OK.

Insert Worksheet tab

Figure 11-1
Inserting a new worksheet.

Deleting Worksheets

If you have created a worksheet in an Excel file that you no longer need, you can delete it. Deleting unnecessary worksheets can save on file size and make the file quicker to open and close.

Choose Home>Cells>Delete (arrow)>Delete Sheet. If any cells in the selected sheet have data in them, a warning message appears, as shown in Figure 11-2. However, a worksheet with no data in it will not display the warning message. Click the Delete button. Use caution when deleting worksheets. The Undo feature does not work with the Delete Sheet function.

Figure 11-2
Deleting a worksheet.

Renaming Worksheets

Because Excel uses the rather generic naming scheme of Sheet1 or Sheet2, you can more easily identify the type of data each worksheet contains if you give your worksheets more descriptive names. Names for sheets can be up to 31 characters long and are not case sensitive; however, a worksheet name cannot be left blank and cannot include these special characters: – * / \ ? : [ ]. Just follow these steps to rename a worksheet:

1. Click anywhere on the sheet you want to rename.

2. Choose Home>Cells>Format>Rename Sheet. The worksheet tab becomes highlighted. Leave it highlighted so that you can replace it with a new name.

3. Type a unique name for the worksheet, as shown in Figure 11-3. Remember that two worksheets in a single workbook cannot have the same exact name.

Figure 11-3
Renaming a worksheet.

4. Press Enter to accept the change.

Keep the Name Short

Be descriptive, but keep the name short. When you have lots of worksheets with long names, it can be more difficult to maneuver from one to the next.

Copying Worksheets

Excel has a terrific timesaver in that if you need a worksheet similar to one you already have, you can copy the worksheet. Then all you have to do in the new worksheet is modify the parts you need changed. You don't need to start at the beginning. The following steps show you how to copy a worksheet:

1. Click anywhere on the worksheet you want to duplicate.

2. Choose Home>Cells>Format>Move or Copy Sheet. The Move or Copy dialog box appears.

3. Check the Create a Copy check box (see Figure 11-4).

Right-Click Worksheet Tab

Optionally, right-click the worksheet tab and select Move or Copy.

Figure 11-4
Duplicating a worksheet.

4. Select where in the order of the worksheets you want the duplicate sheet placed.

5. Click OK. Excel duplicates the sheet and gives it the same name as the copied sheet and numbers it sequentially.

Move a Worksheet

To move a worksheet, drag the worksheet tab left or right.

Moving Worksheets to a Different Workbook

Although it certainly may be what you need, use caution when you move worksheets to other workbooks. Calculations or charts based on worksheet data might become incorrect when you move the worksheet to another workbook.

Copy and Move Limitation

Because worksheet in Excel 2007 and 2010 have more columns and rows than earlier versions, you cannot copy or move a worksheet created in an Excel 2010 (or 2007) workbook to one created in Excel 2003, XP, or earlier.

---

1. Open both the workbook containing the sheets you want to move and the workbook to which you will move the sheets.

2. Click anywhere on the worksheet you want to move. If you don't see the sheet you want, click the tab scrolling buttons until you see it.

Multiple Worksheets

If you want to move or copy multiple worksheets, hold down the Ctrl key and click additional tabs. If you want to move or copy all the existing worksheets to another workbook, right-click a sheet tab and choose Select All Sheets.

---

3. Choose Home> Cells>Format>Move or Copy Sheet. The Move or Copy dialog box opens.

Right-Click Option

Optionally, right-click a selected tab and choose Move or Copy.

---

4. From the To book drop-down menu, shown in Figure 11-5, select the workbook to which you want to move or copy the sheets.

Figure 11-5
Select the workbook you want to move to.

5. If you want to duplicate the sheets to the other workbook, click the Create a Copy check box.

6. Select where in the order of the existing worksheets you want the moved sheet placed.

7. Click OK. Excel moves or copies the worksheets to the other workbook. In Figure 11-6, the sheet named January was moved from the Book1 workbook to the American Construction Company workbook.

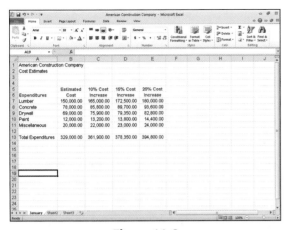

Figure 11-6
Moving a worksheet to a different workbook.

Duplicate Naming Convention

If you opted to copy a sheet to another workbook in which a sheet has the same name, Excel keeps the same name but adds a sequential number to the end.

Hiding Worksheets

A worksheet can be hidden from view but still contain active working formulas and data. Click anywhere on the worksheet that you want to hide and choose Home>Cells>Format>Hide & Unhide>Hide Sheet. Excel hides the worksheet from view. All formula references to a hidden worksheet are still valid even when a worksheet is hidden.

To unhide the worksheet, select Choose Home>Cells>Format>Hide & Unhide>Unhide Sheet. A dialog box like the one in Figure 11-7 appears listing all currently hidden worksheets in the active workbook. Select the worksheet you want to unhide and click OK.

Right-Click Worksheet Tab

Optionally, right-click a worksheet tab and select Hide (or Unhide).

Figure 11-7
Choosing a worksheet to unhide.

Changing Worksheet Tab Colors

Each worksheet tab has its own unique name. Earlier in this chapter, you discovered how you can easily rename sheets. It may be helpful to assign a color to the sheet tabs which can make them easier to locate, especially for a frequently used sheet or in a workbook with lots of worksheets.

To recolor the worksheet tab, click anywhere in that worksheet and choose Home>Cells>Format> Tab Color. The Tab Color gallery that you see in Figure 11-8 appears. Select a color or select No Color to remove a tab color. The color choices you see depend on your current worksheet theme.

Figure 11-8
Assigning colors to worksheet tabs.

Right-Click Worksheet Tab

Optionally, right-click a worksheet tab and choose Tab Color to display a Tab Color gallery.

When a worksheet with a colored tab is the current worksheet, Excel does not display the tab color in full. It displays only a colored line under the tab name. The tab becomes full color when the worksheet is not the active one.

Generating References to Other Worksheets

Sometimes you need to refer to information stored in another worksheet—for example, when you have a workbook with sheets for each company division, along with a worksheet that totals the individual worksheets. You can create a reference in the Totals worksheet that instructs Excel to reference the data in the various monthly worksheets. When you create a reference to different sheet, Excel will use the name of the sheet first, then the cell location. Use the following steps to guide you:

1. Select the cell into which you want to enter a reference.

2. Perform one of the following actions:

   ▶ If you want to display a value located in another cell on the same worksheet, type the equals sign and then the cell address. For example, type =A2. If the value in A2 changes, the cell with the reference to A2 also changes (see Figure 11-9).

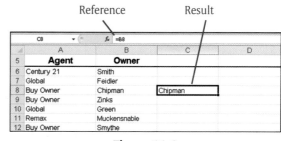

Figure 11-9
Creating a reference to another cell.

   ▶ If you want to display a value located in a cell on a different worksheet but in the same workbook, type the equals sign. Next, click the worksheet tab containing the cell you want to reference and then click the actual cell you want to reference. Press the Enter key. Excel displays the equals sign, the worksheet name, an exclamation point, and the cell reference (see Figure 11-10).

Cross-Referenced Formulas

Formulas referencing other worksheets or other workbooks can also be compound formulas or used in a function.

Figure 11-10
Referencing a cell on another worksheet.

Alternative Method

Optionally, you can manually type the referenced sheet and cell address, but you must be sure to include the exclamation point.

Notice in all of the previous examples, the answer is displayed in the worksheet, but on the Formula bar the originating cell location is displayed. The linked reference is the sheet name followed by an exclamation point and the cell location. If the value in the originating cell changes, the value in the cross reference cell will also change.

Cross-Referencing Other Workbooks

Similar to creating a link to a different worksheet in the current workbook, you can also create links to specific locations in other workbooks. The easiest method to create a workbook link is to have both the origination and the destination workbooks open.

If, when updating links, the originating workbook was renamed, deleted, or moved, an information dialog box will appear notifying you it could not update the link. You have the option of continuing, leaving the data as it was last saved, or clicking an Edit Link button to change the link references.

1. Open the workbook to which you want to refer. For illustration purposes, let's call the file *Original*.

2. Click the desired cell in the workbook where you want to create a reference. Again, as an example, let's call this file *Reference*.

3. In *Reference*, begin the formula or reference with an equals sign.

4. If using a function or formula, enter any portion that you want to precede the cross-reference.

5. Click the cell that you want to reference from *Original*.

6. Finish the remainder of the formula or press the Enter key. Excel displays the equals sign, an apostrophe, and then the *Reference* file name in brackets followed by the worksheet name, a closing apostrophe, an exclamation point, and then the absolute cell reference. For example, [NAMES.xlsx]Sheet1!A2

refers to the value in cell A2 of Sheet1 in the Excel file named NAMES. See Figure 11-11 for an example of a cross-reference.

Figure 11-11

Creating a cross-reference to a different workbook.

Absolute Reference

Excel uses absolute references (with dollar signs) when referring to other workbooks.

When you open a workbook containing a cross-reference, Excel displays a message such as the one shown in Figure 11-12, prompting you with a security warning so it can determine whether to update the cross-referenced cell. Click Enable Content (also seen in Figure 11-12) if you want Excel to check the originating workbook for changes to the referenced cell.

Enable Content button

Figure 11-12

Giving permission to update a cross-reference.

Inserting a Hyperlink

In Chapter 7, "Discovering Word Tools," you saw how you could insert a hyperlink into a Word document which would, when clicked, take you to another document area, another document, an Internet site, or even launch an e-mail. You can accomplish the same task in Excel. Select a cell or graphic object and then choose Insert >Links> Hyperlink. The Insert Hyperlink dialog box appears. If you clicked a blank cell before beginning, in the Text To Display box you can type the text you want the cell to display. If you started with a cell already containing data or an object, you can change the displayed text.

Click ScreenTip

Click the ScreenTip button to enter text you want displayed, such as a prompt or hint that appears whenever the user pauses the mouse over the link.

Select the option you want to use and enter any relevant information. Click OK when you are finished. Figure 11-13 illustrates an Excel worksheet with a hyperlink.

Figure 11-13

An Excel hyperlink.

To remove a hyperlink, right-click the link and select Remove Hyperlink.

Managing Worksheet Views

SOMEONE ONCE WROTE about the importance of seeing and being seen. Although I'm sure that quote referred to people, it also can apply to your Excel worksheets. You need to see them in many contexts. That's what this section does—shows you your worksheets from different perspectives.

Zooming In or Out

The Zoom feature enlarges or shrinks the display of your worksheet to allow you to see more or less of it. Excel can zoom your worksheet in percentages, with the normal display of your worksheet being 100%. Zooming in or out does not affect printing. Chapter 4, "Managing Word Pages," shows you zooming in on a Microsoft Word document.

Choose View>Zoom>Zoom or click the Zoom level button next to the status bar Zoom controls. The Zoom level button displays the current zoom percentage. Select a magnification percentage from the Zoom dialog box. A higher zoom setting makes the text appear larger so you see less on the screen; a lower setting shows more on the screen, but the data appears smaller. Click OK.

Custom Options

Select the Custom option and enter your own setting from 10% to 400%.

You can also use the Zoom control slider to manually set the magnification. Drag the Zoom slider bar to the right to increase magnification or drag it to the left to decrease magnification. Click the Zoom In or Zoom Out buttons on the Zoom control slider, which changes the magnification percentage by 10% for each click of the Zoom In button (see Figure 11-14). The Zoom percentage displays on the Status bar.

Figure 11-14
Zooming in on your data using the Zoom controls.

View Icons

On the Status bar, next to the Zoom controls, you find three View icons you can use to quickly switch among the Normal view, Page Layout view, and Page Break Preview modes.

Changing Worksheet Views

When working with a larger worksheet, it can become difficult to see the entire worksheet on the screen. As you scroll down or across the worksheet, you may lose track of which column or row of data you are entering. Excel contains several tools to help you view your worksheet from different perspectives.

▶ **Page Layout:** Choose View>Workbook Views>Page Layout. As in Figure 11-15, the Page Layout view displays your worksheets on individual pages that correspond to printed pages. A ruler appears on the top and in the header and footer area. See Chapter 12, "Setting Security and Printing Options," for more on headers and footers.

▶ **Normal:** Choose View>Workbook Views>Normal. Excel returns to the default Normal view, which shows one continuous page of columns and rows.

▶ **Page Break Preview:** Choose View>Workbook Views>Page Break Preview. A Welcome to Page Break Preview dialog box appears. Click OK. The Excel mode changes to Page Break Preview, where Excel indicates page breaks with lines (see Figure 11-16). You can drag these lines to modify where pages break. (See Chapter 12 for more on using page breaks.) To return to the Normal view, choose View>Workbook Views>Normal.

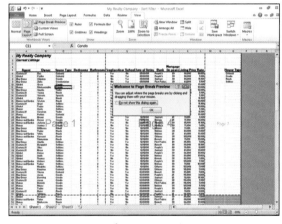

Figure 11-16
Page Break Preview.

Figure 11-15
Page Layout view with headers and footers.

Use Zoom Controls

Use the Zoom controls to increase or decrease magnification.

Hide Message Box

If you do not want to see this dialog box when you enter Page Break Preview, click Do Not Show This Dialog Again.

▶ **Full Screen:** Choose View>Workbook Views>Full Screen. As shown in Figure 11-17, you see only the worksheet itself with its row and column headings, worksheet tabs, and the title bar. The Ribbon, Quick Access Toolbar, and the Status bar are hidden. Press the Escape key. Excel returns to Normal view.

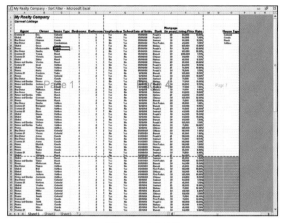

Figure 11-17
Full Screen view.

Freezing Worksheet Titles

When working with a long or wide list, as you add more data you might lose track of which column or row you are entering data into. It would be helpful if you could see which column or row label you are working with. You can freeze the column headings and row labels so they remain visible no matter where you are working in your worksheet.

Choose what you want to freeze:

▶ **Columns:** Select the column to the right of the columns you want to freeze. For example, click cell B1 to freeze only column A.

▶ **Rows:** Select the row below the rows you want to freeze. For example, click cell A4 to freeze rows 1, 2, and 3.

▶ **Columns and rows:** Click the cell below the rows and to the right of the columns you want to freeze. For example, click cell B2 to freeze both column A and row 1.

Choose View>Window>Freeze Panes>Freeze Panes. A thin black line appears to separate the sections. As you see in Figure 11-18, as you scroll down and to the left, row 1 and columns A and B remain visible even though you see rows 40 through 62 in the bottom section and columns G through K on the right. Choose View>Window>Freeze Panes>Unfreeze Panes to remove the freeze from row and column headings.

Figure 11-18
Freezing column titles.

Splitting the Excel Screen

Sometimes you need to see two or more different sections of your worksheet at the same time, but your worksheet is too large to view both sections. Excel includes a feature which allows you to split a window into two or four sections which you can move independently of each other.

Click anywhere in a row and column where you want to split your screen. This is usually somewhere around the middle of the screen. Choose View>Window>Split. Excel splits the window horizontally into two or four panes, each separated from other panes by bars. Each pane has its own set of scroll bars (see Figure 11-19).

Figure 11-19
Splitting a window into multiple panes.

Drag the horizontal split bar up or down, or drag the vertical split bar left or right to resize the window sections, or double-click any part of the bars that divide the panes to remove that particular split.

Choose View>Window>Split again to remove the split.

Hiding Rows and Columns

If you have rows or columns you don't really need to see, or that you don't want to print, you can hide them from view. Hiding them doesn't delete them or make their data inaccessible; it only keeps them out of view. When you hide rows or columns, Excel is actually changing the row height or column width to zero.

Tip

You can hide multiple columns at one time or multiple rows at one time, but you can't hide both columns and rows in a single step.

Select the rows or columns you want to hide and choose Home>Cells>Format>Hide & Unhide>Hide Rows or Hide Columns (see Figure 11-20). Optionally, right-click over a selected column or row and choose Hide.

Select All   Hidden rows   Hidden columns

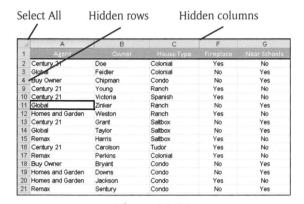

Figure 11-21
Hidden columns or rows.

When you are ready to unhide rows or columns, select the rows or columns on both sides of the hidden rows or columns. If you have hidden column A or row 1, you cannot select columns or rows on both sides. In this situation, click the Select All button to the left of column A and above row 1. Choose Home>Cells>Format>Hide & Unhide>Unhide Rows or Unhide Columns. Again, you can optionally right-click the selected rows or columns and choose Unhide.

Figure 11-20
Select the columns or rows you want to hide.

The selected rows or columns remain hidden. In Figure 11-21, columns D, E & F are hidden from view.

Sorting Data

SOMETIMES WORKSHEETS become quite large, making locating particular pieces of information time-consuming and difficult. If your data is in an array, you may find the data easier to view if it is sorted in a particular manner.

Perhaps you have multiple worksheets, and you want to locate every occurrence of a specific value. Or, maybe you're just a neat freak and want everything to be in a particular order. Excel contains features to help your arrange your worksheets in an easy-to-manage sequence.

Sorting from the Ribbon

Like most Excel tasks, there are two ways to sort your data: the easy way and the powerful way. Sorting from the Ribbon is the easy way, and, although it doesn't provide as many options as the alternative sorting method, you'll find it works for most of your sorting tasks. Just follow these easy steps:

1. For the easiest sorting, create a list in contiguous order and with headings specifying the contents of each column. Figure 11-22 illustrates an ideal data array.

Figure 11-22
Data for sorting.

2. In the column you want to sort by, click any cell containing data. If the data is not in a contiguous list, you must first select the entire list.

Prompt to Include Additional Cells

If Excel finds unselected data in columns next to the selected data, it may prompt you for more information.

3. Choose Data>Sort & Filter>Sort A to Z. (If the current cell contains a value, the button says Sort Smallest to Largest.) Excel sorts the entire list in ascending order. Sorting text data in ascending order sorts text A–Z; sorting numeric information in ascending order sorts low to high (1–10); and sorting dates in ascending order places the earliest date first.

Tip

Excel sorts in the following pattern: numbers, spaces, special characters, including ! " # $ % & ( ) * , . / : ; ? @ [\ ] ^ _ ` { | } ~ + < = > and, finally, alphabetic letters. Blanks are always placed last.

Optionally, choose Data>Sort & Filter>Sort Z to A (or Largest to Smallest). Excel sorts the entire list by descending order. Figure 11-23 shows the House Type column sorted in descending order.

Figure 11-23
Sorting your data.

Working with the Sort Command

Okay, now for the more powerful way of sorting Excel data. The Excel Sort command not only supplies several ways you can sort your data, it provides options for sorting your data horizontally or even whether or not to sort by capitalization. The following steps show you how to use the Sort command:

1. Select or click in the list of data you want to sort.

2. Choose Data>Sort & Filter>Sort. The Sort dialog box opens (see Figure 11-24).

Figure 11-24
The Sort dialog box.

3. If your data includes column headings, make sure the My Data Has Headers option is checked. Excel does not include header rows in the sort process. If the data doesn't include column headings, deselect the option.

4. From the Sort By drop-down menu, select the column by which you want to sort (see Figure 11-24).

5. From the Sort On drop-down menu, choose Values.

6. From the Order drop-down menu, select how you want to sort the data:

   ▶ To sort text values, choose A to Z or Z to A.

   ▶ To sort numeric data, choose Smallest to Largest or Largest to Smallest.

   ▶ To sort by dates, choose Oldest to Newest or Newest to Oldest.

7. Click OK.

You can also sort your data horizontally. Choose Data>Sort & Filter>Sort. Click the Options button and choose Sort Left to Right then click OK. Define your sort choices in the Sort dialog box and click OK.

Sorting by Multiple Criteria

What about those times when, after sorting your data, you have multiples of the same item. For example, if you sort an employee list by last name and you have three employees with the last name Wilson. Well, you can apply a secondary sort, for example on first name. Doing so would then list Barbara Wilson, John Wilson, and then Stephen Wilson. Just follow these steps:

1. Select or click in the list of data you want to sort.

2. Choose Data>Sort & Filter>Sort. The Sort dialog box opens.

3. Select whether to include column headings in the sort.

4. Set up the primary sort criteria as in the previous section.

Sorting Dates

Excel sorts dates formatted with slashes such as 11/22/68, as numeric data. Dates with the day or month spelled out must be sorted differently. See the section, "Sort by Day, Month, or Custom List" later in this chapter.

5. Click the Add Level button.

6. In the Then By section, select the secondary column you want to sort by if two or more items are identical in the first Sort By option (see Figure 11-25).

Figure 11-25
Selecting a second sorting level.

7. Select how you want to sort the second data criteria. Repeat as needed. You can have up to 256 sorting levels.

Delete Sort Level

To delete an entry, select the sort entry and choose Delete Level. You must keep at least one sort entry in the list.

8. Click OK. Excel performs the sort process. Figure 11-26 illustrates data rows sorted first by House Type and then by the number of Bedrooms.

Figure 11-26
Data sorted by multiple criteria.

Ignored Characters

During an Excel sort, apostrophes (') and hyphens (-) are ignored, unless two text strings are the same except for a hyphen. In that situation, the text with the hyphen is sorted as the latter.

Removing Duplicate Records

After sorting your data, you may discover you have some records in the list more than once. You could manually scan the data and delete the extras one by one or, better yet, let Excel remove any duplicate records. Follow these steps:

1. Select or click in the list of data you want to work with.

2. Choose Data>Data Tools>Remove Duplicates. The Remove Duplicates dialog box appears (see Figure 11-27).

Figure 11-27
Easily remove duplicate records.

3. Check or uncheck the columns you want Excel to examine.

4. Click OK. Excel looks for and removes duplicates. A message tells you how many duplicates were removed (if any) and how many unique values remain. In Figure 11-28, you see that five duplicate records were found.

5. Click OK.

Figure 11-28
See how many records Excel removed.

Filtering Data

AFTER YOU CREATE an Excel database and assemble a large amount of data, you probably want to analyze it. You may want to ask yourself questions about your data. "Who are my best customers?" "Which inventory items are provided by a specific supplier and cost less than a certain amount?" "Which employees work the least amount of hours?" Which condos have three bedrooms? Excel includes several tools you can use to answer these questions and study your data so you can make better decisions.

Filtering means that Excel can pull out specific records for review. This provides you with an easy way to break down your data into smaller, more manageable chunks. Filtering does not rearrange your data; it simply temporarily hides records you don't want to review so you can clearly examine those you do.

Creating an AutoFilter

AutoFilter provides a quick and easy way to find and work with a subset of data in a range. A filtered range displays only the rows that meet the criteria you specify for a column. You use the AutoFilter, which includes filtering by selecting from available choices.

Unlike sorting, filtering does not rearrange a range. Filtering temporarily hides rows you do not want displayed. When Excel filters rows, you can edit, format, chart, and print your range subset without rearranging or moving it.

1. After clicking anywhere in your database, choose Data>Sort & Filter>Filter. Excel displays a filter arrow in each database column.

Protected Worksheets

The AutoFilter feature is unavailable for protected worksheets.

---

2. Click the arrow in the column heading from which you want to find a common value. Excel displays a drop-down menu, which includes one of each unique entry (up to 10,000 entries) in the selected column (as you see in Figure 11-29).

Filter arrow

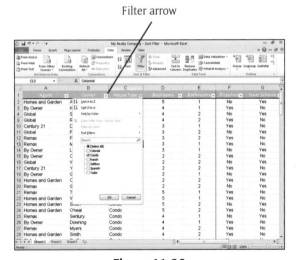

Figure 11-29
Select the item you want to filter.

3. Remove the check mark from Select All. All items become unselected.

4. Click the entry or entries you want to filter and then click OK. Excel displays only the records that match your choice. In Figure 11-30, for example, you see only the Condos. Other record rows are hidden. Also notice that the filter arrows on filtered columns take on a different appearance to indicate that a filter is in use.

Figure 11-30
Filtered data.

From the column containing the filtering you want removed, click the column filter arrow and choose Clear Filter from "field name." If you want to turn off the AutoFilter, choose Data>Sort & Filter>Filter. You can turn the AutoFilter on and off as often as you need to.

Searching for Blank Cells

Suppose you are a coin collector and you have your existing coins and the coins you'd like to obtain all in an Excel database list. One of your columns is for the date you obtained the coins, so for the coins you don't yet have, the date obtained field would be blank. By using the AutoFilter, you can advise Excel to locate only the records where a particular field (whether the house contains a fireplace, in this example) is blank.

Make sure the AutoFilter option is on and your database columns contain filter arrows. Click the arrow in the column heading where you want to find a blank cell. Remove the check mark from Select All and then scroll to the bottom of the list and check the Blanks entry. The Blanks entry only appears if the selected field actually has any blank entries. It should be the only one selected. Click OK, and Excel displays only the records with blank cells in the column you selected, which in Figure 11-31 is the Fireplace column.

Figure 11-31
Locating records with blank data.

Performing a Secondary Filter Selection

Secondary filters are used when you want to be even more specific than with a single filter. With a single filter, you pick, for example, the city of Miami. The secondary filter comes into play when you want to see only the people in Miami with a last name of Schwartz. Here's how you perform a secondary filter selection:

1. Make sure the AutoFilter option is on and your database columns contain filter arrows.

2. Click the column arrow by which you want to filter data first.

3. Choose the data you want to filter. In Figure 11-32, you see only selections that display only the Condos in the House Type column. Note, however, that there are different Agents involved in the Condos.

Figure 11-32
Data filtered using the AutoFilter.

4. To further isolate specific items, click the filter arrow at the top of another column, in this example, Agent.

Additional Filters

Each additional filter is based on the current filter and further reduces the subset of data.

5. Select the field by which you want to perform the second filter. In Figure 11-32, the primary option was to filter by House type of Condo. In Figure 11-33, the data is additionally filtered to show only the By Owner agent.

Figure 11-33
Data filtered twice.

6. Repeat Steps 4 and 5 to further filter by as many fields as necessary.

7. When you're finished working with your filtered data, choose one of these options:

   ▶ To return to the first filter only, click the second filter column arrow and choose Clear Filter from "field name."

   ▶ To return to viewing all records, choose Data>Sort & Filter>Clear.

Don't Mix Data Types

When working with filters, it's best not to mix text, number, and date formats in the same column because only one type of filter command is available for each column. If a mix of formats occurs, the command displayed has the format that is used most frequently.

Choosing Text Comparison Filters

Text comparison is when you specify a range such as "begins with" or "does not equal." Other options might be "exactly" or "contains." Following are the different options:

▶ **Equals or Does Not Equal:** Equals locates all records in which the selected field cells exactly match or don't match the text you specify. For example, if you look for records matching "Chicago," only the records with Chicago appear. Records containing East Chicago, Chicago Hill, Las Vegas, Chicagoan, Seattle, or Boston do not appear. If you chose Does Not Equal you might see East Chicago, Chicago Hill, Las Vegas, Chicagoan, Seattle, or Boston, but not Chicago.

▶ **Begins With or Ends With:** Locates all records in which the selected field cells begin or end with the text you specify. If you chose Begins With, you'll see Chicago, Chicago Hill, and Chicagoan, but not East Chicago, Las Vegas, Seattle, or Boston. If you chose Ends with, you would see the records for Chicago and East Chicago, but not Chicago Hill, Las Vegas, Chicagoan, Seattle, or Boston.

▶ **Contains or Does Not Contain:** Locates all records in which the selected field text contains or doesn't contain the text you specify. The text could be at the beginning, middle, or end of the field cell value.

Click the filter arrow for the text column by which you want to filter data and choose Text Filters. From the following submenu of comparison filters, make a selection. The Custom AutoFilter dialog box you see in Figure 11-34 appears. The comparison filter you selected appears in the Line description box, but you can click the drop-down menu and select a different comparison function. In the first list box on the right, type the data you want to filter and then click the OK button

Figure 11-34
The Custom AutoFilter dialog box.

Choosing Additional Comparison Criteria

When you want your data to meet more than one criterion, Excel can support that as well. For example, you want to locate your clients in Cleveland OR Cincinnati. The OR means that *either* criterion fits what you want. Another example would be if you want to view only the customers in California whose sales are more than a specified amount. In that situation you would use the AND filter. The AND filter specifies that *both* criteria must be met. Take a look at the steps for multiple comparison criteria:

1. Follow the instructions from the previous section "Choosing Text Comparison Filters."

2. Select the And or the Or option.

3. From the drop-down menu, select a second comparison filter.

4. Enter the second comparison filter value. Figure 11-35 shows an example.

5. Click OK to display the filtered records.

Figure 11-35
Choosing a comparison filter.

Use Wildcards

If you need to locate cells that share some of the characters you entered but not others, you can use a wildcard character. Entering one or more question marks finds single characters and entering an asterisk finds any number of characters. For example, if you enter Bos???, you would find Boston, Bosnia, Bosart, and Boshel—any word that begins with Bos but has only six characters.

Reviewing Other Filter Options

Still need more filter options? Excel has plenty of others. You can filter comparison by numbers. For example, you can show the customers who have purchased more than 1,000 units but less than 2,000 units. Filtering by the top ten allows you to show the 10 best (or the 10 worst) territories. Or, you can use filters to display only the employees with the above average work ratings.

Click the filter arrow by which you want to filter and then choose one of the following:

▶ **Filter for Numbers:** Click the filter arrow for the numeric column by which you want to filter data, and then choose Number Filters. A submenu of comparison filters appears. Some of the choices include Equals, Does not Equal, Greater Than, Greater Than or Equal To, Less Than, Less Than or Equal To, and Between (see Figure 11-36). Select the comparison filter you want to use and Excel displays the Custom AutoFilter dialog box. Enter your filter criteria and then click OK.

Figure 11-36
Filtering for number types.

▶ **Filter for Top or Bottom Numbers:** Click Number Filters and choose Top 10. In Figure 11-37, you see the Top 10 AutoFilter dialog box. Select whether you want the Top (highest) or Bottom (lowest) values and, in the second option, select the number of items you want to see (from 1 to 500). In the third option, select whether you want to filter the items by their names or by their percentiles. For example, choose to list the top 10 customers per their sales dollars, or list the top 10% of your customer base. Click OK. Excel displays the records that match your criteria.

Figure 11-37
Filtering for top or bottom values.

▶ **Filter for Above or Below Average Values:** Click Number Filters and choose Above Average or Below Average to filter by numbers that meet either condition. In Figure 11-38, only the records with Ratings above the total average appear.

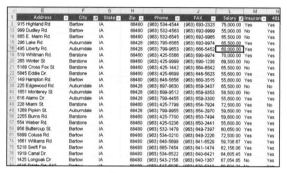

Figure 11-38
Filtering for average values.

Filtering by Date or Time

Another filter option is to filter by date or time. By default, dates in the database are grouped by years, months, and days, in that order. Excel includes two types of date filters: Common and Dynamic. Common filters are those based on comparison operators such as Equal To, Greater Than, Less Than, or Between. Dynamic filters are those for which the criteria can change when you reapply the filter. They include Today, Tomorrow, Next Month, Last Year, and Year-to-Date. Look at the steps needed to filter by a date or a time:

1. Click the filter arrow for the date column by which you want to filter data and choose Date Filters (see Figure 11-39).

Figure 11-39
Available date filters.

2. Select a date filter. If you select a Common filter, you see the Custom AutoFilter dialog box. If you selected a dynamic filter, Excel immediately applies the filter.

Date Range

To filter by a date range, select Between.

---

3. In the box on the right, enter a date or time or, optionally, click the Calendar button to select a date.

4. Click OK. Figure 11-40 shows only those records with dates in 2010.

Figure 11-40
Data filtered by date.

Calendar Year

Years and quarters always start in January of the calendar year.

Splitting Data into Multiple Columns

In Chapter 9, you discovered how you can combine columns using the Excel CONCATENATE function. So if you had a first name (Mary) in column A and a last name (Jones) in column B, you created a formula that resulted in firstname lastname (Mary Jones). Sometimes, you want to break the data down instead of combining it. If you have a column with Mary Jones in it but you really need a column with the first name and another column with the last name, you can have Excel do this task for you.

Look at Figure 11-41. You see data with a combined first and last name. The following steps show you how to break that into two separate columns:

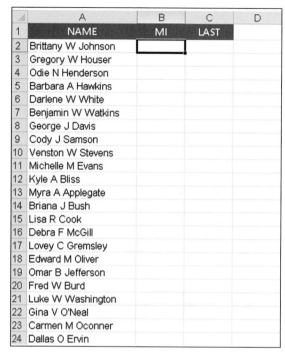

Figure 11-41
Combined data.

1. If necessary, insert blank cells to the left of the cells you want to split. If you will have data in three columns, you must have two blank columns.

2. Select the cells containing the data you want to split into columns.

3. Choose Data>Data Tools>Text to Columns. You see the Convert Text to Columns Wizard.

4. Select Delimited and then click Next.

5. Choose the characters you use to separate your text. In this example, the data is split up by a space, which separates the first and last names, so let's choose space. The preview area shows you how your split data will appear (see Figure 11-42).

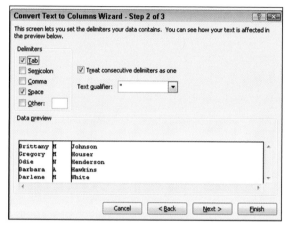

Figure 11-42
The Convert Text to Columns Wizard.

6. Click Next.

7. If you want any specific format for your columns—for example, if you had a ZIP code and you wanted it treated as text instead of numeric or a date as a specific date format—select the column you want formatted and choose a Column Data Format.

8. Click Finish. Excel converts the data into separate columns (see Figure 11-43).

	A	B	C	D
1	NAME	MI	LAST	
2	Brittany	W	Johnson	
3	Gregory	W	Houser	
4	Odie	N	Henderson	
5	Barbara	A	Hawkins	
6	Darlene	W	White	
7	Benjamin	W	Watkins	
8	George	J	Davis	
9	Cody	J	Samson	
10	Venston	W	Stevens	
11	Michelle	M	Evans	
12	Kyle	A	Bliss	
13	Myra	A	Applegate	
14	Briana	J	Bush	
15	Lisa	R	Cook	
16	Debra	F	McGill	
17	Lovey	C	Gremsley	
18	Edward	M	Oliver	
19	Omar	B	Jefferson	
20	Fred	W	Burd	
21	Luke	W	Washington	
22	Gina	V	O'Neal	
23	Carmen	M	Oconner	
24	Dallas	O	Ervin	

Figure 11-43
Separated data.

Use with Caution

This feature isn't perfect. For example, it cannot recognize whether a city (such as New York), includes two words. It puts each word into its own column. You may have to work on the data after you split it up.

Setting Security and Printing
Options

PICTURE YOURSELF AND YOUR FAMILY all snuggled together
sharing the beauty of a blazing fire. You feel safe and warm. As you
share a big bowl of popcorn you reflect how comforting it is, knowing you are sheltered in your home.

To share or not to share. That's what this chapter is about. If you want to
share your workbook with others, you can print it or e-mail a copy of it. If
you don't want to share it, you need to protect your work and keep it safe.

Keeping Workbooks Secure

WORKSHEETS OFTEN CONTAIN numerical information that is confidential in nature, such as financial or payroll data. In today's world of electronic snooping, it's up to you to protect your work against prying eyes. Fortunately, Excel provides a large number of security tools such as password protection, hiding sensitive worksheet areas, or locking data against unwanted changes.

Hiding a Workbook

Suppose you are working on a payroll benefits report and nosy Ned approaches to ask you a question. You don't want him to see your work, so you need to quickly hide it from his view. To shelter your work from curious onlookers, you simply choose View>Window>Hide. Excel hides the current workbook, leaving the Excel program open and visible. If you have another workbook open, you see that workbook but not the hidden workbook.

To redisplay the workbook, choose View> Windows>Unhide. (If no workbooks are hidden, the Unhide button is unavailable.) Excel displays the Unhide dialog box listing all hidden workbooks, as you see in Figure 12-1. Select the workbook to unhide and click OK.

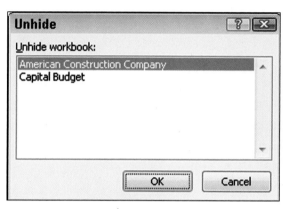

Figure 12-1
Redisplaying a hidden workbook.

Minimize All Windows

Press the Windows key plus the M key to quickly minimize all open items and display the Windows desktop.

Inspecting for Private Information

In Chapter 7, "Discovering Word Tools," you discovered the Document Inspector, which searched through Word documents for metadata. Excel also provides the Document Inspector which can help remove hidden information that you might not want others to see. Just follow these steps:

1. Save the workbook and then click the File tab. From the Info section, click the Check for Issues button and choose Inspect Document. The Document Inspector dialog box appears.

2. Deselect any option you do not want to check and then click Inspect. Excel inspects the document for the selected information.

3. When the inspection is complete, the Document Inspector reappears with information as in Figure 12-2.

Figure 12-2
Remove the items you don't want in the file.

4. Click the Remove All button next to any option you want removed. Excel removes the selected data. After removing the data, the Remove All button next to the option disappears.

No Undo

You cannot undo some changes done with the Document Inspector.

5. Repeat Step 4 for any additional items you want to remove.

6. Click Close, and then click the File tab to return to the workbook.

7. Resave your file.

Protecting Worksheets

You will probably want to ensure that no one can either accidentally or intentionally make unauthorized changes to your data. Excel provides protection at several different levels including protecting the worksheet, specific cells of the worksheet, or the entire workbook.

1. Click anywhere on the sheet that you want to protect and then choose Review>Changes> Protect Sheet. The Protect Sheet dialog box appears, as shown in Figure 12-3.

Figure 12-3
Locking your sheet against unwanted changes.

2. Make sure the option Protect Worksheet and Contents of Locked Cells is checked.

3. Optionally, in the Password to Unprotect Sheet text box, type a password. For privacy reasons, only a series of dots appears. Passwords are case-sensitive.

4. From the Allow All Users of the Worksheet To box, select any options a user is allowed to change without unprotecting the worksheet.

5. Click OK.

6. If you generated a password, a Confirm Password dialog box appears. Retype the password and then click OK again.

When users attempt to change a locked cell, they see an error message such as the one shown in Figure 12-4.

Figure 12-4
No access is allowed to locked cells in a protected worksheet.

Unlocking Cells

You may have a worksheet in which you want only yourself or others to enter data in specific cells and to not have access to formulas or other definite data. You can designate the cells you want editable and leave the remainder of the worksheet protected.

Select the cells you want users to be able to modify and choose Home>Cells>Format>Lock Cell (see Figure 12-5). Because, by default, Excel locks all cells, choosing this option turns the Lock Cells option off. Click the option again to relock the cells again. Protect the worksheet to protect all but the unprotected cells.

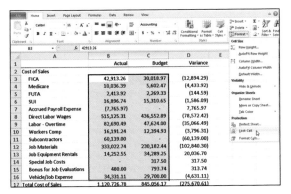

Figure 12-5
Selecting cells you want to unprotect.

Optional Method

Optionally, select Home>Cells>Format> Format Cells, which displays the Format Cells dialog box. Click the Protection tab and deselect the Locked option. Click OK.

Hiding Cell Formulas

You've seen how you can keep others from changing cells by protecting the worksheet, but they can still view the cell contents and formulas. Excel provides a feature with which you can hide the formula so that only the result in the cell is visible. Select the cells containing formulas or information you want to hide. Choose Home>Cells>Format>Format Cells. This displays the Format Cells dialog box. Click the Protection tab and select the Hidden option. Click OK and then protect the worksheet.

In Figure 12-6, although you see the results of the formula in cell B17, the formula bar does not display the actual formula.

No formula seen

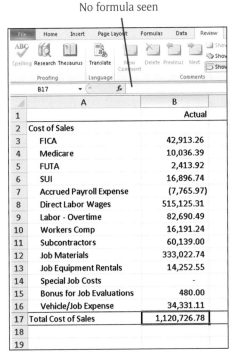

Figure 12-6
Displaying only the formula result, not the actual formula.

Hide Cell Contents

If you want to hide the cell value, color the font white. Choose Home>Font>Font Color.

Marking a Workbook as Final

To protect your workbook against accidental changes, Excel, like Word, includes a feature called Mark as Final. Marking the workbook as final is similar to placing the workbook into a read-only state in that the workbook cannot be changed.

Choose the File tab and from the Info section, click the Protect Workbook button. Choose Mark as Final. Click OK at the acknowledgement message that appears. Excel saves the file and displays a confirmation message. Click OK then click the File tab to return to the workbook. The words Read-Only appear next to the file name on the Title bar (see Figure 12-7). Also notice that all items on the Ribbon are grayed out and unavailable.

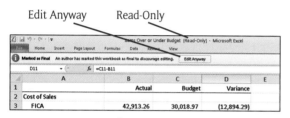

Figure 12-7
Changes cannot be made to a file marked as final.

Marking the workbook as final disables every option in the Ribbon that could change the workbook in any way. The Mark as Final feature is designed to prevent accidental changes and is not permanent. If you find you need to make changes to the workbook, click the Edit Anyway button.

Assigning a File Password

Another method to protect your workbook is applying a password to keep others from even opening the workbook. You can also apply a password to allow them to view it but not make any changes, anywhere in the entire workbook. This type of password protection, called file-level protection, is accomplished through the Save As dialog box. Follow these steps to assign file-level passwords:

1. Choose File>Save As, which displays the Save As dialog box.

2. Click the Tools button and then select General Options. Excel provides two levels of password protection. You can use either or both password options.

3. Type a password in the Password to Open text box (see Figure 12-8). The Password to Open box prevents unauthorized users from even opening the workbook.

Figure 12-8
Assigning passwords to protect the file.

4. Optionally, type a password in the Password to Modify text box. The Password to Modify box prevents users, once the workbook is open, from making any changes.

Read-Only Recommendation

Optionally, check the Read-Only Recommended option to recommend (not require) that the users open the file as read-only, which means before they can save the file, they must assign it a different file name or folder.

When users attempt to open the password-protected file, they see the Password dialog box shown in Figure 12-9. Type the password, and then click OK. If prompted, type the password to allow modifications and click OK. The protected file opens.

Figure 12-9
Enter the password to access the file.

5. Click OK.

6. Retype the password to open, and then click OK. Retype the password to modify, and then click OK.

7. Click Save and then click Yes if you're prompted to overwrite the file.

Checking for Errors

BEFORE YOU PRINT or give your Excel file to someone else, you should check it for spelling errors. You want to eliminate typos that can scream out to the world, "I can't spell." Excel includes a built-in dictionary you can use to check your workbooks for misspellings; however, it can't read your mind, so if you type too instead of two, Excel probably won't indicate that as an error. But, combine the spell check with careful proofreading on your part, and you'll find it becomes a very helpful tool.

Spell Check

Spell Check reviews all cell values, comments, embedded charts, text boxes, buttons, and headers and footers, but it does not check protected worksheets, formulas, or text that results from a formula.

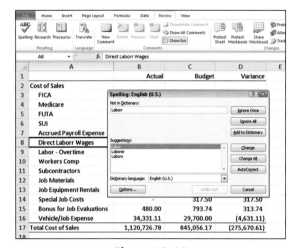

Figure 12-10

Using spell check to improve your worksheet.

Keyboard Shortcut

Optionally, press F7 to launch the Spell Check.

Choose Review>Proofing>Spelling. If there are no errors in the worksheet, a message box appears advising you the spell check is complete; otherwise it displays the Spelling dialog box seen in Figure 12-10, referencing the first error. Choose one of the following:

▶ **Change or Change All:** Choose one of the suggestions; then, click Change to change just this incident of the spelling mistake or select Change All if you think you could have made the mistake more than once.

▶ **AutoCorrect:** Have Excel, in future workbooks, automatically correct the mistake with the selected replacement.

▶ **Ignore Once:** Click this button if you don't want to change the spelling of the highlighted instance of the spelling.

▶ **Ignore All:** Click this button if you don't want to change the spelling of any identical instances of the spelling.

▶ **Add to Dictionary:** Add a word, such as a proper name or medical or legal term, to Excel's built-in dictionary so that Excel won't flag it as a potential error in the future.

If, when you began the spell check, the current cell was not at the beginning of the workbook, Excel asks you whether to check the beginning of the worksheet. When the spell check is complete, a dialog box notifies you. Click OK.

Using Find and Replace

THE EXCEL FIND AND REPLACE feature lets you locate specific worksheet text or formulas and optionally replace the found data with something different. The Find feature can search through formulas, values, or comments. If you select formulas, the Find feature will look through both the underlying formulas and the values for the selected data. If you select values, Excel will look only in the results, not in the formulas. If you select comments, Excel will look only in comments.

Searching for Data

Especially with large workbooks, sometimes it's difficult to locate specific entries. You can let Excel locate the data for you. Choose Home>Editing>Find & Select>Find or just press Ctrl+F. The Find and Replace dialog box appears. In the Find What box, enter the value or word you want to locate.

Click the Options button and specify any desired options (see Figure 12-11):

Figure 12-11
Specify where and what to search.

▶ **Within:** Search just the current worksheet or the entire workbook. By default, Excel searches only the current worksheet.

▶ **Search:** Select whether to search first across the rows first, or down the columns first.

▶ **Look in:** Select whether you want to search through the values or formula results, through the actual formulas, or if you want to look in the comments.

Finding Cell Addresses

Select Formulas when you are looking for a formula that references a specific cell address.

▶ **Match case:** Check this box if you want your search to be case-specific (for example, Daniel instead of DANIEL or daniel).

▶ **Match entire cell contents:** Check this box if you want your search results to only list only the items that exactly match your search criteria.

Click the Find Next button. Excel jumps to the first occurrence of the match. If this is not the entry you are looking for, click the Find Next button again. Excel advises you if it does not locate the data you are searching for. Click the Close button when you have located the entry you want.

Optionally, you can locate all occurrences of the data you want to locate. In the Find and Replace dialog box, click the Find All button. The Find and Replace dialog box expands as you see in Figure 12-12, showing a list of each cell entry that contains your data. You can click any entry to select that cell.

Resize handle

Figure 12-12
See all occurrences of found data at once.

Replacing Cell Data

Excel can locate specific data for you and automatically replace it with different data. Choose Home>Editing>Find & Select>Replace, which displays the Find and Replace dialog box, with the Replace tab on top (see Figure 12-13).

Figure 12-13
The Replace tab.

Type the data you want to replace in the Find What text box. Next, type the replacement data in the Replace with text box. If desired, click the Options button for more Find options. The options that appear on the expanded Replace tab are the same as those on the expanded Find tab. Click Find Next to begin the search. Excel locates the first occurrence of the selected text.

Click Replace if you want to replace the found data with the replacement data. Excel will make the replacement and proceed to the next occurrence; or, click Replace All to have Excel replace all occurrences of the original data with the replacement data. Excel notifies you of the total number of occurrences.

When you're finished, click the Close button.

Adjusting Page Layout

WITH JUST A SINGLE CLICK, you can print your worksheet. But before you print it, you might want to specify what paper size you want to use, how large you want the margins, and whether or not to print the gridlines. You might also only print a portion of the worksheet instead of printing it in its entirety.

Managing Manual Page Breaks

As you have probably already noticed, when you have more data on your worksheet than will fit on a printed page, Excel automatically starts a new page for you. Excel indicates page breaks as dotted lines vertically and horizontally on the screen. You can, however, tell Excel how to manage these page breaks. The easiest way to manage page breaks is through Page Break Preview.

Choose View>Workbook Views>Page Break Preview. Click OK at the Welcome to Page Break Preview message box. Your worksheet appears in Page Break Preview mode and shows blue dotted lines at the natural page breaks (see Figure 12-14).

Hide Message Box

To hide future occurrences of the Welcome to Page Break Preview box, check Do Not Show This Dialog Again.

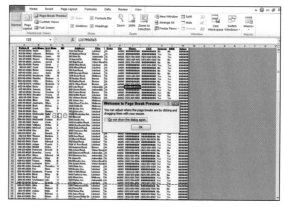

Figure 12-14
Viewing page breaks.

To set page breaks manually, position your mouse over any blue dotted line. The mouse pointer turns into a double-headed arrow, and you can drag the line until it is in the position where you want the page to break. If you drag the page break so the page is longer, Excel scales the page to fit when printing. Manual page breaks appear as solid blue lines.

When you are finished creating manual page breaks, choose View>Workbook Views>Normal.

Specifying a Print Area

When printing, Excel assumes you want to print the entire worksheet area, or just specified pages. If you only want to print a portion of the sheet, you need to specify a specific print range, called the *print area*. This is especially useful if you have several different tables in your worksheet and you only want to print one of them. Setting the print range is a matter of selecting the range and then issuing the command to make that range the print area. Just follow these steps:

1. Highlight the area you want to print.

2. Choose Page Layout>Page Setup>Print Area>Set Print Area. Dotted lines appear around the print area. When you print the worksheet, only the area contained within the dotted lines prints (see Figure 12-15).

To reset Excel to print the entire worksheet, choose Page Layout>Page Setup>Print Area>Clear Print Area.

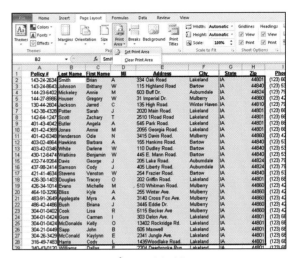

Figure 12-15

Setting the area you want to print.

Setting the Paper Orientation and Size

If your worksheet uses quite a few columns, you might want to change the orientation or paper size. The default size is 8 1/2×11-inch paper in portrait orientation (the short side at the top and bottom). Changing to landscape orientation will print with the long edge of the paper at the top and bottom.

To select the paper orientation, choose Page Layout>Page Setup>Orientation and then select whether you want Portrait or Landscape orientation.

To change the paper size, choose Page Layout>Page Setup>Size. From the drop-down menu of paper sizes that appears, select a paper size. The paper-size choices you see depend on the currently selected printer. The two most common US choices are Letter, which is 8.5×11 inches, and Legal, which is 8.5×14 inches (see Figure 12-16).

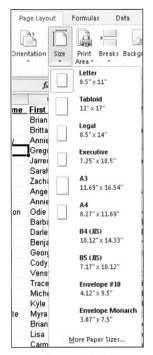

Figure 12-16
Choosing a paper size.

More Paper Sizes

From the Size list, click the More Paper Sizes option to open the Page Setup dialog box. From there you can select additional paper sizes.

Shrinking Worksheets to Fit

Instead of struggling with resizing columns and fonts to make your worksheet fit on a certain number of pages, Excel allows you to scale your document. Scaling makes Excel resize the print area as

needed to fit in the specified number of pages. You can also manually tell Excel to shrink the worksheet by a percentage amount. For example, your worksheet prints on two pages, but there are only three rows on the second page. You can tell Excel to squeeze it just enough so it fits on a single page. Just follow these steps:

Use Minimal Shrinking

Don't try to shrink your document too much. Because Excel shrinks the font, trying to fit too much on a page can make the document typeface too small to read.

---

1. Choose Page Layout>Scale to Fit.

2. From the Width drop-down menu, select the number of pages wide you want to print (see Figure 12-17).

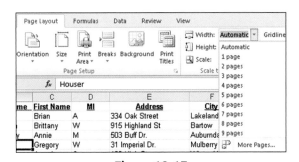

Figure 12-17
Tell Excel how to shrink your document.

3. From the Height drop-down menu, select the number of pages wide you want to print.

Change Scale

Optionally, in the Scale text box, enter a percentage to reduce or enlarge the document. Values range from 10 to 400.

Setting Page Margins

By default, Excel uses a top and bottom margin of .75 inch and left and right margins of .70 inch. You can change these margins to meet your needs. You can select from several predefined settings or you can create your own custom margins. Follow these steps:

1. Choose Page Layout>Page Setup>Margins. Figure 12-18 shows a list of margin options.

Figure 12-18
Select from the margin options.

2. Select from the margin options shown or choose Custom Margins to open the Page Setup dialog box (see Figure 12-19) that enables you to set your own margin options.

Figure 12-19
The Page Setup dialog box.

Center to a Page

From the Page Setup dialog box, click the option Horizontally and/or the option Vertically in the Center on Page section to center the worksheet on the page, regardless of the margins.

Indicating Repeating Rows and Columns

In Chapter 11, "Managing Large Amounts of Data," you learned how to freeze worksheet titles so they remained on the screen even when you scrolled to other areas of the worksheet. If your worksheet will be more than one printed page in height or width, you may want to print one or more rows or columns on each page—in effect, "freezing" titles for each page. To specify which rows and columns should be repeated on each page, follow these steps:

1. Choose Page Layout>Page Setup>Print Titles. The Page Setup dialog box opens.

2. On the Sheet tab, type a dollar sign ($) followed by the row numbers or column letters you want to print as titles in the Print Titles section. Entering $1:$1, as you see in Figure 12-20, repeats rows 1 and 2 at the beginning of each page. If you want a specific column on each page, enter $A:$A (or whatever columns you want) in the Columns to repeat at left box.

3. Click OK.

Collapse Dialog Button

Click the Collapse Dialog button on the right to collapse the Page Setup dialog box so you can select the rows or columns you want to include. Click the button again to return to the Page Setup dialog box.

Figure 12-20

Specifying which columns and rows to print on every page.

Printing Gridlines and Headings

Although by default you see them on your screen, Excel does not print the gridlines that divide the rows and columns. The same is true for the row and column headings. It would be extremely difficult to tell where Column D is if it wasn't referenced at the top. Sometimes you want to print the gridlines or the row and column headings so while viewing the printout, you don't have to rely on any borders you've added.

Choose Page Layout>Sheet Options and select from the following options:

- ▶ **Gridlines:** Check the Print option to print the gridlines surrounding each cell in the worksheet. By default, the Gridlines View option is checked. If you don't want to see the gridlines while you're working on the worksheet, uncheck this item.

- ▶ **Headings:** Check the Print option to print the row numbers or column letters around the worksheet. Figure 12-21 illustrates a worksheet as it would look printed with gridlines and row and column headings.

Change Gridline Color

By default, gridlines are a lighter shade of gray. You can change the gridline color by choosing File>Options. Click the Advanced section and scroll down to the Display options for this worksheet: section. Click the Gridline color arrow and select a different gridline color.

Figure 12-21
A worksheet with gridlines and headings.

Working with Headers and Footers

HEADERS AND FOOTERS are simply text that appears either at the top (header) or bottom (footer) of every page. The type of information you might include in a header or footer might be a report title, the current date, page number, or file name. You typically manage headers and footers through the Page Layout View.

Adding a Standard Header and Footer

You can select from one of the predefined headers and footers or you can create your own. The easiest method is to pick from one of the predefined headers and footers.

1. Choose View>Workbook Views>Page Layout. You see the header area of your worksheet.

2. You may have to scroll to the top of the page where you see the Header area. Headers and Footers are divided into three sections: Left, Center, and Right.

Footer Instead of Header

If you want to work on the Footer, click Header & Footer Tools Design>Navigation> Go to Footer.

---

3. Click in the header section where you want to work (see Figure 12-22). Excel also now displays a Header & Footer Tools Design tab.

Figure 12-22
Click the placeholder text to add a header.

4. Choose Header & Footer Tools Design>Header & Footer>Header (or Footer). A list of predefined headers (or footers) appears, as you see in Figure 12-23.

Figure 12-23
Selecting a predefined header.

5. Select the predefined option you want to use.

The Options group of the Header & Footer Tools Design tab supplies other choices you might want applied to your header or footer. Take a look at each of them (Figure 12-24):

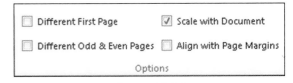

Figure 12-24
Setting options for a header or footer.

▶ **Different First Page:** If you choose this option, Excel won't print the header or footer on the first page.

▶ **Different Odd & Even Pages:** Choose this option if you want a header or footer for the odd-numbered pages of the document different from the one that prints on the even-numbered pages.

▶ **Scale with Document:** This option is selected by default and tells Excel to use the same font size and scaling as the worksheet. If you want the header and footer font size and scaling independent of the worksheet scaling, clear this check box.

▶ **Align with Page Margins:** Choose this option to align the header and footer with the left and right margins of the worksheet. If this is unchecked, the header and footer margins print independently of the worksheet margins.

Creating Custom Headers and Footers

If none of the predefined headers or footers meets your needs, you can easily create your own. While in Page Layout View, choose the desired header or footer section in which you want to work. Type the text you want for the header (or footer), which, as you see in Figure 12-25, you can format just as you would any cell data. You can also choose from any options in the Header & Footer Elements group:

▶ **Page Number:** Insert a code that indicates the page number.

▶ **Number of Pages:** Insert a code that indicates the total number of pages.

Adding Static Text

You can add text to the Page text. For example, "Page &[Page] of &[Pages]" will print "Page 3 of 5" or "Page 1 of 2".

▶ **Current Date or Current Time:** Insert the print date or time of day.

▶ **File Path, File Name, or Sheet Name:** Include file information.

▶ **Picture:** Insert a graphic image such as a company logo.

▶ **Format Picture:** Resize, rotate, or crop a header or footer graphic image.

To continue editing the worksheet, when you are finished working in your header or footer, click a cell outside the header or footer area.

Figure 12-25
Creating your own header or footer.

Printing Your Worksheet

WHEN YOU FINISH COMPILING your worksheet, you'll probably want to print a hard copy or e-mail a copy to someone. Once you have specified any print specifications and options, you can print the worksheet with only a couple of mouse clicks.

Previewing Your Work

You may want to preview the worksheet on the screen before you print, just to make sure you have all the options set correctly. Using the Print Preview feature can save lots of paper by allowing you to see the worksheet on your screen before actually printing it to paper. The following steps walk you through the Print Preview process:

1. Click the File tab and from the Backstage view that appears, choose Print. A print settings section appears on the left and a preview of the worksheet appears on the right.

Keyboard Shortcut

Optionally, press Ctrl+F2 to display the Print preview in Backstage view.

---

2. From the preview area (seen in Figure 12-26), select from the following options.

Previous Page   Next Page

Zoom to Page   Show Margins

Figure 12-26
Taking a sneak peak with Print Preview.

▶ If you have multiple pages, click in the number box and enter the page you want to see, then press Enter; optionally, click the Next Page or Previous Page buttons.

▶ Use the Zoom to Page button in the lower-right to enlarge or reduce the view.

▶ Click the Show Margins button to display or hide the margin lines.

Don't Try to Read!

Don't strain your eyes trying to read the text in the Preview window. You are looking at the overall perspective here, not necessarily the individual cell contents. You cannot edit the worksheet cell contents while in Print Preview mode.

---

3. If you're ready to print your worksheet, continue to the next section, but if you want to return to the worksheet view, click the File tab.

Printing a Worksheet

When your worksheet is complete and you've reviewed it for any changes, you may want to make a hard copy of it to file away or to share with others. Click the File tab and from the Backstage view that appears, choose Print. A print settings section appears on the left (Figure 12-27) and a preview of the worksheet appears on the right. Let's take a look at a few of the print settings:

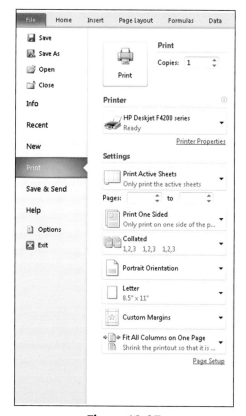

Figure 12-27
The Print window contains many options.

▶ **Copies:** Select the number of copies you want to print.

▶ **Printer:** If you are connected to more than one printer, from the Printer list, you can select which printer you want to use.

▶ **Settings:** The first option allows you to specify whether to print the entire worksheet as determined by the print area or whether to print only specific pages or a selected area. If you want to print only certain pages, enter into the Pages text box, the page numbers separated by a comma or a dash. For example to print only the first three pages, enter 1, 2, 3 or 1-3. Other choices include settings such as margins, orientation, paper size or collating options. The final option is for document scaling.

Choose the options you want and then click the Print button to begin printing.

E-Mailing Workbooks

If you have e-mail access, you can send a workbook directly to another person. Excel copies the workbook contents as an attachment to an e-mail message. Recipients must have Excel installed on their systems to open the workbook file. Although many e-mail applications work fine with this feature, Office works best with Outlook or Windows Mail.

With the workbook open and ready to send, click the File tab and choose Save & Send>Send using E-mail. Then click the Send as Attachment button. Excel launches your e-mail application with the workbook listed as an attachment. Type the recipients e-mail address or click the To button to select from your Outlook Contact List (See Chapter 21, "Working with Outlook Contacts"). Work automatically adds the workbook title as the message subject, but you can change it. Optionally, type a message in the Message body (See Figure 12-28). Click the Send button when you are finished.

Figure 12-28
E-mailing an Excel workbook.

Generating
Excel Charts

PICTURE YOURSELF TRYING TO WORK on a jigsaw puzzle without the box to show you the overall picture. Without seeing the complete picture, the pieces may not come together as you think. It's the same with a chart. Whoever said a picture is worth a thousand words certainly could have been referring to a chart.

Besides, looking at raw data can be boring, misleading, and it's often taken out of context. Everyone likes looking at pictures more than looking at raw data. Charts, sometimes referred to as graphs, provide an effective way to represent your worksheet data by making the associations between numbers easier to see. The chart turns numbers into shapes and enables you to compare the shapes to each other.

Whatever the idea you are trying to convey, charts make it easier. Charts let you almost effortlessly get your thoughts across, and, because different charts may cause you to draw varied conclusions, they may also stimulate questions about your data.

In time past, you've probably used graph paper and spent many hours trying to draw a chart. You'll really welcome the ease with which you can create dozens of chart styles using your Excel data. And you don't have to draw anything. With just a few mouse clicks and a couple of decisions on your part, you have a two- or three-dimensional data diagram.

Creating a Basic Chart

EXCEL PROVIDES TWO METHODS for putting your data into a chart. The first method, which is the really quick way, involves telling Excel where your data is located and pressing a single key on the keyboard. Excel creates a chart that you can then edit or move. Take a look at the first method and the components of a chart.

Editing the Chart

Throughout this chapter you learn how to edit the look and style of a chart.

The steps are very simple. First, select the data (sequential or nonsequential) you want to plot in the chart. See Figure 13-1, in which cells A2 through D6 are selected as an example of sequential data for a chart.

	A	B	C	D	E	F
1	**2009 Sales by Region**					
2	All Colors	Jan	Feb	Mar	Total	
3	East	30	34	13	77	
4	West	26	30	12	68	
5	North	16	9	32	57	
6	South	28	38	15	81	
7	Total	100	111	72	283	
8						
9						

Figure 13-1
Selecting your chart data.

Don't Include Totals

Typically, if you are selecting values such as monthly figures, you don't want to include totals in your chart.

Second, press the F11 key. Excel immediately adds a new sheet called Chart1 to your workbook with the data plotted into a column chart. Each subsequent chart page is numbered sequentially such as Chart2, Chart3, and so forth.

Different Keyboards

Some newer keyboards use a different function for the F11 key. If your F11 key does not produce a chart, use the Insert tab as explained in the next section.

To modify the chart, you first need to know the various components involved in a chart. Figure 13-2 shows you the various components that can make up a chart, and Table 13-1 identifies each of those components.

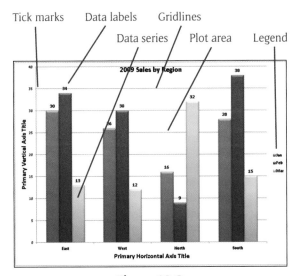

Tick marks   Data labels   Gridlines

Data series   Plot area   Legend

Figure 13-2
Excel chart elements.

Table 13-1 Chart Components

Component	Description
Title	A descriptive name for the overall chart. By default, titles are not added in a basic chart, but you can add them later manually or by using the Chart Wizard.
Horizontal or Category Axis	Column or row headings from your selected data, which Excel uses for Category axis names. In a column chart, the categories display along the bottom. In other charts (such as a bar chart), the category axis displays along the left side.
Horizontal Axis Title	A descriptive name for the Category axis. By default, a category label is not added in a basic chart, but you can add one later manually or with the Chart Wizard.

Component	Description
Category	A single grouping of data on the Category axis. The Category is identified in the legend.
Vertical or Value Axis	A scale representing the zero or the lowest and highest numbers in the plotted data. The Value axis is usually located on the left side on a column chart or on the bottom on a bar chart.
Vertical Axis Title	A descriptive name for the values. By default, a vertical axis label is not added in a basic chart, but you can add one later manually or by using the Chart Wizard.
Legend	The box, usually located on the right, identifies the patterns or colors that are assigned to the chart data series. Notice in Figure 13-3 how the legend explains that one color represents January, another color is for February, and the third color is for March.
Tick marks	The small extensions of lines that appear outside of the gray area that represent divisions of the value or category axis.
Gridlines	These lines extend from the tick marks across the chart area to allow you to easily view and evaluate data.
Series	Excel uses the worksheet cell values to generate the series. Each element, called a data marker, represents a single *(continued)*

Component	Description
	worksheet cell value. Related data markers make up a data series and have the same pattern or color. In Figure 13-4, you can see the comparison of the spreadsheet data to the y-axis and the series values.
Plot area	The background that represents the entire plotted chart area.
Data labels	An optional display of the series numeric values.

Figure 13-3
A chart legend.

Corresponding data

Figure 13-4
Data as displayed in a data series.

Inserting a Chart

THE SECOND TECHNIQUE you can use for creating a chart allows you to set a couple of options as you create the chart. You get to determine where you want the chart and which chart type you want.

When you insert a chart, you can create the chart on its own sheet such as you discovered in the previous section, or you can tell Excel to place the chart on top of the sheet with the data. Excel calls this an embedded chart. No matter where you place your chart, the data is tied to the chart, so if the data changes, so does the chart. Here are the necessary steps:

1. Select the data you want to plot in the chart.

2. Choose Insert>Charts, and click the chart style you want which displays the chart type gallery. Excel can create many chart types;

each compares data in a different manner (see Figure 13-5). Some of the most commonly used chart types include the following:

Figure 13-5
Select the chart type appropriate for your data.

▶ **Column:** Column charts compare values to categories using a series of vertical columns to illustrate the series.

▶ **Bar:** Bar charts, like column charts, compare values to categories but use a series of horizontal bars to illustrate the series.

▶ **Line:** Line charts are similar to bar charts but use dots to represent the data points and lines to connect the data points.

▶ **Pie:** This chart compares parts to a whole. Usually a pie chart has only one data series. Figure 13-6 illustrates data appropriate for a pie chart.

Figure 13-6
Pie chart data.

▶ **Area:** Area charts display the trend of each value, usually over a specified period of time.

▶ **Scatter:** These charts include two value axes, one showing a set of numerical data along the x-axis and the other showing data along the y-axis.

▶ **Surface:** This shows trends in values in a continuous curve.

▶ **Doughnut:** This displays data similarly to a pie chart; it compares parts to a whole but contains multiple series.

▶ **Stock:** Stock charts are usually (but not exclusively) used to illustrate the fluctuation of stock prices. In a stock chart, the data order is very important and usually the row headings are High, Low, and Close (or Open, High, Low, and Close). See Figure 13-7 for an example of a stock chart.

Figure 13-7
Easily track stock progress with a stock chart.

▶ **Radar:** This displays changes in values relative to a center point by comparing the cumulative values of multiple data series.

▶ **Bubble:** These charts are similar to scatter charts but compare three sets of values by displaying a series of circles.

▶ **Cylinder, Cone, and Pyramid:** Excel uses these three chart types to create a column or bar chart using three-dimensional cylindrical, conical, or pyramid shapes.

3. Choose a chart subtype. Depending on the chart type, some chart subtypes show the data series next to each other; others show the data elements stacked on top of each other. Some charts are two-dimensional, and others are three-dimensional. As you see in Figure 13-8, Excel creates the chart on the worksheet where your data resides. The chart is an object on the sheet and floats on top of the sheet. You will discover later in this chapter how to resize, modify, or move the chart. Also, notice in Figure 13-8 that three new Chart Tools tabs appear on the Ribbon.

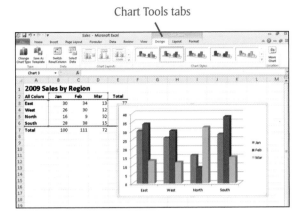

Chart Tools tabs

Figure 13-8
Creating an Excel chart.

Multiple Charts

Workbooks can contain multiple charts. Excel saves all charts as part of the workbook.

Changing the Chart Options

YOU JUST DISCOVERED how simple it is to create a chart. But you probably will want to enhance your chart to improve its appearance. Some of the items you can change include the size, style, color, and placement.

However, like many other Excel features, you must select the area you want to change before you can change it. When a chart is on the same page as the data, and the chart is selected, you see eight dotted handles around the outer edge of the chart as well as a thick colored line. Each chart, no matter where it resides, has two windows. The outer window is a frame in which the chart appears. When a chart is on a sheet by itself, that frame is the entire sheet. When the chart is an object on a worksheet, the frame appears as the box that surrounds the chart.

Click anywhere on the chart to select it, or click outside of the chart to deselect it. If a chart is on its own sheet, you don't need to select it. Just having the chart displayed by clicking the sheet tab makes it eligible for modifications.

Resizing a Chart

When a chart appears on the same page as the worksheet, it may be too small to read the data correctly, or it may be so large that it covers the worksheet data. Either way, it's easy to resize a chart.

Select the chart which displays the eight selection handles. Position your mouse pointer over one of the handles. The mouse pointer changes to a double-headed arrow as you see in Figure 13-9. Drag the handle and you see a dotted line that indicates the new chart size. When you release the mouse button, the chart is resized.

Figure 13-9
Changing the chart size.

Constrain Size Ratio

Hold down the Shift key while you drag the chart to maintain the height-to-width chart ratio.

Changing the Chart Type

If you want to change the chart type, you can select a bar, area, line, pie, or any of the other types, many of which can also be three-dimensional. Be careful when changing the chart type that you don't change the intended chart message. For example, if you change your chart from a pie chart to a bar chart, the emphasis shifts from what each value represents to the values in relationship of the percentage of the whole.

Select the chart and choose Chart Tools Design> Type>Change Chart Type. The Change Chart type dialog box appears. Select the chart type and sub-type you want and then click OK (see Figure 13-10).

Figure 13-10
Choosing a different chart type or subtype.

Moving the Chart

When a chart is on the worksheet page, you can easily move it to any location on the page or you can move it from the data page to its own sheet. You cannot move a chart that's on its own sheet except to move it from its own sheet to the data page.

To move the chart located on the data sheet, to a different location on the data sheet, select the chart and position the mouse over the edge of the chart, but not over one of the handles. Your mouse pointer should be a four-headed arrow. Drag the chart border to a new location. As you move the chart, you see an outline such as you see in Figure 13-11, which represents the new chart position.

Mouse pointer

Figure 13-11
Moving a chart object around on the worksheet.

If you want to move the chart from its own sheet to the data sheet or from a data sheet to its own sheet, just follow these simple steps:

1. Select the chart that you want to move.

2. Choose Chart Tools Design>Location>Move Chart. The Move Chart dialog box seen in Figure 13-12 appears.

Figure 13-12
Changing the chart location.

3. Select a location:

    ▶ **New sheet:** Creates a new worksheet and places the chart on the sheet.

    ▶ **Object in:** Moves the chart to an existing sheet in the workbook. Click the drop-down arrow to select the worksheet to which you want to move the chart.

4. Click OK. Excel moves your chart to the location you specified.

Adding Descriptive Chart Text

A good way to make your chart more readable is to add some descriptive text that helps put the chart into a proper context. The Chart Title appears above or in the chart itself, and provides a brief description of the overall chart. You can also add axis titles to more clearly define your x- or y-axis information.

Adding a Chart Title

To add a chart title, you first select the chart you want to modify and then choose Chart Tools Layout>Labels>Chart Title. A list of options appears. If you choose None, which is the default choice, it means you don't want to display a title. You'll also use this option if you want to remove a chart title. Choose Centered Overlay Title to center the title within the chart plot area. This option retains the existing chart size. Choose Above Chart if you want to center the title above the chart.

Tip

Depending on the data you select when creating a chart, some chart types automatically create a chart title.

Make a selection. A title placeholder box with the words Chart Title (as you see in Figure 13-13) appears on the chart. With the title placeholder selected, begin typing the text you want. The text appears in the worksheet formula bar. Press Enter and Excel replaces the words Chart Title with your text.

Title as you type it   Title placeholder

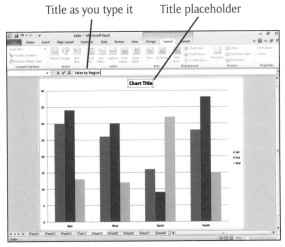

Figure 13-13
Adding a title to the chart.

Optionally, choose Chart Tools Layout>Labels> Chart Title>More Title Options. From the Format Chart Title dialog box seen in Figure 13-14, you can select Fill and then choose any desired background options for the chart title. Excel's Live Preview feature lets you view various options without first selecting them. You can also select from Border Styles, Border Color, Shadows, 3-D Format, and Alignment.

Figure 13-14
Enhancing a chart title.

No 3D Formatting

You can't apply 3D formatting or select a shadow when your title doesn't have a borderline around it.

Adding Axis Text

You can add additional text to either the x- or y-axis that can assist you or someone viewing your chart in better understanding the chart information. For example, adding the text *in millions* to the value axis helps the reader understand that a value of 12 really means 12 million. Or adding a category axis of *2007* might help the reader understand that the January, February, and March they are seeing are from the year 2007.

If you want to add a Category axis title, choose Chart Tools Layout>Labels>Axis Titles>Primary Horizontal Axis>Title Below Axis. Again replace the default text with your own description.

If you want to add a Value axis title, choose Chart Tools Layout>Labels>Axis Titles>Primary Vertical Axis and select a value axis title type. You have several choices for the vertical axis title:

- ▶ **None:** Removes an existing value axis title.
- ▶ **Rotated Title:** The title runs parallel with the y-axis from bottom to top.
- ▶ **Vertical Title:** The title runs from top to bottom with each letter stacked on top of each other.
- ▶ **Horizontal Title:** The title runs horizontally, which makes it easy to read but decreases the chart plot area. Use this title type for very short text.

Figure 13-15 illustrates three positions for vertical axis text and a category axis text.

Figure 13-15
Adding axis text.

Use the Mini Toolbar

Right-click any title, which displays the Mini Toolbar. From there you can change the formatting of the selected title.

Selecting Additional Axis Options

Besides adding a title to the axis, you can also choose a few other options pertaining to the axis. For example, you can choose whether or not to display gridlines to help your reader relate to the values. Besides the default display of horizontal gridlines along the major values, you can also display vertical gridlines, or you can choose not to display gridlines. Choose Chart Tools Layout>Axes> Gridlines. You can add, change, or remove horizontal or vertical gridlines. You can also select More Options to modify the gridline color. Figure 13-16 illustrates a chart with both major and minor horizontal gridlines displayed.

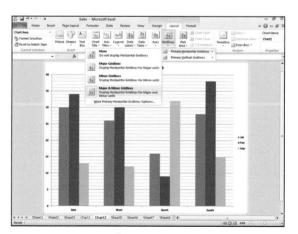

Figure 13-16
Displaying gridlines.

Choose Chart Tools Layout>Axes>Axes to change the way Excel displays either the horizontal or vertical axis. You can choose not to display an axis or you can change the value representation along the vertical axis. Click the More button to change choices such as axis number high or low limits or axis number formatting (see Figure 13-17).

Figure 13-17
Setting value axis options.

Working with the Legend

For most charts, Excel automatically adds a legend that helps explain each series. For example, if you have only red, blue, and yellow bars without a legend, you or your reader wouldn't know what the red bars mean versus the blue or yellow bars. You can turn the legend off, move it around to a different chart area, or change the options associated with a legend.

Choose Chart Tools Layout>Labels>Legend. From there you can select from the seven options seen in Figure 13-18. Remember, if you turn off the legend, you may have difficulty understanding the chart data. Optionally choose More Legend Options, which displays the Format Legend dialog box where you can select a border, fill color, shadow, or a number of other legend options. Also, like chart titles, you can right-click the legend and select formatting options.

Figure 13-18
Modifying the chart legend.

Drag the Legend

Optionally, click anywhere on the legend box to select it and manually drag the legend box wherever you want it.

Adding a Data Table

When you place a chart on the same worksheet as its data, you have one advantage over placing it on its own sheet: you can put the chart right next to the data it represents so you can see firsthand where the chart data comes from. But if you have your chart on its own page, you may want to add a data table.

Data tables appear in the form of a grid beneath the chart and display the numeric data that makes up the chart. They are very helpful if a reader needs to see exact values along with a graphical display, such as when using a 3D chart. The following steps show you how to add a data table:

1. Click anywhere on the chart you want to modify.

2. Click Chart Tools Layout>Labels>Data Table. Options include a choice not to show a data table, show a data table but not show a chart legend, or to show a data table and include the chart legend identifiers.

3. Make a Data Table selection. A data table, as seen in Figure 13-19, displays at the bottom of the chart showing the actual values.

Display Formatting Options

To set data table formatting, right-click the data table and choose Format Data Table.

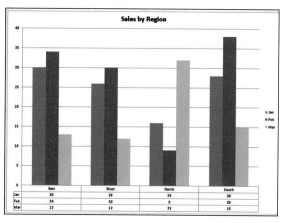

Figure 13-19
Adding a data table.

Displaying Data Labels

Another form of text you can add comes in the form of text to the individual data markers. By default, adding data labels shows only the value of the data point, but you can also include the series name and, depending on the chart style, either the category name or the X and Y values.

1. Select the chart you want to modify and choose Chart Tools Layout>Labels>Data Labels. A menu of data label placement options appears. The options you see depend on your chart style.

Easily Identify Values

You can use Data Labels to help identify the data series values, which are sometimes difficult to read on the y-axis scale.

2. Depending on your chart type, either select Show which turns on the data labels without any options, or choose a placement option. Figure 13-20 shows the data labels with a placement of Outside End.

Figure 13-20

Adding data labels.

3. Choose Chart Tools Layout>Labels>Data Labels>More Data Label Options. The Format Data Labels dialog box appears.

4. If you don't want the data label to be the series value, choose a different option from the Label Options area (such as the series or category names).

5. In the Number area, select a number style for the data labels.

6. Select any additional options and then click OK.

Editing the Chart Data

Suppose that you make a wonderful chart but then decide that you want to include more data, or exclude some of the data you've chosen. Excel provides two ways to change the data area—both of which are very easy.

The first method you can use when you want to quickly add or delete a series to a chart located on the same worksheet as the data. Click anywhere on the chart that you want to edit. Notice that Excel surrounds the chart with selection handles and marks the source data in the worksheet with a colored border. Drag the corner handle of the worksheet source range to add or subtract cells. Be sure your mouse pointer is a double-headed arrow before you drag a corner handle (see Figure 13-21).

Selection handle

	A	B	C	D	E
1	**2009 Sales by Region**				
2	**All Colors**	Jan	Feb	Mar	Total
3	**East**	30	34	13	
4	**West**	26	30	12	
5	**North**	16	9	32	
6	**South**	28	38	15	
7	**Total**	100	111	72	28
8					
9					

Figure 13-21

Changing the data you want plotted.

You can also change the chart data by following these steps:

1. Click anywhere on the chart that you want to modify.

2. Choose Chart Tools Design>Data>Select Data. The Select Data Source dialog box opens with the current chart data selected in the worksheet (see Figure 13-22).

Figure 13-22
The Select Data Source dialog box.

3. Drag in the worksheet to select the new data range. The Select Data Source dialog box collapses so you can easily see your data.

Alternative Method

Optionally, type the cell location in the Chart data range.

---

4. Release the mouse button. The Select Data Source dialog box reappears, and the new data range appears in the Chart data range box.

5. Click OK. The Select Data Source dialog box closes and the chart reflects the new data area.

Altering the Chart Color Style

You've already discovered how you can quickly change many options on your chart. You can also change the look by applying any of the many predefined chart styles. Chart styles are based on the current Excel workbook's theme, and include options such as colors and fonts.

Even if you don't like some of the predefined options, you can still change any chart options individually. Right-click on any element you want to change and select Format (chart item). Most changes can be made directly from the Format dialog box. Just follow these steps to apply a chart style:

1. Click anywhere on the chart you want to modify.

2. Choose Chart Tools Design>Chart Styles and click the More button, which displays the Chart Styles gallery seen in Figure 13-23. This figure illustrates the chart styles based on the Metro theme.

Tip

See Chapter 10, "Making Your Worksheet Look Good," for a refresher on themes.

Figure 13-23
Selecting a chart style.

3. Select a chart style. You may need to scroll down. The available styles vary depending on the chart type.

Enhancing a 3D Chart

Because 3D charts have depth and dimension, you can alter how Excel displays the chart perspective. For example, you can rotate the chart, deepen the floor, or even change the series bevels, lighting, and materials. Let's review the steps required to enhance a three-dimensional chart.

1. Select the 3D chart you want to modify.

2. Choose Chart Tools Layout>Background> 3-D Rotation. The Format Chart Area dialog box, shown in Figure 13-24, appears. The options you see depend on the chart type. Figure 13-24 shows you the options for the column chart you also see in the figure.

Figure 13-24
Changing three-dimensional options.

Change 3D Options

To change the 3D options for a specific chart component, click the chart component. The options in the Format Chart area box apply to the selected component.

3. Click the 3-D Rotation option and choose from options such as the following:

Tip

The options you have available depend on the chart style you selected.

▶ Click the x-axis left or right rotation arrows or enter the degree of left/right rotation (between 0 and 360) you want for the chart in the Rotation box. This rotates the series left or right.

▶ Click the y-axis up or down rotation arrows or enter the degree of up/down rotation.

▶ Click the Perspective up or down arrows to change the "camera" view or the view from the top. On pie charts, you can optionally type the elevation angle (between 10 and 80) in the Elevation text box. Figure 13-25 illustrates changing the depth of the column chart base, which made the bars wider as well as changed the axis rotation and perspective. Compare this chart to the one in Figure 13-24.

Figure 13-25
After changing three-dimensional options.

4. Select options from the available 3-D Format choices such as those you see in Figure 13-26:

Figure 13-26
3-D Format choices.

▶ Choose an option to select a bevel style for the top or bottom of the chart border.

▶ Change the thickness of the bars or height of pie slices by entering a value (between 5 and 500) in the Height box.

▶ Change the Depth option to deepen series bars and the chart floor. This option does not apply to pie charts. Values range from 0 to 2000.

▶ Change the Surface material option.

5. Click Close. The chart appears onscreen, rotated to the angles you selected. Figure 13-27 shows a 3D pie chart before and after changing the height and rotation.

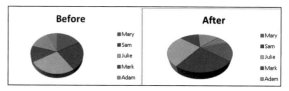

Figure 13-27
Enhancing a pie chart.

Placing a Picture in a Data Series

When Excel creates a chart, the slices, bars, or lines are typically a solid color. Earlier in this chapter you discovered how to change the entire chart style. You could also change the worksheet theme, which would change the chart colors.

One other option is to change the individual data series so that it reflects a specific color other than the default choices. Or you can add a texture or gradient to the colors you select. In some situations, however, you can get your message across even better by using a graphic instead of the solid color bar or pie slice.

1. Right-click the data point you want to modify. A shortcut menu appears.

2. Choose Format Data Series. The Format Data Series dialog box appears.

Different Options

If you are working with a pie chart or a bar or column chart with only one series, the option will say Format Data Point.

3. Click the Fill choice in the list at the left. Fill options appear on the right side.

Change Series Color

If you just want to change the series color, select Solid fill and pick a color.

4. Select Picture or Texture Fill (see Figure 13-28).

5. Click File. The Insert Picture dialog box appears.

Insert ClipArt

Optionally, click the ClipArt button to select a ClipArt object instead of an image.

Figure 13-28
Format Data Point fill options.

6. Locate and select the picture you want to use.

7. Click Insert. The Format Data Series dialog box reappears.

8. Choose whether you want Excel to stretch the picture to fill the series or to multiply them and stack them on top each other. Typically you would use the stretch option if you are modifying a pie chart. Using the stretch option with bar or column charts seriously distorts the image.

9. Click OK. Figure 13-29 illustrates a pie chart where one series was replaced with a photograph, one with a solid color, one with texture, and one with a gradient fill.

Figure 13-29
Liven up your charts with graphic images.

Deleting a Chart

If you create a chart and then decide you don't want it, you can easily delete it. Deleting a chart does not delete any data, only the chart compiled from the data. If the chart is an object on the data page, select the chart and press the Delete key. If the chart is on its own sheet, right-click the chart sheet tab and choose Delete. Click Delete at the confirmation message that appears.

Working with Sparklines

NEW TO EXCEL 2010 are *sparklines*, which are tiny charts that fit into a single cell, typically located near your data. The concept, originally created by Edward Tufte, is often called "intense word-sized graphics".

A sparkline chart provides a quick visual representation of the data showing, at a glance, trends such as the effect of your advertising or whether your sales are growing, stagnant or falling. Sparklines not only make sense as a powerful means to increase the analytical depth of your numbers, they can also add information where space is scarce.

Earlier in this chapter, you discovered how you can create some incredible Excel charts based on your data. Standard Excel charts however, are typically large in size and are separate from the data on which they are based.

Figure 13-30 shows an example of some raw data in an Excel spreadsheet. This data represents sales by color over a 12 month period. If you need to quickly determine sales trend, you'd have to do a lot of calculating.

Figure 13-30
Raw Excel data.

But with the sparklines you see in Figure 13-30, you can see at a glance, how your sales are doing. Notice the sparklines are in the data table which gives context to the numbers.

Figure 13-31
Excel data with sparklines.

With a cell graphic like a sparkline, you can display dynamic information rich data by adding visualization to your raw data.

Adding Sparklines

With Excel, you can create line, column, or win/loss sparkline charts. Line and column charts are similar to the standard Excel line and column charts in that they typically illustrate a trend over a period of time or distance.

Win/loss sparkline charts are comparable to a 100% stacked column chart. The Excel data you use for a win/loss sparkline should be a series of positive and negative numbers. For example, if you want to create a sparkline chart to compare your favorite football team's wins to its losses, you would create data showing a value of minus one for each game lost and a positive one for each game won. The actual value you use doesn't matter. What matters is whether it is a positive value compared to a negative value. Figure 13-32 illustrates data that is used for a win/loss sparkline.

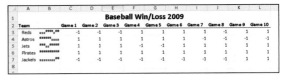

Figure 13-32
Win/loss Excel data.

1. Select the cell next to where your data resides. Sparklines can be in any cell, but placing them next to your data makes them easier to see a visual trend.

2. Click Insert>Sparklines and choose one of the three sparkline types: Line, Column, or Win/Loss. The Create Sparklines dialog box appears. (See Figure 13-33.)

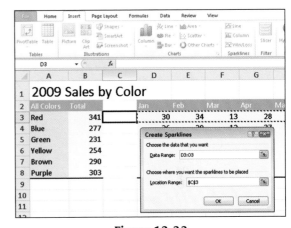

Figure 13-33
The Create Sparklines dialog box.

3. In the Data Range box, either type the cells containing the data you want to plot or drag across the cells with your mouse. The range you selected appears in the Data Range box.

4. If you want the sparkline to appear in a cell different from the one you originally selected, enter, in the Location Range box, the new cell address.

5. Click OK. Excel creates a sparkline chart. A Sparkline Tools Design tab also appears as seen in Figure 13-34.

Sparkline

Figure 13-34
The Sparklines Tools Design tab.

Change Sparkline Type

If you want to change the sparkline type, select the sparkline and choose Sparkline Tools Design>Type and choose a different type.

If you find you want to delete the sparkline, click the sparkline cell and click Sparkline Tools Design>Group>Clear.

Create Multiple Sparklines

You can use the sparkline cell AutoFill handle to quickly copy the sparkline settings to an adjacent data. This creates a sparkline group. Changes you make to one sparkline affect all the sparklines in the group.

Adding Sparkline Markers

Once you create the sparkline you can customize it to highlight important values in the sparkline. For example, you can indicate any negative points, the first point, the last point, the highest point, or the lowest point. You can indicate any one or any combination of the points and if you choose, you can highlight them using different colors.

Simply select the sparkline cells on which you want to add markers and choose Sparkline Tools Design>Show and check the markers you want displayed. In Figure 13-35, you see only the high and low point markers.

High point marker

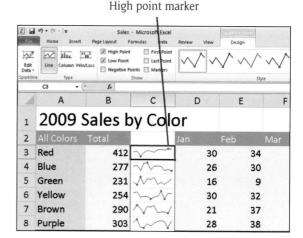

Figure 13-35
Add markers to your sparklines.

Changing Sparkline Styles

Like almost everything else in Excel, you can apply a different design to the sparklines. You can choose from a gallery of predefined styles consisting of line (or bar) color and marker color or you can create your own combination.

Select the sparkline cells on which you want to change the style. If the sparklines are in a group, and you only want to change one of the sparklines, choose Sparkline Tools Design>Group>Ungroup.

Next, choose Sparkline Tools Design>Style and click the More button. You see the gallery of sparkline styles. Select the sparkline style you want. Excel changes all the selected sparklines to the newly selected style. See Figure 13-36.

More button

Figure 13-36
Change sparkline styles.

If you don't want any of the predefined styles, choose Sparkline Tools Design>Style and click the Sparkline Color arrow. From there you can select the color you want. If you choose Sparkline Tools Design>Style and click the Marker Color arrow you can select the marker color you want to use.

Editing Sparkline Data

Like with regular Excel charts, if you change the data values, the dynamic sparklines immediately reflect the change. But what if you want to change the sparkline data range? Relax; it's only a couple of clicks away. Just follow these easy steps:

1. Select the sparklines you want to change and choose Sparkline Tools Design>Sparkline and click the Edit Data arrow. A drop-down menu appears.

2. Choose Edit Group Location and Data if you are working with a group of sparklines, or choose Edit Single Sparkline's Data if you only want to change one of the sparklines. The Edit Sparklines dialog box seen in Figure 13-37 appears.

Figure 13-37
Change sparkline data locations.

3. In the Data Range box, optionally enter the new data area you want to include in the sparklines.

4. In the Location Range box, optionally enter or select a new sparkline location.

5. Click OK.

Part IV
PowerPoint

Very seldom anymore do you attend a conference, seminar, meeting, or trade show without seeing a PowerPoint presentation. That's because PowerPoint is ideal for the presenting of concepts and lecture material. PowerPoint is the feature-laden Microsoft Office program that allows you to create presentations and optional audience handouts. Through the creation of PowerPoint slides, you can add color, images, sounds, animation, and movies to an otherwise text-based presentation. The chapters in this section take you through creating a PowerPoint presentation that will help you get your message across efficiently.

Creating a PowerPoint
Presentation

PICTURE YOURSELF ATTENDING A MEETING. It's a long meeting, and the presenter has been droning on and on about something, but you are not sure about what. Her monotone voice is putting you to sleep, and she just stands there reciting fact after fact about her topic. It all becomes a blur, and you know you aren't getting anything out of this meeting.

Now picture yourself at a meeting with a vibrant presenter who not only gives you the topic facts, but backs them up with colorful charts and illustrations all presented in a logical and interesting manner. This speaker is using a PowerPoint presentation to help get the point across, and, by golly, it's working!

Now it is time for you to give a presentation. If you are not sure where to begin, don't worry. PowerPoint includes quite a few tools to help you take that first step. Actually, you already know a lot more than you think. By working in Word and Excel you have learned about many of the tools you will use in PowerPoint when you create your first dynamic presentation.

Starting with the PowerPoint Basics

EVERY PROJECT NEEDS a starting point, and if you are using PowerPoint for the first time, you will want to begin with a quick exploration of the PowerPoint program window. When you open the PowerPoint application, a blank slide appears and the program is in Normal view.

Perusing the PowerPoint Window

First, I will review a few of the common Office features. Take a look at Figure 14-1. Just like Word and Excel, PowerPoint includes the File tab where you can access your file management commands such as Save, Open, and Print. You also see the Quick Access Toolbar with its Save, Undo, and Repeat buttons. You also see the PowerPoint Ribbon with seven tabs displayed when working with a new PowerPoint presentation. You will see other Ribbon tabs appear as certain processes occur such as adding graphics or tables to your slides.

Down in the lower-right corner you see the familiar Zoom control where you can zoom in for a closer look, and you also see three other View buttons next to the Zoom control. PowerPoint has three working views: Normal, which is the default view; Slide Sorter view, which you will see in Chapter 15, "Editing Your Presentation;" and Slide Show view, which you will work with in Chapter 17, "Presenting Your Presentation." The three View buttons next to the Zoom control take you quickly into any of the three PowerPoint views.

Figure 14-1
The PowerPoint window.

The left pane on the PowerPoint screen is called the Slide list, where you can see the slides in your presentation. As you add multiple slides to the presentation, you will see a scroll bar appear. It is also where you will view and work with your outline. I will cover the outline later in this chapter. The right side pane is the Current Slide window where you perform the actual work on the slides such as adding text or graphics.

The bottom pane is the Notes pane. That is were you can jot down notes to yourself (or to the presenter) as reminders when giving the presentation. I cover creating notes in Chapter 16, "Formatting Your Presentation."

Planning for a Great Presentation

Okay, so this section does not have you actually do anything, but it gives you something to think about. A lot of research has gone into creating the perfect presentation, and here are several tips to help you when planning your presentation:

▶ **Consider your audience.** The way you present information to a group of school children is very different than the way you might present it to your co-workers. (Most of the time, anyway.)

▶ **Keep it simple.** Do not try to shove every thought on to a slide. The slides become jumbled and you lose your audience. Keep the text simple and direct. You can do more explaining as you present.

▶ **Remain focused.** Keep the slides and your speaking focused on the current topic.

▶ **State your intentions.** State what your presentation is about and what you intend to prove with the presentation.

▶ **Make it personal.** Tell the story that illustrates the problem and through the presentation, show how to solve the problem. Provide solutions…not just problems.

▶ **Use graphics such as charts and tables to illustrate your key points.** People like pictures and they understand and retain pictures better than words.

▶ **Don't under- or over-design.** Follow the KISS ("Keep It Simple, Stupid") theory. Although you certainly want some design elements, keep the design elements consistent through the entire presentation and don't add too many so you don't distract your audience. Figure 14-2 illustrates two slides: one with too much design and one so boring it makes you yawn.

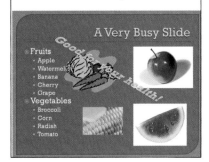

Figure 14-2
Not too much, not too little.

▶ **Know your material.** If you are the one who will present the material, make sure you know it inside and out. Rehearse, rehearse, rehearse.

Keeping those few items in mind will help you get your point across to your audience in just the way you intend.

Understanding the Presentation Process

Although it is certainly not written in stone, the following tasks are the typical actions taken when creating a presentation. Other than the first and last items, the tasks are pretty much interchangeable. Take a look at Figure 14-3, which illustrates the following list:

Figure 14-3
The process of creating a presentation.

▶ **Create the slides:** Although a presentation could consist of a single slide, they rarely do. You can select from the preformatted slide layouts designed to present your information.

▶ **Insert the data:** Once you have some slides, you need to make them project the information you are trying to relay. You do that in the form of text, tables, charts, and shapes.

▶ **Apply a design:** You can create a background for your slides and apply a theme, all of which helps maintain the continuity of your presentation.

▶ **Generate speaker notes:** You can jot down reminders of what you want to say to your audience when you are giving the presentation.

▶ **Prepare for presentation:** To liven up your presentation, you can add multimedia such as video, sounds, or narration, or you can animate the items on a slide.

▶ **Present the presentation:** The culmination of all your work, you present the slides to an audience, during which you can draw on the slides or make them run automatically.

Creating a New Presentation

When you started PowerPoint, you saw a new, blank presentation ready for you to work with. If you do not want to start with the blank presentation provided when you open PowerPoint, you can select from the many pre-designed, pre-formatted PowerPoint templates. These templates illustrate that you need not be an artist to create a good-looking presentation, complete with a background and other images.

Keyboard Shortcut

Press Ctrl+N to create a new blank presentation with a title slide.

Click the File tab and choose New. The Available Templates and Themes window seen in Figure 14-4 launches.

Create button

Figure 14-4
Select the template you want to use.

From the left side, chose a category. PowerPoint can also display choices from the hundreds of templates available from Office.com.

If you just want a plain blank template, from the Blank and recent category choose Blank Presentation and then click the Create button. If you want one of the already installed templates, from the Sample Templates category, choose a template and click Create. If you select one of the templates from Office.com, click the template you want, such as seen in Figure 14-5, and then click the Download button. PowerPoint downloads the template and displays it on your screen.

Download Only Once

You have to download a template only once. The next time you want the template, you see it listed under the Recent Templates category or under My Templates.

Download button

Figure 14-5
Save time by beginning with a predesigned template available online.

Adding New Slides

AFTER YOU CREATE the presentation, you can begin working on the first blank slide for the presentation title, or you can start inserting the slides. Slides use slide layouts, which are preformatted slide designs that help you enter text, graphics, and other things. Some layouts have text placeholders for entering titles and other text, whereas some contain content placeholders for inserting tables, charts, diagrams, pictures, clipart, images, or video.

Inserting Blank Slides

When you insert a slide, you must select the layout that best resembles the slide you want to create. Don't worry...you can later change to a different layout or change any component of the slide.

Choose Home>Slides and click the arrow at the bottom of the New Slide button. A list of slide layouts appears as seen in Figure 14-6. Choose the layout you want. With one exception, all the slide layouts contain some combination of text place-holders or text and content placeholders. It is up to you to decide which of the nine slide layouts you want to use. The following list explains each slide layout and what placeholders it contains:

> **Delete Slide**
>
> Deleting an unwanted slide is as easy as selecting the slide in the Slide pane and pressing Delete.

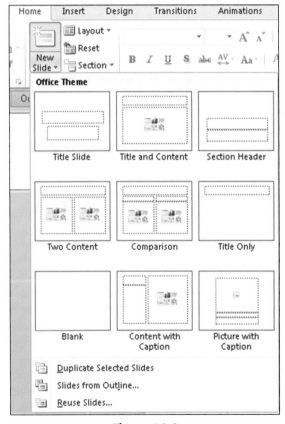

Figure 14-6
Select the layout you want for your new slide.

▶ **Title Slide:** Contains two text placeholders. Typically you use the larger text box for the presentation title and the smaller one for the presentation description.

▶ **Title and Content:** Contains one text placeholder, usually used for the slide title, and one content placeholder.

▶ **Section Header:** Very similar to a Title slide, the section header contains two text placeholders. Section header slides are usually used to break a presentation into separate areas.

▶ **Two Content:** Contains one text placeholder for the slide title and two side-by-side content placeholders.

▶ **Comparison:** Contains three text placeholders and two side-by-side content placeholders. One text placeholder is used for the slide title, and the other two are positioned above the content placeholders.

▶ **Title Only:** Contains one text placeholder positioned for the slide title.

▶ **Blank:** Contains no placeholders.

▶ **Content with Caption:** Contains two text placeholders and one content placeholder. One text placeholder is for the slide title and the other for content explanatory text. Figure 14-7 illustrates a slide created from a Content with Caption layout.

▶ **Picture with Caption:** Contains two text placeholders and a modified content placeholder. One text placeholder is for the slide title and the other is to explain the content placeholder. The content placeholder is modified to insert only pictures.

Figure 14-7
A slide made in the Content with Caption layout.

Viewing Placeholders

As you add slides to your presentation, they appear in the Slide list; however, the Slide list pane does not show placeholders. Only the Slide pane on the right shows the placeholders. To switch to a different slide, simply click the slide in the Slide list.

Copying Slides

To save time and effort, if you have already slides that are similar to a new slide you want, you can duplicate them. You can copy a slide from the current presentation or from another saved presentation.

Copying from the Current Presentation

If you need a new slide similar to one in the current presentation you can save yourself time by duplicating the slide and then editing the duplicate as needed. Just follow these steps:

1. From the Slide list pane, click the slide you want to duplicate.

Duplicate Multiple Slides

If you want to duplicate multiple slides, hold down the Ctrl key as you click on each slide you want to duplicate.

2. Choose Home>Slides and click the New Slide arrow.

Use the New Slide Button

If you don't click the arrow and just click the New Slide button, PowerPoint automatically adds a blank slide in the layout used by the slide above the location where the current slide is being inserted.

3. Choose Duplicate Selected Slides. PowerPoint creates a copy of the slide and inserts the copy directly below the selected slide (see Figure 14-8).

Figure 14-8
Duplicating slides can save you lots of time.

Using Slides from Another File

If you have a saved presentation with slides that can help you in the current presentation, you can copy them, thereby saving lots of time. You have the option of not only copying the slide content, but if you want it, you can also copy the formatting. Just follow these easy steps:

1. Choose Home>Slides and click the New Slide arrow.

2. Click Reuse Slides. The Reuse Slides pane, seen in Figure 14-9, opens on the right side of the screen.

Figure 14-9
Select the presentation you want to copy from.

3. Click the Browse button and choose Browse File.

4. Locate and click the PowerPoint presentation from which you want to select slides.

5. Click Open. All the slides in the selected presentation appear in the Reuse Slides pane (see Figure 14-10).

Keep Source Formatting option

Figure 14-10
Reusing slides from other presentations.

6. By default, the reused slides use the design elements in the currently open presentation. If you also want the design formats in the saved presentation, click the Keep Source Formatting option.

7. Select the slides you want to reuse. PowerPoint inserts the slide into the presentation.

8. When you are finished selecting slides to reuse, click the Close (x) button to close the Reuse Slides pane.

Adding Slide Objects

NOW THAT YOU HAVE SELECTED a slide layout, it is time to begin adding data to the slide. That data can be in the form of text, whether titles or bullets, photographs or clipart, charts or diagrams, tables, or just drawn shapes. In this section, you learn how to add each of these elements to your slide. In Chapter 15, you will see how to edit the objects after you add them.

The sections that follow first assume you want to add the object into the slide placeholder, but you can add any of these objects anywhere on the slide. I also give you instructions on how to optionally place the object on the page without using the content placeholder.

Including Text on Slides

Think of each text placeholder as a miniature Word document in that you just begin typing your text. The text stays constrained to the placeholder, but, if needed, PowerPoint wraps the text around in the placeholder box. The default font is determined by the slide layout and the current theme, but you can change it as needed to suit your purpose.

Begin by clicking any text placeholder. The placeholder text (which, by the way, does not print) disappears and a blinking insertion point appears. Type the desired text and use the same editing techniques as you discovered in Chapter 2, "Getting Started with Word." Typically, if you are working on a title text placeholder, you only want one or two lines of text since the font size is already very large.

If you want to freely place text on a slide without using a placeholder, you use a text box. Choose Insert>Text>Text Box. Bring your cursor to the slide and draw a box about the size you want the entire block of text. When you release the mouse button, the text box appears with a blinking insertion point where you type your text. If the text box is too small, you can continue typing, although all the text may not display. In Chapter 15, you will see how to move or resize the text box.

Content placeholders display a "Click to add text" guideline. If you want to create a list of bullet points for the slide, click the "Click to add text" line and begin typing. Each time you press Enter, the slide displays another bullet, as you see in Figure 14-11. Click anywhere outside of the content placeholder to deselect the placeholder boundaries.

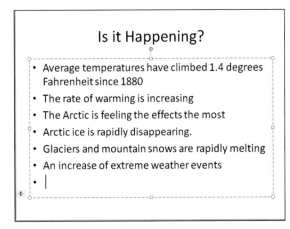

Figure 14-11
Press the Enter key to display a new bullet point.

Attaching Graphic Images

When working with a content slide, you can, as you just discovered, add bullet point text. Another element type you can add to a content slide is a graphic image. Graphic images come in the form of pictures, which are usually in the form of a photograph but could be any saved graphic image or clipart that is a graphic and is small in size, usually in the form of an illustration or line drawing.

A slide content placeholder has six icons in the middle as you see in Figure 14-12. As you hover your mouse over each icon, the icon brightens and a ScreenTip appears to describe the type of content. The six content icons are Insert Table, Insert Chart, Insert SmartArt Graphic, Insert Picture from File, ClipArt, and Insert Media Clip.

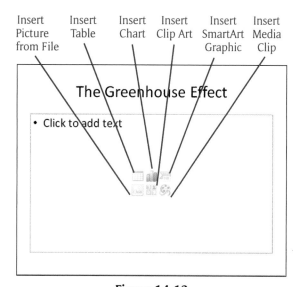

Figure 14-12

Click to insert content into a content placeholder.

Adding Clipart

While most Office applications have the ability to insert clipart into a file, adding clipart to a slide, especially one with quite a few bullet points, brings both interest and distractions to an otherwise dull slide. Office ships with hundreds of clipart images and thousands more are available online, free from Microsoft. Office stores clipart in collections with keywords so you can easily locate the image you want. Whatever the topic, you are sure to find a clipart image that complements it. Here is how you can add clipart to a slide content placeholder:

1. Choose the slide you want to place clipart and in the content placeholder, click the Clip Art icon. If you do not want the clipart in the content placeholder, but just as a separate screen object, choose Insert>Images>Clip Art. Either way, the Clip Art pane appears on the right side of the screen.

2. In the Search For box, type a word or short phrase that best describes the image you want. For example, typing *planet* brings up a collection of artwork ranging from globes to astronauts.

3. Click the Go button. Office displays the available clipart that matches your request (see Figure 14-13).

4. Click the image you want. The image appears in the slide as you see in Figure 14-14.

5. Click the Close button to close the Clip Art pane.

Figure 14-13
Click the clipart graphic you want to use.

Tip

Chapter 15, "Editing Your Presentation," shows you how to move, resize, and otherwise manage graphic images.

Adding Saved Pictures

If you have a digital photograph or other graphic image such as a company logo, you can place it on the slide as well. To insert an existing graphics file into your slide, follow these steps:

1. In the content placeholder for the slide you want a picture, click the Insert Picture from File icon. If you do not want the image in the content placeholder, but just as a separate screen object, choose Insert>Images>Picture. The Insert Picture dialog box opens.

2. Locate and select the image you want to insert.

3. Click Insert. PowerPoint inserts the image you selected into the content placeholder or elsewhere on the slide (see Figure 14-15).

Figure 14-14
The clipart image appears in your slide.

Figure 14-15
Adding a picture to the slide.

Inserting Tables

If you want to present your data in a row and column, use a table on the slide. Tables are a great way to display the numerical facts that backup your topic. In Chapter 5 "Working with Columns and Tables," you discovered information about inserting and managing a table in Word. Many of Word's table features are mirrored in PowerPoint.

Begin by selecting the slide on which you want the table and then clicking the Insert Table icon on the content placeholder. The Insert Table dialog box appears prompting you for the number of columns and rows you want in your table. Enter the numbers you want and click OK. If you need more columns or rows, or less, you can change that after you create the table. PowerPoint inserts the table into your document. If you already have applied a design to your presentation, the table picks up the styles and colors associated with that design.

> ## Ribbon Table Command
>
> If you do not want to use the content placeholder, you can optionally choose Insert>Tables>Table, which provides a grid where you can select the table size.

Just like a Word table, you add any text into the individual cells by typing the text and then either clicking in the next cell or using the Tab or Shift+Tab keys to move around the table (see Figure 14-16).

Table object borders

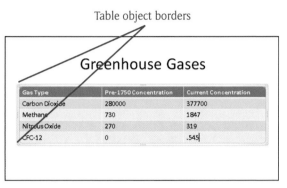

Figure 14-16
Illustrate data in a table.

Because the table is an object in the slide, when a table is active you see a border surrounding it. The border has a series of dots in each corner and at the middle of the top, bottom, left, and right sides. In the next chapter, you will see where you can use the border and the border dots to move or resize the table. You can inactivate the table by clicking anywhere outside of the border and reactivate it by clicking anywhere in the table.

When you insert a table, and while the table is active, PowerPoint adds two contextual tabs to the Ribbon: Table Tools Design and Table Tools Layout, both of which you see in Figure 14-17. The Table Tools Design tab helps you manage the overall table appearance, and the Table Tools Layout tab primarily helps you manage the table plan.

Figure 14-17
The Table Tools tab.

You will find the Table Tools Layout tab is very similar to the Word Table Tools Layout tab. It includes tools with which you can insert and delete rows, merge and split cells, change row height and column width, and manage text directions.

The PowerPoint Table Tools Design tab also is almost identical to the Word Table Tools Design tab. From there you can select styles, borders, and fill options for your table.

Building Charts

Chapter 13, "Generating Excel Charts," is an entire chapter devoted to creating charts. The charts you create in a PowerPoint slide are very similar with one difference. In PowerPoint, you decide on the chart first, then you enter the data. The following shows the steps involved:

1. From the slide you want to place a chart, click the Insert Chart icon on the content placeholder, or, if you are not using a content placeholder, choose Insert> Illustrations> Chart.

Chart Steps

If you want to place a chart in you Word document, you also can choose Insert> Illustrations>Chart. The remaining steps are identical in both Word and PowerPoint.

---

2. From the Insert Chart dialog box seen in Figure 14-18, select the chart style you want and then click OK. Your PowerPoint window resizes itself to half the screen and an Excel worksheet window with sample data in it appears on the right.

Figure 14-18
Choosing a chart style.

3. Edit the worksheet data so the labels and values portray the data you want shown. As you make the changes, the chart in the PowerPoint window immediately reflects the changes (see Figure 14-19).

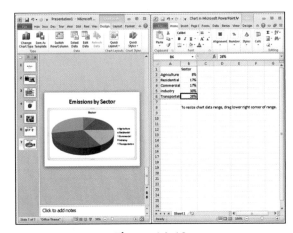

Figure 14-19
Enter the chart data into the Excel worksheet.

4. When you finish editing the data, close the Excel window. You do not need to save changes as they are already saved in PowerPoint.

5. The PowerPoint window displays three Chart Tools tabs (Design, Layout, and Format) while the chart is selected, so you can edit the chart design as you learned for editing an Excel chart.

Edit Data

To edit the chart data, choose Chart Tools Design> Data>Edit Data, which reopens the data in the Excel window.

Creating SmartArt

Another element you can place on a content slide is called *SmartArt*. SmartArt objects are diagrams that show relationships, product cycles, workflow processes, and such. Using a diagram allows your viewers to better visualize a concept or idea.

Tip

SmartArt diagrams are also available in Word and Excel.

First you must select the diagram type and then you can customize it to meet your specific needs. There are eight basic diagram types, although each type contains quite a few variations. Here are the diagram types:

▶ **List:** Use this type for describing related items, usually sequential or showing a progression.

▶ **Process:** Use this type for describing how a concept or physical process changes over time.

▶ **Cycle:** Use this type to show progress from one stage to another when the process repeats itself. Figure 14-20 is a classic example of a cycle diagram.

▶ **Hierarchy:** Use this type to describe relationships between items or people. A company organization chart is an example of a Hierarchy diagram.

▶ **Relationship:** Use this type to describe how two or more items are connected to each other.

▶ **Matrix:** Use this type for showing the relationship between the whole and its components.

▶ **Pyramid:** Use this for showing proportional or interconnected relationships.

▶ **Picture:** Use this type to lay out a series of pictures.

Office.com

PowerPoint lists Office.com in the diagram types, however, this option isn't really a diagram type, but rather a source for additional miscellaneous diagrams.

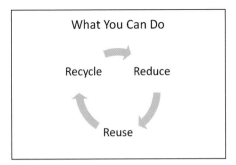

Figure 14-20
A cycle diagram created from SmartArt.

Begin by clicking the Insert SmartArt Graphic icon in the content placeholder or by choosing Insert>Illustrations>SmartArt. The Choose a SmartArt Graphic dialog box seen in Figure 14-21 appears. Select the diagram type you want, and then from the List section, choose the diagram subtype and click OK. The illustrations in this section show a hierarchy organization chart.

Figure 14-21
Choose the type of SmartArt you want to create.

Removing Shapes

Later in this chapter you will see how you can add additional shapes to your diagram. If, however, your diagram has shapes you do not want or need, you can easily delete them. In Figure 14-22, you see an organization diagram that automatically begins with a high level, an assistant level, and three sublevels. If you don't want the Assistant box, for example, you can remove it. Simply click

the border edge of the shape you want to remove. When the shape is selected, you see eight selection handles around the box. Press the Delete key to delete the unwanted shape.

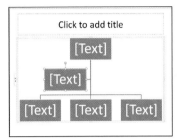

Figure 14-22
Deleting unwanted shapes.

Adding Text to a Diagram

Notice that each box in the diagram has a text placeholder. To add text to your diagram you could click each individual placeholder and type the desired text. A faster way, however, is to use the Text pane that appears on the left side of the diagram (see Figure 14-23). Selection handles surrounding the graphic shape are tied to your insertion point location on the Text pane. As you enter text, it automatically resizes to fit in the selected diagram shape.

Figure 14-23
Entering text into the Text pane.

Working with Hierarchy Levels

In the Text pane, when you press Enter, another blank line and a corresponding shape appear on the slide. Since a hierarchy diagram (such as an organization chart), usually includes different levels, called branches, PowerPoint by default provides several higher headings and a few lower headings. You can promote or demote these headings as needed. In the Text pane, click anywhere in the line you want to promote or demote and do one of the following:

► Press the Tab key to demote to a lower level. Optionally, choose SmartArt Tools Design>Create Graphic>Demote.

► Press the Shift+Tab key to promote to a higher level. Optionally, choose SmartArt Tools Design>Create Graphic>Promote.

As you promote or demote the text, the slide graphic immediately reflects the changes (see Figure 14-24).

Figure 14-24
Promoting and Demoting in an organization chart.

Adding Diagram Shapes

The SmartArt Tools Design tab contains a button to add shapes; however, in most situations it is generally easiest to add shapes using the Text pane. Simply click at the end of the text in the shape located before where you want the new shape. Press Enter and the Text pane provides another line for typing and a shape to go with it. You can then add as many shapes as you want.

Unlike the hierarchy type diagrams, the list, process, cycle, relationship, and matrix diagrams do not have branches, which means they travel in a single direction. Look at the Text pane and diagram in Figure 14-25 where you see three shapes forming a circle. When working with these types of diagrams, all the Text pane lines are on the same level.

Figure 14-25
A single-level Text pane.

When adding shapes to a hierarchy diagram, you have additional decisions to make such as at what level you want the new shape placed. If you are adding a peer-level shape, you use the Text pane. Click at the beginning of the line where you want the new shape and press the Enter key. On the resulting blank line, type the text for the new shape.

If, however, you want to add an assistant-level shape, follow these steps:

Tip

The Add Assistant feature is available only if you are working with an Organization Chart.

---

1. In the Text pane, click the line for the shape to which you want to add an assistant.

2. Choose SmartArt Tools Design>Create Graphic and click the Add Shape arrow. A list of choices appears.

3. Choose Add Assistant. The Assistant box appears. In the Text pane, instead of a bullet point like the other shapes, the Assistant appears at the bottom of the list with a right-angled arrow (see Figure 14-26).

Assistant

Figure 14-26
Adding an assistant.

Changing the SmartArt Layout

If after working on your diagram you decide you should have chosen a different style, you do not have to start all over. Choose SmartArt Tools Design>Layouts and select from the layouts. As you pause your mouse over any layout, Live Preview displays your chart as it would appear in the new layout. In Figure 14-27, you see the original organization chart changed to a Circle Picture Hierarchy.

Figure 14-27
Select a different layout.

Figure 14-28
Selecting a new shape.

Remember that only an organization chart can have an assistant, so in this example, choosing a different layout forces the assistant to a peer level.

Changing Shapes

If you want to call special attention to a certain area of your diagram, you can change the shape. Optionally, you can change the shapes for all the diagram shape objects. For example, you want the assistant to be in the form of a circle instead of the square cornered box. Or perhaps you want a box to have rounded corner boxes instead of the square corners.

Select the shape you want to change and choose SmartArt Tools Format>Shapes>Change Shape. A gallery of shapes like the one you see in Figure 14-28 appears. Choose a new shape and the diagram reflects the change.

Text Size Change

Changing shapes may force the text size on all the shapes to change. If your shape size needs modified, choose SmartArt Tools Format>Shapes and choose Larger or Smaller.

Changing a Diagram Style

If you want to add a little style to your diagram, you can select from a variety of predefined styles that are coordinated and would look good with your current diagram layout. You can also change the colors assigned to the diagram. The color choices available depend on the PowerPoint presentation theme. You learn how to apply designs and themes in Chapter 16.

If you want to change the diagram colors, choose SmartArt Tools Design>SmartArt Styles>Change Colors. A drop-down gallery similar to what you see in Figure 14-29 appears. Again, as you pause your mouse over any choice Live Preview shows you how it looks on your diagram.

Figure 14-29
Adding a little color to your diagram.

If you want to change the box styles, such as adding shadows, embossing or three-dimensional angles, choose SmartArt Tools Design>SmartArt Styles and click the More button. Select from the choices you see. In Figure 14-30, you see the diagram with an intense color depth and shadows.

Figure 14-30
Adding diagram special effects.

You can also change an individual shape color or effects by selecting the shape and choosing SmartArt Tools Format>Shape Styles and choosing from the number of different options provided which include the shape fill color, outline attributes, and shape effects. See the Assistant shape in Figure 14-31.

Figure 14-31
Changing the individual shape attributes.

Working with Outlines

THROUGHOUT THIS CHAPTER, you discovered how to create a presentation by adding slides one at a time. Another, and typically much faster, method for creating a presentation involves using an outline. You first worked with outlines in Word in Chapter 7, "Discovering Word Tools." Working with a PowerPoint outline is very similar. In fact, you can create your presentation based on an outline that you saved in Word.

The pane on the left side of a presentation has two tabs. The first tab is for the Slide list pane, but behind that tab is the Outline tab. Click the Outline tab to begin working with the presentation outline in the Outline pane.

The best way to begin the outline is to create the slides and their titles. PowerPoint treats the first line of outline text as the first slide title. Usually the first slide in a new presentation is a title slide layout, so on the first line you should type a title for your presentation. When you press the Enter key the insertion point moves to the next line and PowerPoint creates another slide, which by default is in a Title and Content layout. Again, the text you type in the outline becomes the slide title. You keep typing the slide titles until you have the slides you want. Figure 14-32 illustrates the Outline pane with the slide titles.

Figure 14-32
Typing in the Outline pane.

The second level in a PowerPoint outline is for items such as subtitles and bullet points. Click at the end of the slide you want to add a subtitle or bullet point. Press Enter to create a new line and press the Tab key. Pressing the Tab key indents the text and makes it into a second level heading. If the current slide is in a Title layout, the second level text becomes a subtitle, or if the current slide is a Title and Content layout, the second level text becomes bullet points as you see in Figure 14-33.

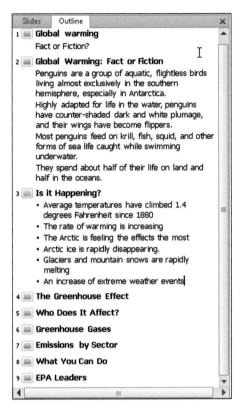

Figure 14-33
Adding bullet points in the outline.

Move Backward

To shift second level text back to first level text, press Shift+Tab.

Editing Your
Presentation

PICTURE YOURSELF ASSEMBLING A BICYCLE. You have all the parts laid out in front of you and you slowly begin putting all the pieces together. Carefully and meticulously, you adjust the seat and handle bars so everything is right where you need it, and then you add the decals and emblems for a few final flourishes.

Whether you create your presentation from a blank beginning or from one of the PowerPoint templates that provide some rather impressive slides, you will want to make modifications to any presentation you create. This chapter is about editing. You have created the slides you need, and now you need to adjust the slide content until everything is in just the right place.

Changing Views

HAVE YOU EVER HEARD the old expression that sometimes you can't see the forest for the trees? When your presentation has a number of slides, sometimes you become so concentrated on the individual slides that you need to sit back and look at your presentation from another perspective. Fortunately, PowerPoint includes a couple of different ways to do just that.

Working in Slide Sorter View

Depending on your task, you will probably switch frequently between the three main PowerPoint views. Up to this point you have been working in the Normal view. When you are editing the individual slide elements, you can work best in the default Normal view.

However, for a good overall look at the presentation and an easy way to manipulate entire slides, it is easiest in the Slide Sorter view. The Slide Sorter view provides a thumbnail size view of each slide in the presentation. You cannot edit slide content in Slide Sorter view, but you can change the order in which the slides appear as well as easily delete slides.

Change to Slide Sorter view by clicking the Slide Sorter icon from the View icons or by choosing View>Presentation Views>Slide Sorter. Figure 15-1 shows a presentation in Slide Sorter view.

Figure 15-1
Viewing slides in the Slide Sorter view.

The third main view, Slide Show view, lets you present the show in its entirety. You will work in Slide Show view in Chapter 17, "Presenting Your Presentation."

Viewing Slides in the Slide Sorter

From the Slide Sorter view you can view the overall effects of your presentation, including the ability to view a slide close up or in other color modes. Here are a couple of your options:

▶ Use the zoom controls at the bottom to zoom the slide collection to a larger or smaller size. Optionally, if your mouse has a scroll wheel, hold down the Ctrl key and roll the scroll wheel forward to enlarge the view or roll it backward to shrink the view (see Figure 15-2).

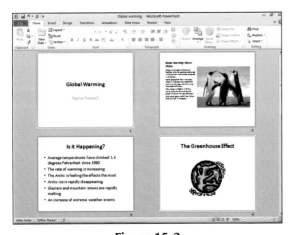

Figure 15-2
Zoom the slides in or out.

▶ Double-click a slide to display the slide in Normal view.

Selecting Slides

Before you can manipulate the slides, you need to select them. Simply click once on an individual slide. Selected slides have a heavy border around them. If you want to select multiple slides, do one of the following:

▶ To select a sequential group of slides, click once on the first slide, hold down the Shift key, and click the last slide in the group. All the selected slides display a heavy border around them.

▶ To select a non-sequential group of slides, click once on the first slide, hold down the Ctrl key, and click on each additional slide you want. In Figure 15-3, slides 3, 5, and 6 are selected.

Figure 15-3
Selecting slides.

Deleting Slides

Using the Slide Sorter view makes deleting slides only a keystroke away. Simply select the slides you do not want and press the Delete key. Optionally, after selecting the unwanted slides, press Delete.

Undo Errors

If you accidentally delete the wrong slides, immediately click the Undo button on the Quick Access Toolbar or press Ctrl+Z.

Rearranging Slides

You might decide that you would rather display slides in a different order than you originally created. First select the slide you want to move and then drag the slide into a new position. As you drag the mouse, a solid line indicating the new slide position appears between two slides, as seen in Figure 15-4. When you release the mouse button, the selected slide moves into the new position.

Figure 15-4
Moving a slide in the Slide Sorter view.

Figure 15-5
The Grayscale tab.

Exploring Other View Options

If you are planning on printing your slide show and you only have a black and white printer, you might want to see how it would look before you print it. PowerPoint provides a couple of other views to see how your presentation looks in grayscale or black and white.

▶ From either Slide Sorter view or Normal view, choose View>Color/Grayscale>Grayscale to see how your presentation would look in shades of gray. A new tab as seen in Figure 15-5 appears while in Grayscale mode. Using the Grayscale tab in Normal view you can select any individual slide object and adjust its tone. Choose Grayscale>Close>Back to Color View to return to color mode.

▶ Choose View>Color/Grayscale>Black and White to see how your presentation would look in black and white. Figure 15-6 shows a slide in its full color mode, in grayscale mode, and in black and white mode. Similar to grayscale mode, a new tab appears while in black and white mode. Use the Black and White tab to adjust any image. Choose Black And White>Close>Back to Color View to return to color mode.

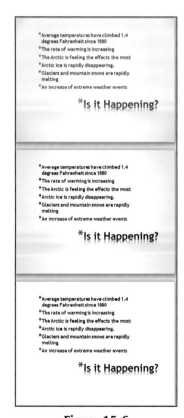

Figure 15-6
A slide in color mode, grayscale mode, and black and white mode.

Modifying Slide Layouts

WHEN YOU FIRST CREATE a new slide, you must choose a slide layout; however, as you work on the slide, you might find that you want to change the layout. For example, you might need to change a Title and Content layout slide to a Two Content slide.

You can change layouts from either Normal view or Slide Sorter view. Select the slide or slides you want to change and choose Home>Slides>Layout. A gallery of slide layout options appears as you see in Figure 15-7. If you have a design applied to your presentation, the available layouts reflect the design.

Choose the layout you want. The slide layout changes and all objects are rearranged. Depending on the layout and the current view, you may see new placeholders.

Figure 15-7
Choosing a different layout.

Adding Multimedia and WordArt to Your Presentation

I N THE PREVIOUS CHAPTER you discovered how to place objects into the slide, primarily by using the content placeholder icons. One content placeholder icon not discussed in the last chapter was multimedia, which includes audio or video files. In this section, you discover how to add multimedia to your slide as well as a creative art object called WordArt. You will also learn how to add and format your own lines and shapes to any slide.

Inserting Multimedia

Multimedia is described as the use of computers to present text, graphics, video, animation, and sound files in an integrated way. PowerPoint by itself is a multimedia application because it can use those file types in a presentation. For the purpose of this book, the term multimedia file will refer to an animation, video, or sound file.

You can insert a multimedia file either in a content placeholder or anywhere on the slide. Because multimedia files typically have an action or sound associated with them, sometimes you will only see an icon that represents the file. The media action or sound in the file becomes apparent whenever you run the presentation in a slide show.

Inserting Sounds

If you have a sound file that you want to play when viewing a particular slide, you can add it to the slide. Because sound files typically have no picture associated with them, you see only an icon on the slide in the shape of a speaker. To insert a

sound file, first select the slide on which you want the sound file. Next, choose Insert>Media and either click the Audio button or click the arrow on the Audio button. Clicking just the Audio button displays the Insert Sound dialog box, and clicking the arrow displays additional options as you see in Figure 15-8.

Figure 15-8
Choosing a sound clip.

Choose one of the following:

▶ Just like clicking directly on the Audio button, the Audio from File option displays the Insert Audio dialog box seen in Figure 15-9. From there you locate the sound file you want to use and click Insert. A sound icon with audio controls under it appears in the middle of your slide. You can click the sound icon and drag it anywhere you want on the slide. Two Audio Tools tabs also appear.

Figure 15-9
Locate the sound you want on your slide.

▶ Choose Clip Art Audio, which opens the Clip Art pane and displays a list of sound files included with Microsoft Office and available from Office.com. Optionally, enter a category, such as insects, in the Search For box, and then click Go to filter the sound files that appear. Click the sound file icon to insert it into your slide, or, if you want to hear the sound before you insert it, pause your mouse over a sound file and from the arrow that appears, choose Preview/Properties. The Preview/Properties dialog box appears and your sound plays. Close the Preview Properties box and if you want the sound file on your slide, click its icon. Figure 15-10 shows the Clip Art pane. After you choose the sound you want, a sound icon with audio controls and two Audio Tools tabs appear.

▶ Choose Record Sound if you have a microphone hooked up to your system and want to record your own sound file.

Audio icon

Figure 15-10
Select a sound from the Clip Art pane.

The Audio Tools Playback tab, as seen in Figure 15-11, provides tools for you to preview the sound, adjust the sound volume, and choose other sound options.

Figure 15-11
Change sound preferences from the Audio Tools Playback tab.

Inserting a Video Clip

Placing a video clip onto a slide is very similar to adding a sound clip. However, you do get more than just an icon when you insert a video clip. You get the first image on the video. You can select your video from a saved file on your computer or from the Clip Art gallery, which also checks for videos from Office.com. Choose Insert>Media> Video or click the Video drop-down arrow. Clicking the arrow gives you the option of adding Video from File or Video from Clip Art organizer. Clicking the Video icon is the same as choosing Video from File. It displays the Insert Video dialog box. You locate and select the movie you want and choose Open.

Alternative Method

If you have a content placeholder on the slide, you can click the Insert Media Clip icon which also displays the Insert Video dialog box.

PowerPoint places the movie in the middle of the slide and displays the movie image in the middle of the current slide. Like a sound file, if you select the movie image it becomes selected and the Video Tools Format and Video Tools Playback tabs appear where you can manage the video file (see Figure 15-12).

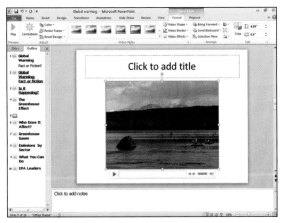

Figure 15-12
The Video Tools Format tab.

Designing with WordArt

Adding text and art to a slide is one way to add visual excitement, but if you're the creative type or if you want your text to have more impact,

WordArt might be your solution. With WordArt, you can take headings or key words and add decorative color schemes, shapes, and special effects. The following steps show you how to create a WordArt object.

1. Select the slide on which you want the WordArt and choose Insert>Text>WordArt. A gallery of options appears as you see in Figure 15-13.

Tip

You can add WordArt to any Word, Excel, PowerPoint, or Publisher document. In Publisher, choose Insert>Text>WordArt. The choices in Publisher are slightly different than in Word, Excel, or PowerPoint.

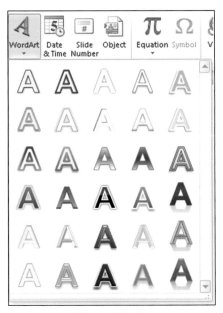

Figure 15-13
The WordArt gallery.

2. Select a style. A WordArt text placeholder box appears on the slide and a Drawing Tools Format tab appears.

3. Type the text you want, and when you are finished click outside of the WordArt text box to see your WordArt object (see Figure 15-14). Limiting WordArt to a single line of text is a good idea; the elaborate formatting can make lengthier text difficult to read.

Edit Text

To edit the text, simply double-click anywhere in the WordArt text and make a correction.

Figure 15-14
Creating WordArt.

4. Click the Drawing Tools Format tab. If you do not see the Drawing Tools Format tab, click once on the WordArt box.

Partial Text Change

To change only a portion of the WordArt, highlight the portion you want to change before you make the change.

5. Use the tools in the WordArt Styles group to modify the WordArt text characteristics. All options include Live Preview, so as you hover your mouse pointer over any option, you see its effect on your WordArt object:

▶ Styles changes the text style from the one you selected in Step 2.

▶ Text Fill changes the text color, gradient, or pattern.

▶ Text Outline modifies the outer edges of the text.

▶ Text Effects applies special effects such as shadow, reflection, rotation, bevel, and transformation (see the next section).

6. Optionally apply a background to the WordArt object, by choosing Drawing Tools Format>Shape Styles and then click the More button. A gallery of themed styles appears as you see in Figure 15-15. Select a background option or click the Other Theme Fills arrow to select from several gradient options.

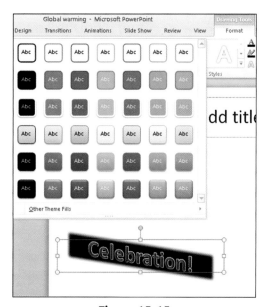

Figure 15-15
Select a style for the object.

Drawing Shapes

Even if you do not have an artistic bone in your body, you can still draw with the Microsoft Office drawing features. You can draw arrows, boxes, stars, circles, callouts, and dozens of other objects. The Shapes feature is available in Word, Excel, PowerPoint, and Publisher.

Follow these steps to draw a shape:

1. Select the slide on which you want to draw.

2. Choose Insert>Illustrations>Shapes. A gallery of shapes appears as seen in Figure 15-16.

3. Choose the shape you want. The gallery closes and your mouse pointer turns into a small black plus sign.

4. Click and drag in the slide until the shape that appears is about the size you want (see Figure 15-17). When you release the mouse button, the shape object becomes selected.

Figure 15-16
Selecting a predefined shape.

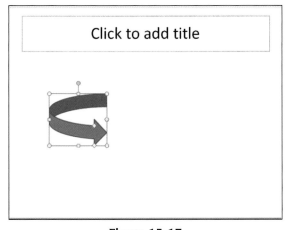

Figure 15-17
Drawing shapes.

After you draw the shape you can apply many style changes to it. After you select the object, choose Drawing Tools Format>Shape Styles. From there, you can:

▶ **Click the Shape Styles More button and select from the available styles.** The choices you have depend on any theme you have assigned to your presentation (see Figure 15-18).

▶ **Click the Shape Fill option to change the object fill.** Choices include solid fills, gradients, pictures, and textures.

▶ **Click the Shape Outline option to change the border around the object.** You can select a border color, size, and style.

▶ **Click the Shape Effects option to add special effects such as shadows, borders, or rotation (see Figure 15-19).**

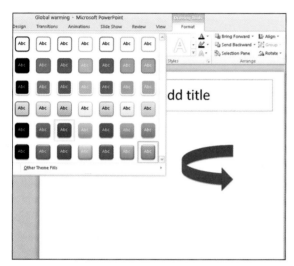

Figure 15-18
Changing a shape style.

Figure 15-19
Adding shape effects.

Managing Objects

NOW THAT YOU HAVE all of these objects on your slides, you probably need to manipulate them a little. You can move them to a different location, adjust their size, change brightness or contrast, or just delete an object you don't want. If you have multiple objects, you can align them, group them, or even place one object on top of or beneath another. In this section you discover how to take any of those actions.

Edit Slide Text

If you want to edit the text on a slide, simply click in the text you want to edit. If the text is in a text placeholder, you can also edit it in the Outline pane.

Moving Objects

If an object is not where you want it, you can easily move it to another place on the slide. Click the image to select it and then position the mouse pointer over any part of the selected image *except* the selection handles or the green rotation handle. The mouse pointer has four arrow heads. Drag the image to the desired position. As you see in Figure 15-20, a lightly transparent version of the object indicates the new position. When you release the mouse button, the object moves to the new location.

Figure 15-20
Dragging the object to a new position.

If you want to move the object just a little bit, you may find it easier to use the keyboard. After selecting the object, use the up, down, left, or right arrow keys to nudge the object into a different position.

Use Cut and Paste

If you want to place the object on a different slide, use the cut and paste features.

Deleting Objects

Okay, this process is so simple it really doesn't deserve its own section, but putting it in one makes it easier for you to find. To delete an unwanted object, click the object's border and press the Delete key.

Resizing Objects

The object may not fit on the page exactly as you envisioned it. You can easily make the object smaller or larger. Just follow these steps:

1. Select the object you want to resize. The selection handles appear around the object.

2. Position the mouse pointer over one of the eight handles. Do not select the green rotation handle. Your mouse pointer turns into a white double-headed arrow. See Figure 15-21.

3. Drag a selection handle in one of the following manners:

▶ Drag a top or bottom handle to change the object height.

▶ Drag a left or right side handle to change the object width.

▶ Drag a corner handle to resize both the height and width at the same time.

4. When the object is the desired size, release the mouse button.

Rotating Objects

Most graphic objects appear onto the slide in a horizontal or vertical position. And most of the time, that's exactly what you want. But in some cases, tilting the object at a fashionable angle provides just the right touch to a slide. PowerPoint objects come with a rotation handle with which you can rotate an object clockwise or counterclockwise.

Select the object you want to rotate and position the mouse pointer over the green rotation handle. Drag the rotation handle clockwise or counterclockwise until the graphic object is at the angel you want. Notice in Figure 15-22 that the mouse pointer turns into a circular arrow.

Mouse pointer

Figure 15-21
Resizing an object.

Rotation handle   Mouse pointer

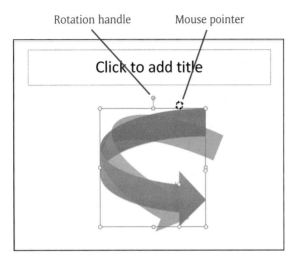

Figure 15-22
Rotating an object.

Flipping an Object

If you want to reverse the direction of a picture or other object, you can flip it vertically or horizontally. Take a look at the bird in Figure 15-23. In the picture on the left the bird is facing left, but on the right side image, which is the same photograph, the bird is facing right. To flip an object, select the object and choose Home>Drawing>Arrange>Rotate and choose Flip Horizontal or Flip Vertical.

Figure 15-23
Flipping an image.

Aligning Multiple Objects

If your slide contains multiple graphic objects, like the ones you see in Figure 15-24, you may want some of them to line up with each other. PowerPoint includes a tool to make aligning objects quick and easy. Just follow these steps:

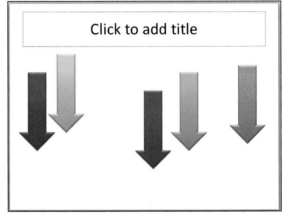

Figure 15-24
Multiple objects that need aligning.

1. Select the first object you want to align and then hold down the Ctrl key and select each additional object.

2. Choose Home>Drawing>Arrange>Align. A menu of alignment options appears.

3. Choose one of the following alignment options:

   ▶ **Align Left:** Aligns the objects along their left edges

   ▶ **Align Center:** Centers the objects horizontally along their middles

   ▶ **Align Right:** Aligns the objects along their right edges

   ▶ **Align Top:** Aligns the objects along their top edges

▶ **Align Middle:** Centers the objects vertically along their middles

▶ **Align Bottom:** Aligns the objects along their bottom edges

Two additional options on the alignment choices apply when you have three or more objects selected. Distribute Horizontally calculates the total space from the left edge of the left most object to the right edge of the right most object and evenly divides the space between the selected objects. Distribute Vertically calculates the total space from the top edge of the top object to the bottom edge of the bottom object and evenly divides the space between the selected objects.

In Figure 15-25, I aligned the object tops and distributed the space horizontally.

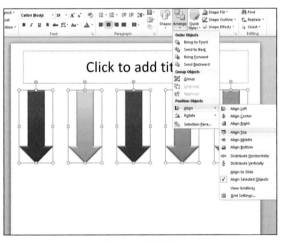

Figure 15-25
Selecting an alignment option.

View Gridlines

Optionally, from the Align options, choose View Gridlines to display a grid that you can use to manually align the objects.

Stacking Objects

When you have multiple objects, sometimes you want them to overlap. Depending on the order in which the images were created, you may have one object covering up another object you don't want covered. In Figure 15-26, you see a chart, an arrow, and a circle, with the circle being the topmost object. In this sample, the circle should be on the bottom and the arrow on the top, making the chart in the middle of the three objects.

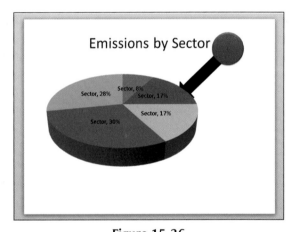

Figure 15-26
Incorrectly stacked objects.

When you restack objects, you can send an object back one object at a time or push it to the lowest object. Or, you can bring an object forward one object at a time or bring it to the top of the stack. Follow these steps:

1. Select the object you want to reorder.

2. Choose Home>Drawing>Arrange.

3. Choose one of the Order Objects options: Bring to Front, Send to Back, Bring Forward, or Send Backward.

Now take a look at the objects in Figure 15-27.

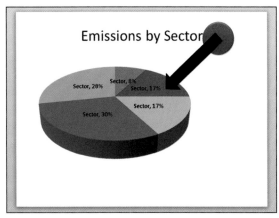

Figure 15-27
After changing the stacking order.

Grouping Objects Together

You can group multiple objects together to form a single object, which makes moving, resizing, and reshaping objects much easier. For example, instead of resizing each of four objects individually, you can group them and resize only one. A really nice feature about the group function is that if you need to you can easily ungroup the object, make any desired individual changes, and then quickly regroup them.

Select the objects you want grouped together and choose Home>Drawing>Arrange>Group. In Figure 15-28, you see three independent objects on the left and one grouped object on the right. If you want to ungroup the object, select it and choose Home>Drawing>Arrange>Ungroup. To regroup, select any one of the original objects and choose Home>Drawing>Arrange>Regroup.

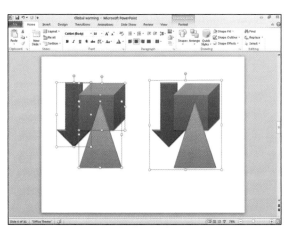

Figure 15-28
Grouping objects.

Using Picture Tools

When you place a picture on a slide (or a Word file or Excel worksheet), you get quite a few options to perform some fairly sophisticated tasks. You can adjust the image brightness and contrast, apply a color accent, give it a frame, or rotate it three-dimensionally. You can even crop it to get rid of unwanted areas. You accomplish all of these picture tasks by using the Picture Tools Format tab that appears on the Ribbon when you select a picture. Figure 15-29 shows you the Picture Tools Format tab.

Figure 15-29
The Picture Tools Format tab.

Making Picture Adjustments

The Adjust group contains seven options. The first option, the Remove Background feature, is new to PowerPoint 2010, and allows you to remove background detail from an image allowing only a selected portion to remain visible. Begin by selecting the picture you want to modify and from the Picture Tools Format tab, in the Adjust group, click the Remove Background button. Your screen changes, similar to the one seen in Figure 15-30. PowerPoint guesses the image background and turns it magenta. The image foreground remains visible.

If you need to adjust the image boundaries so it better fits the area you want, drag any of the selection lines so the selection box contains the image portion you want. If you want to be more specific in the areas you want to keep, click Background Removal> Refine>Mark Areas to Keep and draw around the areas you want. You can also click the Mark Areas to Remove button and draw around areas you don't want. Each time you draw an area, you see a white marker. If you mark an area in error, click the Delete Mark button and click the marker you don't want.

When you are finished, click Background Removal>Close>Keep Changes. PowerPoint removes the background. You can then add effects such as shadows, reflections, or glows to the remaining image portion. See Figure 15-31 where I added shadows to the flowers and placed a black rectangle under them.

Selection border

Figure 15-30
Removing the background area.

Figure 15-31
After removing the background.

Other picture adjustments include:

► The Corrections button displays a gallery where you can adjust the image brightness and contrast. The original image begins at 0% and you can make the image up to 40% brighter or darken it by 40%.

► The Color button applies a coloring effect such as sepia, black and white, or other color variations.

► The Artistic Effects button displays a gallery where you can apply cool effects such as texture, water sponge, or photocopy. Pause your cursor over any effect to see the effect on your picture.

► The Compress Pictures button applies a compression algorithm to all the presentation pictures in order to reduce the document size.

► The Change Picture button displays the Insert Picture dialog box where you can replace the current picture.

► The Reset Picture button undoes any editing and formatting you performed on the selected picture. Trust me...this button will become your friend!

Working with Picture Styles

The Picture Styles group on the Picture Tools Format tab offers a gallery of styles with preformatted shapes and three-dimensional effects. Click the More button to see the complete gallery, as shown in Figure 15-32.

Figure 15-32
Applying a picture style.

In the same group you also have options to change the picture shape and border or to add effects. Through the Picture Shape option you can make your picture take the shape of an arrow, circle, callout, or any of the many different shapes. The Picture Border allows you to assign a color to the frame around your picture. The Picture Effects option provides options for adding shadows, glows, soft edges, and other options. You discovered the effects options when working with objects earlier in this chapter.

Cropping the Picture

The process of cropping removes unwanted portions of an image.

1. Select the picture you want to crop and then choose Picture Tools Format>Size>Crop. Your mouse pointer turns into a cropping tool, and instead of selection handles the picture has cropping handles.

2. Drag a cropping handle to begin the crop-ping process. As you drag the mouse, the mouse pointer changes to a black cross. You may need to crop from several sides of your image. As you drag a cropping handle, a line appears representing the new picture edge, as you can see in Figure 15-33.

Too Much Crop?

If you crop too much off the image, drag the cropping handle the opposite way. What you cropped reappears.

3. Click the Crop button or press the Esc key to turn off the cropping feature.

Mouse pointer

Figure 15-33
Drag from an image edge.

Formatting Your
Presentation

PICTURE YOURSELF WALKING down the grocery aisle. You immediately recognize many products because of their appearance. The soup brand you use touts a half red and half white label. Your favorite peanut butter has red, blue, and green stripes with white lettering, and your usual laundry detergent is in a big orange bottle. What you count on is the consistency of the brand label. Think about it. When certain delivery people walk into your presence, you know who they represent because of their uniform appearance.

Uniformity is also important when creating a presentation. It not only shows professionalism, but maintaining consistency helps your audience know that you are still working on a particular topic. What you don't want, however, is a completely boring presentation where all slides look the same. A certain amount of variety is important, but the basic design on a presentation topic should be consistent. This chapter is about the look and consistency of a PowerPoint presentation. You will discover how to quickly apply a professionally designed theme to your presentation as well as modify that look or even create your own.

Changing Views

POWERPOINT COMES SUPPLIED with a gallery of themed designs, and more are available from Microsoft Office Online. Themes come with a preset font, coordinated color palette, background, and placeholder arrangement, and with a single click you can apply all these attributes to every slide in your presentation. You can change to a different theme at any time.

The theme you select sets the tone for your entire presentation. If you are giving a presentation on an arctic oil exploration you probably want a presentation with cooler color tones, but if you are giving a presentation on global warming, you want one with warmer colors. For vibrant presentations, use one with bright distinctive colors shades. Choosing a theme is a very personal choice. Only you can decide which one is right for your presentation.

To apply one of the predefined themes, choose Design>Themes and click the More button. A gallery of themes appears as seen in Figure 16-1.

Figure 16-1
Choosing a theme.

As you pause your mouse over any theme, Live Preview shows you in the Slide pane what your slides would look like with the new theme. Select the theme you want, and all slides in your presentation take on the new look. Figure 16-2 illustrates the same slide with three different themes beginning with the original Office theme that appears when you launch PowerPoint.

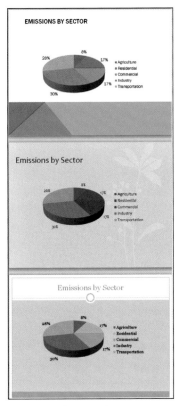

Figure 16-2
A slide with different themes.

The templates you discovered in Chapter 14, "Creating a PowerPoint Presentation," are all based on different themes. One time-saver is to choose one of the templates and then fit your presentation to the template. Better yet, modify the theme so it fits your presentation.

Changing Theme Options

S UPPOSE YOU APPLY the theme, but you want to modify the theme colors or font. You can easily change options using the Design tab, and the changes affect the entire presentation. Begin by applying the theme of your choice. For an example, in Figure 16-3, you see the Concourse theme as it is applied to the entire presentation. Notice on the status bar that PowerPoint displays the current theme name.

Current theme

Figure 16-3
After applying a theme.

Choosing a Background

While a predefined theme already has a background, you can easily select something different. For a background you can have a solid color, a transparent color, a gradient blend of two colors, a texture, or a picture.

By default, background changes apply to the current slide or all slides. If you want to change the background for a group of slides, for example to indicate the presentation is changing focus, from the Slide Sorter view, select the slides you want to change before changing the background. The following steps walk you through changing the slide background.

1. Choose Design>Background>Background Styles. A gallery of styles appears as seen in Figure 16-4. As you pause your mouse over an option, Live Preview shows you the result on the current slide.

Figure 16-4
Choosing a background style.

2. If you want one of the background styles, select it. The background applies to all your slides. If you want to create your own background, choose Format Background, which displays the Format Background dialog box, and continue with these steps.

3. If not already highlighted, click the Fill option on the dialog box's left side.

4. Choose one of the following options:

   ▶ **Solid Fill:** This option provides a single uniform color. Click the Color button and select a color. As you choose a color, you immediately see it on the current slide. Optionally, drag the transparency slider to the right to lighten the color hue.

   ▶ **Gradient Fill:** This option gives the background a mixture of two colors gradually blending into each other. When you choose this option, the dialog box changes to provide the options you see in Figure 16-5. Select the two colors you want to blend. You can also control the Type, which is the direction the colors blend together, and the Gradient stops, which control how smoothly they blend.

Figure 16-5
Creating a background gradient fill.

Figure 16-6
Choosing a background texture.

▶ **Picture or Texture Fill:** This option provides a means to select either a texture for the background or an image. If you want a texture, click the Texture button and select an option from the gallery seen in Figure 16-6. If you want a picture for your background, either click the File button and choose your picture or click the Clip Art button and choose the clipart you want for your background. You can also adjust the transparency and other options for the texture or image.

▶ **Pattern Fill:** This option provides a variety of pattern styles ranging from polka dots to cross hatch marks. Patterns consist of two colors and the option provides buttons where you can select a background color and a foreground color.

Don't Distract the Audience

Using pictures for a slide background can be extremely distracting from the slide content, especially if the image has lots of colors. Use this feature sparingly, and if you do use it, adjust the transparency so the image is light in the background.

5. If you want the new background for all the slides, choose Apply to All. If you just want the choice for the current slide, click the Close button.

Reset Button

Click the Reset Background button to start over.

Applying Theme Effects

PowerPoint also has Theme Effects you can apply to your presentation. Theme effects are the attributes applied to lines and filled objects. When using an arrow, for example, you can certainly change the individual arrow effects, but if you have multiple arrows or other shapes, you probably want them to have a consistent appearance throughout the presentation.

Choose Design>Themes>Effects and click the theme effect you want to use from the gallery seen in Figure 16-7.

Figure 16-7
Choosing a theme effect.

Working with Slide Masters

YOU ALREADY KNOW that consistency in a presentation is important. For example, in each slide layout, the fonts and font sizes are consistent, the placeholder frames are in the same position, and all the bullet point items have the same style bullet.

Often, one of the themed templates is almost, but not quite, right for your presentation. Perhaps a color is slightly different than you really want, or you want your company logo on each slide, or maybe you want a different font than supplied with the template. If your presentation already has a lot of slides, it would be tedious to place the logo or change the font or color on each and every slide.

Instead, you can work with the Slide Master. Think of the Slide Master as the control center for the presentation. The Slide Master view controls the fonts, sizes, bullet styles, colors, alignments, spacing, and more for each slide type of your presentation. It is also where you place any art, such as a logo, that you want on every slide in exactly the same position and in the same size.

Choose View>Master Views>Slide Master. As seen in Figure 16-8, on the Slide List pane, you have the various masters for each slide layouts and a master slide and in the slide pane, you have the current slide layout master. Switching to Slide Master view presents a Slide Master tab with tools for working with the Slide Master.

If you already have slides in your presentation, the Slide List pane can show you which slides are used by each layout. Pause your mouse over a layout to reveal the information. As you also see in Figure 16-8, as the cursor pauses over the Title and Content slide, a ScreenTip appears indicating that the layout is used by slides 3 through 8.

Slide master   Slide layout masters

Figure 16-8
Working with Slide Masters.

In the Slide List pane, the top slide is called the Slide Master and the ones below it are the individual slide layout masters. Changes you make to the master slide affect all layouts, but you can still individualize a specific layout by choosing the slide layout master you want modified and making changes to it.

To make any changes to the master, select the master you want to modify and if the item you want to modify is in a placeholder, select the placeholder. Using the instructions you learned in previous chapters, do any of the following:

► Insert an image such as a logo.

► Move, delete, insert, or resize a placeholder.

► Change the font, font size, color, or other font attributes.

► Add borders to any placeholder.

► Modify the bullet style. See the next section for instructions on changing bullet styles.

Figure 16-9 shows the Slide Master after the following edits, and because the edits were done on the Slide Master instead of a layout master, the changes apply to all slides.

Figure 16-9
After editing the Slide Master.

► The title font type is changed to Cooper Black.

► The title font color is changed from gray/black to blue.

► A shadow is added to the title text.

- ▶ A graphic is added in the lower-left corner.
- ▶ The content section bullet style is changed from a round bullet to an arrow.

If you want to make changes to an individual slide layout master, select the slide layout master and make the desired change. In Figure 16-10, clipart is added to the Title Slide layout master, giving the bottom of the slide layout a different appearance than the rest of the slide layouts.

Figure 16-10
Changing options on a specific layout.

Close Master

When you are finished modifying the Slide Masters, choose Slide Master>Close>Close Master View.

Modifying the Bullet Style

If you want to select different bullet style other than the standard, you can choose from a bullet style gallery or even use a picture. You can also change the bullet color.

From the Slide Master, select the content place-holder and choose Home>Paragraph and click the arrow next to Bullets. A gallery of bullet styles appears as shown in Figure 16-11.

Single Slide Bullet Change

If you want to change the bullets for a single slide, instead of the Slide Master or a specific slide layout, choose the slide from the Normal view instead of the Slide Master view.

Figure 16-11
Selecting a different bullet style.

Either select one of the bullet styles shown or click the Bullets and Numbering option to display the Bullets and Numbering dialog box (see Figure 16-12). From the Bullets and Numbering dialog box you can change the bullet size or color, select from hundreds of bullet styles, or choose a picture to use as a bullet.

Bullet size   Bullet color

Figure 16-12
The Bullets and Numbering dialog box.

To choose different bullet styles, click the Customize button, which displays the Symbol dialog box. Select the symbol you want to use. Optionally, from the Font drop-down menu, choose a different font. Many fonts display different symbols such as the Wingdings symbols you see in Figure 16-13. Click the OK button after you select a symbol. Click OK again if you are finished and want to close the Bullets and Numbering dialog box.

Change Number Style

If you are using numbering on your slides, you can change the number style from the Bullets and Numbering dialog box. Click the Numbered tab to make your selection.

Figure 16-13
The Wingding font provides lots of bullet style choices.

Close Master View

When you are finished modifying the Slide Masters, choose Slide Master>Close>Close Master View.

Generating Footers

In earlier chapters, you discovered how, in a Word or Excel document, you could place a header at the top of every page and place footers at the bottom of every page. PowerPoint also lets you create headers and footers for all your slides. In fact, by default, all new blank presentations come with some type of header and/or footer placeholders. Take a look at the Slide Master in Figure 16-14 where you see the placeholders at both the top and the bottom of the Slide Master. In the Slide Master, optionally drag the placeholders to other positions or delete them if you do not want them.

Placeholders

Figure 16-14
Positioning the footer placeholders.

However, even though the slides have footer place-holders, the option to display the footer is turned off. You must activate the footer and make a few decisions about its format. From either Normal view, Slide Sorter view or Slide Master view, choose Insert>Text>Header & Footer. The Header and Footer dialog box appears with the following items on the Slide tab:

▶ **Date and Time:** Check this option if you want the date and optional time printed on your slides. When you select this option, you see other choices become available. The Update Automatically option creates a dynamic date so whenever you print the slides or view them in a slide show, you see the current date. Click the date format drop-down arrow to display a variety of date formats and choose the format you want. The Fixed option allows you to manually type a specific date that is static and does not change.

▶ **Slide Number:** Check this option if you want the slide number printed on your slides.

▶ **Footer:** Check this option if you want additional text printed on each slide. In the text box, type the text you want. Figure 16-15 shows a company name for the footer text.

Figure 16-15
The Header and Footer dialog box.

▶ **Don't Show on Title Slide:** Click this option if you do not want to see the header or footer on the title slide. Most presentations do not show headers or footers on the title slide.

Notes and Handouts

Click the Notes and Handouts tab to set the options for the speaker notes or audience handouts. See the next section for creating the speaker notes and see "Printing Audience Handouts" later in this section.

Select the options you want and click Apply to All. If you have a particular slide (other than a title slide) on which you don't want the header or footer, select that slide, redisplay the Header and Footer dialog box, turn off the options you don't want, then choose Apply, which applies the options to only the current slide.

Creating Speaker Notes

WHEN YOU CREATE your presentation, you typically keep the actual amount of readable information on the slide to a minimum by just adding bullet points to present your ideas. Then you, as the presenter, elaborate more on those points, or optionally then break each point down to its own slide.

To assist you in keeping track of what you want to say when a particular slide comes up, you can enter notes, which are sometimes called speaker notes. Entering information in the PowerPoint notes area helps you remember the information you want to relay to your audience. You can then print a hard copy of those notes along with a copy of the slide for your reference.

Entering Speaker Notes

Located below the current slide is an area called the Notes pane. In Normal view, you could just click anywhere in the Notes pane and begin typing your text, but since the area is pretty small, it is to your advantage to resize the Notes pane. Drag up the separator bar that you see between the slide and the Notes pane. This gives you more room for the notes, although it makes the slide appear smaller. You can move this separator bar up or down as needed (see Figure 16-16).

Separator bar

Figure 16-16
Type your notes in the Notes pane.

Another and probably easier way to work on your speaker notes is to view the Notes page. Choose View>Presentation Views>Notes Page. You see a full screen view with half the page taken by the slide and the other half with a placeholder you can click into and easily type your text (see Figure 16-17).

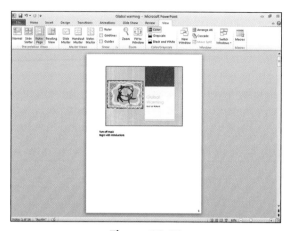

Figure 16-17
Entering notes in the Notes page.

Editing the Notes Master

Like the Slide Master that controls the slide design and layout, PowerPoint provides a Notes Master. Choose View>Master Views>Notes Master. From the Notes Master seen in Figure 16-18, you can change the default font, perhaps making it larger and easier to read when in a dimly lit room. You

can move the placeholders, for example, if you prefer the note text on top and the slide on the bottom. Any formatting option you can apply in the presentation, you can also apply in the Notes Master. When you finish setting up your parameters for the Notes Master, choose Notes Master>Close>Close Master View.

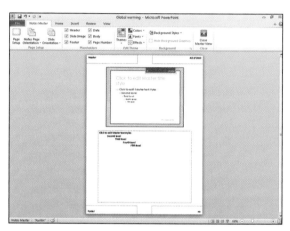

Figure 16-18
Changing the Notes Master.

Finishing Your Presentation

YOU'VE PUT A LOT OF WORK into creating your presentation and you are almost ready to present it. Before you do, however, you want to check it for errors. You may also want to print some or all of the presentation.

Checking Your Spelling

Ouch! Nothing can detract more from your presentation than misspelled words. Word and Excel have a tool for checking your spelling, and so does PowerPoint. Like Word and Excel, PowerPoint underlines any potential misspellings with a wavy red underline. You can correct the spelling errors as you type by right-clicking the misspelling and choosing from the shortcut menu options. You can also check the entire presentation at once. Choose Review>Proofing>Spelling, which immediately launches the Spelling dialog box that stops at the first misspelled word (see Figure 16-19).

Figure 16-19
Checking for misspellings.

Select a correct spelling and choose Change or Change All, add the word to your dictionary, or ignore the misspelling once or throughout the entire presentation. The spell check runs through the presentation and the Masters and then notifies you when it is complete. Click OK to acknowledge the message.

Printing Your Presentation

The big day has finally arrived and it is time to give your presentation. Most of the time, presentations are given on a computer screen, in the form of a slide show, which you will discover in the next chapter, "Presenting Your Presentation." Sometimes, however, you just want to print your presentation.

Preparing to Print

When printing, you have quite a few options from which you can choose. You can print the slides, the outline, the notes, and handouts. Click the File tab and choose Print. The Backstage view print panel seen in Figure 16-20 appears. Here are some of the choices available in the print panel:

Click here to specify what to print

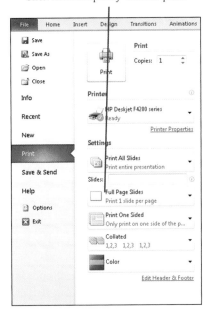

Figure 16-20
The print panel.

▶ **Copies:** Specify the number of copies you want printed and whether you want them collated.

▶ **Printer:** Choose the printer you plan on printing to.

▶ **Other Settings:** Specify other settings, such as whether to print all slides, a preselected group of slides, or the current slide. Optionally, you can specify whether to print double-sided (if your printer has the capability); print-collation order; what you want to print such as the slides, the outline, the

Notes pages, or the handouts; and whether to print in color, grayscale, or pure black and white. If you select color and you're printing to a non-color printer, PowerPoint prints in grayscale.

Print Range of Slides

When choosing to print a range of slides, enter the slide numbers separated by a comma for individual slides, or a dash for a range of slides.

On the right side of the screen, as seen in Figure 16-21, you see the Preview panel. From here you can click the Next Page or the Previous Page button to view the other slides. You can also use the Zoom slider to enlarge or decrease the preview view.

After making your selections, either click the Print button to print your presentation with the options you chose or click the File tab to return to the presentation slides.

Creating Audience Handouts

One of the printing options was for audience handouts. Handouts are thumbnail size versions of your slides that you distribute to your audience. You have the choice of printing one, two, three, four, six, or nine slides to a page.

Handout Page Lines

If you select three slides to a page, PowerPoint automatically prints lines on the right side of the page for your audience members to write their own notes.

PowerPoint also includes a Handout Master, as seen in Figure 16-22. Choose View>Master Views>Handout Master where you can customize the handout layout including fonts, headers, footers, page numbers, and orientation. After you make any desired changes to the Handout Master, close the Handout Master by choosing Handout Master>Close>Close Master View.

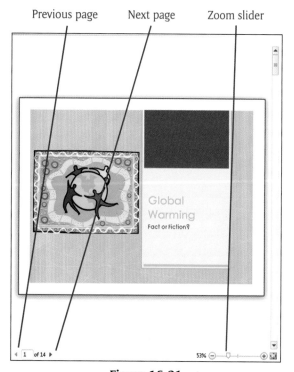

Figure 16-21
The Preview panel.

Figure 16-22
The Handout Master.

When you are in the print panel and you choose to print your handouts, you choose the number of slides you want to print per page and whether you want them in a horizontal or vertical format. Figure 16-23 shows the sample presentation's audience handouts printed three per page.

Figure 16-23
Give your audience handouts to follow your presentation.

17

Presenting Your
Presentation

PICTURE YOURSELF STANDING PERFECTLY STILL. Now talk but don't move. Or move stiff and robotic like. It's difficult isn't it? If you are like most people, you naturally move your hands when you speak. You don't need to sing and dance…just get the point across effectively.

You can also make your slides move as they speak by applying transitions and animations. PowerPoint calls the movement from one slide to the next *transitions*. Transitions add mild excitement to the presentation by creating special movements as one slide turns into the next slide. Notice I said *mild* excitement.

You are finally ready to give your presentation to your group, so you just apply a few finishing touches to it. This chapter shows you how to prepare, start, and lead a slide show presentation, as well as give it your own comments in the form of annotations. You also see how you can package the slide show so it can run repeatedly by itself or from a CD that you give to a user.

Adding Transitions and Animations

I'T'S TIME TO SHAKE THE BUSH (or rather the presentation) and wake up your audience by rolling a few objects across the screen during the slide show. You can make each slide fade into the background as the next one appears, or you can make bullet points appear one at a time. You can create simple transitions such as just replacing one slide with another, or you can select from a number of really fancy transitions.

Setting Slide Transitions

Transitions are wonderful in a presentation if used in moderation. However, some presentations have so many different transitions that they tend to distract the audience with the *Wow!* factor instead of the content. Some transitions are simple in that one slide simply replaces another or dissolves into the next slide, or you can use a transition called Checkerboard, where the slide spins onto the screen in small blocks. In fact, there are 35 transitions you can use.

Although you can use Normal view, transitions are easiest to setup while in the Slide Sorter view. When assigning transitions, you not only can assign a transition visual effect, you can set a speed for the transition to occur and you can assign a transition sound. Follow these steps to assign slide transitions:

1. Select the slides to which you want to apply a transition effect.

2. Choose Transitions>Transition to This Slide, and click the More button. A gallery of slide transitions appears (see Figure 17-1).

Figure 17-1
Assigning a slide transition.

3. Select the transition you want. A selected slide previews the transition effect.

Transition Indicator

In the Slide Sorter view, slides with transitions have a small star-shaped transition icon under the slide. In Normal view, the transition icon appears beside the slide in the Slide list pane.

4. Optionally, choose Transitions>Timing> Sound drop-down menu. A list of available sounds appears (see Figure 17-2). Select the sound you want associated with the transition or choose Other Sound if you want to select a sound stored on your computer.

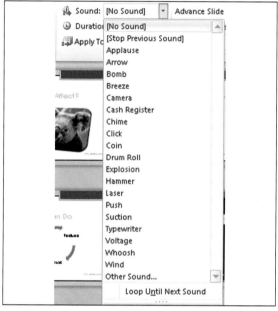

Figure 17-2
Choosing a sound for a transition.

Loop Your Sound

If you want the sound repeated until the next slide, also click Loop Until Next Sound. Please, for the sake of your audience, use this feature sparingly!

---

5. Choose Transitions>Timing>Advance Slide and specify how the slide should advance to the next slide:

▶ Choose On Mouse Click if you want the transition to occur when you click the mouse button.

▶ Choose After if you want the transition to occur automatically after a specified time.

▶ In the After box, enter a number of seconds the slide should display before advancing to the next slide. As shown in Figure Figure 17-3, if you select a timed advance, the number of seconds displays under the slide.

Transition icon   Slide timing

Figure 17-3
Enter the slide timing.

Add Both Options

You can also check both options so you can still manually advance the slide if you want to.

---

6. If you want the selected options to apply only for the currently selected slides, you don't have to do anything else, but if you want the same transitions applied to all slides in the presentation, choose Transitions>Timing>Apply To All.

Remove Transition

To remove a transition, select the slide, choose Transitions>Transitions to This Slide and click the None option.

Assigning Predefined Animations

An animation is similar to a transition, but a transition moves from one slide to another, whereas an animation moves an individual object on or off the screen within a slide. PowerPoint comes with quite a few preset animation schemes.

1. If necessary, switch to Normal view by choosing View>Presentation Views>Normal. You cannot assign animations in Slide Sorter view because you cannot select the component you want to assign an animation.

2. Display the slide you want to assign an animation and then select the component you want to animate. It could be a slide title or any graphic element. You will see in the next section how to animate a bullet list, and later in this chapter I show you how to apply an animation effect to an individual chart element such as a series or category.

3. Choose Animations>Animations and click the More button. A gallery of options appears. Select from the Animation gallery seen in Figure 17-4.

Figure 17-4
Pick an object animation type.

4. Hover your mouse over any of the animation choices to see your selected object with the animation. Click the animation you want.

Tip

Since an animation is a transition for an element, when you view the presentation in the Slide pane or the Slide Sorter view, slides with animations have a small star-shaped icon next to or under the slide.

Animating Bulleted Lists

Often when giving a presentation using a bulleted list, one point leads into another. By applying animations to certain bullets, you can talk about the main slide items, and then with a click of the mouse illustrate the secondary slide list items.

1. If necessary, switch to Normal view by choosing View>Presentation Views>Normal and display a slide with bulleted text.

2. Select the bullet list component and choose Animations>Animations.

3. Click the More button and select an animation.

4. Click Animations>Animations>Effect Options. You can have the bullets all arrive at once, or by the first level paragraphs. With the latter option, the next level arrives when you click the mouse or a specific timing interval occurs. See Figure 17-5.

Figure 17-5
Animating bulleted lists.

Remove Animation

To remove an animation, select the object and choose Animations>Animations>More>None.

Animating a Chart by Components

If you use charts in your presentation, you can animate the chart series or the chart categories. For example, if you have a bar chart that shows the number of clients you have in each of your four stores, you could choose to display one store at a time. The following steps show you how to apply an animation effect to a chart:

1. If necessary, switch to Normal view by choosing View>Presentation Views>Normal and display a slide with a chart.

2. Select the chart you want to animate and choose Animations>Animations.

3. Click the More button and select an animation.

Animation Indicator

Slides with animations display with a number on them but the number does not print or display during a slide show.

4. Choose Animations>Animations>Effect Options. The actual options you see depend on the chart type. For example, a column chart shows all options but a pie chart only lists two of them. See Figure 17-6.

Figure 17-6
Choosing a chart animation.

- ▶ **As One Object:** This option applies the animation choice to the entire chart.
- ▶ **By Series:** This option applies the animation to each data series, displaying one data series at a time.
- ▶ **By Category:** This option applies the animation to each category, displaying one category at a time.
- ▶ **By Element in Series:** This option applies the animation individually to each data marker in each series.
- ▶ **By Element in Category:** This option applies the animation individually to each data marker by category.

5. Hover your mouse over any option to see its effect on your chart, and then make a selection.

Additionally, depending on the animation type you select, when you select Animations>Animations> Effect Options, you see options for the effect. Take a look at Figure 17-7, where you see not only the chart options, but also options for the Spin animation.

Figure 17-7
Choosing animation options.

Rehearsing Timings

Why should you rehearse your slide show? Just as actors must repeatedly rehearse their roles, you should rehearse your presentation. The more you rehearse, the more comfortable you become with the task. Besides making you more comfortable, rehearsing can help you examine the amount of time you spend on each slide. If you have only a specified amount of time, you can determine if your presentation is too short or too long. It also lets you look at each individual slide timing and helps you determine if a particular slide is necessary or whether it would be better served if combined with another slide.

Finally, if you are not sure how much time to allocate for each slide, you can play the slide show and let PowerPoint record your timing as you rehearse your speech.

The following steps show you how to rehearse your presentation and record the timings.

Prepare Your Notes

Before you begin your practice, you will want to prepare your speaker notes or any other tool you plan on using during the presentation.

---

1. Choose Slide Show>Set Up>Rehearse Timings. The slide show begins, as you see in Figure 17-8, and a Record bar appears in the top-left corner of the screen.

2. Practice your speech about the current slide and then click one of the following:

   ▶ **Next:** Advance and begin timing the next slide.

   ▶ **Pause:** Temporarily stop recording the timing.

   ▶ **Repeat:** Restart the timing and rehearsal for the current slide.

3. When you complete the rehearsal and have gone through all the slides, the dialog box appears advising you of the total presentation length and asking you if you want to save the slide timings. Click Yes if you are happy with the timing or click No to discard the timings. You can start the rehearsal process again.

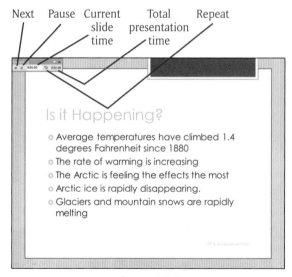

Figure 17-8
Rehearsing slide timings.

Running Your Presentation

THE BIG DAY HAS ARRIVED. You have completed the hard work, so now all you have to do is sit back and enjoy the show.

Setting Up the Slide Show

Before you actually give the presentation, you should set up a few parameters. The Set Up Show dialog box provides most choices you could want to use. Choose Slide Show>Set Up>Set Up Slide Show. The Set Up Show dialog box seen in Figure 17-9 appears with a large variety of slide show options.

Figure 17-9
The Set Up Show dialog box.

▶ **Show Type:** Determines whether to show the presentation in a window or full screen.

▶ **Show Options:** Determines whether to repeat the show until you manually stop it and whether to show any animations or narrations. Also allows you to choose a pen color for annotations you make with the electronic felt tip pen. Red is generally the best choice because most people can see it easily.

▶ **Show Slides:** Determines which slides you want to include in the presentation slide show.

▶ **Advance Slides:** Determines whether to advance the slides manually or using the timings you set up for the individual slides or during rehearsal.

▶ **Multiple Monitors:** If you are showing the slide show on multiple monitors, it controls which monitor to use for the slide show.

Select any desired options and then click OK.

Starting the Slide Show

Finally! You are ready to view your presentation in a slide show. You can actually launch the slide show from several places:

▶ Click the Slide Show view button at the bottom of the presentation window.

▶ Choose Slide Show>Start Slide Show>From Beginning.

Keyboard Shortcut

To launch the slide show with the keyboard, press the F5 key.

Figure 17-10 illustrates the slide in full screen view during the slide show.

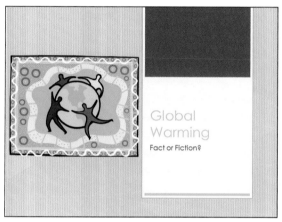

Figure 17-10
A PowerPoint slide show.

When your slide show completes, a black screen appears advising you to click the mouse button.

Navigating Slides

If you assigned timings to your slide show and during the Slide Show setup you elected to use the timings, you don't have to do anything but sit back and watch the show. That is…unless you want to take control over the timings. You can use either the mouse or the keyboard to control the actions in your slide show.

Navigating with the Mouse

When you are in the midst of a slide show presentation, your mouse pointer hides itself until you move the mouse. Then, if you position the mouse over the lower-left corner of the slide, you see the slide show controls. They are fairly transparent until you point directly to one of the four buttons: Previous, Pen, Slides, and Next. Table 17-1 shows you the four buttons and their functions.

Table 17-1 Slide Controls Functions

Button	Name	Function
⬅	Previous	Jumps to the previous slide
✎	Pen	Displays the pop-up menu seen in Figure 17-11 where you can choose annotating pen options
🗏	Slides	Displays a pop-up menu for making slide selections
➡	Next	Jumps to the next slide

Figure 17-11
Pen options from the slide show controls.

Other mouse options include simply clicking the left mouse button, which advances you to the next slide. If you click the right mouse button, a shortcut menu appears such as you see in Figure 17-12, from which you can make additional choices. Many audience members, however, find seeing the shortcut menu in the middle of a presentation extremely distracting.

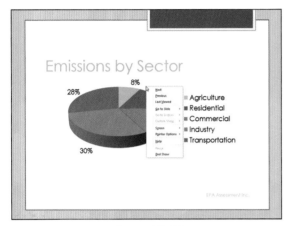

Figure 17-12
Right-click shortcut menu.

Navigating from the Keyboard

Sometimes navigating with the mouse while giving the presentation can be difficult and is often annoying to the audience. A PowerPoint slide show includes quite a few intuitive keystrokes you can use to maneuver in the presentation. Table 17-2 shows you some of these keystrokes.

> ## Jump to a Slide
>
> To go to a certain slide, enter the slide number and press Enter.

Table 17-2 Slide Show Keystrokes

Press This	Get This
N	Next animation or next slide
Spacebar	Next animation or next slide
P	Previous animation or previous slide
Ctrl+P	Change pointer to pen
Ctrl+A	Change pointer to arrow
E	Erase annotations
S	Stop (pause) (Press S again to resume)
B	Pause and show black screen (Press B again to resume)
W	Pause and show white screen (Press W again to resume)
Esc	End the presentation

Pausing the Presentation

Perhaps during the presentation an audience member asks a question that you need to address. You can temporarily pause the presentation and optionally blank out the screen so the audience focuses on you and what you have to say.

If you have an occasion where you want the audience to *not* look at the presentation screen—for example, if you want listeners to concentrate on something you are saying—you can temporarily blank the screen. The slides timings do not advance. If you just want to pause the presentation, press the letter S or click the Slide control button and choose Pause. To resume the presentation, press the letter S again or click the Slide control button and choose Resume. When you pause the presentation, the presentation remains visible on the screen.

If, however, you don't want the audience to see the presentation screen during the pause, you can turn the screen to black or white. If you look carefully, you can see the control buttons in the lower-left screen corner. To pause the presentation and turn your screen black, press the letter B (or W for white) or, optionally, click the Slides control button and choose Screen>Black Screen (or White Screen). To resume the presentation, press the letter B (or W) again or, optionally, click the Slide control button and choose Screen>Unblack Screen (or Unwhite Screen).

Annotating Slides

During the presentation you can draw on your screen with an electronic pen or highlighter. You might draw to underline words or check off key points as you discuss them. You actually have two types of pens: a Ballpoint pen that provides a thin line, or a Felt Tip pen that draws thicker, heavier lines. Additionally, the Highlighter draws wide, fairly transparent lines.

To annotate your slides, choose the pen you want to use from the Pen control button. You can also choose the pen ink color and even switch colors in the middle of the annotating. The keystroke to switch to the pen is Ctrl+P.

Draw on your screen. The drawn image appears on the slide. Take a look at Figure 17-13 where you see some annotations made with a red felt-tip pen.

Figure 17-13
Annotating your slides.

To cancel the pen and return to the normal arrow pointer, simply press the Esc key once. Be sure to only press Esc once. Pressing it a second time cancels the slide show.

Erase Annotations

To erase the screen annotations, press the letter E or click the Pen control button and choose Eraser or Erase All Ink on Slide.

When the slide show ends, a prompt appears asking you if you want to keep your annotations. Choose Keep or Discard. If you choose to keep them, PowerPoint adds the drawing as objects on the slide.

Part V
Access

Many database applications are designed with a programmer in mind and are not intuitive to the novice
user. Access, the Microsoft Office database application,
is one of the most powerful database programs that
exist, but with its Ribbon and interactive Wizards, you
don't have to be a programmer to design your own database. Access helps you track and report information
easily. The chapters in this section show you how you
can use the power of Access to build database solutions
to track contacts, events, issues, assets, tasks, and
more. You'll like the Navigation Pane, which provides
quick access to all your tables, forms, and other Access
objects—all of which you can create with a couple of
mouse clicks.

Creating an Access
Database

PICTURE YOURSELF GETTING READY for an antique sale. You need a list of all the items and you also want to record pertinent information such as their date and estimated value. Instead of reaching for a pad and paper, you create an Access database. A database is described as a comprehensive collection of related data organized for convenient access. You can use a database for organizing things like customer lists or inventory lists. One advantage of using a database is that all of the information is kept together. You don't have to access multiple files to get to your data.

You actually use databases every day. Every time you look up a recipe from your recipe book, you've looked in a database. Each time you look up a phone number in your Outlook contact list, you're using a database. Even though entire books are written about using Access, you'll find the Access application of Office a powerful but easy-to-use database. In this chapter, you learn how to create a database, add, edit, and delete records and be introduced to the sometimes-confusing database terms.

Understanding Database Terms

THERE ARE LOTS OF TERMS associated with databases and just the terms alone scare some people away from working with Access. But it's not as bad as it sounds. There's just a few basic database terms you should become familiar with before you begin creating and working in an Access database such as the one you see in Figure 18-1. Let's take a quick look:

Figure 18-1
A sample database.

▶ **Database.** A database is a collection of information that is similar in nature. A telephone book, a list of your videos, and an inventory list are all examples of a database.

▶ **Records.** A record is all the information about one item. For example, in an address book, the entire sheet of information about Diane Koers is the record.

▶ **Fields.** Fields are categories of information. In the address book example, the last name and fax number are examples of fields.

▶ **Tables.** A table is a matrix, similar in appearance to a spreadsheet, that's used to store database information. All databases require at least one table whereas many databases require several tables, linked together; such as one to store a client's address and telephone numbers and another one to track all the phone calls made to the client.

▶ **Forms.** A form is used for easy data entry. Forms usually display one record at a time.

▶ **Primary Key Field.** A primary key field is where Access stores unique, one-of-a-kind data. Every database table should have a primary key field.

▶ **Queries.** A query is a subset of data that meets certain criteria. An example might be a query of all clients named Smith who live in the city of Chicago.

▶ **Reports.** A report summarizes data in a format suitable for printing. A mailing label is an example of a report.

▶ **Objects.** The general term for all the tables, queries, forms, and reports that you create for your database.

Exploring Access

IFFERENT THAN MOST other Office applications, Access doesn't automatically start with a blank window ready for you to enter data. You have to first tell the program you want to create a new database or if you want to open an existing database. Other initial differences between Access and Word, Excel, or PowerPoint include that Access only allows you to have one database open at a time and you have to give a new database a name at the onset of creating it. Follow these steps to explore an Access database screen:

1. Open the Access application by choosing Start>All Programs>Microsoft Office>Microsoft Access 2010. Access opens by displaying the Available Templates window you see in Figure 18-2.

Sample templates

Figure 18-2
Creating a new database.

2. For the purpose of exploring a database, before you create your own, click Sample Templates. A gallery of templates appears as seen in Figure 18-3.

Faculty   Database name   Create button

Figure 18-3
Selecting a sample template.

3. Click Faculty. On the pane on the right side of the screen, Access suggests a name for the database.

4. If you want to give the database a different name, enter it in the name box.

5. Click Create. The sample predesigned database opens in Table view. See Figure 18-4.

Navigation Pane   Security warning

Figure 18-4
The sample Faculty List database.

When you open one of the sample templates provided with Access, in order to protect your computer, Access displays a Security Warning. You will see this warning whenever you open a database that was created somewhere other than your own computer. Make sure you know where the database originated and that it is safe, then click Enable Content.

This Faculty database doesn't have any records in it yet, but the main screen you are seeing is called the Faculty List table. The name appears at the top of the table (also called a datasheet), which looks very much like an Excel worksheet but doesn't have the column letters and row numbers you see in Excel. Instead, the columns have names that describe the content of each column.

In staying consistent with other Office products, the top of the Access window has a Ribbon with various tabs and groups. Depending on the steps you take in the database, you may see additional tabs appear.

Along the left edge of the screen is the *Navigation Pane*. When in its collapsed state, all you see are the words Navigation Pane and a double arrow at the top of it. Click the double arrow and the Navigation Pane expands as you see in Figure 18-5. The expanded pane displays all the tables, forms, queries, and reports that belong to the database. The white icons represent tables or forms and the green icons represent reports. Double-click any icon and the pane on the right expands to display the element.

Forms and Tables   Reports

Figure 18-5
Expanded Navigation Pane.

As an example, if, on the Faculty database, you double-click Faculty Details from the Navigation Pane, you see the Faculty Details form shown in Figure 18-6.

To access a report, from the Navigation Pane, double-click the report icon you want. For example, in Figure 18-7, you see the Faculty by Department report.

Figure 18-6
An Access form.

Figure 18-7
An Access report.

You'll discover several locations in which you can enter data for your database and one of these is in a form window. When you finish with a form window, you can return back to the main screen by clicking the form's Close button (X).

Creating a New Database

A S YOU'VE SEEN in the previous section, you can use one of the Access template databases. If it meets your needs, you can simply start entering your records. You can also customize the database if you find there is a field you need that isn't in there or perhaps a number of fields you don't want. Chapter 19, "Modifying an Access Database," will show you how to modify a database, whether it's one you've opened from a template, or one you created yourself.

And now that you've seen what a database looks like, it's time to create your own. Follow these steps:

1. Open Access. If you have Access already open, click the File tab and choose New.

2. From the Available Templates category, click Blank Database.

3. On the right side of the screen, enter a name for your database. If you don't give it a name, Access automatically creates it with the name Database1, Database2, and so forth.

4. Click the Create button. The Navigation Pane and a blank datasheet table appears. See Figure 18-8.

Figure 18-8
A new blank database.

Creating a Table

The first thing you must decide when you create a database is what kind of information you want to track. Are you creating a database of your DVDs? If so, you'll want fields such as Movie Name, Date, Genre, and perhaps Rating. If you are creating an address list, you'll probably want at least a Name, Address, City, State, Zip, and several Phone Number fields. And if you're creating a database of items in your home, you might want a Description, Location, Purchase Date, Purchase Price, and maybe even a Photo field.

When you're planning which fields you want to include, here are a few guidelines to assist you:

▶ **Be descriptive.** A field called First Name is a lot more meaningful than a field called FN. You might know what FN stands for, but if someone else were to use your database, they might not have a clue what it represents.

▶ **Have plenty of fields.** Break up fields such as address into smaller fields such as Address, City, State, and Zip. If you want to sort or extract information from the field, it's much easier if the data is in its own field. Same thing goes for names—break a name into segments such as First Name, Middle Initial, and Last Name.

▶ **Plan ahead.** Try to think of fields you might use in the future. It's much easier to add a field when first creating the database than it is to add a field later.

Since Access provides you with the first table for your database, that's a good place to begin. Assigning field names and renaming and deleting fields are accomplished through Design View. Follow these steps:

Tip

As an example throughout the next several chapters, I'm going to create and work with a small address book database.

1. Click Home>Views and click the View arrow. Then select Design View. A Save As dialog box prompts you for a table name.

2. Enter a table name (I'm calling mine Addresses) and click OK. Access renames the beginning default table and displays the table in Design View, as seen in Figure 18-9.

Figure 18-9
Table in Design View.

3. By default, Access gives the first field a name of ID and it's an auto-numbering field. It's a primary key field and this means that each record you enter will be assigned a unique number. If you don't plan on entering your own unique ID field, I recommend you leave the default one alone. Click your mouse on the line below ID.

Primary Key Field Indicator

Notice the key in the leftmost column of the ID which indicates this is the primary field key. If you want a different field as the primary field key, click in the field you want and choose Table Tools Design>Tools>Primary Key.

4. Type a name for the next field. Field names cannot be longer than 64 characters.

5. Press the Tab key. The highlight moves to the Data Type field.

6. You need to tell Access what type of information this field will hold. Will it be text, dates, currency values, numeric data, or something else? Click the Data Type arrow and choose a data type from the drop-down menu you see in Figure 18-10.

Primary key field

Figure 18-10
Selecting a field type.

▶ **Text:** Use this for entering information such as a name or street addresses. Text fields can be a maximum of 255 characters.

▶ **Memo:** Use this for storing longer descriptions, up to 65,535 characters.

▶ **Number:** Use this to store raw numbers. Number fields can be used in calculations.

▶ **Date/Time:** Use this to store dates such as Sales Date or Birth Date or times such as Ending Time or Manufacturing Time.

▶ **Currency:** Use this to store raw numbers, but format the numbers as currency with dollar signs. Currency fields can be used in calculations.

▶ **AutoNumber:** Use this for Access to create sequentially unique numbered fields.

▶ **Yes/No:** Use this for storing information that answers the questions Yes or No, On or Off, or True or False. Access will display the field with a check box. When checked it means "Yes" and when unchecked it means "No".

▶ **OLE Object:** Use this to embed information from an outside source, such as a photo, or auxiliary Word or Excel document.

▶ **Hyperlink:** Use this field type to store hyperlinks to other documents or Websites.

▶ **Attachment:** Use this to create an attachment to an outside document. Similar to, but more efficient than, OLE objects.

▶ **Calculated:** Use this if you need a calculation derived from at least one numeric field in the same table.

▶ **Lookup Wizard:** Use this for providing a drop-down menu with choices to select from. For example, if you have an inventory item that comes in four colors, you might have a "Color" field set up as a Lookup Wizard. Then the person doing the data entry picks the color from a list.

Enter Long Description

Optionally, enter a description of the field in the Description column.

7. Click in the next field and enter a field name and data type. Use as many fields as needed to complete your database. Each field name must be unique. See Figure 18-11 for an example.

Figure 18-11
Creating multiple fields.

Field Properties

See Chapter 19 for information on changing the Field Properties displayed at the bottom of the Design View window.

8. Click the Save button on the Quick Access Toolbar. You don't have to save your records in a database as Access does that automatically for you, but you do have to save design changes.

9. Click Home>Views>View (arrow)>Datasheet View. You see the table, but the column headings now appear as your individual field names, as you see in Figure 18-12.

To close the table, click its Close box.

Close box

Figure 18-12
A table ready for data.

Creating a Form

You've created the table fields which you must do before you can create a form. A form is simply another way to look at the fields. After you enter records into your database, in the table view, you'll see them one on top of the other, but when you view them in a form view, you see one record at a time. Creating a basic form is so easy, you won't believe your eyes!

Click Create>Forms>Form. Access automatically creates a form using all the fields in your table and gives the form the same name as your table (see Figure 18-13). Don't worry too much about the appearance of the form. In Chapter 19, you'll discover how you can change the look of the form, remove unwanted fields, and resize and move fields wherever you want them.

Figure 18-13
A form ready for data.

Click the Save button or press Ctrl+S. The Save As dialog box appears. From here you can give the form a new name or keep the existing one. Click OK. The Form now appears as another object on the Navigation Pane. See Figure 18-14.

Addresses table   Addresses form

Figure 18-14
The Navigation Pane with two objects.

To close the form, click its Close box.

Creating Reports

At the beginning of this chapter, I mentioned that a report summarizes data in a format suitable for printing. Just as easily as you created a form, you can create a basic report. The default report format lists the records in a layout similar to your datasheet table. But reports are easily customizable and Chapter 19 will show you in detail how to do just that.

To create a basic report, from either the Form or the Table, click Create>Reports>Report. Instantly, Access creates a report for your data, as you see in Figure 18-15. The report contains a header that prints at the top of each page, showing the report name, date, and time.

Figure 18-15
A basic report.

Click the Save button or press Ctrl+S to save the report. As with the form, if you want to, you can give the report a different more descriptive name. Once you save the report, it appears as an object on the Navigation Pane.

To close the report, click its Close box.

Working with Records

ONCE YOU HAVE your database field set up, you'll want to begin entering records. Remember that a record is all the information about one item. So when you are entering data in an address book, you should have all the information about the record readily available. It can be tedious to get all your records entered, but to successfully use your database, you need to be able to add, edit, and delete records.

Adding Records

Access provides two methods to enter your data. You can either enter data on the datasheet table or you can enter it in the form. Which method you use is entirely up to you.

Tip

A database is different from many other types of files in that you don't have to click the Save button each time you add a record. Access automatically saves the data each time you add or edit a record.

Entering Data in Datasheet View

The advantage of entering data on the data sheet is that you can view multiple records at one time allowing you to visually compare the records. Follow these steps:

1. Open the datasheet by double-clicking its icon on the Navigation Pane.

2. Click Home>Records>New or click the mouse in the first available row. The first available row has an asterisk beside it.

3. Make sure the insertion point is blinking in the field you want to enter and type the data for the first record.

4. Press the Tab key to move to the next field and enter its data. (See Figure 18-16.) You can press Shift+Tab to move back to the previous field. When you have entered all the field information you want for that record, Access automatically takes you to the next row where you can enter the next record.

Figure 18-16
Entering records.

5. If your database has a Yes/No field in it, you see a check box for the field. Click the check box if the instance is true, otherwise leave it unchecked.

6. If your database has a date field in it, you can type the date as mm/dd/yy or mm/dd/yyyy or you can click the calendar icon and choose a date. See Figure 18-17.

Figure 18-17
Entering a date.

Entering Data in Form View

If your database has more than a few fields, when you enter data in the Datasheet View you have to keep scrolling right or left to see all the fields. If you enter data in the Form view, you don't have to scroll to see all your fields. They all appear on one main screen unless you happen to have dozens of fields, in which case you might need to scroll up or down. Use the following steps to enter your records in Form View:

1. Open the form by double-clicking its icon on the Navigation Pane.

2. Click Home>Records>New or click the New Record button at the bottom of the window (seen here).

3. Make sure the cursor is blinking in the field you want to enter and type the data for the first record.

4. Press the Tab key to move to the next field and enter its data. See Figure 18-18. Just like entering data in Datasheet View, you can press Shift+Tab to move back to the previous field.

Figure 18-18
Entering records in Form View.

5. When you have entered all the field information you want for that record, press the Tab key. Access automatically takes you to a new blank record.

Viewing Records

Once you have your records entered, you'll want to be able to look at them. Access gives you two distinct views to use when viewing records: Form View and Datasheet View.

Viewing in the Datasheet

In Datasheet View, you'll see many records on a single sheet, similar to an Excel spreadsheet. Use your horizontal scroll bars to scroll right or left and see additional fields, or use the vertical scroll bar to view additional records. You won't see a vertical scroll bar if your database doesn't have more records than the screen can show and you won't see a horizontal scroll bar if your database doesn't have more fields than the screen can show. In Figure 18-19, you see only a horizontal scroll bar.

Figure 18-19
Viewing records in Datasheet View.

You can easily edit any field in Datasheet View. Just drag across and highlight the existing information, type the change, and press Enter.

To assist you in navigating through your records, Access also provides view controls at the bottom of the window. See Figure 18-20. Using these buttons lets you quickly jump to the first record, next record, previous record, and last record. You also see a Filter indication and a Search box. You'll take a look at those shortly.

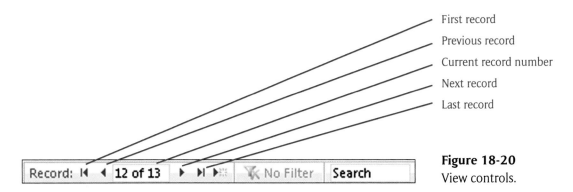

First record

Previous record

Current record number

Next record

Last record

Record: I ◀ 12 of 13 ▶ ▶I ▶❊   ☓ No Filter   Search

Figure 18-20
View controls.

Navigating Around in a Form

Form View allows you to see one record at a time and like in Datasheet View, you can easily edit any record. You locate the record you want, drag across and highlight the field information you want to change, and then type the new changes. When you press Tab or click out of the current field, Access saves your changes.

Also like the Datasheet View, you have view controls at the bottom of the window, which allow you to quickly navigate to the first record, next record, previous record, and last record. The view controls also show you the current record number and the total number of records. See Figure 18-21.

View controls

Figure 18-21
Viewing records in Form View.

Deleting Records

You can delete the entire record or just the data in a particular field record. When you delete a record, the entire record is gone from both the Datasheet View and the Form View. The method you use depends on which option you want and what view you are currently using:

▶ If you are in Datasheet View, and you want to delete only the data in one field of a single record, highlight the record cell data by clicking once on the data cell, and then clicking once on the border surrounding the data. (See Figure 18-22.) Next, press the Delete key or choose Home>Records> Delete. No warning is given, and the field empties. You can undo (Ctrl+Z) this if you deleted the wrong field information.

A selected field

ID	First Name	Middle Initi	Last Name	Address 1	Address 2	City	State
1 Barney	R	Fife	1742 Main		Mayberry	NC
2 Barney	F	Rubble	91 Gladstone S		Bedrock	US
3 Diane	M	Koers	14 South Chart		Some City	US
4 Diane	S	Lowe				
5 Dino	R	Lowe	1302 West 10th Apt 3C		Carmel	IN
6 Dorothy	M	McNeely	123 West Main		Jasper	IL
7 Elvis	A	Presley	Graceland Man		Memphis	TN
8 Fred	F	Flintstone	89 Gladstone S		Bedrock	US
9 Funky	U	Fred				
10 George	G	Jetson	Skypad Apartm		Orbit City	US
11 James	W	Stewart			Beverly Hills	CA
12 Marilyn	R	Monroe			Hollywood	CA
13 Paul	E	Newman	167 Ranch Driv		Hidden Valley	CA
14 Daniel		Scott	309 Wekiva Wa		Cincinnati	OH
(New)						

Figure 18-22
A selected field.

▶ If you are in Datasheet View, and you want to delete an entire record, click the mouse on the small box to the left of the first field. If you were looking at this in Excel, it would be the row number. See Figure 18-23. Then press the Delete key or choose Home> Records>Delete. Access displays a confirmation message. **Use caution!!** Once you delete a record, you cannot undo it. Click Yes if you really want to delete the record.

Record selection box

![A selected record datasheet view]

Figure 18-23
A selected record.

▶ If you are in Form View and you want to delete only the data in one field of a single record, display the record and drag your mouse across the field data you want to delete. Then either press the Delete key or choose Home>Records>Delete. No warning is given, and the field empties. You can undo (Ctrl+Z) this if you deleted the wrong field information.

▶ If you are in Form View and you want to delete an entire record, display the record you want to delete, press the Tab key, which highlights the next available field. Then choose Home>Records and click the Delete

arrow. From the resulting menu seen in Figure 18-24, choose Delete Record. Access displays a confirmation message. Use caution!! Once you delete a record, you cannot undo it. Click Yes if you really want to delete the record.

Figure 18-24
Deleting records in Form View.

Tip

If any of the information in the record you are deleting is tied to other tables in the database, the confirmation message warns you that deleting this record will also affect those tables.

Finding Records

When you have a lot of records in your database, it sometimes becomes difficult to find the one you're looking for. Access provides two methods to help you locate a particular piece of information. In one method, the fastest one, you just start typing at the bottom of the Datasheet window, in the Search box. See Figure 18-25. You can use this from the Datasheet or the Form View. As you type, Access jumps to the first record that matches what you typed.

Search text   Text found in record

Figure 18-25
Searching from the Search box.

The second method has you use the Find command. The Find command is useful when you want to seek out text that you may have trouble visually locating. The Find command doesn't change any text; it simply locates and highlights the specified text for you. And with the Find command, you have a number of options from which you can choose. The Find command is easiest used with the Datasheet View.

Follow these steps:

1. Open the table or form you want to search.

2. Choose Home>Find>Find or press Ctrl+F which displays the Find and Replace dialog box you see in Figure 18-26.

Figure 18-26
The Find and Replace dialog box.

3. In the Find What box, enter what you're looking for.

4. Choose from the additional options as desired:

   ▶ **Look in:** Choose whether you want to search in the current field or the current document, which includes the entire table.

   ▶ **Match:** Choose from Whole Field, which means the text you entered in Step 3 is the complete and only word (or phrase) in its field. With Whole field selected, entering *Jet* will not find *Jetson*. Choose Any Part of Field if you mean the text entered in Step 3 is just a portion of the field. For example, if you enter *read* in the Find box, Access will also locate words like *bread* or *reading*.

   ▶ **Search:** Select a direction to search. Choices are Up, Down, or All. If you choose up or down, Access searches from the point of the current record.

   ▶ **Match Case:** Check this to locate instances that match the uppercase and lowercase letters as you entered in the Find box. For example, if you typed *West*, Access will not locate *west* or *WEST*.

5. Click Find Next. Access highlights the first occurrence of the found data.

6. Click Find Next again to locate the next occurrence of the data.

7. Access notifies you when no more matches can be found. Click OK, then click Cancel.

Using Replace

If you want to replace the found data with something different, click the Replace tab and enter the text you want to find. In the Replace With text box, enter the data you want to replace it with. Click Find Next and if you do indeed want to replace the data, click Replace.

Sorting Records

When you enter your data records, you don't have to worry about entering them in any special order. That's because Access provides a simple-to-use sort function. The process of sorting rearranges your records so that they are in alphabetical, numerical, or date order. Sometimes sorting your data helps you find the information you want quicker.

You can sort your data in two ways: ascending or descending. When you sort in ascending order, the records are sorted alphabetically from A to Z, numbers are sorted from smallest to largest, and dates are sorted from earliest to latest. If you sort in descending order, just the reverse happens. Text is sorted from Z to A, numbers are sorted from largest to smallest, and dates are from latest to earliest.

To sort your records, from Datasheet View, first click anywhere in the field by which you want to sort. Don't select the entire field—just click in that field

of any record. Next click Home>Sort & Filter and then choose Ascending or Descending. Access sorts the records for you. In the sorted column heading, you see an up or down arrow. An up arrow indicates the records are sorted by that field in Ascending order and a down arrow indicates the records are sorted by that field in Descending order.

Take a look at Figure 18-27. The records are sorted in ascending order by Last Name.

Sort indicator

Figure 18-27
Sorting your records.

Multiple Sort

You can sort your records on more than one field. You perform one sort, then another and if desired, another. But you must sort them in reverse order. For example, suppose you have an employee database and you want to sort the employees by Department, then by Hire Date, then by Last Name. You would first sort by Last Name, then perform the second sort by Hire Date, and finally perform the third sort by Department.

When you no longer want your records sorted, you can choose Home>Sort & Filter>Remove Sort. The records will return to the order in which they were entered.

Filtering Records

After you create an Access database and assemble a large amount of data, you probably want to analyze it. You may want to ask yourself questions about your data. "Who lives in California?" "Which SciFi movies do I own? "Which inventory items are provided by a specific supplier and cost less than a certain amount?" "Which employees work in the Memphis office?" Access includes the ability to filter, which you can use to answer these questions and study your data so you can make better decisions.

Filtering means that Access can pull out specific records for review. This provides you with an easy way to break down your data into smaller, more manageable chunks. Filtering does not rearrange your data; it simply temporarily hides records you don't want to review so you can clearly examine those you do. Filtering in Access is similar to filtering in an Excel worksheet. You learned about filtering Excel data in Chapter 11, "Managing Large Amounts of Data."

The filtering process in Access is very similar to that in Excel. By default, a datasheet has filter arrows already displayed. You use the filter by selecting from available choices. A filtered range displays only the rows that meet the criteria you specify for a field. The following steps show you how you can filter records:

1. Click the arrow in the field heading from which you want to find a common value. Access displays a drop-down menu, which includes one of each unique entry (up to 10,000 entries) in the selected column (as you see in Figure 18-28).

Figure 18-28
Filtering records.

2. Remove the check mark from Select All. All items become unselected.

3. Click the entry or entries you want to filter and then click OK. Access displays only the records that match your choice. In Figure 18-29, you see only the records with a city of Hollywood. Notice that the filter arrows on filtered columns take on a different appearance to indicate that a filter is in use.

Figure 18-29
Filtered records.

Clear Filter

To clear the filtering, from the column containing the filtering you want removed, click the column filter arrow and choose Clear Filter from "field name."

There are many other functions you can perform with filters, including searching for fields that are blank, performing secondary filters, and using comparison filters. Text comparison is when you specify a range such as "begins with" or "does not equal." Other options might be "exactly" or "contains". As I mentioned earlier, the filtering in Access is very similar to that in Excel. See Chapter 11 for lots more information about filtering.

			STOCK	
			CONS GAME	
			CONTINENTL	
			COOPER	
			COPLEX	
			CORDUKES	
			CORPEX	
			COSMOS	
			COUNT	
			COUNTRY RD	0.00
			COUNTY	0.4
			COVENTRY	1.00
			CPH INVEST	3.48
			CPI GROUP	0.38
			CPT GLOBAL	0.73
			CRANE GRP	0.53
			CRANSWICK	8.47
			CREDITCORP	

Modifying an Access
Database

PICTURE YOURSELF WATCHING a stock ticker. The stock prices change frequently and your job is to keep track of the current price. So you enter the new price into your database. The problem is that whoever designed your database didn't make it easy for quick data entry. You wish you could modify it to better fit your needs.

Sometimes a database basic forms and tables will provide everything you need, but other times, you find yourself wishing for additional fields, or other tables and forms. Each database can be modified to meet your requirements. In this chapter, you learn how to add and delete fields from a table and modify forms.

Designing Table Appearance

B Y DEFAULT, when you create a table, the fields appear in the order you created them and they are all the same general width, regardless of the field type or size.

Changing Table Field Width

On some tables, you may find fields that aren't wide enough to display the information they contain such as an address field. Other fields are too wide and are wasting precious screen space, perhaps a State field. You can easily adjust the table field column width, however, changing the table field width does not affect the allowable number of characters in the field. It only changes how you see the table.

In Access, you can change a table field width the same way you can in Excel. Position your mouse pointer over the right side of the field name, along the gray bar. When the mouse is in the correct position, it changes into a black double arrow with a bar through it. (See Figure 19-1.)

Drag the gray bar to the right to make the field column wider or drag it to the left to make it narrower. As you drag the mouse a black line running down the screen indicates the new field width.

Mouse pointer

Figure 19-1
Changing field width.

Click the Save button on the Quick Access Toolbar. If you forget to click the Save button, when you close the table, Access asks you if you want to save your changes. Click Yes if you want to save them, or No if you don't.

Formatting Tables

In Access, you began with a blank datasheet and then added your data. But in its generic form, a table can sometimes be difficult to read. Perhaps the fonts are too small, or the data doesn't line up in a way that makes it easy to read. In fact, a datasheet is just plain boring.

Fortunately, similar to Excel, Access includes a variety of features with which you can make the datasheet more interesting and easier to read. Change the fonts, or make the numbers easier to read by adding numeric formatting. Liven up your worksheet with effective use of borders, lines, and color. Whoever said "Looks aren't everything" wasn't staring at an Access datasheet.

If you look at the Home tab, in the Text Formatting group shown in Figure 19-2, you see quite a few options with which, by now, you are probably very familiar.

Figure 19-2
The Text Formatting group.

Many choices in the Text Formatting Group apply to the entire table and a few apply to only the current column. Still others apply only to certain type fields such as a memo field. Let's take a look at some of the more commonly used formatting features:

Font: The default font is Calibri. Click the arrow beside the font to choose a different one. Font options apply to the entire table.

Font Size: The default size is 11. Click the arrow beside the font size to choose a larger or smaller font. Font size options apply to the entire table.

B **Bold:** Click the button to activate the feature. Click the button again to deactivate the feature. Bold applies to the entire table.

I **Italics:** Click the button to activate the feature. Click the button again to deactivate the feature. Italics applies to the entire table.

U **Underline:** Click the button to activate the feature. Click the button again to deactivate the feature. Underline applies to the entire table.

Alternate Row Color: Click the arrow next to the icon and select a shading color. Access shades every other row on the table making it easier to see the data. Figure 19-3 illustrates a table with alternating row color. Choose No Color to remove any row color.

Figure 19-3
Alternating row color.

A **Font Color:** Click the arrow next to the icon and select a color for all data in the table. Font color choices apply to the entire table.

Background Color: Click the arrow next to the icon and select a background color for all cells in the table. Background color choices apply to the entire table.

≣ Align Text Left: Horizontally aligns the data along the left edge of the field.

≣ Center: Centers the data horizontally in the middle of the field. If you change the field column width, the data remains centered to the new column width.

≣ Align Text Right: Horizontally aligns the data along the right edge of the cell.

⊞▾ Gridlines: This button controls which, if any, gridlines appear on the table. You get a menu of options as seen in Figure 19-4.

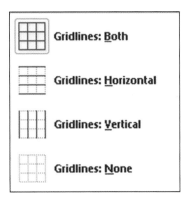

Figure 19-4
Gridline options.

Change Default Formatting

If you want all new datasheets to appear with specific formatting, click the File tab and choose Options. From the Access Options dialog box, click Datasheet and specify the options you want. Click OK when you are finished.

Another way to perform most of the previous formatting along with a few others is using the Data Formatting dialog box. Click the Home>Text Formatting Dialog Box Launcher which displays the Datasheet Formatting dialog box seen in Figure 19-5. From here you can change the gridline color, background color, and a number of other effects. All choices in this dialog box apply to the entire table. Make your selections and then click OK.

Click the Save button on the Quick Access Toolbar.

Figure 19-5
The Datasheet Formatting dialog box.

Moving Table Fields

The table lists the fields in the order you created them, but if you want to change the order of the fields, you can easily do so.

Select the field column you want to move by clicking on the field heading. Position your mouse over the column heading so the mouse pointer is a white arrow pointing left. See Figure 19-6.

Mouse pointer

Figure 19-6
Reordering the table fields.

Press the mouse button down until you see a thick line on the left side of the field column. Drag the mouse until the thick line is to the right of the column you want in front of it. In Figure 19-7, I am moving the field Cell Phone so that it will be right after the Home Phone field. When you release the mouse button, Access moves the field and all its data to the new position.

Click the Save button on the Quick Access Toolbar.

Mouse pointer

Figure 19-7
Moving the field to a new position.

Hiding Table Fields

If your table has fields that you don't particularly want to view, but you don't want to delete them because you use the data elsewhere, you can hide them from view. And just as easily, you can unhide them when you want them. If the field is used in any calculation, Access still performs the calculation even though the field is hidden. Follow these steps to hide a field:

1. Open the table containing the field you want to hide.

2. Click the field column heading, which highlights the entire field.

3. Choose Home>Records>More. A menu of options appears. See Figure 19-8 where I have selected the Middle Initial field that I want to hide.

Figure 19-8
Hiding fields.

4. Choose Hide Fields. The field disappears from your view.

5. Click the Save button on the Quick Access Toolbar.

Alternative Method

You can also hide a field by right-clicking the field heading you want to hide and choosing Hide Fields.

When you want to view the column again, choose Home>Records>More and choose Unhide fields.

Modifying Table Structure

WHETHER YOU CREATED your database from the beginning or started with an Access template, you'll probably find yourself wishing you had additional fields. That's not a problem because you can add as many new fields as you want. And if your table has any fields you decide you don't want, you can easily remove them.

Adding Fields to a Table

After you create your database, if you decide you need additional fields; go right ahead. Each Access 2010 database table can contain up to 255 fields. And like many Access features, there's a quick and easy way to add fields and then there's a way that takes a few extra steps, but gives you more flexibility.

The "quick and easy" method is to open the table to which you want to add a field. Then right-click the column heading where you want the new column. From the resulting shortcut menu you see in Figure 19-9, choose Insert Field. Access immediately inserts a new text field and gives the field a generic name like Field1, Field2, Field3, and so forth. You can rename the field by right-clicking the field name and selecting Rename Field. Type a new field name and press Enter. Click the Save button on the Quick Access Toolbar.

Figure 19-9
Inserting a new field.

But what if you want a new numeric or date field? Although using the "quick and easy" method is great, it doesn't give you the opportunity to choose a field type or other field attributes. The second method involves going into the Design View and from there you have a great amount of control over the new field.

Follow these steps to add a new field through Design View.

1. Open the table you want to add new fields to, then choose Home>Views>View (arrow)>Design View. Access switches to Design View. This is the same view you used when you first created your table.

2. Click the gray box to the left of the field where you want to insert the new field. The field becomes selected. See Figure 19-10.

Selected field

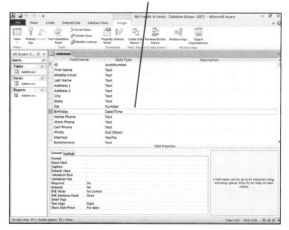

Figure 19-10
Select where you want the new field.

3. Choose Table Tools Design>Tools>Insert Rows. Access inserts a blank row.

4. In the Field Name box, enter a name for the new field.

5. In the Data Type box, select a data type.

Add a Field at the Bottom

If you just want to add a new field to the bottom of the list, just begin typing the field name in the Field Name column and select a data type.

6. Click the Save button on the Quick Access Toolbar.

7. Click Table Tools Design (or Home)>Views> View (arrow)>Datasheet View to return to your normal table view.

Deleting Table Fields

When you delete a field, Access deletes not only the field but all data stored in the field. And you cannot "undo" the action. Because the act of deleting a field is potentially harmful, Access prompts you for confirmation before deleting any field and its data.

Just as when you add a field, Access provides a quick and easy method to delete fields. From the open table, right-click your mouse over a field and choose Delete Field. A confirmation message appears. Click Yes.

Checking Field Properties

Besides a data type, every field you create in your database has properties that determine attributes which control a variety of field characteristics. These traits include how many characters can be entered in a field, verification that a field meets assigned values, the number of decimal places, and more. You manage all field properties through the Design View. Choose Home>View>Views (arrow)>Design View. Field properties for the selected field appear at the bottom of the screen. The choices that appear depend on the field type you're working with. Let's take a look at a few of the field properties.

Save Property Changes

Be sure to click the Save button after making any field property change.

Field Size

The Field Size option only appears for Text and Numeric data types. If you are working with a text field, the maximum number of characters is 255, but if you want it restricted to a smaller number,

say five characters for a Zip Code, then you enter 5. If your data type is numeric, click in the Format box. Access provides the Field Size drop-down menu. Most users leave the numeric data size as the default Long Integer.

Format

The format option primarily controls how numbers, dates, and times appear in the table. If your data is numeric, click in the Format box and choose one of the options seen in Figure 19-11.

Click this area to display the drop-down arrow

Figure 19-11
Select a numeric type.

If your data is a Date/Time type, you get a drop-down menu to select from like the one you see in Figure 19-12.

Figure 19-12
Select a date/time type.

Click here to start the Input Mask Wizard

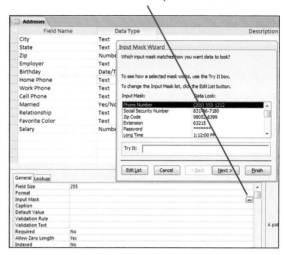

Figure 19-13
The Input Mask Wizard.

Input Mask

Used with Text and Date field types, you can create a template with punctuation marks that can make your data entry easier. Input masks are often used with telephone numbers or social security numbers so they appear in a commonly used format and also help prevent many data entry errors.

In the Input Mask text box, you enter a 0 where you want numbers and any punctuation marks or spaces where they belong. For example, to enter a mask for telephone numbers, you enter (000) 000-0000 and for social security numbers, you enter 000-00-0000.

If you need additional help with creating a mask, click the three dots on the right side of the Input Mask text box. You may be prompted to save your table and then the Input Mask Wizard seen in Figure 19-13 appears. Choose an option then click Next. Review the questions on the second page of the Wizard and click Next. Review and select any options from each Wizard page and then click Finish.

Default Value

You can save data entry time if a particular field has a frequently used text entry, value, number, or even an abbreviation. By entering default data, all new records will have the data, which of course, you can override when you enter the record.

Validation Rule

Validation Rules are an invaluable tool for avoiding data entry errors. For example, suppose you are keeping an employee database and all salaries fall between $40,000 and $150,000. By creating a data validation rule restricting the salary between those two numbers, the data entry operator can't accidently enter a salary of $350,000.

Most validation rules use the Greater Than (>), Less Than (<), Equal to (=), or Not Equal To (< >) symbols and you can combine the Greater Than or the Less Than with the Equal to. So in the previous example, you need a validation rule that says the data must be greater than or equal to 40,000 and less than or equal to 150,000. The expression (rule) you would enter is >=40000 AND <=150000.

You can type the expression in the Validation Rule text box or you can click the three dots in the box. The Expression Builder dialog box appears. Enter your expression in the top box then click OK. See Figure 19-14.

Figure 19-14
The Expression Builder.

Additional Functions

The Expression Builder box also has additional functions you can use to create validation rules. Click the Help button for more information.

Validation Text

If someone enters data that violates your validation rule, Access displays a message. You can customize the message by entering a statement in the Validation Text box. What you enter is what the users see if they enter data that doesn't fit the requirement, regardless of whether you enter the data in Datasheet View or Form View. See Figure 19-15.

Validation text   Attempted entry

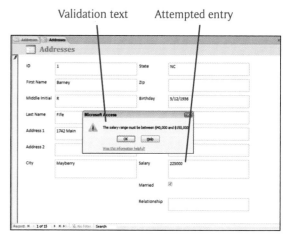

Figure 19-15
A validation error message.

Required

By default, any field of any record can be blank. In the required box, if you choose Yes instead of No, Access will not let you leave the record until an entry is made in the required field. For example, if you require that a State be entered for each record and you try to access another record without entering a State for the current record, a warning message appears like you see in Figure 19-16.

Figure 19-16
The field entry required error message.

Text Align

This option determines how the text is aligned in a field column. You can change this option by choosing an alignment option from the Text Formatting group on the Home tab.

Show Date Picker

Anytime you set a field data type to Date/Time, Access displays the little calendar to the right where you can select a date. However, if you don't want the calendar, you can set this option to Never. The data entry person must then type the date in the format you specify.

Lookup

This option is one of my personal favorites. You may not have noticed it, but each field properties section displays an additional tab, the Lookup tab where you can determine the entry type you want to use:

> ▶ **Text box:** The default choice, a text box simply lets the data entry person type the entry.

> ▶ **List box:** A list box provides a drop-down menu from which the data entry person must choose one option. No other choices are acceptable. Figure 19-17 illustrates a sample lookup list.

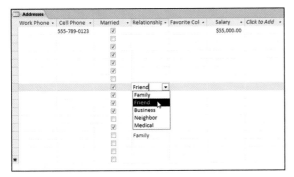

Figure 19-17
Sample lookup.

> ▶ **Combo box:** Combo boxes let the data entry choose multiple selections from a drop-down menu. See Figure 19-18 for a sample combo box lookup.

Figure 19-18
Sample combo box.

The following steps show you how to set up Lookup options.

1. From the Design View, select a text field in which you want to create a lookup.

2. From the Field properties, click the Lookup tab.

3. Click the Display Control arrow and choose List Box or Combo Box, depending on which option you want. A variety of additional properties appear.

4. Click in the Row Source Type field, click the arrow, and choose Value list.

5. Click the Allow Value Edit Lists option and choose Yes.

6. If you are using a Combo Box, click Allow Multiple Values and select Yes. If you are creating a List, leave this option set to No.

7. Click in the Row Source box, and click the three dots on the right. The Edit List Items dialog box appears.

8. Enter the list you want for the field as seen in Figure 19-19. You can enter as many items as desired.

Allow Multiple Values   Allow Value List Edits   Click here to display the Edit List Items dialog box

Figure 19-19
Creating a lookup list.

9. Click OK.

10. Click the Save button to save your changes.

Modifying a Form

WHEN YOU CREATE a form (Create> Forms>Form), Access places every field in your table on the form and places them in a columnar format. And while that may be just fine for you, you may want to mix things up a bit.

Changes you make to tables such as adding or removing fields do not necessarily reflect on your forms. So you might want to modify a form to match those database changes. However, you do not have to display all fields on your form!

Typically forms have a descriptive text label next to the field. The label describes and identifies the field . All changes to the forms are made in Form Design. Open the form you want to modify and choose Home>Views>View (arrow)>Design View.

Deleting a Field from a Form

When deleting a field from the form, no data will be lost. This just means that the field data cannot be accessed from the form. A form is simply a different way you can view the database information.

From the Design View seen in Figure 19-20, select the field you want to delete. A heavy border surrounds the field. Press the Delete key to delete the field from the form. You probably will want to delete the field label as well, so click the label to select it and press the Delete key.

Text   Field label   Database field   Selected field

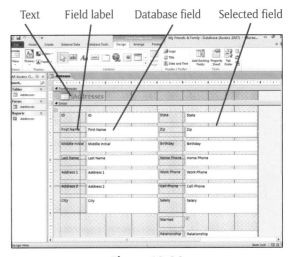

Figure 19-20
Working in Form Design.

If you want to delete all the fields and start over, press Ctrl+A, which selects everything on the form. If you have any selected fields or labels you don't want to delete, hold down the Ctrl key and click on those items to deselect them. In Figure 19-21, all items but the header items are selected. Press the Delete key to remove the selected fields and labels.

Figure 19-21
Deleting all fields.

> ## Oops!
>
> If you accidentally delete the wrong field from your form, use the Undo button on the Quick Access Toolbar or close the form without saving any changes.

Adding a Field to a Form

If you decide to start over and create your own form, you'll probably need to add fields back onto the form. To add fields, you need to see the Field List. When the Field List is displayed, all available fields appear and you can easily place them on your form. Follow these steps to add a field to your form:

1. From Design View, display the field list by clicking Form Design Tools Design>Tools> Add Existing Fields. A Field List appears.

2. Click the field you want and drag it onto the form. As you drag it, your mouse pointer has a small box under it like the one seen in Figure 19-22.

Mouse pointer has a small box

Figure 19-22
Adding a field to the form.

3. Release the mouse button where you want the field. Both the field label and the field appear on the form. You'll see in the next section how to move the fields and the labels around.

4. Continue adding any desired fields and their labels. You can delete any unwanted field labels.

5. Click the Save button on the Quick Access Toolbar.

Moving a Form Field

If you need a field or a field label in a different position, Access makes it easy to move. The way you move objects around depends on whether you want to move the field and heading together or separate.

> ▶ **If you want to move both the field and the heading together, click on the field itself, then position the mouse pointer over the heavy orange border surrounding the field until the mouse becomes a four-headed arrow.** Then drag the border

until the field is in the new position. Moving the field by the orange border moves both the field and the title simultaneously. When you are dragging the field, it looks like only the field is moving, but when you release the mouse button the heading will move into place as well.

▶ **If you want to move just the field (separate from the heading), click the field to select it, then position the mouse pointer over the box in the upper-left corner.** Drag the gray box until the field is in the new position. Moving the field by the box moves only the field and not the label.

▶ **If you want to move just the label (separate from the field), click the label to select it, then position the mouse pointer over the box in the upper-left corner.** Drag the box until the heading is in the new position. Moving the heading by the gray box moves only the heading and not the field.

Drag this to move both the field and heading

Drag this to move only the heading

Drag this to move only the field

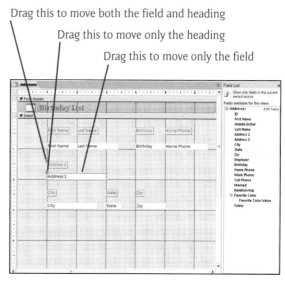

Figure 19-23
Moving fields around on the form.

Nudge to Move

To move the fields or field headings with the keyboard, select the field or heading and press the up, down, left, or right arrow keys.

Figure 19-23 shows fields and their headings moved into different positions on the form. Be sure to click the Save button on the Quick Access Toolbar.

Resize Fields

If you need to resize a field, select the field and drag one of the six handles surrounding the field. Drag from a corner handle to resize both height and width. Drag from the right or left middle handle to change the height only or drag from the top or bottom middle handles to change the field width.

Changing the Form Theme

Access uses the themes common to most other Office applications. Themes contain professionally designed color combinations and font, and because you can have practically as many forms as you want, you can apply different themes to different forms. Access uses a default theme named Clarity.

To change a form theme, from the form Design View, choose Form Design Tools Design>Themes> Themes. A gallery of available themes appears, as you see in Figure 19-24. Click the Theme you want.

Figure 19-24
Select a different theme.

Click the Save button on the Quick Access Toolbar.

Adding a Form Background

If changing the theme doesn't glitz up your form enough, you can add a background picture to the form. Go to the form Design View and choose Form Design Tools Format>Background> Background Image>Browse. The Insert Picture dialog box appears. Navigate to and select the picture you want for the form background and click OK. Access inserts the picture on the form background. Click the Save button on the Quick Access Toolbar.

When you add a background picture, Access keeps the form fields white so they sit on top of the picture and you can still see the data. The labels, however, are a different story. If your picture has a lot of color in it as you see in Figure 19-25, notice that the field labels are almost impossible to read.

Figure 19-25
Add a background picture.

To remedy that problem, while in the form Design View, select the field labels either one at a time, or select multiple labels by holding down the Ctrl key while choosing the labels. Then choose Form Tools Format>Font and choose an appropriate font color. In Figure 19-26, I made the field labels larger, white, and bold.

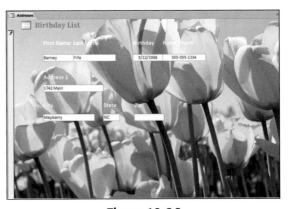

Figure 19-26
After changing the label color.

What about if you add a background and then decide you don't want it after all? Can you remove it? You can remove it, but doing so is not very intuitive. Use the following steps to remove a form background.

1. From the form Design View choose Form Design Tools Format>Background> Background Image. An Image Gallery appears. See Figure 19-27. The Image Gallery is a collection of recently used database images.

2. Right-click the image you no longer want for your background and choose Delete. The image no longer appears in the Image Gallery, but your form still shows the background.

3. Click the Save button on the Quick Access Toolbar.

4. Switch to Form View by choosing Home> Views>View>Form View. The background image disappears from the screen.

Figure 19-27
Removing a background picture.

Part VI
Outlook

Microsoft Outlook is a collection of integrated messaging and contact-management programs that allows you to do all the things the other Personal Information Management (PIM) programs do, and it also makes it easier than ever to have your information work together. For example, you can use the Contacts portion of Outlook when creating e-mails or when creating a mail merge in Word. You can use the Calendar portion to remind you of upcoming important events and you can use Outlook's Task feature to help keep yourself organized. The chapters in this section guide you through the ever-helpful functions available in Microsoft Outlook.

Communicating with
Outlook E-Mail

PICTURE YOURSELF SITTING AT YOUR COMPUTER, exchanging e-mail with co-workers, family, and friends, or perhaps even finding romance, as Tom Hanks and Meg Ryan did in the movie *You've Got Mail*.

Using Microsoft Office Outlook, the most widely used e-mail program, you can quickly and easily enter the world of electronic communication. With Outlook's e-mail, you can perform the basics of sending, receiving, and reading e-mail, but Outlook goes far beyond those basics in providing you with features. In addition to forwarding e-mail and sending and receiving e-mail attachments, you can manage the mail you receive. And if you're like most of us; you get a lot of e-mail.

And, besides providing you with e-mail capabilities, Outlook acts as a personal information manager, providing you with a calendar on which you can enter meeting information, helping you keep track of names, addresses (both snail-mail and e-mail), and phone numbers, and letting you create a to-do list for those things you know you're going to forget if you don't write them down.

Looking at the Outlook Window

WHEN YOU FIRST OPEN OUTLOOK, the Outlook Today page appears, showing you what's on your calendar for today, tasks on your to-do list, and a summary of your e-mail situation (see Figure 20-1). Across the top of the window, you see the Outlook Ribbon with tabs and groups like other Office products.

Navigation Pane   Customize Outlook Today

Figure 20-1
Viewing your agenda in the Outlook Today window.

The Navigation Pane runs down the left side of the screen, and you click the buttons in the Navigation Pane to switch to different areas in Outlook. For example, to work with Outlook's to-do list, click Tasks or to manage your appointments, click Calendar. When you click Mail, Outlook highlights Personal Folders in the Navigation Pane and continues displaying the Outlook Today page. You use the items listed below Personal Folders to help you work with e-mail.

Customizing Outlook Today

You can customize the Outlook Today page by clicking Customize Outlook Today in the upper-right corner of the window. Outlook displays the Customize Outlook Today page (see Figure 20-2).

Figure 20-2
Set options for the Outlook Today window.

▶ If you remove the check from the When Starting, Go Directly To Outlook Today box, Outlook doesn't display Outlook Today when you open the program. Instead, Outlook displays your Inbox, which contains e-mail messages you receive.

▶ You can click the Choose Folders button to display the Select Folder dialog box, which you can use to select folders to appear on the Outlook Today page. I recommend you at least display the Inbox, Drafts, Sent Items, Deleted Items, Junk E-mail, and Outbox folders.

▶ In the Calendar section of the Customize Outlook Today page, specify the number of calendar days you want shown on the Outlook Today page.

▶ In the Tasks section, identify the tasks you want to appear on the Outlook Today page and then identify how you want Outlook to sort them.

▶ In the Styles section, you can control the layout and appearance of the Outlook

Today page. The default, called Standard, is a three-column layout. You can select to use a two-column layout, a one-column layout, or you can select the Summer or the Winter layout, which both use a two-column layout but present a different appearance of the Outlook Today page.

When you finish setting Outlook Today options, click Save Changes to see the effects of your changes.

Working with E-Mail

THINK OF E-MAIL as electronic letter writing. Using e-mail is a quick and easy way to keep in touch with people both nearby and far away. And, for reasons I can't begin to explain, writing an e-mail seems to take less time than writing a letter. There's no question that e-mail is here to stay.

To use e-mail, you need an Internet connection, an Internet Service Provider (ISP), and an e-mail address. Your computer must contain hardware—a modem or a network card—to support an Internet connection. Your Internet Service Provider (ISP) tells you what equipment your computer needs to use the service (and often provides you with some or all of the equipment) and also gives you an e-mail address.

Other E-Mail Accounts

You also can sign up for an e-mail address that isn't connected to a specific ISP. For example, Microsoft offers free Hotmail e-mail accounts and Google offers free Gmail e-mail accounts. Using these accounts, you can collect e-mail using an Internet browser such as Internet Explorer, or you can collect the e-mail in Outlook.

Once you sign up for service with an ISP, set up your Internet connection, and obtain an e-mail address, you're ready to start using the e-mail capabilities in Outlook.

Setting Up an Account

The first time you open Outlook, a wizard may appear and prompt you to set up an e-mail account. If you started Outlook and skipped this step, you can set up e-mail accounts at any time. Follow these steps (if you already see the Setup Wizard, you can skip steps 1 and 2):

1. Click the File tab and from the Info tab, click Account Settings and click Account Settings again. The Account Settings dialog box appears.

2. From the E-mail tab, click New. The Add New E-mail Account window appears.

3. Click Next and type your name, your e-mail address, and your password on the Auto Account Setup screen of the wizard (see Figure 20-3).

Figure 20-3

Configuring your e-mail.

4. Click Next. Outlook configures your e-mail account. Be patient. The process may take a few minutes.

5. Click Finish.

If Outlook is unable to automatically configure your e-mail account, go back to the Auto Account Setup screen and choose the Manually Configure Server Settings or Additional Server Types options. Outlook displays the screen you see in Figure 20-4. Your ISP will provide you with the Incoming Mail Server and Outgoing Mail Server (SMTP) information and specify whether you need to check the Require Logon Using Secure Password Authentication (SPA) check box. You can click the Test Account settings to check to see if your information is valid, or simply click Next.

Figure 20-4

Manually configure an e-mail account in Outlook.

After you click Finish, Outlook displays the Account Settings window, and you can see your e-mail account as you see in Figure 20-5. Click the Close button.

Figure 20-5
Your e-mail account appears in the Account Settings dialog box.

Now you're ready to start working with e-mail.

Reading Incoming Mail

To receive incoming e-mail, you don't need to do anything special other than open Outlook. By default, Outlook automatically checks for incoming e-mail for you.

Check for Messages Now

Expecting a particular message? You can click Send/Receive>Send & Receive>Send/Receive All Folders to tell Outlook to check for messages now.

When you click Mail in the Navigation Pane, you see a window divided into three panes (see Figure 20-6). The left pane is the Navigation Pane, of course. The center pane contains the folder contents, called the message list. The right pane, called the Reading pane, displays the content of any message you select

in the center pane. And, to the right of the message content pane, Outlook displays the To-Do Bar, which you can display to get a quick overview of upcoming appointments and tasks without leaving the Mail pane in Outlook. See Chapter 23 for details on the To-Do Bar.

Inbox   New message indicator   Message list

Figure 20-6
Outlook's Inbox, where new mail appears.

E-mail messages accumulate in the Inbox. The number that appears in parentheses beside the Inbox, and any of the folders in the Personal Folders section, represents the number of unread messages in the folder. The sender's name of an unread message in the middle pane appears in bold when you examine the list of messages. The total number of messages in the Inbox appears in the lower-left corner of the screen.

Tip

Although I'm talking specifically about the Inbox in this section, the information here applies to messages in any folder listed in the Personal Folders section of the Navigation Pane.

Outlook organizes messages in the Inbox based on when you received them. It groups them together such as Today, Yesterday, Last Week, or Last Month. If you cannot see messages from other time periods, click the plus sign (+) beside the time period.

To select a message so that you can view its content, click the message in the message list. Outlook displays the message's content in the Reading pane so that you can read it. After you click another message or folder, Outlook automatically marks the message as "read," removing the boldface type from the sender's name in the middle column.

You can double-click a message to open it in a separate window, like the one shown in Figure 20-7, but there aren't many reasons to do so. As you'll see later in this chapter, you can do pretty much whatever you need to do with any message from the Reading pane.

Click here to download pictures   Blocked pictures

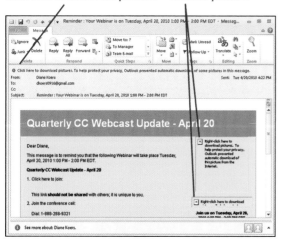

Figure 20-7
An open e-mail message.

In Figure 20-7, you may have noticed a bunch of X's in boxes in the message content in the right pane. The X's represent pictures in the e-mail message that Outlook isn't displaying. By default, Outlook blocks and doesn't download pictures in e-mail messages to help you avoid getting e-mail from spammers.

Tip

Spam is unwanted e-mail typically sent out in bulk. It usually contains pictures and may try to sell you something. Spammers don't always use legitimate e-mail addresses—often they find a domain name (the part of your e-mail address that appears after the @ sign) and simply use a program to create possible e-mail addresses, in the hopes that some will actually be legitimate. The messages often include links to pictures or sounds on the Internet. If the pictures or sounds are automatically downloaded, you may be verifying your e-mail address for the junk e-mail sender. The junk e-mail sender watches for valid e-mail addresses and then sells them to other spammers, increasing the amount of spam you receive. At best, spam is annoying; at worst, it's offensive, time-consuming to handle, and can give your computer a virus.

You can view the pictures in any e-mail message if you right-click any of the boxes at the top of the message and, from the menu that appears, select Download Pictures (see Figure 20-8). Outlook downloads and displays the pictures. If you preview another message and return to the one with downloaded pictures, they will still appear.

Figure 20-8
Download pictures from an e-mail.

Replying to a Message

Many e-mail messages you receive will require a response from you. What makes replying easy is that you don't need to know the recipients e-mail address to reply to a message. Here comes one! And, it's asking you for information. To reply to an e-mail, follow these steps:

1. Click Mail in the Navigation Pane.

2. Click the folder containing the message to which you want to reply.

3. In the message list, click the message to which you want to reply.

4. Click Home>Respond>Reply. Outlook opens a window containing the original message, and the insertion point appears above the original message, waiting for you to type your reply (see Figure 20-9).

5. Type your reply.

Send button

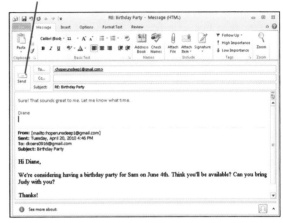

Figure 20-9
Replying to an e-mail message.

6. Click the Send button to the left of the recipient's e-mail address. Outlook places the message in your Outbox. The next time Outlook automatically checks for incoming messages, it will send your reply and store a copy of it in the Sent Items folder.

Forwarding a Message

Suppose Mary just sent you an e-mail message that contains information that you know would be valuable or interesting to John. Without having to retype the e-mail contents, you can forward the message to John by following these steps:

Tip

These steps assume that you have stored e-mail addresses in your Contacts list (you can read about creating contacts in Chapter 21). If you have not stored an e-mail address in your Contacts list, type the e-mail address of the person to whom you want to send the message in Step 5. Then, skip to Step 10.

1. Click Mail in the Navigation Pane.

2. Click the folder containing the message you want to forward.

3. In the message list, click the message you want to forward.

Tip

If you forward a message that contained images that you didn't download, the pictures are not forwarded to your recipient.

4. Click Home>Respond>Forward. Outlook displays the message in a window, with the Insertion point appearing in the To box (see Figure 20-10).

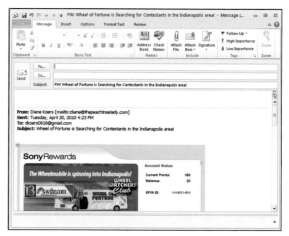

Figure 20-10
Forwarding a message.

5. Click the To button. Outlook displays the Select Names: Contacts dialog box shown in Figure 20-11.

Figure 20-11
Use this dialog box to select contacts when you forward a message.

6. Click the name of the person to whom you want to forward the message. Or, you can type some characters of the person's name and Outlook will find the nearest match.

7. Once you have highlighted the correct contact's name, click the To -> button. Outlook adds the recipient in the To -> text box.

8. Repeat Steps 6 and 7 for each recipient to whom you want to forward the message.

9. Click OK. Outlook redisplays the message window.

10. Optionally, in the body of the e-mail, add any additional message.

Delete Other Addresses

Do your friends a huge favor! If the e-mail you are forwarding has other people's e-mail addresses in it, delete those names and e-mail information from the message before you click the Send button!

---

11. Click Send. Outlook places the message in your Outbox and sends it the next time it checks for new messages. Outlook stores a copy of the sent message in the Sent Items folder.

Deleting a Message

Once you finish reading a message, replying to it, and forwarding it, you may want to delete it. The concept here is that you don't need the message around for anything anymore. To delete a message, click it in the message pane of the Inbox (or whatever folder contains the message) and then click Home>Delete>Delete or press the Delete key on your keyboard. Outlook moves the message to the Deleted Items folder.

What Folder?

Depending on what e-mail you are using, you may see a Deleted Items folder or a Trash folder. In the example of using Gmail, Outlook calls it a Trash folder.

In the interest of good housekeeping, you should periodically empty the contents of the Deleted Items folder. To delete the messages in the Deleted Items folder, right-click the Deleted Items folder and choose Empty Folder from the resulting shortcut menu shown in Figure 20-12. A confirmation message will appear; click Yes.

Figure 20-12
Cleaning up the Deleted Items folder.

Creating a New Message

Although you can't send physical objects such as a sample of your product, you can send letters, pictures, and computer files. So if you have something that you want to tell somebody and you don't have a message to reply to or forward, it's not a problem. Create your own message by following these steps:

1. Click Mail in the Navigation Pane.

2. Click Home>New>New E-mail. Outlook displays an empty message window.

3. Type the e-mail address of the person to whom you want to send a message in the To box or, if you've stored the e-mail address in your Contacts list, click the To button. Outlook displays the Select Names: Contacts dialog box.

4. Click the name of the person to whom you want to send the message. Or, you can type some characters of the person's name and Outlook will find the nearest match.

5. Once you have highlighted the correct contact's name, click the To -> button. Outlook adds the recipient in the To -> text box.

Send to Multiple Contacts

You can send a message to multiple recipients. If you're using the Contacts list, just keep selecting names. Outlook separates them with a semicolon. You can also select contacts for the Cc: line. The Cc: (which stand for Carbon Copy) is a secondary recipient. Finally, you can enter contacts on the Bcc: line. Recipients on the To: and the Cc: line cannot see the names listed on the Bcc: line, which, by the way, means Blind Carbon Copy.

6. Repeat Steps 5 and 6 for each recipient to whom you want to send the message.

7. Click OK. Outlook redisplays the message window.

8. In the Subject line, type something that summarizes the purpose of the message. Although you don't have to put a subject in the message, many e-mail programs automatically consider them spam and may either delete them or put them into a special junk mail folder.

9. In the large white message box, type your message as seen in Figure 20-13. You can format your text by selecting it and choosing options from the Format Text tab.

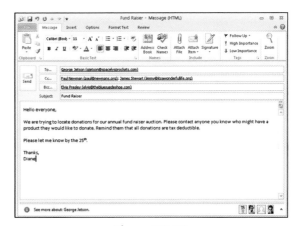

Figure 20-13
Creating a new message.

Spell Check

Nothing makes you look as bad as a misspelled word. Double-check your spelling by choosing Review>Proofing>Spelling and Grammar.

10. Click Send. Outlook places the message in your Outbox and sends it the next time it checks for new messages. Outlook stores a copy of the sent message in the Sent Items folder.

Working with E-Mail Attachments

YOU'VE HEARD ABOUT attachments: they are files that come along with an e-mail. In fact, you've probably heard never to open an attachment unless you know the person sending it and you're expecting the attachment. That's good advice, by the way. Following that advice will help you avoid getting a computer virus.

You can receive and you can send files attached to an e-mail message.

Receiving an E-mail Attachment

Before we begin working with attachments, let's learn **Attachment Rule #1: Never, never, never, open an attachment from someone you don't know.** The attachment may contain a virus that could corrupt your entire computer. Your anti-virus program screens the attachments, and Outlook screens the attachments, but they can't catch all of the malicious items that come through e-mail. So use extreme caution when working with attachments. Now...did all that scare you? Good! That means you'll be careful.

Okay, now let's assume you receive an attachment from someone you know and you expected the attachment. Now what? Click the e-mail message containing the attachment to select it. You'll notice that a paperclip appears next to the subject line of the message, above the time the message came in (see Figure 20-14).

Attachment icon   Attachment

Figure 20-14
An e-mail message with an attachment.

In the Reading pane, you'll see two choices below the address information; one for the message and one for the attachment. Click the Message icon to preview the message. Click the attachment icon and if the attachment is a readable file, you'll see a preview of it. (See Figure 20-15.) Double-click the attachment to open it in the program that created it. If the attachment is from a Microsoft Office application, the file will open in Protected View.

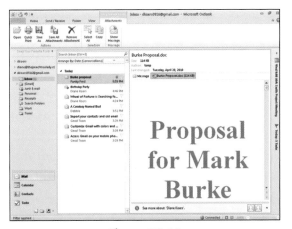

Figure 20-15
Previewing an attachment.

Tip

If you don't have the program that created the attachment installed on your computer, you'll see an error message. You won't be able to open the attachment until you install the program that created it or a viewer for that program.

If you need to save the attachment you receive for future reference, you can right-click it and choose Save As. In the Save Attachment window, navigate to the folder on your computer where you want to keep the attachment and then click the Save button. Once you've saved the attachment on your computer, you can delete the e-mail if you don't need the information in the message portion.

Sending an E-Mail Attachment

Okay, now it's your turn. You need to send a file to someone. Or, you want to send an Outlook item (task, contact, and so on) to someone. No problem. Follow the steps to create, reply to, or forward an e-mail message described earlier in this chapter, but don't click the Send button yet. Choose Message>Include (see Figure 20-16) and then click one of the items shown in Table 20-1.

Attach File   Attach Items   Signature

Figure 20-16
The Message Ribbon.

Click Attach Item Arrow

To attach a business card, calendar, or Outlook item, you must first click the Attach Item Arrow.

After you select and attach the appropriate item, click the Send button. Outlook places the message in your Outbox and sends it the next time it checks for new messages. Outlook also places a copy of the sent message in the Sent Items folder.

Table 20-1 Attachment Options

Ribbon Button	Purpose	Action
	Attach a file	Navigate to the location where the file is stored on your computer and select the desired file to attach.
	Attach an Outlook item	Navigate to the Outlook folder containing the item and select the desired Outlook item.
	Attach an electronic business card	Select a contact from your Contacts list.
	Attach your Outlook calendar	Specify the calendar timeframe (the recipient doesn't need to use Outlook to see your calendar).
	Attach an electronic signature	Clicking this button lets you both create and attach the signature.

Creating an E-mail Signature

An e-mail signature is an address or phrase that you want to include at the bottom of your e-mail messages. Perhaps your company name, address and phone number, or your favorite famous quote. You can create many signatures and then chose signatures for different e-mail recipients.

Create your own signature by following these steps:

1. Click the File tab and choose Options. The Outlook Options dialog box opens.

2. From the topic section on the left, choose Mail. The dialog box displays Mail options. See Figure 20-17.

Signatures button

Figure 20-17
Viewing Mail options.

3. Click the Signatures button. The Signatures and Stationary dialog box appears.

4. Click the New button. In the resulting box, enter a name for the signature such as Diane, or Company, then click OK.

5. In the Edit Signature Box, type and format your signature clause. See Figure 20-18 for an example.

Save button

Figure 20-18
Creating an e-mail signature.

6. Click the Save button, then click OK twice.

When you are ready to use the signature, from the New, Reply, or Forward message, click Message> Include>Signature and select which signature you want to use. See Figure 20-19.

Figure 20-19
Using an e-mail signature.

Using Personal Folders to Manage E-Mail

Earlier you discovered that you can use the Personal Folders to help you organize e-mail. If you're like me, you may find yourself collecting e-mail from a variety of people on a particular subject. I like to keep my "same subject" e-mail stored in a folder, so, I create my own folders that appear along with the other folders listed under Personal Folders. To create a new folder, follow these steps:

1. Click Mail in the Navigation Pane.

2. Choose Folder>New>New Folder. Outlook displays the Create New Folder dialog box (see Figure 20-20).

Figure 20-20
Creating a new folder.

3. Type a name for the new folder.

4. Open the Folder Contains list to specify the types of Outlook items you'll store in the folder. To store e-mail messages, select Mail and Post Items.

5. In the Select Where to Place the Folder box, choose the top-level folder (usually your name) to create a folder at the same organizational level as the Inbox.

6. Click OK. Outlook adds the folder in the Folders list.

7. To move items to the folder, simply click the message you want to move, and drag it until it's on top of the new folder, as shown in Figure 20-21, and then release the mouse.

Mouse pointer   Selected item

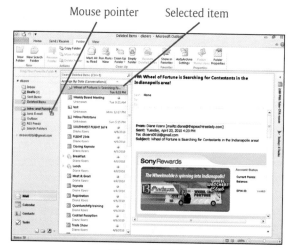

Figure 20-21
Moving items to the new folder.

Working with Outlook
Contacts

PICTURE YOURSELF GETTING RID OF YOUR ROLODEX, no longer typing or writing contact information on hundreds of little cards that get mashed and smashed as you use them. Imagine knowing exactly where to easily find street addresses, phone numbers, and e-mail addresses without hunting for your address book, wherever you put it. And, best of all, picture yourself no longer typing e-mail addresses because you can have them automatically filled in. These are just some of the advantages of using Outlook's Contacts folder.

In Microsoft Office Outlook, your contacts are those whose information you need to keep handy for future reference. Outlook stores all this information in a folder: the Contacts folder.

Exploring Your Contacts Folder

THINK OF THE CONTACTS FOLDER as a huge Rolodex without the frayed edges on the cards. Click Contacts in the Navigation Pane to display the Contacts folder. In Figure 21-1, you see the Business Cards view of the Contacts folder. This view most closely resembles the Rolodex.

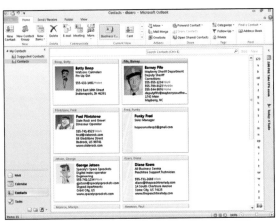

Figure 21-1
The Business Cards view.

Tip

You can use your Outlook contacts in a Word Mail Merge. See Chapter 6, "Using Word for Mail Merge," for details.

Down the right side of the screen, you see the alphabet. Clicking a letter of the alphabet quickly takes you to the contacts beginning with the letter. For example, if you click the letter Y, you would see your contacts for Andrew Young, or Sarah Yetz.

As mentioned in Chapter 20, "Communicating with Outlook E-Mail," Outlook has a new look for Office 2010. Instead of a toolbar, you see the Office Ribbon, which contains different tabs. On each tab are groups and each group then has its own icons for different purposes.

Adding a New Contact

What type of information can Outlook store in an Outlook contact? You can store the obvious information such as name, home, business, and other addresses and phone numbers. But you can also store e-mail addresses, Web pages, manager, departments, assistant information, nickname, spouse information, hobbies, and the list goes on and on.

Entering General Contact Information

So how, you're wondering, do you create a contact? Follow these steps:

1. Click Contacts in the Navigation Pane.

2. Choose Home>New>New Contact. Outlook displays an empty Contact window.

3. Fill in the window, supplying information such as name, company, and job title. As you fill in information, Outlook displays a preview of the contact information (see Figure 21-2).

Add Contact Picture   Preview

Figure 21-2
Creating a contact.

Figure 21-3
Choose a phone number type.

4. You can store up to three e-mail addresses for each contact. Click the E-mail down arrow, choose an e-mail and enter the e-mail address. If you enter an incorrectly formatted e-mail such as forgetting to put the @ symbol, Outlook displays an error message.

5. In the Phone number fields, you see four boxes for phone numbers; however, if you click the down arrow next to any of the phone number fields, you see where you can specify the phone number field you want. There are 19 of them, as shown in Figure 21-3.

6. In the Addresses field, you can click the arrow and specify up to three separate addresses. If you enter what appears to be an incomplete or unclear address, Outlook displays an error message, prompting you to check the address.

7. Optionally, click in the Notes field and type any miscellaneous information you want to store regarding the contact.

8. If you have additional information or you would like to assign a picture to the contact, proceed to the next section. If you are finished entering contact information, click Contact>Actions>Save & New if you want to create another contact. Otherwise, click Contact>Actions>Save & Close. Outlook saves the contact and displays it in any of the Contacts folder views.

Showing a Contact Photo

The age old disease CRS (Can't Remember Stuff) hits all of us at one time or another. Sometimes you just can't remember who a particular contact is and why you added them to your contact list. Often, seeing a photo of the person jogs your memory just enough to remember the contact. You can add a photo to any contact.

From the Contact window, click the Add Contact Picture box, just to the right of the Name field. The Add Contact Picture dialog box opens. Navigate to and click the picture you want and choose Open. Outlook places the picture in the box. See Figure 21-4.

Figure 21-4
Add a contact photograph.

More Contact Information

If you want to store additional information about the contact's work position or personal information, Outlook provides a screen for that. Simply click Contact>Show>Details. The Details screen seen in Figure 21-5 appears where you can enter additional contact information.

Birthdays and Anniversaries

If you enter a birthday or anniversary date for the contact, Outlook automatically creates a recurring entry on the calendar. See Chapter 22, "Using the Outlook Calendar," for more information on the Outlook calendar.

Figure 21-5
Additional contact information.

And if those fields aren't enough for you, click Contact>Show>All Fields. In the Select From drop-down menu, choose All Contact Fields. A list of every contact field appears as seen in Figure 21-6. Enter any additional information you want to store. Scroll down...there are lots of fields.

Figure 21-6
All contact fields.

Return to Main Screen

Choose Contact>Show>General to return to the main contact screen.

Editing Contact Information

You've found a little spare time and you've decided to use it to update your contacts by supplying missing information. The method you use to open a contact's window to add or change information depends on the view of the Contacts folder you use.

- ▶ In any view of the Contacts folder, right-click the contact and choose Open.

- ▶ In the Business Card view, double-click any contact.

- ▶ In the Card view, double-click the contact's name to open the contact information in the Contact window. Or, you can single-click any field and make changes to it. Click outside the field when you finish.

- ▶ In the Phone or List view, double-click an entry to display the contact information in a Contact window. Or, click the field you want to edit twice, and you can make changes directly onscreen. When you use this method, click the field twice slowly; otherwise, Outlook will assume you're trying to double-click.

Once you open the contact, you can edit any of the contact information. When you are finished modifying a contact, click Contact>Actions>Save & Close.

Delete a Contact

If you no longer want the contact stored in your contact list, from any of the contact views, click once on the contact you want to delete and choose Home>Delete>Delete or press the Delete key on your keyboard. Be careful! There is no warning and the contact is immediately deleted.

Adding Contacts from E-Mails

You also can add contacts to the Contacts folder from an e-mail you received. Follow these steps:

1. Click Mail in the Navigation Pane.

2. Display the e-mail message that contains the contact you want to add to the Contacts folder.

3. In the Reading pane, right-click the sender's e-mail address and choose Add to Outlook Contacts (see Figure 21-7). In the Contact window that appears, Outlook fills in the contact's name and e-mail address.

Figure 21-7
Add a contact using an e-mail message.

4. Enter any remaining contact information.

5. Click Contact>Actions>Save & Close.

Assigning Categories to Contacts

Outlook provides six color categories that you can assign to contacts so that you can organize and display contact phone information by categories that are meaningful to you. You decide what the various colors mean, and, when you create a contact, you can assign the contact to a color category.

Begin by selecting the contact you want to categorize. You can select multiple contacts by holding down the Ctrl key and clicking the contacts you want. Then choose Home>Tags>Categorize. A list of color categories appears as seen in Figure 21-8.

Figure 21-8
Assigning a category.

Choose the category you want. If it's the first time you've used that category, a Rename dialog box appears asking what you want to call the category. For example, instead of calling it the Green category, you might call it the Family category.

> ## Multiple Categories
>
> You can assign multiple categories to a contact.

Viewing the Contacts Folder

Outlook's Contacts folder goes beyond the capabilities of the Rolodex, because you can display the information in a variety of ways. Use the options that appear in the Ribbon under the Home tab, Current View group, to change the appearance of the Contacts folder. Figure 21-9 shows you the Card view, which displays cards that vary in size, depending on the information you've stored for the contact. Card view includes the names of the fields you're viewing.

Card view

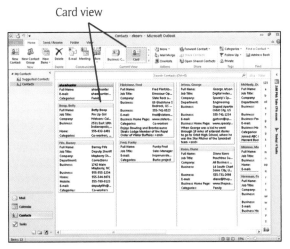

Figure 21-9
The Card view.

Mouse pointer

Figure 21-10
After widening the columns.

In Card view, and depending on your screen resolution, Outlook displays three or four columns in this view, and you'll notice that you can't really read the information stored about the contact. But, you can increase the space allotted to each contact. Place the mouse pointer over one of the lines between the columns, and the mouse pointer changes to a double-headed arrow.

Drag the mouse pointer to the right. You'll see dark lines for each of the column dividers, and when the column is as wide as you want it, release the mouse button. Outlook widens the space allotted to each contact so that you can see more (or less) information per contact (see Figure 21-10). You can use the horizontal scroll bar to view the cards on the right.

The Phone view, shown in Figure 21-11, is terrific for helping you focus on finding a phone number.

Phone view

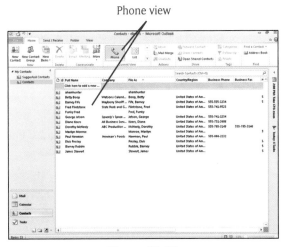

Figure 21-11
The Phone view.

The List view, seen in Figure 21-12, lists the contacts in a list format with column headings at the top of the window. You can click any column heading to sort the list by that column.

List view

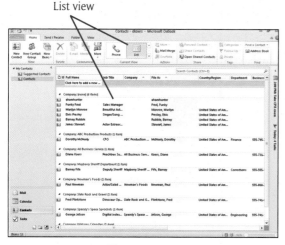

Figure 21-12
The List view.

Customizing a Contact Folder View

Suppose you have hundreds of names in your contact list and you would like to see only your family members. You can create your own customized Contact view. Just follow these steps:

1. Choose Home>Current View and click the More button.

2. Choose Manage Views. The Manage All Views dialog box appears, shown in Figure 21-13.

Figure 21-13
The Manage All Views dialog box.

3. Click the New button. The Create a New View dialog box appears.

4. Enter a name for the new view; for example, Family Members, and then click OK. The Advanced View Settings dialog box opens.

5. Click the Columns button. The Show Columns dialog box seen in Figure 21-14 appears. The Show Columns dialog box gives you the opportunity to select fields that will be visible in the view.

Figure 21-14
Adding or removing fields from the new view.

Figure 21-15
Use the Filter dialog box to select contacts.

6. To add a field to the view, click the field in the left column (Available Columns), and then click the Add button. To hide a field from the view, click the field in the right column (Show These Columns in This Order) and click Remove. You can also select a field and move it up or down the list by clicking the Move Up or Move Down button. Click OK when you are finished. You return to the Advanced View Settings dialog box.

7. Click the Filter button where you can control which contacts should appear in the new view. When you don't set any filters, Outlook displays all contacts in the view. In Figure 21-15, I want to display only the contacts that are categorized as Family, so I click the More Choices tab, click the Categories button, and choose the Family category.

8. Click OK twice.

The Advanced View Setting dialog box has several other choices:

▶ **Group By:** Controls the way Outlook groups contacts in a view. When you choose a field in the Group Items By list, the subsequent Then By list becomes available.

▶ **Sort:** Controls the way Outlook sorts the contacts.

▶ **Other Settings:** Controls settings like fonts, column sizes, grid lines, and group styles.

▶ **Conditional Formatting:** Controls fonts used for various types of contacts. Outlook sets up font rules for some kinds of contacts by default, so that these kinds of contacts are identifiable by the font Outlook uses. You can use this dialog box to add your own rules about the appearance of certain kinds of contacts. When you click Add, the Condition button becomes available. When you click it, Outlook displays the Filter dialog box to identify the contacts to whom you want to apply the font rules.

▶ **Format Columns:** Controls the format of the fields that appear in a view.

8. Click OK twice. The Home>Current View gallery now includes your customized view. Just click the view to see the selected contacts. See Figure 21-16.

New view option

Figure 21-16
View contacts in the customized list.

Creating a Contact Distribution Group

Suppose that you find yourself sending the same e-mails to a specific group of contacts. For example, you may like to share jokes with a specific group of people, or you may be participating in a project and you need to communicate with the project team regularly. You can set up a Contact Group in Outlook.

Using an Outlook Contact Group you can simultaneously select several contacts—those included in the contact group—when you address an e-mail.

When you fill in the recipient of the e-mail, you select your contact group, and Outlook automatically fills in the e-mail addresses of each contact included in the group, saving you lots of time.

To create a contact group, follow these steps:

1. Click Contacts in the Navigation Pane.

2. Choose Home>New>New Contact Group. Outlook displays a Contact Group window as shown in Figure 21-17.

Figure 21-17
Use this window to set up a contact distribution group.

3. In the Name box, type a title for the group. Use something simple, but descriptive such as Smith Project or Joke group.

4. Choose Contact Group>Members>Add Members>From Outlook Contacts. Outlook displays the Select Members dialog box shown in Figure 21-18.

Figure 21-18
Select contacts to include in the group.

5. Click a name in the list and then click the Members button. Outlook displays each included contact's name in the box beside the Members button.

6. Repeat Step 5 for each contact you want to add to the contact group.

7. Click OK. Outlook redisplays the Contact Group window, and the name and e-mail address of each contact you selected in Steps 5 and 6 appears in the window.

8. Click Contact Group>Action>Save & Close.

The group appears as a contact in your contact list. To use your contact group to send an e-mail, create a new e-mail message or forward an existing message. Click the To button and, in the Select Names dialog box that appears, select the name you gave your distribution list and click OK. Then, fill in the rest of the e-mail as described in Chapter 20.

Mapping a Contact's Location

If you store a street address for a contact, Outlook can help you view a map of the address. Follow these steps:

1. Click Contacts in the Navigation Pane.

2. Open the contact's window, which you see in Figure 21-19.

Map It button

Figure 21-19
Open the contact's window.

3. Click the Map It button. Outlook opens a Bing window in Internet Explorer and displays a map, pinpointing the contact's street address (see Figure 21-20).

Aerial button

Figure 21-20
Bing displays the map.

Along the top of the map, click the Aerial button and choose Bird's Eye to zoom in from a satellite view as seen in Figure 21-21.

Figure 21-21
Bird's Eye View.

Printing Contact Information

I F YOU WANT TO PRINT your contacts, Outlook provides a variety of styles in which you can print them. Click the File tab and from the Backstage view, click Print. Your screen looks similar to the one seen in Figure 21-22. From the second column, you have several choices:

Preview window   Preview buttons

Figure 21-22
Printing your contacts.

▶ **Print:** Click this to print contacts using the current settings. Most people choose this option last; after they select the printer, print options, and settings.

▶ **Printer:** If you have multiple printers, click this option to choose which printer you want to use.

▶ **Print Options:** Click this to set printing options such as number of copies, which pages, and whether to print all contacts or only selected contacts.

▶ **Settings:** Choose a contact layout that you want to use. A preview of the selected layout appears on the right side of the screen.

Preview Buttons

You can use the view buttons at the bottom of the Preview window to change the Preview perspective.

Using the Outlook
Calendar

PICTURE YOURSELF MANAGING a schedule that is meeting-intensive. You have meetings at the office and away from the office, in the city where you live, and on the road. Sometimes you initiate a meeting; other times, you are included by others in a meeting. And, the original date and time for a meeting changes, sometimes more frequently than you'd expect.

You need a calendar for your appointments, but the manual calendar you've been keeping just isn't filling your needs. You do everything in pencil because of potential changes, and your book has become so messy that some days you're having trouble reading it. And that's not even counting the tasks you need to accomplish in addition to the meetings—you need to be able to manage both your workload and your schedule so that you know when you need time *outside* meetings to accomplish other things on your plate.... Enter Outlook's Calendar.

Exploring the Calendar

THE CALENDAR VIEW in Outlook integrates with your e-mail and your tasks so that you can manage more than just your appointments. It lets you view your workload—both appointments and tasks—from a variety of perspectives, and it is neat and clean—no more messy erasures.

Understanding the Calendar Views

Click Calendar in the Navigation Pane to view the calendar. Outlook displays one of the five Calendar views of the Calendar folder. You can change the Calendar views by choosing Home> Arrange or View>Arrangement and selecting one of the following:

▶ The Day view (see Figure 22-1) shows you the appointments you have today along with tasks on your task list that haven't yet been completed.

Tip

You can read more about tasks in Chapter 23, "Tracking Tasks with Outlook."

Figure 22-1
A daily view of your calendar.

▶ The Work Week view of the calendar, seen in Figure 22-2, shows Monday through Friday's appointments and tasks.

Figure 22-2
The Work Week calendar view.

▶ The Week view (Figure 22-3) shows appointments from Sunday through Saturday.

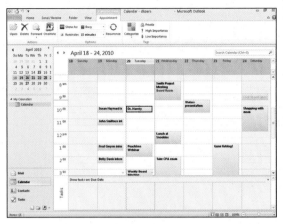

Figure 22-3
The full week calendar view.

▶ The Month view, shown in Figure 22-4, provides a monthly view of your calendar.

Figure 22-4
The monthly calendar view.

▶ The Schedule view illustrates daily appointments, broken down by time. See Figure 22-5.

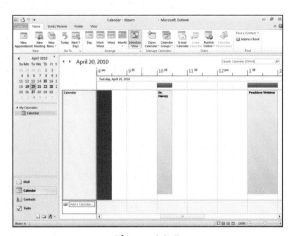

Figure 22-5
The Schedule calendar view.

In addition to these views, Outlook provides several other views of the calendar. You can switch views by choosing View>Current View>Change View and clicking a new view. For example, in the List view (see Figure 22-6), Outlook lists all appointments stored on your calendar, even those in the past.

Figure 22-6
View all your appointments in list format.

After changing to one of the extra views such as List view, to return to a standard calendar style you must choose View>Current View>Change View>Calendar.

Adding Holidays

When you first start using Outlook, you won't find any holidays on the calendar, but you can take care of that issue. Follow these steps:

1. Choose File>Options. Outlook displays the Outlook Options dialog box.

2. From the first column, click Calendar. The right side displays calendar options as seen in Figure 22-7.

Add Holidays button

Figure 22-7
The Outlook Calendar Options dialog box.

3. Click the Add Holidays button. The Add Holidays to Calendar dialog box appears (see Figure 22-8).

Figure 22-8
The Add Holidays to Calendar dialog box.

4. Place a check in the box beside the country whose holidays you want to appear on your calendar. You can select more than one country. A message appears when Outlook is finished.

5. Click OK twice to close each dialog box. Outlook displays the standard holidays of the country you selected on the calendar.

Working in the Calendar Folder

WHEN YOU WORK in the Calendar folder, you can set up appointments—both one-time appointments and recurring appointments. You also can create events and schedule (and cancel) meetings.

Setting Up Appointments with Reminders

You can easily add an appointment to your Outlook Calendar by following these steps:

1. Click Calendar in the Navigation Pane. Outlook displays your calendar.

2. Click Home>New>New Appointment. Outlook displays a new appointment window (see Figure 22-9).

Reminder arrow

Figure 22-9
Create an appointment and set up a reminder for it.

Alternative Method

Alternatively, double-click any time in the calendar to display the New Appointment window.

3. Fill in the subject. This information will appear on your calendar.

4. If you want, fill in a location.

5. Select a start date and time. Outlook fills in the end date and time automatically, but you can change them.

Tip

Optionally, display the appointment date on the calendar and double-click the appointment time to open the Appointment window with the time and date already entered.

6. Write any notes about the appointment in the description box.

7. Outlook automatically adds a reminder that will appear 15 minutes before the appointment time. To change the reminder time, choose Appointment>Options, click the Reminder drop-down arrow, and select a time.

8. Choose Appointment>Actions>Save &
   Close. Outlook adds the appointment to
   your calendar.

If you set a reminder, at the specified time prior to
your appointment, Outlook will play a sound and
display a reminder onscreen like the one shown in
Figure 22-10. Click Dismiss to make the reminder
go away or click Snooze to make it go away and
redisplay in five minutes.

Figure 22-10
A typical reminder.

As mentioned earlier, by default, Outlook assigns a
15-minute reminder to all appointments. If you
prefer a different amount of time, you can change
this default. Choose File>Options. In the Calendar
section, a check appears beside Default Reminder
(see Figure 22-11). Open the list box beside the
Default Reminder check box and select a different
amount of time.

Default reminder time

Figure 22-11
Set the default reminder time.

Recurring Appointments

So, the manager of the project you're working on has
decided on a weekly staff meeting for the next 12
weeks for status updates. Instead of adding the
appointment to your calendar 12 times, you can set
up a recurring appointment by following these steps:

1. Click Calendar in the Navigation Pane.
   Outlook displays your calendar.

2. Click Home>New>New Appointment.
   Outlook displays a new appointment window.

3. Fill in the subject. This information will
   appear on your calendar.

4. If you want, fill in a location and write any
   notes about the appointment in the description box.

5. Optionally, set a reminder by choosing Appointment>Options>Reminder and selecting a reminder time.

6. Choose Appointment>Options>Recurrence. Outlook displays the Appointment Recurrence dialog box seen in Figure 22-12.

Figure 22-12
Use this dialog box to create a recurring appointment.

7. Set a recurrence pattern. The options in the right portion of the Recurrence Pattern section change, depending on the option you select in the left portion of the section.

8. In the Range of Recurrence section, you can specify an end date.

9. Click OK. Outlook redisplays the appointment window. Just below the Location, you'll see information about how often the appointment recurs (see Figure 22-13).

Recurrence notation

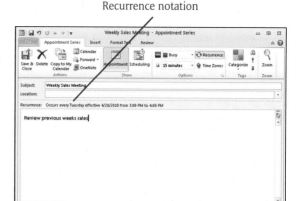

Figure 22-13
When you create a recurring appointment, Outlook provides you with recurrence information.

10. Choose Appointment>Actions>Save & Close. Outlook adds the appointment to your calendar.

Scheduling an Event

An event differs from an appointment by Outlook's definition because an event lasts all day. Outlook treats holidays as events. Your birthday is an event. To create an event, follow these steps:

1. Click Calendar in the Navigation Pane. Outlook displays your calendar.

2. Choose Home>New>New Item>All Day Event. Outlook displays an Event window, with a check in the All day event check box (see Figure 22-14).

Figure 22-14
Creating an event.

Events

Figure 22-15
Events don't appear near a time slot.

3. Fill in the subject and the date and, if appropriate, a location and any notes you need in the Description box.

4. If appropriate, you can choose Event> Options>Recurrence and set up information to make the event recurring. For details, see the previous section.

5. Choose Event>Actions>Save & Close. Outlook displays the event at the top of the day on which it occurs; visually representing that no time is associated with the event (see Figure 22-15).

Requesting a Meeting

You can use request a meeting with a contact who also uses Outlook. When you request a meeting, Outlook generates an e-mail that contains meeting information. Typically you and the contact work for the same company. If your company uses Microsoft Exchange Server and shares calendars, you can check schedules for shared calendars to find a meeting time that suits everyone.

When you request a meeting, you initially set up an appointment. To request a meeting with someone who also uses Outlook, follow these steps:

Tip

There is no technological reason why you cannot request a meeting with a user who doesn't use Outlook. But, when you send a meeting request to a user who doesn't use Outlook, sometimes the resulting e-mail message looks like gibberish to the recipient.

1. Click Calendar in the Navigation Pane.

2. Click Home>New>New Meeting. Outlook displays an Invited Event window.

3. Fill in the meeting subject and location information.

4. Set the proposed meeting's start and stop times and, if appropriate, provide additional information in the message area. See Figure 22-16.

Figure 22-16
Fill in the meeting request window.

5. Click the To button. Outlook displays the Select Attendees and Resources dialog box (see Figure 22-17).

Figure 22-17
Select meeting participants.

6. Click the name of a person you want to attend the meeting. Or, you can type some characters of the person's name and Outlook will find the nearest match.

7. Choose one of the following and Outlook adds the recipient in the appropriate text box.

   ▶ Choose Required if this person must attend the meeting.

   ▶ Choose Optional if the person's attendance is optional.

   ▶ Choose Resources if you are selecting a resource.

8. Repeat Steps 6 and 7 for each meeting participant to whom you want to e-mail the meeting request.

9. Click OK. Outlook redisplays the meeting window, listing Required and Optional attendees in the To box and Resources in the Location box. If you typed a location in the box previously, Outlook asks you if you want to replace the location information.

10. If your company uses Outlook and Microsoft Exchange Server and shares calendars, choose Invited Event>Show>Scheduling, and use the tab that appears to help you find the best time for the meeting and to add others to the meeting request.

11. Click the Send button. Outlook saves the meeting on your calendar and places an e-mail in your Outbox for each meeting attendee. The e-mail will be sent the next time Outlook checks for new mail.

Tracking Meeting Request Responses

You can easily identify when someone has responded to a meeting request. Open the meeting on your calendar by double-clicking it. Just above the To line, Outlook displays an overall status on meeting responses. You can choose Meeting>Show> Tracking to see the status of individual responses to the meeting request (see Figure 22-18).

Figure 22-18
Review who has responded to your meeting request.

Cancelling a Meeting

Occasions will arise when you need to cancel a meeting. Open the meeting on your calendar by double-clicking it. Choose Meeting>Actions>Cancel Meeting. Outlook changes the Send Update button to the Send Cancellation button (see Figure 22-19).

Figure 22-19
Cancelling a meeting.

Click the Send Cancellation button, and Outlook creates an e-mail message addressed to all meeting participants that cancels the meeting—the subject line of the message is the original subject line, preceded by the word "Canceled." Outlook places the message in your Outbox and sends it the next time Outlook checks for new mail.

Figure 22-20 illustrates the recipients' cancellation message if they are also using Outlook.

✕ Remove from Calendar

Canceled: Fund Raiser

Diane Koers [dkoers0916@gmail.com]

Required: Funky Fred; Dino Lowe; Diane Koers
When: Thursday, April 22, 2010 3:00 PM-4:00 PM.
Location: Board Room C

Description:

Please let me know if you can attend the planning meeting for the Thomson fund raiser. We need everyone's input.

Thanks,

Diane

Figure 22-20
A cancellation e-mail.

Tracking Tasks with
Outlook

PICTURE YOURSELF WITH A PILE OF LAUNDRY that never seems to end and keeps getting bigger and bigger. You need to find a way to keep track of all your tasks, and whether you're at work or home, you'd really like some sense of accomplishment when you get something done so that you'll feel like you're making a dent in the pile.

Using a combination of Outlook's Tasks folder and the To-Do list, you can easily create tasks and easily track progress. You can create "one-time" tasks and recurring tasks. You can convert an e-mail into a task, and you can assign tasks to others and still monitor the task progress. This chapter explores the ways Outlook can help you keep that pile of work under control.

Outlook considers tasks and to-do's different but the same. Is that an oxymoron? You'll see... Then, later you'll take a look at the To-Do Bar.

Working with Tasks

TASKS ARE A GREAT FEATURE of Outlook, but are also vastly underused. Tasks can help you meet deadlines or alert you when something needs your attention. Let's explore the ways you can use tasks in Outlook:

- ▶ Add tasks
- ▶ Create recurring tasks
- ▶ Set a task's priorities
- ▶ Attach documentation to a task
- ▶ Set a task's progress
- ▶ Assign tasks to others
- ▶ Delete tasks

Adding Tasks

Tasks are items that you need to track until completion.

Outlook provides two methods to enter tasks. One way, the short way, is where you just briefly mention the task. The other method allows you to elaborate in much greater detail about the task. Let's begin with the short way.

From the Navigation Pane, click Tasks. You see the My Tasks section at the top of the Navigation Pane. Tasks are divided into two sections: To-Do List and Tasks. Outlook distinguishes between tasks and to-do's. A *task* is an item you create in the Outlook's Tasks folder to track an activity until you complete

it. A *to-do* is any Outlook e-mail message, task, or contact flagged for follow-up. By default, Outlook flags all tasks for follow-up, so, all tasks are also to-do items.

Click the Tasks option as seen in Figure 23-1. A list of tasks appears as seen in Figure 23-1. Notice that Outlook displays past-due tasks in red.

My Tasks   To-Do List   Tasks   Click here to add a new task

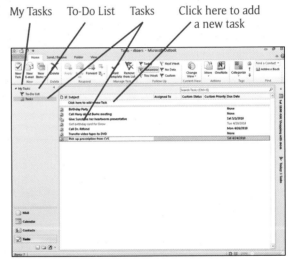

Figure 23-1
My tasks list.

Click the top line in the tasks list, where it says "Click here to add a new Task." Type brief information about your task such as Pick up dog food or Call Harry about Burke meeting. Press Enter and you've just created a new task. And you did it quickly.

That was easy, but it didn't give you much information about your task, and quite honestly, many tasks are just that easy and don't need additional information. However, if you want to be more thorough and enter starting and due dates, prioritize the task, or be more descriptive about the task, use the following steps:

1. Click Tasks in the Navigation Pane.

2. Click Home>New>New Task. Outlook displays a new Task window (see Figure 23-2).

Figure 23-2
Creating a new task.

3. Type a subject. The subject you type will appear in all views of the Tasks folder or the To-Do List.

4. Select a start date. Outlook automatically assigns the same due date to the task.

Start Date Is Optional

You don't have to assign a start date to a task, but, from a time-management perspective, you are more likely to get the task done if you assign a date to it.

5. If appropriate, select a status other than Not Started. Click the Status arrow for a list of options.

6. You can set a priority for the task—Low, Normal, or High—and then use any of several views to sort tasks by priority.

7. If you've started the task, you can fill in the % Complete box with an estimate of how far along the task is.

8. You can have Outlook remind you about the task by placing a check in the Reminder box. Then, select a date and time for the reminder.

9. Type any notes about the task in the description block.

10. Choose Task>Actions>Save & Close. Outlook saves the task.

You also can create a task from an e-mail message. Click Mail in the Navigation Pane and then find the message you want. Drag the message onto the Tasks button in the Navigation Pane (see Figure 23-3).

Mouse pointer   Selected e-mail

Figure 23-3
Dragging an e-mail message into the Tasks folder.

When you release the mouse button, Outlook opens a Task window with the title of the subject of your e-mail. By default, Outlook doesn't assign a start date, due date, status, priority, or percent complete; and Outlook doesn't create a reminder— but you can do all of those things. Outlook *does* display the content of the e-mail message in the description block of the task (see Figure 23-4).

Figure 23-4
Creating a task from an e-mail message.

When you choose Task>Actions>Save & Close, Outlook adds the task to the Tasks folder using the subject line of the task (which was also the subject line of the e-mail).

In Figure 23-5, you see a variety of tasks. Tasks have an icon next to them that indicate special situations. For example, if the task is delegated to someone else, the task icon has people on it.

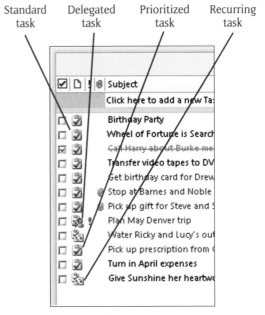

Figure 23-5
Tasks with different sources and specifications.

Flag for Follow-Up

Flag tasks for follow-up (thereby creating to-do items) by clicking the task and choosing Home>Follow Up. Outlook offers you time frames: Today, Tomorrow, This Week, Next Week, No Date, or Custom. Outlook reminds you of a follow-up task, depending on the time frame you selected. For example, if you select follow-up for "Tomorrow", you see a reminder at the start time of the next day.

Editing Tasks

You can easily edit a task if you find you need to make changes. For example, you can edit a task to update its progress by making changes to both the Status and the % Complete fields. Or you can elaborate on the "quick task" that you entered earlier. Click the Tasks button in the Navigation Pane and select a view where you can see the task. Then, double-click any portion of the task's entry. Outlook displays the task in the Task window. Make your changes and choose Task>Actions>Save & Close.

Microsoft Office Project

If you're a Microsoft Office Project user, Project can import task information from Outlook, including the Status and % Complete fields.

For example, to record work on a task, you can make changes to the Status and % Complete fields. You also can record actual work, mileage and billing information, and the date completed by. To do so, while viewing the task, choose Task>Show> Details (see Figure 23-6). Then, fill in fields as appropriate and click Tasks>Actions>Save & Close.

Figure 23-6
Recording task progress.

Completed Tasks

When you complete a task, from the Tasks pane, click the desired task and choose Home>Manage Task>Mark Complete. Outlook marks the task complete and makes it unavailable. If you just want to delete a task, click Home>Manager Task>Remove from List. If you created the task from an e-mail message, Outlook warns you that deleting the task will also delete the e-mail.

Creating a Recurring Task

Just like the Energizer Bunny, you've got a task that you need to do over and over again. For example, you need a reminder to water your vacationing neighbors' plants every day. Or perhaps you need a reminder at the end of each month to file your sales tax and payroll reports. You can create a recurring task by following these steps:

1. Click Tasks in the Navigation Pane.

2. Click Home>New>New Task and create a new task but don't click Save & Close yet.

3. Choose Task>Options>Recurrence. Outlook opens the Task Recurrence dialog box (see Figure 23-7).

Figure 23-7
Use this box to set up a recurring task.

4. Select a recurrence pattern option—Daily, Weekly, Monthly, or Yearly—and the choices to the right of those options change to match your selection.

5. You can set a start and end date for the tasks in the Range of Recurrence section.

6. Click OK. Outlook redisplays the Task window, which now contains a message above the subject line that describes the recurrence.

7. Click Task>Actions>Save & Close.

Attaching Documentation to a Task

Suppose that you've got a task to do and you've got information in a Word document, an Excel spreadsheet, or any other document that pertains to the task. You can attach the file to the task and then open it from the task in Outlook. No more hunting. Follow these steps:

1. Click Tasks in the Navigation Pane.

2. Follow Steps 2 to 9 in the section "Adding Tasks" to set up the task. Or, edit an existing task by double-clicking it.

3. Choose Insert>Include>Attach File. Doing so displays the Insert File dialog box shown in Figure 23-8.

Attach File

Figure 23-8
Attaching a document to a task.

4. Navigate to the folder that contains the document you want to attach, select it, and click Insert. Outlook displays an icon representing the file in the description portion of the task (see Figure 23-9). You can attach multiple documents.

Figure 23-9
A task containing attachments.

5. Choose Task>Actions>Save & Close.

To open the associated file from within Outlook, open the task and double-click the document icon.

Assigning Tasks to Others

Good managerial skills dictate that you have the ability to delegate. In Outlook, you can delegate a task to another Outlook user. Outlook refers to this process as making a task request, and you can select options to keep an updated copy on your task list and to receive a status report when the task is complete. Follow these steps to assign a task to someone else:

1. Click Tasks in the Navigation Pane.

2. Add or edit a task, making sure that you leave the Task window open (see Figure 23-10).

Assign Task button

Figure 23-10
Add or edit a task.

3. Choose Task>Manage Task>Assign Task. Outlook changes the appearance of the Task window, giving you the opportunity to supply an e-mail address (see Figure 23-11).

Figure 23-11
Assigning a task to someone else.

4. Click the To button. Outlook displays the Select Task Recipient: Contacts dialog box.

5. Click the name of the person to whom you want to send the task request. Or, you can type some characters of the person's name and Outlook will find the nearest match.

6. Once you have highlighted the correct contact's name, click the To -> button. Outlook adds the recipient in the To -> text box.

7. Repeat Steps 5 and 6 for each recipient to whom you want to assign the task.

8. Click OK. Outlook redisplays the Task window with the recipients' e-mail addresses in the To box.

9. Enter any optional message in the task note window and click Send. Outlook places the task request in your Outbox and sends the task request the next time it checks for incoming and outgoing e-mail.

A recipient of a task request can accept or decline the task. The task request arrives as an e-mail message (see Figure 23-12), and when the recipient opens the message, he or she is prompted to accept or decline the task. Outlook sends the originator of the task request a message that indicates the task request has been accepted or declined. If the recipient accepts the task, Outlook places it in the recipient's Tasks folder.

Figure 23-12
The recipient of a task request.

Outlook keeps a copy of the task on your task list and notifies you and updates the task in your Tasks folder each time the person to whom you assigned the task updates the task. When the task is complete, Outlook automatically sends you a status report when the person handling the task marks it complete.

If the recipient of the task request declines the task, the sender of the task request receives an e-mail notification that the task request has been declined.

Exploring To-Do's

WHEN YOU CLICK ON TASKS from the Navigation Pane, you see two folders under a main folder entitled My Tasks. The two subfolders are for Tasks and To-Do's. Outlook offers these two folders for viewing the Tasks folder, because it distinguishes between tasks and to-do's. When you click Tasks in the Navigation Pane, Outlook displays your To-Do List as you see in Figure 23-13.

So, when you initially click the Tasks button in the Navigation Pane, you're seeing all to-do items, not just tasks. You can view *only* tasks if you click Tasks in the My Tasks portion of the Navigation Pane. Then, Outlook limits the view to show you only tasks. Compare the To-Do list of Figure 23-13 with the Tasks list in Figure 23-14 to see the difference between tasks and to-do's.

Figure 23-14
My Task list.

Extra To-Do item

Figure 23-13
My To-Do list.

Other views provide varying information about the items displayed or organize the items in different ways. Click the Task list and choose Home>Current View>Change View or View>Current View>Change View. A gallery of views such as seen in Figure 23-15 appears. Let's compare the different views:

Figure 23-15
Available Task views.

▶ Detailed view shows a completed check box, the source icon, an icon for the priority assigned to the item, attachment icons, the item's subject, status, due date, modified date, date completed, folder, categories, and follow-up flag.

▶ Simple List view shows the source icon, completed check box, task subject and due date, categories, and follow-up flag.

▶ To-Do List view shows the list separated by date with a Reading pane on the right.

▶ Prioritized view groups the items together by priority. You set a to-do priority from the Task window by choosing Task>Tags>High Importance or Task>Tags>Low Importance.

▶ Active Tasks view shows source icon, priority, attachment, subject, status, due date, % complete, categories and follow-up but limits the items displayed to only those that are not yet complete.

▶ Completed Tasks view shows only completed items.

▶ Today view shows only the items that are past due or due today. No items with a future date appear in this view. You see the icon, completed check box, subject, due date, category, and follow-up flag.

▶ Next Seven Days view shows icon, priority, attachment, subject, status, due date, % complete, category, and follow-up flag, but only items that are due in the next seven days appear. Past due items and items due in the far future are hidden.

▶ Overdue view shows the same information as the Next Seven Days view but limits the items displayed to only those that are overdue.

▶ The Assigned view organizes tasks by the person to whom they are assigned. If a task is not delegated to someone else, it doesn't appear in the view. See Figure 23-16.

Figure 23-16
Assigned task view.

▶ Server Tasks view shows tasks listed on the server. These views are useful if your organization uses Microsoft Exchange Server and shares Outlook information.

Creating Notes

OUTLOOK CONTAINS A NOTES feature with which you can create the equivalent of an electronic sticky note. Click the Notes button at the bottom of the Navigation Pane. Outlook displays the Notes pane. Double-click any blank spot on the Notes pane and a Note box appears. Just start typing as you see in Figure 23-17. When you finish, click the close box (X) in the upper-right corner of the note.

You can attach an Outlook item, such as a note, to a To-Do by opening the To-Do and choosing Insert>Include>Outlook Item. Then, select the Outlook folder containing the item you want to attach and, within that folder, select the item. See Figure 23-18.

Notes button

Figure 23-17
Writing Notes.

Outlook Item

Figure 23-18
Attaching a note to a task or a to-do.

Using the To-Do Bar

THE OUTLOOK TO-DO BAR, is sort of your "day at a glance" tool, although it often shows you more than one day. It integrates all the Outlook views and is available in all Outlook views, so any time, any place, you have access to the things you need to act upon. The Outlook To-Do Bar, which is minimized by default, runs down the right side of the screen (see Figure 23-19).

To open the To-Do Bar, click the Expand button at the top of the bar, and Outlook shows you the complete To-Do Bar, which summarizes your upcoming meetings and tasks (see Figure 23-20).

Minimize button

Figure 23-20
The To-Do Bar provides a snapshot of your upcoming schedule.

View the To-Do Bar in Calendar View

The To-Do Bar isn't automatically visible in the Calendar view, but you can turn it on with a click of the mouse. Click Calendar in the Navigation Pane and choose View> Layout>To-Do Bar>Normal.

Other Applications

The To-Do Bar also includes items from Office OneNote and Office Project.

To-Do Bar   Expand button

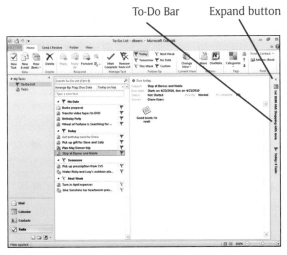

Figure 23-19
The To-Do Bar appears minimized when you view the Mail, Contacts, and Tasks folders.

The To-Do Bar is more than just something you can look at for a quick update. You can click any date on the calendar to switch to the Calendars folder in Outlook for that date. And, you can add to-do's to the To-Do Bar. For example, to create a to-do item for an e-mail, drag the e-mail into the appropriate timeframe on the To-Do Bar. The to-do will appear both on the To-Do List (when you click the Tasks button in the Navigation Pane and then click To-Do List under My Tasks) and on the To-Do Bar. And, you can right-click the flag of any to-do and choose Mark Complete to clear it from the To-Do List and the To-Do Bar.

You can add new tasks directly in the To-Do Bar by typing in the "Type a new task" text box. If you want to resize the amount of space allocated between the calendar appointments and the tasks, drag the separating bar, seen in Figure 23-21, up or down until the sections are the size you want.

To minimize the To-Do Bar and move it back to the right, click the Minimize button. If you want to completely hide the To-Do Bar from a particular view, choose View>Layout>To-Do Bar>Off.

Separating bar

Figure 23-21
Resize the space in the To-Do Bar.

Part VII
Publisher

Publisher is the often-overlooked application in Microsoft Office. In fact, it doesn't come with all Office versions. In the past, when you wanted to create a publication, you needed a professional printer to help you with layout and graphic design. Not any more. With Publisher, you can create brochures, business cards, calendars, and lots of other printed items. And you do not need to be a professional printer. You only need an idea. The chapters in this section help you take your ideas and turn them into publications!

You're Invited!

For: New Year's Party

January 1st

8:00 p.m.

Creating a Predesigned Publisher
Publication

PICTURE YOURSELF PLANNING A BIG PARTY. You have so much to do and so little time. One task on your to-do list is creating the invitations. You could go to your local party store and buy ready-made invitations, or you can design your own quickly and easily using Microsoft Publisher.

To create these publications without going through a lot of trouble, you use one of the supplied publication designs. A publication design gives you the structure for creating the type of publication you want. The designs provide placeholders for graphics and text, similar to the place-holders you worked with when creating PowerPoint slides.

Selecting a Publication Template

DIFFERENT FROM MOST other Office 2010 applications, when you first launch Publisher (Start>All Programs>Microsoft Office>Microsoft Publisher 2010), you don't see a blank document ready for you to begin working. Instead, you get the Available Templates window that includes hundreds of predesigned templates on which you can base the document you want to create (see Figure 24-1). Starting with a template is by far the easiest way to create a document in Publisher.

Figure 24-1
Selecting a publication template.

Select a publication type:

▶ If you select Blank 8$^1/_2$ × 11 or Blank 11 × 8$^1/_2$ templates, you can begin creating your own publication from the beginning. Click the template you want and it appears on your screen.

▶ If you select More Blank Page Sizes, you see a collection of other sizes along with an option to create your own custom size. And if you scroll down farther, you'll see blank templates by publication type and by manufacturer. You also see options to customize the template, which you'll review later in this chapter. Click the template you want and click the Create button.

▶ If you select My Templates, you see a list of your publications that you have previously saved and can choose one of them as a template. Select the template you want and click the Create button.

▶ The Most Popular section provides sample common layouts that many Publisher users like to use. When you select a category, such as brochures, a more detailed list of brochure templates appears. Since most of these templates originate from Office.com, click the template you want and click the Download button. The template will appear on your screen. In Figure 24-2, clicking the Greeting Cards category displays greeting card choices.

Back button   Download button

Figure 24-2
Viewing additional templates.

▶ The More Templates category offers even
more Publisher template categories. Like
the Most Popular section, click the template

type you want, and then click the template
you want. A preview appears in the upper-
right corner. Be sure to scroll down the
screen; there are usually dozens of samples
for each publication type. Click the
Download button after you've selected the
template you want and the template will
appear on your screen.

Wrong Category?

If you chose the wrong template category,
click the Back button to return to the previous screen.

Viewing the Publisher Window

IN OFFICE 2010, the fine folks at Microsoft
brought Publisher up on a par with the other
Office applications. Publisher now has a Ribbon
from which you make your selections and since the
Ribbon is new to Publisher let's just take a brief
look at it.

As you see in Figure 24-3, the Ribbon contains tabs
(task-orientated screens). The tabs are divided into
subsections called groups, which break the tasks
into smaller areas. As you click a different tab, the

Ribbon changes to reflect options pertaining to the
selected tab. Also, as you select various elements in
your publication you may see additional contextual
tabs such as Drawing Tools or Text Box Tools.

Figure 24-3
The Publisher Ribbon.

Some Ribbon buttons display a down arrow, which means there are more choices available. And in some options, you must click the More button, which displays a gallery of choices. For example, if you click Page Design>Schemes and click the More button, you see the color scheme gallery.

Many group options include an icon at the bottom-right edge of the group option. Clicking the Dialog Box Launcher opens a related dialog box.

Customize the Ribbon

See Chapter 1, "Discovering Office Common Features," to customize the Ribbon.

Other elements seen in the Publisher window shown in Figure 24-4 include:

Navigation Pane   Rulers   Dialog Box Launcher

Figure 24-4
The Publisher window.

▶ **Title bar:** Across the top you see a title bar that shows the program title and the document title.

▶ **File tab:** The first tab on the Ribbon, the File tab is where you see the Backstage view and access many common file functions such as Open, Save, and Print.

▶ **Quick Access Toolbar:** The Quick Access Toolbar provides fast and easy access to the Save, Undo, and Redo commands. Like with other Office applications, you can customize the Quick Access Toolbar. See Chapter 1.

▶ **Horizontal and Vertical rulers:** Because many publications require precise placement of text and objects, you see both horizontal and vertical rulers to assist you.

▶ **Frames:** Frames are placeholders for text and objects. You'll learn lots more about frames throughout this chapter.

▶ **Navigation Pane:** Some publications can be quite lengthy. The Navigation Pane helps you find a particular page quickly and easily. See the next section, "Using the Navigation Pane" for more information.

▶ **Status bar:** Along the bottom of the Publisher window you see a status bar that tells you if your Caps Lock is on, along with a variety of other options such as the current page number and zoom controls.

Using the Navigation Pane

The pane on the left side of the screen is the Navigation Pane. When you first create a new publication, thumbnails of the publication pages appear in the Navigation Pane. In Chapter 14, "Creating a PowerPoint Presentation," you worked with the Slide List pane. The Publisher Navigation Pane is very similar to the PowerPoint Slide List pane.

Click any page displayed in the Navigation Pane to display it in the main working window. Use the Navigation Pane vertical scroll bar as necessary to scroll up or down and view additional pages. You can expand or collapse the Navigation Pane by clicking the Collapse arrow seen in Figure 24-5. You can then expand the Navigation Pane by clicking the expand arrow. You can also resize the Navigation Pane, which makes the thumbnails larger or smaller. Position your mouse over the right edge of the Navigation Pane, between the vertical scroll bar and the vertical ruler, until the mouse pointer turns into a double-headed white arrow. Drag to the right to enlarge the Navigation Pane or drag to the left to make it smaller.

Collapse arrow   Resizing bar

Figure 24-5
The Navigation Pane.

Understanding Frames

When you created a PowerPoint presentation, after selecting a slide layout, you saw the placeholders where you entered text or added objects. A Publisher publication also uses placeholders, some for text and some for objects, except that in Publisher they are referred to as frames. In Figure 24-6, you see a frame at the top with the words Catalog Title, and there are several more in the page, prompting for more text information. The picture is a frame for a graphic. A little later in this chapter, you will place pictures in a graphic frame.

Text frame   Picture frame

Figure 24-6
Placeholder frames.

Customizing Your Publication

I'M GOING TO TAKE A STEP backwards here. When you open Publisher and select a template, many choices display, on the right side of the screen, a section where you can customize the publication to better fit your needs and save you time. When they created the publication template, the designers at Microsoft supplied a group of coordinated colors and fonts; however, you can choose different colors and fonts in the Customize section. See Figure 24-7 for an example of a template with customization options. Some templates even display additional options such as for the page layout.

Also, since many publications use common information such as a company name or phone numbers, rather than retyping this information each time you create a publication, you can store this information in the Business Information section. Then, when needed, Publisher automatically populates the publication fields.

Entering Business Information

You can have several business information sets. Perhaps you have one for your company that includes your boss's name, and maybe you have one that you use for the school PTA and of course you have one you use for yourself! You enter the business set information and Publisher stores the business information sets for future use as well as in the current publication.

If you have already created a business information set, click the Business Information down arrow and choose the set you want. If you have not yet created a business information set, or want to create a new one, click the Business Information down arrow and choose Create New. You see the Create New Business Information Set dialog box.

Font scheme   Color scheme   Business information

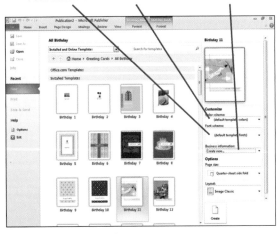

Figure 24-7
Customizing your publication.

Enter any relevant information in the Create New Business Information Set dialog box, replacing the existing text with your information. If you have a company logo, you can add it by clicking the Add Logo button, locating and selecting your logo, and choosing Insert. See Figure 24-8.

Figure 24-8
Enter your information for the business information set.

Edit Business Information

If you need to edit the business information set, while in any publication, choose File> Info>Edit Business Information then click the Edit button.

In the Business Information set name, enter a descriptive name for this group of information and click the Save button. The business information set now appears in the drop-down menu for this publication and future publications.

Changing the Color Scheme

When you create a publication based on a temple, it contains a scheme of colors that harmonize with each other. By default, Publisher assumes you want to use the original color designs; however, if you want to change the colors to a different theme, click the Color Scheme down arrow, which displays color groups as they are associated with the different Office themes as you see in Figure 24-9. Choose the colors you want for your publication.

Figure 24-9
Choosing a color scheme.

Tip

You are not limited to only the colors in your selected scheme; however, they appear as the starting point when selecting color for text or shapes.

Choosing a Font Scheme

Each publication, when it was originally designed, included a set of fonts that complement each other, and by default, Publisher assumes you want to use the original fonts. You can, however, customize the font scheme more to your liking or more appropriate for your actual publication. If you want to change the font scheme, click the Font Scheme down arrow, which displays fonts as they are associated with the different Office themes (see Figure 24-10). Choose the font scheme you prefer.

Figure 24-10
Select the font group you want to use.

Presenting View Options

AS YOU WORK on your publication, you will find yourself needing to look at it from several perspectives. Perhaps you want to view the detail, or look closer at the ruler, or stand back and look at the overall appearance. Publisher has several options to help you take a better look.

Setting Down Ruler Guides

The Publisher window provides rulers across the top and left sides. When working on your publication, you often will want to place a frame in a very precise position on the page. The rulers, with markings in eighths of an inch, guide you in placing your objects.

However, with the rulers being at the far left or at the top it is sometime difficult to line up to a specific position unless you have your publication greatly zoomed in. (You will learn about zooming the screen in the next section.) A better way to work with the rulers is to use ruler guides, which can go anywhere on the page.

Ruler guides are non-printing light green lines that you use for visual alignment. You turn them on or off as needed. Choose Page Design>Layout>Guides, which displays a guide gallery as seen in Figure 24-11.

Figure 24-11
Choose a guide to help you align objects.

Choose the guides you want. In Figure 24-12 you see one horizontal and one vertical guide. You can easily move the guide by positioning your pointer over the guide until the pointer turns into a double-headed arrow. Drag the guide until it is where you want it.

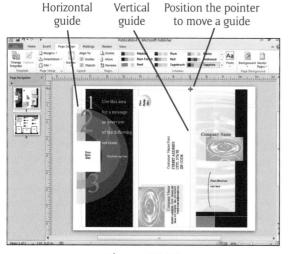

Figure 24-12
Use ruler guides to align objects.

Notice the guide line displays very lightly on the ruler, and as you move the guide, you see it move on the ruler as well. This helps you tie the guide to the ruler for exact object positioning. If you look on the status bar you can also see the exact position of your pointer.

When would you use the ruler guides? Well, one example might be when you need to place the bottom of a picture at precisely 2.75 inches from the top. Place a horizontal guide at 2.75 inches and then drag the picture so its base sits on the guide. Another example when you might use a guide is that at the 2-inch vertical mark, you want to draw a box exactly 1.75 inches tall by 3.25 inches wide. Place two vertical and two horizontal guides so they are the exact dimensions apart and then draw your box in between the guides (see Figure 24-13).

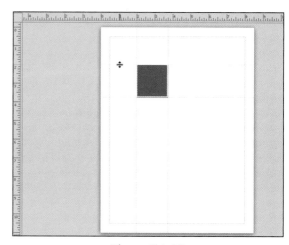

Figure 24-13
Use ruler guides to help you specifically size an object.

Add as many horizontal and vertical guides as needed. When you no longer need them, choose Page Design>Layout>Guides>No Ruler Guides, which clears all the guides. If you just want to remove individual guides, drag the unwanted guide to the ruler on the top or left.

If you want to hide the rulers, choose View>Show>Rulers. Choose View>Show>Rulers again to redisplay the rulers. Hiding the rulers does not hide the ruler guides.

Zooming for a Better View

As you create your publication, you will probably need to see the details a little more clearly. When you are viewing the entire page, it can be difficult to read the print. Fortunately, it is very easy to zoom in and zoom out on any section of your publication. In fact, there are several ways you can zoom into or out of your document:

▶ Choose View>Zoom>100%.

▶ Choose View>Zoom. Click in the Zoom box, enter a zoom percentage, and then press the Enter key.

▶ Choose View>Zoom>Whole Page and see the publication full page. Depending on your monitor, this is usually at a 40–50% zoom.

▶ Click the Zoom In button on the status bar to zoom in closer on your publication. Each click zooms in a little more (see Figure 24-14).

▶ Click the Zoom Out button to decrease the zoom on your publication. Each click zooms out a little more.

▶ Click the Zoom slider, which provides zoom percentages ranging from 10% (really, really tiny) to 800% (enormous—stand back!). You can also choose Whole Page, which generally zooms to the 50% level, or Page Width, which zooms in enough to see the entire width of the document.

▶ If your publication has more than one page, click Two-Page Spread, which allows you to see facing pages. Figure 24-15 shows facing pages with pages 2 and 3.

Figure 24-15
Viewing pages side by side.

Single Page   Two Page   Zoom box   Zoom Out   Zoom In

Figure 24-14
Zooming in for a closer look.

Working with Text

I F YOU ARE READY to begin editing the publication so it contains the content you want, you probably want to begin by entering the text content. One of the first tasks is changing the sample text provided in the template with your own text.

Entering Text in a Text Box

Highlight the text in the text box by either dragging across it completely or by clicking the text box to select it and pressing Ctrl+A. While the text is still highlighted, begin typing your own text. Your text replaces the highlighted sample text. Some publications, such as newsletters, include linked text frames, meaning that as you type the text, if needed, it will automatically flow into the next linked text frame. You can tell where the next frame is located when you click on a frame and look at the icon below it. If there is an arrow pointing to the right, then more text flows into a linked text box elsewhere in the publication. The last linked text box has an icon above it with an arrow to the left to indicate linkage to a previous text box. If the frame does not have an icon with an arrow below it, the box is not linked to other boxes, or is the last box in the group.

Making the Text Fit into the Frames

A huge challenge is making your text fit in the text frame. If the text you entered is too long for the text box, what happens? You actually have quite a few ways to control what happens to the extra text. You can do any of the following:

▶ Shrink the text size so it fits into the box (see Figure 24-16). Be cautious with this option, because if you have a lot of text to shrink, it may make it too small to read easily. Although this is usually the default option, you can select it by clicking Text Box Tools Format>Text>Text Fit>Shrink Text on Overflow.

Shrink Text on Overflow

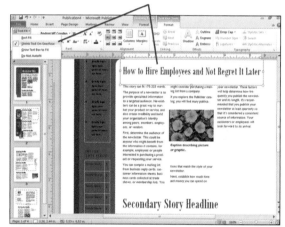

Figure 24-16
Don't make your text too small to read!

▶ Edit the text and remove any unnecessary wording. Editing text in a Publisher frame is just like editing text in a Word document.

▶ Make the text frame larger. Choose Text Box Tools>Format>Text>Text Fit>Grow Text Box to Fit.

- ▶ Adjust the character spacing in the text. See "Adjusting Character Spacing" later in this chapter.

- ▶ Let the extra text fall into another frame. (See the next section.)

Making Text Flow Across Frames

Notice that most placeholder text shows you approximately how many words will fit in the story frames. When you enter more text than will fit within a frame, you see an icon near the bottom of the text frame. The icon is there to remind you that the entire story is displayed across two or more frames. How many frames it flows across is dependent on the template you are using.

Figure 24-17 shows how Publisher will automatically go to the next frame when the first column becomes full. The frames are linked together so Publisher knows they are filled with the same story. Frames could be linked on the same page, or could be on different pages.

As you pause your mouse over the story, the frame appears as dotted lines. If you click in a frame, the first frame for example, you see the icon pointing right, which indicates the story continues to the next frame on the right. If you were to click in the second frame, it too would have an arrow pointing right, indicating there is yet more to the story in the next frame to the right. And if you click in the third frame, there is no arrow because that's the end of the story.

What's a Story?

A story refers to text that fits across multiple frames.

Link indicator

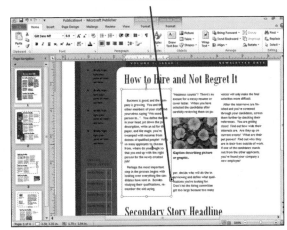

Figure 24-17
Linked text boxes.

Formatting Text

When using a predefined publication, most of the formatting is already set up for you, but sometimes you want to make changes. The Publisher Ribbon contains all the tools you need. Formatting text in a Publisher text box is identical to formatting text in a Word document. You select the text you want to change and click the options you want. Refer to Chapter 3, "Making a Word Document Look Good."

Figure 24-18
Character formatting options.

In Figure 24-18 you see the Home>Font group, which includes:

- ► Font
- ► Font Size
- ► Increase Font Size
- ► Decrease Font Size
- ► Clear Formatting
- ► Bold
- ► Italics
- ► Underline
- ► Subscript
- ► Superscript
- ► Change Case
- ► Character Spacing (see the next section for more information on Character Spacing)
- ► Font Color

Adjusting Character Spacing

When working with headlines you may find you have a lot of unused space, or perhaps your headline is just a little too long. You can tinker with the character spacing to add or remove space between characters. If you want to adjust the space between all selected characters, it is called tracking; if you want to adjust the space between two specific characters, it is called kerning. Begin by selecting the text you want to adjust and then choose Home>Format>Character Spacing. You see the menu in Figure 24-19.

Character spacing

Figure 24-19
Adjusting character spacing.

From the Character Spacing menu, choose a Tracking preset option and then click OK. Choices include:

- ► **Normal:** Keeps the text at 100% of its original tracking.
- ► **Very Tight:** Reduces the tracking space by 25% of Normal.
- ► **Tight:** Reduces the tracking space by 12.5% of Normal.
- ► **Loose:** Expands the tracking space by 12.5% of Normal.
- ► **Very Loose:** Expands the tracking space by 25% of Normal.

Too Much Text?

If you have a block of text that doesn't quite fit into a frame but is not enough to go into another frame, try reducing the character spacing.

One other option is to choose your settings through the Character Spacing dialog box. Choose Home>Format>Character Spacing>More Spacing. The Character Spacing dialog box seen in Figure 24-20 appears from which you can select custom settings.

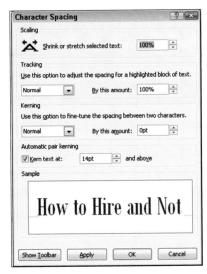

Figure 24-20
The Character Spacing dialog box.

Using the Mini Toolbar

Like other Office applications, Publisher now contains a semitransparent Mini Toolbar designed to provide quick access to many text, paragraph, and object formatting features so you don't have to move your cursor so far to select the commands from the Ribbon.

The Mini Toolbar appears whenever you select some text. As your cursor points to the selected text, the transparent toolbar appears. As you move your pointer so it rests on top of the toolbar, the Mini Toolbar appears in full opacity (see Figure 24-21).

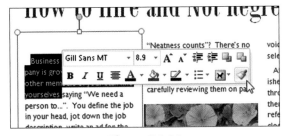

Figure 24-21
Save mouse movement by using the Mini Toolbar.

Available choices on the Mini Toolbar include:

- ▶ Font
- ▶ Font Size
- ▶ Grow Text
- ▶ Shrink Text
- ▶ Increase Indent
- ▶ Decrease Indent
- ▶ Bring Forward
- ▶ Send Backwards
- ▶ Bold
- ▶ Italic
- ▶ Underline
- ▶ Center
- ▶ Font Color
- ▶ Shape Fill
- ▶ Shape Outline
- ▶ Bullets
- ▶ Wrap Text
- ▶ Format Painter

Turn Off Mini Toolbar

If you find the Mini Toolbar distracting, you can turn it off. Click the File tab and choose Options. Click General and remove the check mark from Show Mini Toolbar on Selection.

Adding Bullets and Numbering

If you have text that needs bullets or numbering, you can also add those from the Ribbon. Select the text to which you want to add bullets or numbering and choose Home>Paragraph and click the

Bullets button or the Numbering button. The default bullet or numbering style is applied to your text. If you want a special style bullet or numbering, choose Home>Paragraph>Bullets (or Numbering) arrow, which displays a menu from which you can select. See Figure 24-22 for a look at the Bullets menu.

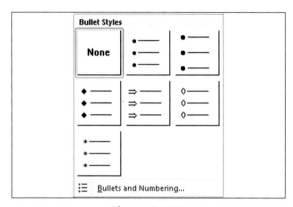

Figure 24-22
Selecting a bullet style.

Changing Alignments

Just like in Word, you can change the alignment of your text. Horizontal alignment manages the text between the left and right margins of a text box. Vertical alignment manages the text between the top and bottom margins of a text box.

In Chapter 3, you discovered you can change the horizontal alignment by selecting the text you want to change and clicking one of the four alignment buttons from the Home>Paragraph area. In

Publisher, you have the same four choices—Align Text Left, Center, Align Text Right, and Justify—all available on the Paragraph Group of the Home tab. You can change a headline, all of the text, or a selected story paragraph. You cannot change the alignment for only part of a paragraph.

Alignment Shortcut Keys

All horizontal alignments have shortcut keys. For Align Text Left, use Ctrl+L; for Center, use Ctrl+E; for Align Text Right, use Ctrl+R; and for Justify, use Ctrl+J.

Adjusting Paragraph Spacing

Another text adjustment commonly used is the spacing before and after paragraphs. Between the paragraphs, instead of placing a full blank line that is determined by the font size, many publications use a fixed amount of space based on point size. The easiest way to control the setting is through the Paragraph dialog box and, like horizontal alignment options, applies to the entire paragraph. Just follow these easy steps:

1. Select the paragraphs you want to format.

2. From the Home tab, click the Paragraph Dialog Box Launcher. The Paragraph dialog box seen in Figure 24-23 appears.

Figure 24-23
Setting paragraph spacing.

3. Using the Indents and Spacing Tab, set an amount of space you require either before the first line of a paragraph or after the last line of a paragraph, or both.

4. Click OK to apply the settings.

Change Line Spacing

From the Paragraph dialog box, you can also set the line spacing, which is the space between individual paragraph lines.

Inserting Drop Caps

A drop cap is a large capital letter typically at the beginning of a story, although you could have a drop cap in any paragraph. Adding drop caps adds a touch of elegance to your story and often captures a reader's eye.

Click the paragraph for which you want a drop cap. You don't have to actually select any part of the text. Publisher will automatically make the first letter in the paragraph the drop cap. Choose Text Box Tools>Format>Typography>Drop Cap, which displays the Drop Cap gallery as shown in Figure 24-24. Scroll through the various drop cap styles. Pause your cursor over any option to see a preview of your paragraph with the drop cap. Click the one you like.

Figure 24-24
Choosing a drop cap style.

Working with Graphics

I N CHAPTER 15, "Editing Your Presentation," you learned how you can manipulate graphics. Among the options you discovered were how to move, resize, and rotate graphics. Graphics work the same way in Publisher. You select the graphic image, and, using the selection handles, you manipulate the graphic to the size or position you want.

Publisher templates come with sample graphics. However, like the text in the text frames, the graphics in the graphic frames are only samples. You will most certainly want to replace the graphic with one more appropriate to your publication.

A graphic frame may contain only a picture, or it may be two frames grouped together—one for the picture and another text frame for a picture caption. To replace the sample image with your own, follow these steps:

1. Click the graphics frame to select it. The Picture Tools Format tab appears.

2. Choose Picture Tools>Format>Adjust> Change Picture>Change Picture. The Insert Picture dialog box seen in Figure 24-25 appears.

Change Picture button   Selected graphic

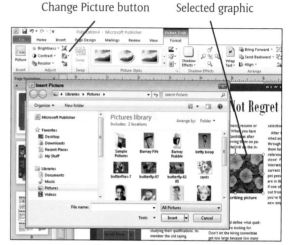

Figure 24-25
Changing the graphic.

3. Locate and select the picture you want and choose Insert. Publisher replaces the existing picture with your newly selected picture.

Other Picture Options

The Picture Tools Format tab also has buttons to adjust the image brightness or contrast, crop the picture, change the style, and many other typical graphic options. Pause your cursor over any button to see a ScreenTip explaining the button's purpose. Also refer to Chapter 15.

Designing Your Own
Publication

PICTURE YOURSELF ON THE BEACH, playing in the wet sand. You want to build a sand sculpture, so with an idea in mind, you begin with a handful of sand and slowly transform the wet glob into a work of art.

In the previous chapter you discovered how easy it was to begin with a template that met your needs and just plug in your own text and graphics. The pattern was already laid out and meticulously designed. Most of the time, using a predesigned template is the fastest and easiest way to produce your publication. However, when nothing seems to fit just what you have in mind, you can create your publication from the beginning.

Starting Your Publication

IN THIS CHAPTER, you begin with a blank page and transform it into a beautiful publication. You will discover how to add your own frames and manipulate them into positions appropriate for your task. You can add as many pages as desired to your publication and fill them with the information you want the world to see.

Planning a Design

The first thing you must do is spend a little time planning your project. Ask yourself questions such as the following:

► What size paper do I plan on using?

► In what orientation will I need the paper?

► Will I use multiple columns?

► Will I print this myself or take it somewhere to be commercially printed?

► What types of things do I want to say?

► Which fonts would look good for the intended audience?

The best thing you can do is begin with a pencil and a blank piece of paper. Sketch out a rough idea of what you want. It doesn't have to be perfect, but it will certainly give you a good place to start. Take a look at Figure 25-1. On the top you see the rough design of a publication, and on the bottom you see the final publication. Planning ahead with pencil and paper will save you time and frustration when you begin working with your publication in Publisher.

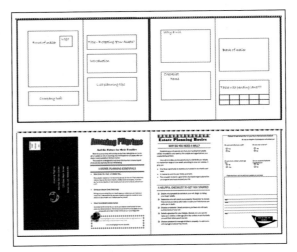

Figure 25-1
Sketch out your ideas before you begin.

Selecting a Paper Size

The next thing you must do is start Microsoft Publisher and select your blank paper size. Choose File>New if you do not already see the Getting Started with Microsoft Office Publisher 2010 window. From the Available Templates section, click More Blank Page Sizes and then choose one of the blank page sizes you see in Figure 25-2. Be sure to scroll down. There are hundreds of blank page sizes—something for every project.

Select the one best suited for your project, and then choose the color and font scheme and the business information set you want to use. If you forgot what the color and font schemes or the business information sets were about, refer back to Chapter 24, "Creating a Predesigned Publisher Publication." After making your selections, click the Create (or Download) button.

Figure 25-2
Begin by choosing the paper size for your publication.

The sample publication created in this chapter is a fold-out brochure so that even though the entire brochure is on a single sheet of paper, the brochure really contains four pages: a front panel, the left inside panel, the right inside panel, and the back panel. On some publication sizes, Publisher may prompt you to insert the additional pages. Choose Yes.

Setting the Margins

Depending on the layout you selected, the first page of the blank publication appears on your screen with blue lines, which are the page margin guides. Technically, a publication doesn't have exact margins other than the ones built into some printers, such as a laser printer, so the margin guides are just that—guides. You use the guides to ensure that your text and graphics do not stray off the page edge.

Hide Margin Guides

You will find the margin guides very helpful in placing objects on the screen; however, you can turn them on and off by choosing View>Show>Guides.

You can change the margin guides at any time; however, it saves time if you change them before you begin placing objects on your screen. Choose Page Design>Page Setup>Margins. A list of margin options appears as seen in Figure 25-3.

Figure 25-3
Managing the page margins.

From here you can select one of the pictures margin settings or you can click Custom Margins and choose your own setting. The Layout Guides dialog box seen in Figure 25-4 appears. Use the spinner boxes to change the Left, Right, Top, and Bottom margin guides. When you are finished, click the OK button

Figure 25-4
Creating custom margins.

Working with Frames

EVERYTHING YOU PUT ON your publication appears in a frame. The entire publication is made of combinations of five frames: text frames, picture frames, table frames, WordArt frames, and Design Gallery frames. (You will discover the Design Gallery later in this chapter.)

Inserting Frames

You are ready to begin placing frames for the objects you want on the publication. You can place the frames one at a time as you need them, or you can lay out the frames in approximation to your sketched drawing. The choice is up to you, but, personally, I prefer the latter method. It seems to keep me better organized.

You insert frames by choosing options located on the Insert tab.

Modify Frame

Don't worry if the frame you create isn't the right size or in the right position. In the next section, you'll discover how easy it is to adjust the frame.

Depending on the option you select, the following occurs:

▶ **Text Box:** Use the Text Box for headings, paragraphs, or stories. The Text Box tool doesn't ask you for more information. You simply click Insert>Text>Draw Text box, drag a rectangular shape in the publication, and then release the mouse button when the frame is approximately the right size. When you release the mouse button, the frame appears with eight selection handles and a rotation handle. Click in the text frame and begin typing your text as seen in Figure 25-5.

Figure 25-5
Inserting a table frame.

▶ **Insert Table:** Use a table to portray facts in a column and row format. After you click Insert>Tables>Table, you drag the mouse across the squares that represent the number of rows and columns you want in your table. See Figure 25-6. A table appears in the publication.

▶ **Insert WordArt:** In Chapter 15, "Editing Your Presentation," you first discovered WordArt to place on a PowerPoint slide. Publisher's WordArt is very similar, although

the options are a little different. Choose Insert>Text>WordArt to display the WordArt gallery seen in Figure 25-7. Choose the option you want and type the text you want.

Figure 25-6
Inserting a table frame.

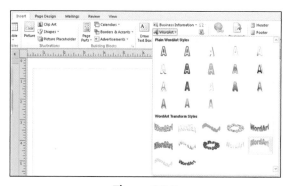

Figure 25-7
Adding WordArt.

▶ **Picture Placeholder:** When you click Insert>Illustrations>Picture Placeholder, Publisher displays a frame with an icon in the middle as you see in Figure 25-8. Click the icon and you see the Insert Picture dialog box where you locate and select the picture you want to use. Click the Insert button to fill the frame with the selected picture.

Click here to insert a picture

Figure 25-8
Inserting a picture frame.

▶ **Clip Art:** Office ships with hundreds of clipart images and thousands more are available online, free from Microsoft. Office stores clipart in collections with keywords so you can easily locate the image you want. Click Insert>Illustrations>ClipArt. In the Clip Art pane that appears on the right side of the screen, in the Search For box, type a word or short phrase that best describes the image you want. Click the Go button. (See Figure 25-9.) Click the image you want in your publication.

Figure 25-9
Inserting clipart.

▶ **Shapes:** Even if you do not have an artistic bone in your body, you can still draw with the Shapes feature. You can draw arrows, boxes, stars, circles, callouts, and dozens of other objects. Click Insert>Illustrations>Shapes and choose a shape from the Shape gallery. Drag in the document until the shape that appears is about the size you want (see Figure 25-10). See Chapter 15 for more information about working with shapes.

Mouse pointer

Figure 25-10
Drawing shapes.

Draw Perfect

To constrain the shape so it is equally sized, such as a perfect circle or a completely straight line, hold down the Shift key when drawing.

▶ **Page Parts:** New to Publisher 2010 are Page Parts, which include publication elements such as heading bars, pull quotes, sidebars, and others. Click Insert>Building Blocks> Page Parts and choose the element you want. In Figure 25-11, you see a pull quote, which I selected from the Page Parts gallery. You use pull quotes to highlight clips of text used in a story.

Pull quote

Figure 25-11
Adding Page Parts.

Click here to select the calendar month

Figure 25-12
Placing a calendar in your publication.

▶ **Calendars:** If you are creating a flyer or publication that requires a calendar, Publisher includes a variety of daily or monthly calendars. Click Insert>Building Blocks>Calendars and either choose a calendar from the displayed gallery or choose More Calendars where you see the Building Block Library seen in Figure 25-12. From here you can choose a daily calendar or a monthly calendar. If you choose a monthly calendar, on the right panel, select the month you want to display. Click the Insert button.

▶ **Borders & Accents:** You often see border art around a scrapbook page, but you can also add it to your publication. Border art is typically a repeating series of small graphics that encompass a frame. Not every publication type should have border art, as it can make the publication look frivolous. However, if you are printing a coupon or some other lively piece of information, border art may be just what you need. Click Insert>Building Blocks>Borders & Accents. A gallery of options as seen in Figure 25-13 appears. Select the one you want, or click the More Borders and Accents option.

▶ **Advertisements:** Click Insert>Building Blocks>Advertisements to display a collection of color-coordinated objects (see Figure 25-14) that you can easily add to your publication. Many Publisher users find them very helpful for filling in blank spaces. But you will also find ready-made coupons, reply forms, and other useful items. And because they are objects, you can manipulate them as you would any other object.

Figure 25-13
Inserting a border.

Modifying Frames

Whether you already have text or graphics in the frame, once you have the frame in place, you can easily modify its size or position. You have discovered that with other Office objects you select the object and then you can manipulate it. Since a Publisher frame is also an object, you modify it using the same standard techniques:

▶ To delete a frame, select the frame and press the Delete key.

▶ To move a frame, select the frame, move the mouse pointer over the frame edge (but not a handle), and then drag the frame to a different position. Make sure the mouse pointer is in the shape of a four-headed arrow as seen in Figure 25-15 before you drag the frame. You can also use the arrow keys to "nudge" a frame up, down, left, or right a small amount.

Mouse pointer as four-headed arrow

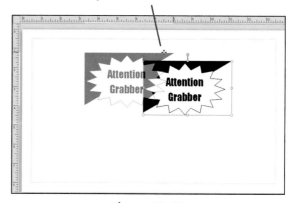

Figure 25-15
Moving a frame.

Figure 25-14
Using Publisher's advertisements.

▶ To move a frame to a different page, select the frame and then choose Home> Clipboard>Cut or press Ctrl+X. Display the page you want the frame placed in and choose Home>Clipboard>Paste or press Ctrl+V.

▶ To change the frame size, select the frame and position the mouse over a selection handle. When the mouse pointer appears as a double-headed arrow, drag the handle until the frame is the size you want (see Figure 25-16). Use the middle handles to drag straight up, down, left, or right, and use the corner handles to change both the height and width. If you have text in a text frame, when you resize the frame the text rewraps to fit the new size. If you have a graphic in a picture frame, be cautious when dragging a side handle as doing so can distort the image proportions.

▶ To rotate a frame and its contents, use the green rotation handle. Position the mouse pointer over the handle until the mouse pointer turns into a small semicircle. Drag the rotation handle until the frame is at the angle you want. See Figure 25-17 for an example.

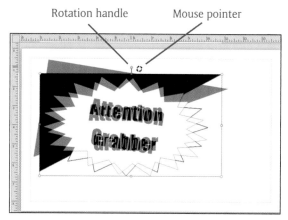

Figure 25-17
Rotating a frame.

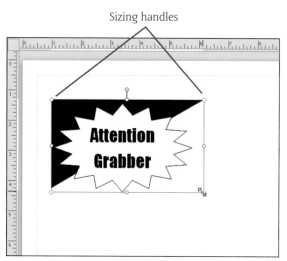

Figure 25-16
Resizing a frame.

Working with Frame Styles

Even though onscreen you see dotted lines surrounding a frame, those lines do not print. They are there to help you visualize the frame location relative to other screen items. Adding a border or background shading to a text frame is a great way to make the frame stand out and attract attention. A border surrounds the frame but does not affect what is inside the frame, and adding background shading fills the entire frame area with a color. To save you time, Publisher offers border and shading combinations in a gallery of predefined styles. The following steps show you how to add borders and background shading to your text frames.

Although you can add borders and shading to any type of frame, typically you use it with text frames.

1. Select the frame you want to modify.

2. Choose Drawing Tools Format>Shape Styles and click the More button. A gallery of styles appears. The choices and color you see depend on the color options you selected when creating your publication.

3. Pause your mouse over any option to see its effect on your frame as you see in Figure 25-18, and then click the option you want.

Figure 25-18
Selecting a Shape Style.

4. If you want a different border around the frame, choose Drawing Tools>Format>Shape Styles and click the Shape Outline arrow. From here you can select a different color, thickness, style, and other options.

5. If you want a different shading for the frame interior, choose Drawing Tools>Format> Shape Styles and click the Shape Fill arrow. A gallery appears including colors, pictures, gradients, textures, and patterns. In Figure 25-19, you see choices for a texture fill.

Figure 25-19
Fill your frame with a pattern.

Use Light Colored Text

If you choose a dark background color or pattern, you will probably want to change your text color to a light or white color.

Working with Text

I N CHAPTER 24, you discovered several general Publisher functions you use with publication text. Most of those functions such as applying fonts and font attributes you can use in almost any Office application. In this section, you discover some functions that you typically only see in Publisher; functions that are designed to make your publication look great and help keep your readers interested.

Inserting a File

If you have a story created in a Word document, you can easily bring the story into Publisher. When you bring in the file, it retains the formatting from the Word document, which you can keep or change.

Other File Types

You can also insert a file created in WordPad and Notepad.

You can either insert the file into an existing text box or you can let Publisher create one for you. If you don't have a text box ready for the story, when you insert the file, Publisher creates a text box in the middle of the page. If the story requires more than one page, Publisher continues the story onto additional pages, using page-wide linked text boxes. To insert a file, just follow these easy steps:

1. Display the publication page on which you want to insert the file.

2. Choose Insert>Text>Insert File. The Insert Text dialog box appears.

3. Navigate to and select the file you want to insert.

4. Click OK. Publisher creates a text box with the document text in it. See Figure 25-20.

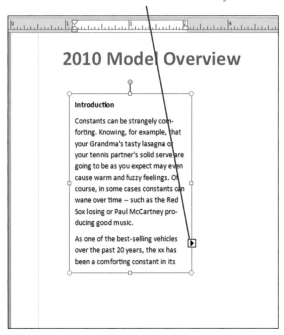

Click here to view more of the story

Figure 25-20
Inserting a Word file.

Generating Text into Columns

In Chapter 5, "Working with Columns and Tables," you discovered how to create columns in a Word document, which provide a newspaper-like feeling to your document. Publisher has columns as well. The difference is that Publisher columns fall within a text frame and apply to the story in the selected frame. In Word, the columns stay in effect until you tell Word otherwise.

To create columns, select the text frame you want to modify and choose Text Box Tools Format>Alignment>Columns. Select the number of columns you want. In Figure 25-21, you see the story on the current page as it appears in three columns. The continuation story on the next page remains in one column so if you want it in multiple columns as well, you need to repeat the choose Text Tool Format>Alignment>Columns command.

Figure 25-21
Breaking a story into columns.

If you want more than three columns, or if you want to control the amount of spacing between the columns, choose Text Tool Format>Alignment>Columns>More Columns. The Columns dialog box appears from which you can choose from one through 63 columns and you can adjust the spacing between the columns as desired. Click OK when you are finished.

Changing Text Vertical Alignment

In Chapter 24, you saw how you can change the text horizontal alignment by using the commands on the Home tab. The Text Box Tools tab also contains tools to convert the horizontal alignments, but these tools are also used in conjunction with the vertical alignment. You can align the text vertically to the top of the story to the middle of the frame or to the bottom of the frame. By default, Publisher aligns text horizontally to the left and vertically to the top.

When you choose a vertical alignment option, Publisher aligns all the text in the frame. Strangely enough, though, it modifies the horizontal alignment to the current paragraph. And in most stories, you won't want some paragraphs centered and some right aligned or left aligned. So, what you need to do is select all the text in the frame before you make an alignment modification. Follow these steps:

1. Select the entire frame text by clicking in the frame and choosing Home>Editing>Select>Select All Text in Text Box, or by pressing Ctrl+A.

2. Choose Text Box Tools Format>Alignment and select an option. Figure 25-22 shows you the available alignment options.

Align Top Left: Aligns the text vertically to the top of the text box and horizontally along the left margin.

Align Top Center: Aligns the text vertically along the top of the text box and horizontally centered to the margins.

Align Top Right: Aligns the text vertically along the top of the text box and horizontally along the right margin.

Align Center Left: Aligns the text vertically centered in the text box and horizontally along the left margin.

Align Center: Aligns the text vertically centered in the text box and horizontally centered between the margins.

Align Center Right: Aligns the text vertically centered in the text box and horizontally along the right margin.

Align Bottom Left: Aligns the text vertically along the bottom of the text box and horizontally along the left margin.

Align Bottom Center: Aligns the text vertically along the bottom of the text box and horizontally centered between the margins.

Align Bottom Right: Aligns the text vertically along the bottom of the text box and horizontally along the right margin.

Figure 25-22
Choosing a vertical alignment.

Modifying Text Direction

Sometimes you need your text to run in a different direction than the typical horizontal placement. Perhaps you want a banner to run down the side of your page, or you need one of those little signs with the tear-off tabs at the bottom. Publisher lets you set the text direction so it runs vertically. Use this feature only with short lines of text. You don't want to read an entire story vertically!

Click in the text box you want to modify. You must click in the box, not just have it selected. Choose Text Box Tools Format>Text>Text Direction. Publisher toggles the text between vertical and horizontal. You will probably need to resize the text box to make it fit properly. See Figure 25-23 for an example.

Text direction

Figure 25-23
Changing text direction.

Adding Text to a Shape

Any shape object other than arrows and lines can have text applied. You *could* create a text frame and move it inside the object, but that typically makes for a lot of work. A much easier way is to let Publisher enter the text and automatically place it in the shape.

Right-click the shape and choose Add Text from the shortcut menu. A blinking insertion point appears in the object where you can type your text. You can then select the text and use any formatting tool to enhance it as you wish. See Figure 25-24.

Figure 25-24
Type text in the drawn shape.

Wrapping Text Around a Graphic

By controlling how you wrap text around a frame or graphic, you can make your publication look much more professional. If you look at the graphics in

Figure 25-25, you see the same graphic three times inside the text. With the graphic on the top, the Square wrap option wraps text around the graphic in a square pattern. The center graphic uses the Tight option, and you see the text wrapped tightly around the graphic, which leaves less whitespace between the text and graphic.

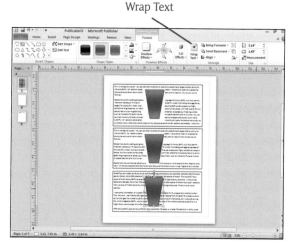

Figure 25-25
Making text and graphics play nice together.

The bottom graphic illustrates the None option, where the graphic overlays on top of the text. Through wrap, which is not shown in Figure 25-25, is the default.

To change the way the text wraps around a graphic, select the graphic and choose Drawing Tools Format>Arrange>Wrap Text. Select the text wrapping option you want.

Working with Pages

S OME PUBLICATIONS CONTAIN only a single page when you create them. Others may contain two, four, or more pages. If you have too many pages, you can delete the extras; and if you need more, you can easily add them.

Inserting New Pages

As you continue working on your projects, you may find you need additional pages. If, for example, your community newsletter has extra articles, you can add pages as needed. Just follow these steps:

1. Choose Insert>Pages and click the Page arrow. A menu of options appears.

    ▶ Choose Insert Blank Page to insert a simple blank page.

    ▶ Choose Insert Duplicate Page to create a copy of the current page.

    ▶ Choose Insert Page, which displays the dialog box seen in Figure 25-26 where you will make additional decisions. The choices you see depend on your publication type. In this example, because the current document is a Newsletter, you get the Insert Newsletter Pages dialog box.

2. Click the page drop-down menu and choose the type of page you want to insert. See Figure 25-27.

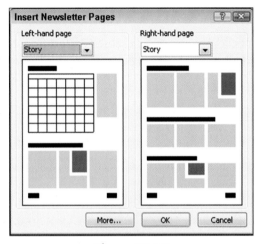

Figure 25-26
An Insert Page dialog box.

Figure 25-27
Choose a page type.

3. Optionally, click the More button. The Insert Page dialog box shown in Figure 25-28 appears.

Figure 25-28
An Insert Page dialog box.

4. Choose how many new pages you want to insert.

5. Select whether you want the new pages placed before or after the current page.

6. Determine whether you want the new pages blank, with a text box, or as a duplicate of a specified page.

7. Click the OK button. The new page appears on the Navigation Pane.

Deleting Unwanted Pages

To delete extra pages you don't need in the publication, display the page you do not want and choose Page Design>Pages>Delete. Depending on what you are deleting, the following occurs:

▶ If the page is a single page, not part of a two-page spread, and the page contains no objects, Publisher simply deletes the page with no questions asked.

▶ If the page is a single page but contains objects, a warning message indicates that the selected page contains objects. Click Yes to delete the page.

▶ If the page is part of a two-page spread, you see the Delete Page dialog box seen in Figure 25-29, prompting you whether you want to delete both pages or just the left or right page. Make a selection and click OK. If the page (or pages) contains objects, you are prompted with a warning message.

Figure 25-29
Which page do you want to delete?

Depending on the publication type, you may also see an additional warning message. Click OK to continue.

Moving Pages

If you created a page and then decided you want it in a different position in the publication, you can move pages from one place to another. You use the Navigation Pane. If necessary, resize the Navigation Pane so you can see which page you want to move. Select the page you want to move and drag it up or down the Navigation Pane. As you move it, you see a heavy black line and an outline of the page you are moving. See Figure 25-30. Move the black line so it is on in the position where you want the page. Release the mouse button and Publisher moves the page.

Selected page   New position

Figure 25-30
Moving pages.

Adding Page Backgrounds

For many publications, a really cool trick is to add a color or gray shaded background to a page. Like filling shapes, you can add backgrounds with colors, gradients, textures, patterns, or even a picture! Follow these steps to apply a background:

1. Display the page you want to format.

2. Choose Page Design>Page Background> Background. The Background gallery appears, as you see in Figure 25-31.

Figure 25-31
Adding a background to a page.

3. Click the one you want, or choose More backgrounds where you can choose additional gradients, patterns, textures, or a picture.

Preparing for Printing

W HEN YOU PACK YOUR CAR for a vacation, you probably have a checklist— either a mental list or a physical one. Did you turn off the stove? Did you pack the sunscreen? And don't forget, even Santa checks his list twice! All types of issues come to mind as you run through the list. When you finish your publication, before you go to the trouble and possible expense of sending it to recipients, you want to make sure it is just right.

Before you actually print your document, you will want to check it for flaws—both text spelling flaws and potential design flaws. Publisher contains several tools to help keep your document in tip top shape.

Checking Your Spelling

Like other Office applications, Microsoft Publisher includes a feature to check for misspelled words. As you type text in your publication, Publisher operates the spell checker tool in the background and identifies problems by displaying a wavy red line under them. Right-click on an unrecognized word and choose from the possible replacement words.

If you want to check the entire publication in a single round, you can choose Review>Proofing> Spelling or press the F7 key. The Check Spelling dialog box appears with the first error. By default, the Spell Check checks only the currently selected story, but you can either click the Check All Stories option in the Spell Check dialog box, (see Figure

25-32) or choose Yes if Publisher prompts you to check the other stories. When the spelling check process is complete, click Yes to the informational box that appears.

Figure 25-32
Making your publication free of spelling errors.

Running the Design Checker

Just before you produce your publications you should run the Design Checker. The Design Checker examines the publication and looks for potential items such as stories with undesignated overflow, frames out of the print area, text boxes with no text, missing Web links, invisible objects, or even pictures that are out of proportion, missing, or have poor resolution.

Depending on the publication destination, the Design Checker can run a general design check, or look for special problems a commercial printer might run into with the file, or problems you might encounter if you e-mail or create a Website from the publication.

Follow these steps:

1. Click the File tab and from the Info tab, choose Run Design Checker. The Design Checker task pane seen in Figure 25-33 appears and lists the potential problem areas it located.

Figure 25-33
Running the Design Checker to look for problem areas.

Figure 25-34
Design Checker offers solutions.

2. Click directly on an item to jump to and select the questionable area. You can the fix the problem, however, in some cases, the Design Checker offers an automatic fix. Instead of jumping to the problem area, click the down arrow next to a problem as seen in Figure 25-34. You can choose to Go To This Item, which takes you back to the problem, or Publisher may offer a fix for the problem.

3. Click Explain, and a Publisher Help window appears with information about the problem and its possible solutions.

Control the Design Checker Behavior

To see or control the Design Checker behavior, click the Design Checker Options hyperlink in the Design Checker pane. You can control how the Design Checker displays found errors, and which potential design errors it should look for.

Preparing to Print

Before you print your document, you should preview it on the screen so you can sit back and look at how document layout settings such as the margins will look in the printed document. In the preview, although you can only view the document and cannot edit it, you can tell quite a bit about it from a different perspective. The following steps walk you through the Preview process:

1. Click the File tab and, from the Backstage view that appears, choose Print. A print settings section appears on the left and a preview of the publication appears on the right.

2. From the preview area (shown in Figure 25-35), select from the following options:

   ▶ If you have multiple pages, click in the page number box, and then click the Next Sheet or Previous Sheet buttons to view additional pages.

   ▶ Use the Zoom controls in the lower-right to enlarge or reduce the view or click anywhere in the Preview window to zoom in or out.

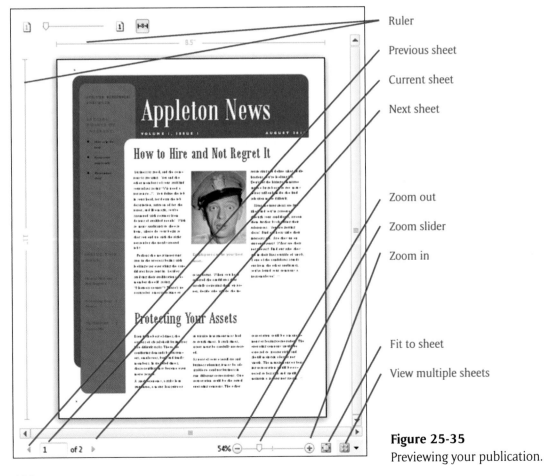

Ruler

Previous sheet

Current sheet

Next sheet

Zoom out

Zoom slider

Zoom in

Fit to sheet

View multiple sheets

Figure 25-35
Previewing your publication.

If you need to return to the publication, click the File tab.

Printing Your Publication

When your document is complete and you've reviewed it for any changes, you may want to make a hard copy of it to file away or to share with others. Click the File tab and, from the Backstage view that appears, choose Print. A Print Settings section appears on the left and a preview of the worksheet appears on the right. The Print settings section seen in Figure 25-36 illustrates the many printing options. Take a look at a few of them:

Figure 25-36
Print settings.

▶ **Copies:** Select the number of copies you want to print.

▶ **Printer:** If you are connected to more than one printer, you can select which printer you want to use from the Name drop-down menu.

▶ **Settings:** Determine which pages you want to print. If, from the Navigation Pane, you select the pages you want before you display the Print dialog box, you can choose Print Selection to print only those pages. If you want to print only selected pages, choose Print Custom Range and enter the page numbers separated by a comma or a dash. For example to print only the first three publication pages, enter 1, 2, 3 or 1-3. Other settings include options such as paper size.

Choose any desired options and then click the Print button to begin printing.

E-Mailing from Publisher

Microsoft Publisher's e-mail capabilities are tied to the e-mail program you use with other applications, such as Outlook or Windows Mail. You learn about e-mailing with Outlook in Chapter 20, "Communicating with Outlook E-Mail." To send your publication via e-mail, choose File>Save & Send where you see the Backstage view's Save & Send options shown in Figure 25-37. Notice that next to each button is an explanation of its options.

Figure 25-37
Share your publication via e-mail.

If you choose to send only the Current Sheet, not as an attachment, but embedded as HTML text in the body of the e-mail, Publisher generates an e-mail message where you enter the recipient's e-mail address and a subject. Publisher also checks for potential design flaws that may occur when sending it as an e-mail.

If you choose to Send All Pages, the Send All Pages as Message dialog box appears and advises you of how it will assemble the publication in the e-mail. It also advises you that some formatting content may be lost and prompts you to save your file. Make your selections and click OK. Publisher generates an e-mail message where you enter the recipient's e-mail address and a subject. Publisher also checks for potential design flaws that may occur when sending it as an e-mail.

If you choose Send as Attachment, Publisher prompts you to save the publication, and then generates a new e-mail message where you enter the recipient's e-mail address and a subject. The publication is attached as a Publisher document. In order to read or edit the publication, the recipient must have Publisher installed on her computer.

In most situations, the best way to e-mail a publication is as PDF file. That way the recipient can't change the publication, only read it. From the Save & Send Backstage view, choose Send as PDF. Publisher then generates a new e-mail message where you enter the recipient's e-mail address and a subject. The publication is attached as a PDF file, as seen in Figure 25-38.

Send button   PDF attachment

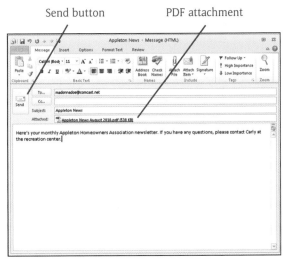

Figure 25-38
Enter a recipient and send the e-mail.

When you are ready to send the e-mail, click the Send button.

Index

Symbols/Numbers

characters (Excel cells), 186
3D Excel charts, 269–270

A

absolute references (Excel)
    formulas, 167
    workbooks, 213
Access
    Compatibility Mode, 13
    databases
        creating, 353, 356
        forms, 355, 360
        navigating, 354–355
        overview, 352
        records. See records
        reports, 355, 360–361
        tables, 356–359
        templates, 353–355
    files. *See* files
    forms
        backgrounds, 386–387
        deleting fields, 383–384
        inserting fields, 384
        moving fields, 384–385
        themes, 385–386
    records
        creating, 361–363
        datasheets, 361–364
        deleting, 364–365
        filtering, 368–369
        forms, 362–364
        searching, 365–367
        sorting, 367
        viewing, 363–364
    tables
        deleting fields, 378
        field alignment, 381
        field dates, 381
        field formats, 378–379
        field input masks, 379
        field lookup, 381–382
        field size, 372, 378

        field validation rules, 379–380
        field validation text, 380
        field values, 379
        formatting, 372–374
        inserting fields, 376–377
        moving fields, 375
        required fields, 380
        viewing fields, 375–376
    window, 353–355
accounts (Outlook), 393–395
adding
    Outlook contacts, 408–411
    Outlook tasks, 434–436
    Word text, 25–26
address blocks (Word Mail Merge), 103
alignment
    Access table fields, 381
    Excel cell text, 192–195
    PowerPoint slide objects, 314–315
    Publisher text, 461–462, 476–477
    Word text, 45–46
animations (PowerPoint), 340–344
annotating PowerPoint presentations, 347
appointments (Outlook), 425–427
arranging PowerPoint slides, 303–304
assigning Outlook tasks, 439–440
attachments (Outlook), 401–403, 438
attributes (Word), 38
auditing Excel formulas, 179–181
AutoFill (Excel), 148, 166
AutoFilter, 223–224
AutoSum (Excel), 169–172
axes (Excel), 263–265

B

backgrounds
    Access, 386–387
    Excel, 196–197
    PowerPoint, 324–325
    Publisher, 473–474, 481
backspacing, 26
Backstage view, 8–9
bar codes (Mail Merge), 96

black and white PowerPoint slides, 304
blank cells, 224
bookmarks (Word), 117–118
borders
    Excel cells, 196
    Publisher frames, 473–474
    Word text, 46
Building Blocks (Word), 120–123
bulk mailing (Mail Merge), 96
bullets
    PowerPoint, 328–329, 341
    Publisher, 460–461
business information sets, 452–453

C

calendar (Outlook)
    appointments, 425–427
    events, 427–428
    holidays, 424
    meetings, 428–431
    reminders, 425–427
    views, 422–424
capitalization
    Excel
        cells, 144
        formulas, 164
        functions, 168
    Outlook e–mail, 397
    Publisher, 462
    sorting data, 220
    Word, 29–30, 77
categories (Outlook contacts), 412
cells. *See also* columns; data
    Excel
        ### characters, 186
        alignment, 192–195
        AutoFill, 148
        blank, 224
        borders, 196
        capitalization, 144
        case sensitivity, 144
        colors, 188–189, 196–197
        conditional formatting, 201–203